principles of
Psychological Measurement

principles of
Psychological
Measurement

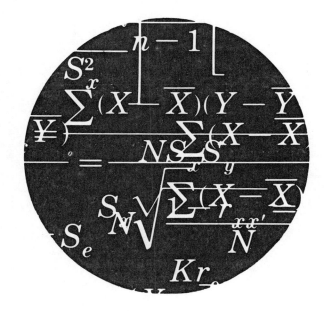

Elmer Lemke
Illinois State University

William Wiersma
University of Toledo

HOUGHTON MIFFLIN COMPANY   BOSTON
Dallas   Geneva, Ill.   Hopewell, N.J.   Palo Alto   London

Preface

This book is designed primarily for a first course in psychological measurement, whether the course is offered at the undergraduate level or deferred until the graduate program. Any professional in psychology must be able to acquire and use quantitative information. A knowledge of the basic principles and methods of measurement is essential. Therefore, it follows that understanding these principles and methods is an important component of professional training. This text, and conscientious study, should start the student toward mastery of the essential principles and methods.

This text is divided into three general sections. The first three chapters comprise the introduction. This section includes some basic procedures necessary for the quantification of measured characteristics. The next five chapters provide the basic theoretical principles. Although these chapters have a theoretical orientation, all theory is well illustrated with practical examples. Finally, the concluding three chapters comprise a test utilization section. Here the emphasis is on the study of a selected number of tests in terms of basic principles previously illustrated, stressing the practical aspects of test development. After covering the entire text, the student should not be left with fragmented concepts of measurement, but should achieve adequate closure in synthesizing and applying measurement concepts.

The use of this text requires basic mathematical preparation. A knowledge of elementary algebra should be adequate, and no prior statistical knowledge is presumed. Obviously, whenever quantification is considered, numbers and their manipulation are involved. However, the emphasis in this text is on underlying ideas and concepts. Computation is discussed in connection with necessary skill development and in illustrations for the support of understanding. It is assumed that most students in an introductory course have had little, if any, systematic presentation of measurement principles and methods.

The basic organization of the book has a developmental sequence. However, the text can be used as a reference work, and parts of it can be considered independently. For example, an individual might want to consider only a theoretical part, such as the two chapters on reliability.

At various places in the text, especially in the more technical parts, important principles or concepts are restated in bold type. This is done only where the continuity of the discussion is not affected. These principles can be easily identified and used for review and clarification.

There are two types of exercises at the end of each chapter, which reflect the important principles contained in the text. They comprise a check so the student may determine whether or not the basic concepts are known. Responding correctly to these exercises does not insure complete mastery of the chapter content, but they do serve as an aid to learning. The exercises provide considerable opportunity for individual study, with the rate and amount of study adjusted to fit the needs of the individual student. The student can check the correctness of responses and receive immediate feedback on performance.

The general purpose of the text is to provide the student or reader with a background in the concepts, purposes, and skills underlying measurement. The book is not written as a "cookbook" of measurement operations, nor is it intended as a compendium of available instruments. It is an introductory text that minimizes advanced, specialized measurement topics, but will provide a foundational knowledge base. It should be used to that end.

Preface for the Student

This book is basically organized into three major sections: introduction and basic operations, theory, and application. Since there is considerable overlap between these major considerations of the content, the text is not subdivided. Instead, we have used the chapters as the major divisions of content. Measurement contains many specific concepts and operations; we have tried to present these concepts and operations, and then put them together into a meaningful whole. This contrasts with presenting a "big picture," and taking it apart to identify the pieces. Measurement itself is not an end, but the means to an end, and the objective of this text is to provide you with an understanding of the underlying principles and procedures that have extensive potential application.

Chapters 2 and 3 discuss the necessary background in basic statistics and in score manipulation. These chapters are heavily oriented toward the operations used in analyzing and transforming scores and score distributions. Although these chapters precede what we might call measurement theory per se, their content is very important in providing the background for understanding the basic operations prerequisite to measurement theory and its development.

Chapters 4 through 8 contain the essential theoretical measurement concepts. There is considerable emphasis on reliability and validity. Although these chapters contain measurement theory, there are many applicable illustrations and references throughout.

The final three chapters, 9 through 11, have a broader focus in that they deal with the measurement of human characteristics. The problems of measuring these characteristics are discussed, and tests are selected to illustrate these measurements. These chapters discuss basic measurement principles in the context of a few tests, and present the utilitarian and investigative aspects of measurement activity in general.

At various places in the text, especially in the more technical parts, important principles or concepts are restated in bold type. They can be easily identified and used for review and clarification.

At the end of each chapter, there is a list of Suggested Readings for those who would like more information about topics discussed in the chapter. They are followed by two types of student exercises. These exercises check your understanding of the material covered in the chapter. Correctly solving these exercises should not only indicate mastery of the chapter content, but should aid in understanding it. If you have difficulty responding correctly to these exercises, you should review the appropriate sections of the text, as they cover the most important points in each chapter. Answers to arithmetic and short-response exercises appear in the narrow column on the same page as the questions. This column should be covered before working the exercises on the page.

Following the text, there is a Glossary of measurement terms (starting on p. 271). All terms contained in the Glossary appear in the text, but it provides a convenient and useful summary. The Bibliography (starting on p. 277) should be useful for reference purposes. Finally, Appendixes A and B include certain statistical tables and information necessary for developing and illustrating the text material.

Contents

Preface   v

Preface for the Student   vii

Chapter   1. Introduction to Measurement   1

    2. Basic Measurement Statistics   11

    3. Transformations   41

    4. Reliability   64

    5. Reliability Estimation   84

    6. Criterion Validity   109

    7. Content and Construct Validity   133

    8. Factor Analysis: A Procedure for Identifying Psychological Constructs   150

    9. Measurement of Human Abilities   172

    10. Measurement of Interests and Personality   208

    11. Test Construction   240

Glossary   271

Bibliography   277

Appendix A. Table of the Normal Curve   282

Appendix B. Summation: Notation and Operations   284

Name Index   295

Subject Index   297

Introduction to Measurement 1

The tasks and problems related to measurement are very real to individuals in both the physical and behavioral sciences. Measurement serves as a prerequisite, not only for scientists conducting research, but also for practitioners seeking to apply the theories and methods that lead to the products of research. Thus, concern with measurement is not reserved for the scientist or researcher in a discipline, it is also the concern of the practitioner and the professional. This book is directed to the aspiring researcher or practitioner.

There are several possible approaches to organizing the information relative to measurement. The table of contents will give readers an overview of how the information is organized. There are, however, more subtle modes of organization present in most texts. One approach is to develop extensive category systems for skills, purposes, theory, and operations. Another is to set up a "theory and application of theory" cycle for various principles and their applications. This text does not place major emphasis on categorization. Theoretical considerations may be supported by applications, but there was no conscious attempt to adhere to a definite cyclic format. Rather, the organization of content follows what we consider a mixture of theory, statistical skills, and application that reflects a logical development. This is an attempt to avoid fragmentation of principles and to provide the student with a broad and integrated base of knowledge.

The matter of definition is always important when theory is involved and where there is considerable emphasis on the precision of principles and methods. Definition in the context of measurement is extremely important. We have made every attempt to provide adequate definition, in terms of both coverage and precision. The student should be especially careful in identifying and understanding definitions. Such care will enhance understanding of the entire text.

All words do not have consistent meaning for all people. Measurement is no exception. In measurement, methods as well as theories are continually being developed and refined. Because measurement problems are complex, many procedures of measurement are not as precise or as extensively developed in the behavioral sciences as they are in the physical sciences. Nevertheless, psychological measurement has begun to arrive at a mature level of applicable theory and procedures. In order to be an intelligent practitioner, the student should be aware of the basic principles of psychological measurement that follow.

Meaning of Measurement

The measurement of various phenomena, however crude, has been around for a long time. Its presence has been motivated more by necessity and practicality than by fascination, although in areas like astronomy, initial measurement was most certainly motivated by curiosity. The cave man undoubtedly made some crude measurements in converting an animal skin to an article of clothing. Through the ages certain arbitrary units evolved, such as the foot and the cubit, that were attempts at facilitating and even standardizing measurement.

Any number of similar definitions of measurement might be secured by various means. When we consider the verb *measure,* we usually associate it with determination of the dimension, capacity, extent, etc. of something specific. To measure the floor of a room is to determine its length and width and, correspondingly, its area. To determine the room's capacity, we develop a description of its volume. When we measure time, we deal with its appropriate units. In all cases we express the result quantitatively, that is, in numbers. To say merely that an object is curved or red or light is not to "measure" the object. Such phrases may aid description but, not being quantitative, they are not in themselves measurement.

Stevens (1951) has defined measurement: "In its broadest sense, measurement is the assignment of numerals to objects or events according to rules [p. 1]." A very important part of Stevens's definition is "the rule" in any specific case. Simply assigning numerals does not make the process quantitative. Football players are assigned numerals for the convenience of identification, but this is, at best, qualitative measurement. Although the process of football numeral assignment may not be random, it does not generally designate quantification. Therefore, in this text, we will qualify the rule of measurement as being a quantitative process—*one that will result in numbers with quantitative meaning.* Thus, in our discussion we will restrict the term *measurement* to quantitative description. This characteristic enables us to take advantage of the many benefits provided by operations with numbers and the corresponding mathematics underlying such operations. It should be noted that a broader definition of measurement could be given.

We might note some additional characteristics of measurement in general, as implied in the definition. Measurement is a neutral procedure with neither "good" nor "bad" connotations. Value judgments, so to speak, depend upon the unique needs and purposes of the situation. In any given situation, the adequacy of the "rule" determines the adequacy of the measurement. Stevens's definition also implies that if we can identify the rule, measurement of anything is, at least, theoretically possible. Rules are commonly set up on some rational, empirical basis.

Many processes come under the umbrella of this definition. It is easy to measure certain physical objects with adequate instruments. We talk about securing length, height, and distance, for example. We can see a football field and observe that it is long. We can measure its length with an appropriate device. Such measurement procedures are commonplace and very real to everyone. But the definition also includes more abstract and elusive processes. It also includes the measurement of achievement, anxiety, ability, and a host of other characteristics of individuals, either singly or in groups. We can see a person and observe that he is anxious, for example. If we had an appropriate device, we could measure his anxiety. Such constructs measured in the behavioral sciences may not have physical existence in the same way that a football field exists. Yet the general procedure, as implied by the definition, is similar to that in the physical sciences. Of course, in terms of the underlying rationale, the specific, operational process may be much more difficult to structure and apply. So long as we understand the definition of measurement as the assignment of numerals to objects or events according to rules, we should avoid erroneous conceptions and conclusions in the more abstract measurement situations.

Nature of Psychological Measurement

Psychological measurement is generally indirect. That is, we typically measure behavioral characteristics by inference rather than by direct manipulation or observation. We do not physically extract the IQ of a child and examine it. Rather, we infer intelligence from selected behavioral observations. Of course, the behavior we elect to observe is determined by our current conceptions of intelligence. Achievement, attitudes, personality characteristics, special abilities, etc. are all measured in an indirect manner, inferred from behavior or behavior categories.

The indirect approach to psychological measurement is necessitated, to a large extent, by the nature of the organism's characteristics. Many characteristics are, in fact, abstractions of behavior. The reason we infer that an individual is motivated or anxious, for example, is simply because of a variety of cues. The function of measurement is converting these cues to quantitative measures.

Psychological measurement, for the most part, is relative rather than absolute. The units of scholastic achievement, intelligence, aptitude, or motivation are not based on a scale in which there is an absolute zero, such as is the case with weight or height. The meaning or interpretation of a score on a test or performance measure is based on its relationship to some criterion or criteria. The criteria may or may not be based on the performance of a given group. For example, suppose a student scores 68 percent correct on a measurement test. Regardless of how anyone else did on the test, the 68 percent correct has meaning when the test is studied to determine an individual's grasp of objectives embedded in the test content. We say a test is criterion-referenced when interpretation of results is based on mastery or nonmastery of a set of objectives reflected by the test content.

We can also interpret a performance measure by comparing it to the scores of some defined group. Such a group may be considered either typical or atypical, depending on the situation. In the case of the measurement test, we might ask, How does this score compare with the average performances of the class? With all students who have taken the test? With all students with an IQ above 125 who have taken the test? We use the added information about comparable groups for the interpretation of the score. When we use this approach, measurement is relative—it is norm-referenced—and this type of interpretation is widely used. However, it should be recognized that a score can have some meaning when it is criterion-referenced. Many test interpretations are undertaken by using both norm- and criterion-referencing.

All measurement, even in the physical sciences, involves error. Only the most naive individual would argue that his measurements are absolutely accurate. Errors can develop in various ways, such as error in observation or error inherent in the measuring instrument. Yet, it would be folly to advocate discontinuing psychological measurement because of the presence of error. Instead, we try to delineate the causes and extent of error, and in some situations, we may be able to eliminate at least part of it. Understanding the sources of error and recognizing the limits of accuracy comprise an important part of the measurement theory to be presented.

This section considered four characteristics of psychological measurement as defined in this book: (1) measurement tends to be indirect, (2) measurement tends to be quantitative, (3) measurement often is relative, and (4) an element of error is always present. With these characteristics, we might conclude that psychological measurement is difficult at best, and beset with problems. Certainly, to some extent this is true, and much remains to be done in terms of both theoretical development and practical application. However, a great deal of progress has been made in developing the concepts of measurement and in overcoming both practical and theoretical difficulties. Thus, measurement is not a static area of study, but one that is dynamic in both its present status and its potential for development. It must be understood that this book delineates principles about which there is still much discussion at the theoretical level. Nevertheless, an understanding of these principles will result in a much more informed practitioner, and will also provide a foundation for further study of the theoretical issues.

Purpose of Psychological Measurement

If we consider why we measure anything, the reasons seem so intuitively obvious that they hardly merit discussion. The very definition and nature of measurement gives its general purpose: that of quantitative description. We are concerned with the study and assessment of human behavior. Thus, the general purpose of measurement is to aid us in this study.

To be more specific about why we measure anything, we must always specify the *purpose* associated with our measurements. For example, the teacher wants to know Johnny's reading level as he enters the third grade to better ascertain the effectiveness of past instruction and prepare a future course of action. The psychologist wants anxiety measures on a group of patients for the prediction of behavior, or to prepare a course of action that may affect future behavior. For example, if an individual exhibits a high degree of anxiety, the psychologist may try to keep the individual in situations that produce low or no anxiety. A counselor wants aptitude information on counselees. In certain settings, decisions about promotion, assignment, continuation, or termination are based on measurement results. Measurement is used to assist in such decision making.

Another useful application of measurement is in research. Adequate measurement is recognized as an essential part of quantitative research, such as theory building, theory testing, etc. Whatever the application, it should be obvious that purpose is an overriding consideration associated with each application. Any time a test is given, the purpose for giving the test and the decisions to be reached should be delineated clearly.

Need for Psychological Measurement

Psychological measurement eventually is operationalized in the form of some type of test or assessment instrument. Although we can identify various uses of test results, questions about test validity—whether the test measures what it is supposed to measure—can often be raised. Indeed, the testing movement has always had some critics, but by the early 1960s, this criticism had increased, and the widespread use of test results was being questioned because of possible serious social consequences.

To be sure, difficulties may be encountered in specific measurement, testing, or assessment situations. There may be a risk of the misuse of information. To guard against such misuse, decisions about the use of specific tests should be made by competent persons, usually a psychologist with the appropriate training. At least the individuals that prescribe the tests should be familiar with them and their supporting research.

Test items and tests themselves become dated and their usefulness may change over time. Certain kinds of tests or assessments are susceptible to faking. (For example, an individual may respond in a socially desirable manner even though this is not his true feeling.) These weaknesses may be inherent in some measurement instruments, but, again, a thorough knowledge of the test and its research background minimizes misuse and misinterpretation.

Psychological measurement to a large extent involves human subjects. Anastasi (1967, p. 297) has recognized the objection that psychological tests may represent an invasion of privacy. This problem has commonly been associated with personality tests, but it can also apply to other types as well. Certainly almost everyone would agree that the individual must be protected against unnecessary invasions of his privacy. This is true not only for routine testing, but also in research situations. The American Psychological Association's Ad Hoc Committee on Ethical Standards (1973) dealt with this problem and developed a statement of procedures and ethics. In this way the research and development of psychological assessment can continue with a minimum risk that any individual's privacy will be jeopardized or misused. To prohibit certain tests or items, or destroy test score records, would be an overreaction that would seriously damage research and development of psychological assessment, also eliminating its established and beneficial uses.

Anastasi (1967, p. 297) suggests two major considerations applicable to overcoming objections to psychological testing in individual situations: (1) the purpose for which the testing is conducted, and (2) the relevance of the information sought to the specific testing purpose. Once these two considerations are clearly identified and the testing situation is structured to meet them (within the range of appropriate procedures), the objections to the testing or assessment tend to be overcome.

The specific need for psychological measurement varies from situation to situation. Of course, these needs are closely related to the specific purposes discussed earlier. However, a general summary statement of the need for psychological assessment/measurement/testing can be given by:

> The nature of man and of society makes it necessary that we attempt to assess psychological characteristics. Individual human beings differ from one another in a variety of ways: society requires a variety of diverse contributions from its members. The more accurately we can judge each person's suitability for potential roles consistent with his interests, the more successfully a society will function. Accurate assessment brings benefits to the individual as well by enabling him to locate the particular kinds of situations in which he can function most effectively as he seeks education, employment, medical and psychological services, and fuller personal development [American Psychological Assn., 1970, p. 264].

In psychology there is a great deal of emphasis placed on securing all types of information through measurements. Thus, it seems reasonable to consider the types of phenomena we attempt to measure. For example, think about the measurement of intelligence. Eysenck (1953b, pp. 19–20) suggests that the first thing we must recognize when considering intelligence is that it is not real. Loevinger (1957) suggests that human abilities must be real in some sense; and Kaiser (1960), in a critique of a measurement and statistics text, points toward an overemphasis on the "real" existence of intelligence.

What We Measure

We have previously noted the complexities of behavioral measurement; now we suggest that the major reason for these complexities is that we measure constructs, not entities. In the behavioral sciences we attribute structure to behavior and infer constructs from this structure. In the discussion that follows, we will use the terms *construct, trait,* or *attribute* to refer to inferences from behavior or behavior categories. It is important that the student distinguish between *entity* and *construct,* and understand our meaning of construct, trait, or attribute. One example of a construct, trait, or attribute is numerical ability. We give a test of numerical operations to a group and observe that some individuals score higher than others. Next, we infer that some people have greater numerical ability than others. Thus, we infer an ability from the observed behavior—the test.

One of the purposes of measurement is appraisal of human behavior, which quickly leads to the distinction between aptitude, achievement, and ability tests. Although consensus about these terms varies, Wesman (1968) lends the greatest credibility to these distinctions. While stressing that what we do intellectually reflects learning, he emphasizes that the differences between aptitude, achievement, and ability tests *lie in the purposes for which they are used.* If we wish to determine how much a student has learned, we are dealing with the measurement of achievement. If we wish to predict a specific future performance, we are dealing with aptitude. Similarly, if our intent is to assess present intelligence, we are dealing with an ability test. While one test could be used for all of the purposes delineated, most tests are designed for rather specific purposes. The preceding distinction may not completely clear some rather muddy water, but it is an important first step. In later discussion, similarities and differences between achievement and intelligence testing will be discussed further, as will the distinctions between intelligence and aptitude testing. What is important now is that the student realize that the distinction is based on the major purpose for which the test is used.

Human behavior may also be differentiated as cognitive or noncognitive. We usually associate cognitive behavior with knowledge and, perhaps, ability. Noncognitive behavior includes personality, attitudes, and social interaction. This may appear to be a clear-cut distinction, but it becomes blurred when operational measurement is attempted. Some measuring instruments try to provide cognitive information when scored one way, and noncognitive information when scored another way. Personality has been used to refer to the sum total of an individual's mental and emotional characteristics. However, in this text, the term *personality* refers to the subset of noncognitive characteristics.

In summary, a host of constructs are measurable in psychology. Those constructs with which we are most concerned can be classified by purpose, and as cognitive and noncognitive. This section has been designed to clarify terms and to make the student aware of important issues in the measurement of human behavior. Deciding what constructs to measure in order to meet certain purposes, the cognitive and noncognitive organization of constructs, and the effective use of test information will be discussed in later chapters.

Suggested Readings

Coombs, C. H. A theory of data. *Psychological Review,* 1960, 67, 143–159.

Stevens, S. S. On the theory of scales of measurement. *Science,* 1946, 103, 670–680.

Stevens, S. S. (Ed.) *Handbook of experimental psychology.* New York: Wiley, 1951, Chapter 1.

Stevens, S. S. Problems and methods of psychophysics. *Psychological Bulletin,* 1958, 55, 177–196.

Individual Review Questions

1. A broad definition of measurement is: measurement is the assignment of _____ to objects or events according to _____.

2. In qualifying the broad concept of measurement, the numerals assigned by the rules have _____ meaning.

3. With the qualification suggested in the preceding question, the general purpose of measurement is _____ _____.

4. Numerals are assigned to race horses on a random basis. According to the concept of measurement discussed in the chapter, this procedure *would/would not* be considered quantitative measurement.

5. In contrast to the measurement of many physical objects by direct observation, measuring psychological variables is often done by _____.

6. When we infer ability from an individual's test score, we are _____ ability to that individual.

7. The ability that we attribute to a person is often called a _____.

8. A construct reflects an unobservable process that must be _____ from a test score.

ANSWERS

1. numerals; rules
2. quantitative
3. quantitative description
4. would not
5. inference
6. attributing
7. construct
8. inferred

9. Psychological measurements reflect unobservable processes. We say we are measuring attributes or constructs and not physical _____ .

10. The nature of most psychological measurements requires that the measurements are _____ and indirect.

11. One of the characteristics of relative, indirect measurements is that there is no _____ point.

12. An individual is given a paper-and-pencil "test" to determine the extent of his anxiety by considering his responses to situations posed in the test. This is an example indicating the *indirect/relative* nature of psychological measurement.

13. To make an intelligence test score meaningful, it must be compared to another score. This is an example of the _____ characteristic of psychological measurements.

14. Test scores are sometimes interpreted by comparing a given score to other scores in a group. This type of interpretation is called _____ -referenced measurement.

15. Test scores are sometimes interpreted by constructing test items to reflect certain instructional objectives. These items are then studied to determine degree of mastery or nonmastery in what is called _____ -referenced measurement.

16. Norm-referenced measurement stresses the _____ position of a score in a normative group.

17. Criterion-referenced measurement places stress on the mastery or nonmastery of a group of test items reflecting some _____ objective.

18. In norm-referenced measurement, the group to which a particular score is compared is called a _____ group.

19. Criterion-referenced measurement usually focuses on the _____ of a group of items reflecting an instructional objective.

20. Personality and attitudes are examples of *cognitive/noncognitive* behavior.

21. Measures of interests are samples of *cognitive/noncognitive* behavior.

22. Reasoning ability is an example of *cognitive/noncognitive* behavior.

23. Noncognitive abilities are examples of _____ inferred from observable behavior.

24. The term *cognitive* is usually associated with the term *attitude/knowledge/personality*.

ANSWERS
9. entities
10. relative
11. zero
12. indirect
13. relative
14. norm
15. criterion
16. relative
17. instructional
18. norm
19. mastery, or nonmastery
20. noncognitive
21. noncognitive
22. cognitive
23. constructs, or abilities, or traits (any one)
24. knowledge

Study Exercises

1. Distinguish between direct and indirect measurement.
2. Discuss the relative nature of some psychological measurement.
3. Give some examples of how error might enter into psychological measurement.
4. Discuss the notion of a "construct" or "attribute" in psychological measurement.
5. Which of the following are constructs?
    a. Intelligence
    b. Anxiety
    c. Lever pressing
    d. Motivation
    e. Change in heart rate
6. Distinguish between achievement, ability, and aptitude tests.
7. Distinguish between an entity and an attribute.
8. Distinguish between criterion-referenced and norm-referenced measurement.

ANSWERS
5. Intelligence; anxiety; motivation

Basic Measurement Statistics

2

Measurement has been defined as the quantitative description of human behavior. However, in order to efficiently and successfully describe human behavior, it is necessary to have a mastery of some basic statistical concepts. This chapter presents these basic statistical concepts and techniques.

The subjects[1] and phenomena in psychological measurement generally have characteristics that are either constant or variable for the group under study. If a characteristic is the same for all subjects, we say it is a *constant*. For example, age is considered a constant if a psychologist is studying reaction times of only 18-year-olds. Grade level is a constant if a teacher is measuring the science achievement of fifth graders. Any number of examples could be given, and in most measurement situations, one or more characteristics are constant.

A *variable* is a characteristic that can take on different values for different subjects. In the preceding example, it is unlikely that all 18-year-olds would have the same reaction times. Therefore, reaction time is a variable. The fifth-grade

Constants and Variables

---

[1]In this text we use the term *subjects* to mean the individuals involved in the measurement effort—the individuals being measured. For example, if 40 introductory psychology students were measured on a concept attainment task, they would be the subjects of the study.

group would undoubtedly demonstrate at least some differences in science achievement scores, thus making science achievement a variable. Again, any one situation may involve one or more variables.

Variables are often assigned classifying names that can be somewhat descriptive, but that can also be quite arbitrary. Also, when some type of empirical or implied cause-and-effect relationship exists between two variables, they can be contrasted as independent and dependent variables. *The independent variable affects the dependent variable.* This terminology is often found in what has been classically defined as experimental work. Often, independent variables are classifying variables, such as K different treatments or n different age levels. The letters n and K indicate integers of 2 or greater.

Other descriptive names may be ascribed to variables. For example, we sometimes talk about *organismic variables,* which are variables associated with the organism under study. Age and sex are organismic variables. *Environmental variables* and *instructional variables* are other descriptive examples whose meanings are self-explanatory. In measurement, generally it is the variables with which we are most concerned, but a knowledge of the constants is also important for a correct interpretation of the situation.

Measurement Scales

A cursory examination of the measurements made in psychology quickly reveals that all *levels of measurement* are not the same. There are different scales involved in different types of measurement, and, of course, these must be considered. Considerations involve the operations or computations that can be performed on the numbers, and the interpretations made from such numbers. For example, does measurement of attitude have the same operational status as measurement of weight? Can the same operations be applied to a measure of anxiety as to a measure of intelligence?

In considering different measurement scales, we are basically concerned with the use of numbers. Numbers are sometimes used in ways that involve both quality and quantity; to make our consideration complete, we will include some of these uses in briefly structuring a hierarchy of scales.

Numbers may be used as classification labels, such as numbers on football players' jerseys. In this case, we are using the lowest scale in our hierarchy, a nominal scale. *The nominal scale is simply categorization without order.* Objects or subjects are categorized into two or more groups that indicate only difference with respect to one or more characteristics. Another example of a nominal scale would be the classification of people according to profession. The numbers assigned to the categories imply no quantitative operations. Thus, nominal scale data can only be qualitatively grouped. Nominal data are qualitative data.

The next scale in our hierarchy is the ordinal scale. In addition to indicating difference with respect to a characteristic, *the ordinal scale implies order.* The ordering is in terms of least to most, high to low, or something of the like. However, while order is implied, the concept of equal distance between points is not. The numbers assigned on an ordinal scale provide only relative position in terms of ranks. An example of a variable measured on an ordinal scale is a set of intelligence test scores. Such scores imply only that a higher score reflects more of a trait than a lower score. Equal intervals between scores of, say, 108, 109, and 110 cannot be assumed.

If, in addition to order, we have *equal units or intervals established on our scale*, we have an *interval scale*. Equal units mean that we know how far apart individuals are with respect to the construct being measured. For example, in our scale of measurement, the difference between two individuals scoring 35 and 40 on the amount of some attribute they possess is the same difference as two individuals scoring 48 and 53 on the same attribute. That is, the actual score differences are perfectly related to the amounts on the attribute when we have a true interval scale. The necessary condition for an interval scale is that the equal unit can be adequately established in the scale. Temperature is an example of a variable measured on an interval scale.

This brings us to the final scale of our hierarchy, the ratio scale. *The ratio scale has all the characteristics of the interval scale plus a true zero point.* With a true zero point, we know the distance of each individual from this point. Measuring weight on the usual types of scales is an example of ratio scale measurement. Since a score of zero on a time scale means no time, time scores are also ratio scales. An example of a time score is length of time required for successful performance of a given task. In contrast, it does not make sense to say that a score of zero on an intelligence measure means no intelligence. In addition to the equal unit required of the interval scale, *a ratio scale must be so ordered that a score of zero actually means total absence of the attribute measured.*

Most psychological measures defy any easy categorization into ordinal or interval scales. There are, in essence, no absolutely "correct" or "true" units for any measurement scale. Rather, intervals are established on the basis of convention and usefulness. The concern is not whether to use the measurement scale intervals in statistical analyses, but which intervals will prove the most useful. The assumption of interval scale measurement for most psychological measures is challenged by some. However, many writers (e.g., Nunnally, 1970, pp. 20–21) have argued against the challenge. The assumption of the interval scale provides the option of more powerful methods of statistical analysis. These more powerful statistical methods, which assume interval scales, therefore, are considered appropriate unless the data were originally secured by a ranking procedure clearly resulting in ordinal scale measurement.[2]

[2]For additional discussion of measurement scales and their properties, see Glass and Stanley, 1970, pp. 12–14.

Variables can also be defined as discrete or continuous. *A variable is discrete if it can assume only certain values in the range of measurement.* In contrast, *a continuous variable, theoretically, can take on any values in the range of measurement.* Infinite, precise measurement would be necessary for complete continuity. In actual measurement, all scales have discrete increments, since it is operationally impossible to have a scale with an infinite number of gradations. The important distinction is in the theoretical continuity of the variable. For example, we consider intelligence to be a continuous variable, even though our measurements identify only a finite number of points on the scale.

Distributions and Their Descriptions

In measurement we are often interested in the scores of a group of individuals on some attribute. If the scores on this attribute happen to be the same, we say we have a constant; if they vary, we have a variable. Suppose we gather some test data on ten individuals. Their scores are: 1, 2, 2, 3, 3, 3, 3, 4, 4, 5. The attribute is a variable, because the scores are not the same.

We can also distinguish between discrete and continuous variables. Mental ability is a continuous variable. That is, it can be thought of as being theoretically continuous even though the measurements are discrete, that is, in chunks. In order to graph the measurements of a continuous variable, we let the discrete score of 2 range from 1.5 to 2.5, the score of 3 range from 2.5 to 3.5, etc. In this way, we cover the entire range of the continuous variable. Figure 2.1 presents these test scores plotted against the frequency of occurrence. This representation is commonly called a *histogram*.

Let us consider the description of a distribution. If someone asked you to describe a histogram, how would you do it? It takes three elements to describe a distribution: shape, location, and dispersion. In this figure, the shape of the histogram is symmetrical. We will have more to say about shape later. For the present, let us focus on location and dispersion.

Measures of Central Tendency

Measures of central tendency answer the question, Where do the scores tend to be located on the scale of measurement? Measures of central tendency are location indices. There are several measures of central tendency: the *mode*, the most frequently occurring score; the *median*, the midscore; and the *mean*, the arithmetic average. In Figure 2.1, note that the mean, median, and mode are scores of 3. In this book, the mean will be the measure of greatest importance and the one we will consider most frequently. However, there are situations in which the mode or median might be used to greater advantage.

The mean is symbolized in this book as $\overline{X}$, pronounced X bar. The bar indicates that the value we are considering is the arithmetic average of the scores we call X. If we had a second set of scores, 3, 3, 2, and 1, called Y, the mean is denoted $\overline{Y}$. In this latter example, the mean (2.25), median (2.5), and mode (3) are not all the same. These values are identical in some symmetrical distributions. Nevertheless, in this example, each one does indicate a position of central tendency.

The mean, a measure of location or central tendency, is the arithmetic average of a group of scores.

Before leaving measures of central tendency, let us also consider the computation of $\overline{X}$ and some additional symbolism. To compute $\overline{X}$, we added the scores and divided by the number of scores. The formula to describe these operations is:

$$\overline{X} = \Sigma X/N. \qquad (2.1)$$

The symbol Σ simply means *sum*, and ΣX means *sum the scores called* X. Then, we divide the sum by the total number of scores, designated by N. It is important that the student understand the operations indicated by these symbols because we will quickly develop additional formulas based on these simple beginnings.

Suppose, for the purpose of illustration, we consider a distribution of 40 scores. The scores and their frequencies are presented in Table 2.1. The mode is 39, as determined by simply inspecting the distribution. If we let X represent the score for the ith individual in the distribution, the mean is determined by

Figure 2.1 **Histogram of a Variable Labeled** X

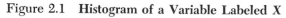

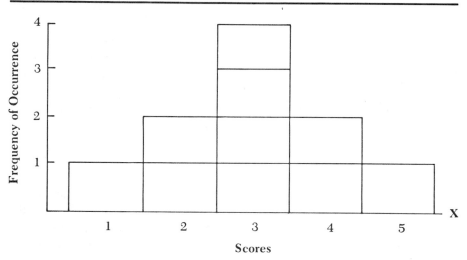

Table 2.1 **Frequency Distribution of Scores**

Score	f	Score	f
35	1	42	3
36	3	43	2
37	2	44	2
38	2	45	3
39	7	46	1
40	4	47	3
41	5	48	2

$$\sum_{i=1}^{40} X_i/40.$$

The notations under and over the Σ indicate that we begin adding with the first and terminate with the fortieth or final score. Applying this formula to the data of our distribution, we find that the total sum of the 40 scores is 1,649. Dividing this sum by 40, we get a mean of 41.225, or, rounded off to tenths, 41.2. In symbol form this operation is written as

$$\sum_{i=1}^{40} X_i/N = 1649/40 = 41.2.$$

In contrast to the mean, the median is determined by the point below which 50 percent of the scores lie, or, in this case, below which we find 20 scores. By counting the frequency, we see that the twentieth score is a 41. However, in this case, the twentieth through the twenty-fourth scores, inclusive, are scores of 41. In order to get a closer estimate of the median, we consider the score 41 as covering the interval of 40.5 to 41.5. In determining the median, we take the lower end of the interval representing the score in which the median falls, and add the proportional part (one out of five) of the interval that we need to reach the median score. Applying this procedure, we find that the median for this distribution is 40.7. The median is computed:

$$\text{Median} = 40.5 + 1/5 = 40.7.$$

As indicated earlier, in a symmetrical distribution, the mean and median would coincide. There is a difference of .5 between the two for this distribution, the mean having the greater value. An important difference between the mean and median is that the mean is affected by extreme scores, whereas the median is not.

The median is always the midpoint of the distribution, and the scores affect the median only as they are located above or below it. A small number of deviant or extreme scores, or even one such score, can affect the mean markedly. If it is desirable to eliminate the effect of such a score, the median is the preferred measure of central tendency.

Consider an example of the mean being affected by extreme scores. Suppose we have a distribution of seven scores: 3, 4, 4, 4, 4, 5, 25. The median of this distribution is the middle score, the fourth score from either end of the distribution, and, computed by the method above, is 4.13. However, the mean for this distribution is 49/7 or 7. Note that the mean is larger than six of the seven scores in the distribution. In this case, the median is much more centrally located, and is a better indicator of the concentration of scores in the distribution.

Measures of Dispersion

When we consider the dispersion or spread of a distribution, we are dealing with measures of variability. If all children age 12 had the same height, there would be no great concern with the height of 12-year-olds. It is the variation of a characteristic within a group of subjects that generates the interest. Researchers search for variable characteristics, devise measures for the characteristics, and attempt to explain the variation.

Measures of variability, in contrast to measures of central tendency, are intervals (or their squares) rather than points. While there are a number of measures of variability, we will consider only three: *range, variance,* and *standard deviation.*

To illustrate the concept of range, consider the sets of scores: $X = 1, 2, 2, 3, 3,$ 3, 3, 3, 4, 4, 5; and $Y = 1, 1, 1, 1, 2, 3, 4, 5, 5, 5, 5$. Figure 2.2 presents the histograms for these two sets of scores. Inspecting the histograms, we can see that X and Y have equal means. However, while the distributions are symmetrical, it should be obvious that the two distributions are different—they differ in dispersion. One simple measure of this dispersion is called *range*. Range is determined by subtracting the smallest from the greatest score and adding 1. In this example, the range is 5 for both the X and Y distributions.

Range is a crude measure of dispersion based only on extreme scores. A more appropriate measure of dispersion would utilize *all* the scores in a set, and thus would reflect the greater dispersion found in the Y variable. The measure that will better reflect dispersion in a variable is called variance (S^2), and it is calculated using the following formula:[3]

[3]Variance, by definition, is $\Sigma(X - \overline{X})^2/N$. Many textbooks use $N - 1$ instead of N in the denominator when computing variance or standard deviation. The $N - 1$ is used when an unbiased estimate of a population variance is being computed in an inferential statistics context. In the discussion here, variance is generally used in a descriptive, not inferential, sense, hence the use of N in the denominator.

$$S_x^2 = \frac{\Sigma(X - \overline{X})^2}{N} = \text{variance of } X.$$

$$(2.2)$$

$$S_y^2 = \frac{\Sigma(Y - \overline{Y})^2}{N} = \text{variance of } Y.$$

S^2 is the general symbol for the variance, whereas S_x^2 specifically refers to the variance of the variable called X. Table 2.2 presents the computation for S_x^2.

To compute the variance, we first subtract the mean from all the scores, giving us deviation scores $(X - \overline{X})$. It is a property of the mean that the sum of the deviations is 0. Note that subtracting the mean from a set of scores simply tells us how many units each score is above or below the mean. Figure 2.3 presents the histogram of the scores with the mean subtracted. Note the difference between the raw score scale (X) and deviation score scale $(X - \overline{X})$. The deviation score scale, for example, tells us that raw scores of 4 and 5 are one and two units above the mean, respectively. Variance is the average of these squared deviation scores.

Consider again the X and Y variables of Figure 2.2. Suppose the X scores represent the height, in feet, of 11 dogs. The mean height of the dogs is 3, while a dog 5 feet high is 2 feet higher than the mean height. Now, the deviation scores clearly give us a linear distance from the mean, or a one-dimensional measure of dispersion. Blommers and Lindquist (1960, p. 140) suggest that when we find $(X - \overline{X})^2$, we are talking about squared distances, or, in this case, squared feet.

Figure 2.2 Histograms Showing Relative Dispersion on Two Variables Labeled X and Y

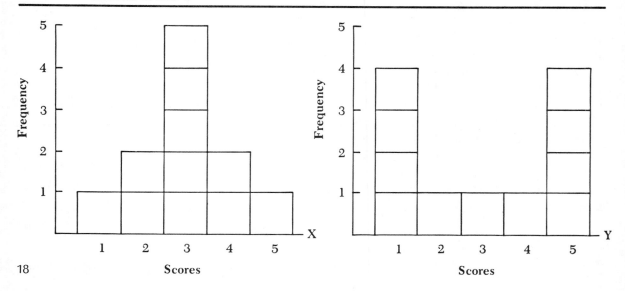

Table 2.2 **Illustration of the Computation of Variance:
Deviation Score Formula**

Individuals	X	$X - \overline{X}$	$(X - \overline{X})^2$
A	1	-2	4
B	2	-1	1
C	2	-1	1
D	3	0	0
E	3	0	0
F	3	0	0
G	3	0	0
H	3	0	0
I	4	1	1
J	4	1	1
K	5	2	4
			$\overline{12}$

$$S_x^2 = \Sigma(X - \overline{X})^2/N = 12/11 = 1.1.$$

Thus, variance is a two-dimensional measure of dispersion—the average squared deviation about the mean—as opposed to deviation scores, which are one-dimensional measures.

If you were to compute S_y^2, the variance of the Y scores, you would find it to

Figure 2.3 **Histogram Showing Raw and Deviation Score Units**

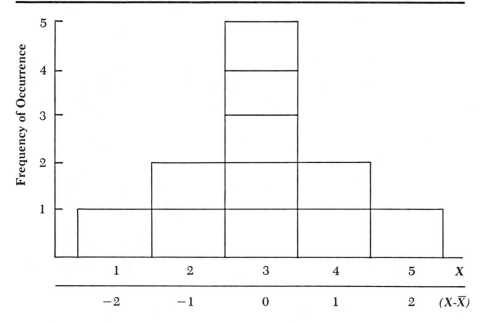

Table 2.3   Illustration of the Computation of Variance: Raw Score Formula

Individuals	X	X^2
A	1	1
B	2	4
C	2	4
D	3	9
E	3	9
F	3	9
G	3	9
H	3	9
I	4	16
J	4	16
K	5	25
$\Sigma X = 33$		$111 = \Sigma X^2$

$$\frac{\Sigma X^2 - (\Sigma X)^2/N}{N} = \frac{111 - 1089/11}{11}$$
$$= 12/11 = 1.1.$$

be 3.1. Clearly, 3.1 is greater than 1.1, the variance of the X distribution. Figure 2.2 confirms this greater dispersion in the Y variable. Thus, in variance, we have a measure of dispersion that reflects the difference in dispersion in the X and Y variables.

Often the variance of a set of scores is desired, and the mean is found to be a mixed number or noninteger. In this situation, formula 2.2 becomes impractical to use,[4] and the following computational formula can be substituted:

$$S_x^2 = \frac{\Sigma X^2 - (\Sigma X)^2/N}{N}. \tag{2.3}$$

Although not as easy to use as formula 2.2, formula 2.3 utilizes only raw scores and is extremely practical when a desk calculator or computer is available. Table 2.3 presents the computation of the variance of X from formula 2.3, and shows that formula 2.3 gives the same result as formula 2.2. As a matter of fact, formula 2.3 can easily be derived from formula 2.2; that is, their equivalence can be shown.

Variance, a two-dimensional measure of dispersion, is the average of the squared deviations from the mean.

Since variance is a two-dimensional measure of the dispersion, it follows that we can take the square root of S_x^2 and go from a measure in two dimensions back to a measure of dispersion in one dimension—a linear measure. This measure is called standard deviation (S_x).

[4]Not only can the squaring of deviated nonintegers become tedious, but when these deviations are squared, if the mean has been rounded off, we may have an accumulation of rounding errors.

To place deviation scores, variance, and standard deviation in perspective, let us review our discussion of dispersion. We selected a set of scores: $X = 1, 2, 2,$ $3, 3, 3, 3, 3, 4, 4, 5$, from which we subtracted the mean to get a set of deviation scores: $X - \overline{X} = -2, -1, -1, 0, 0, 0, 0, 0, 1, 1, 2$. Now, deviation scores are perfectly good scores; but, no matter how great the dispersion, the average deviation score is always 0. However, if we square and average these scores, we circumvent this limitation, and get a measure of dispersion called variance. Although an extremely important index (as we shall see shortly), variance has the undesirable characteristic of being in squared units. When we take the square root of S^2, we get a one-dimensional linear measure of dispersion called *standard deviation*. Standard deviation is an interval on the measurement scale, a linear measure of dispersion in the same metric or measure as the scores.

In the set of scores that we called X, the variance was 1.1, which yields a standard deviation of approximately 1.05. Now, 1.05 is a linear measure of dispersion; it can be represented on the score scale of the histogram as shown in Figure 2.4. One way we use standard deviation is to plot it from the mean. For the distribution of scores called X, a score of 4.05 is one standard deviation above the mean, a score of 5.10 is two standard deviations above the mean, etc. Since a standard deviation is a linear distance on the base line of the distribution, we

Figure 2.4   Histogram Showing Linear Units on the Score Scale

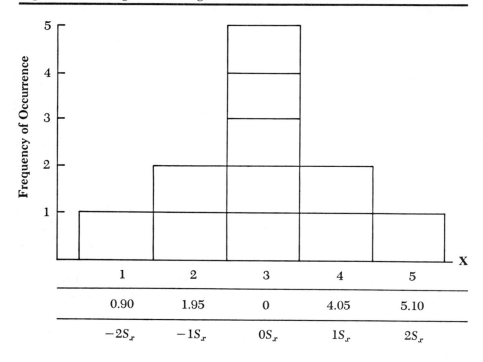

Table 2.4 **Illustrative Example of How the Standard Deviation Reflects the Metric of the Raw Scores**

Individuals	U	$U - \overline{U}$	$(U - \overline{U})^2$	Individuals	T	$T - \overline{T}$	$(T - \overline{T})^2$
A	1	-2	4	A	10	-20	400
B	2	-1	1	B	20	-10	100
C	3	0	0	C	30	00	000
D	4	1	1	D	40	10	100
E	5	2	4	E	50	20	400
			10				1,000

$$S_u{}^2 = 10/5 = 2.0$$
$$S_u = 1.414$$

$$S_t{}^2 = 1000/5 = 200$$
$$S_t = 14.14$$

can compute: the mean plus one-half standard deviation $[\overline{X} + .5(1.05) = 3.53]$; the mean plus one and one-half standard deviations $[\overline{X} + 1.5(1.05) = 4.58]$; one and eight-tenths standard deviations below the mean $[\overline{X} - 1.8(1.05) = 1.11]$; etc.

Standard deviation is a linear measure of dispersion that is found by taking the square root of the variance:

$$S_x = \sqrt{\Sigma(X - \overline{X})^2/N}.$$

It is interesting that when we plot standard deviations with respect to the mean, they begin to have empirical value. For many distributions of test scores, two or three standard deviations from the mean encompass most test scores. This is one reason for the present discussion. Adding and subtracting standard deviations from the mean will come to have more conceptual and empirical meaning later.

A standard deviation is often described as a measure of dispersion in the metric of the scores. To find the meaning of the "metric of the scores," we compute the standard deviations for the following sets of scores: $T = 10, 20, 30, 40, 50$; and $U = 1, 2, 3, 4, 5$. Table 2.4 presents the computation, and shows that when the measures are in units, the standard deviation is in units; when the measures are in tens, the standard deviation is in tens. Thus, standard deviation reflects the metric of the scores.

In this example, suppose we want to interpret a score of 5. By itself the score means nothing; however, if we were told that the mean is 3, then a score of 5 begins to have meaning because we know it is two units above the mean. The next question is whether two units above the mean is a large or small distance relative to the other scores. If the standard deviation is 0.5, then two units is four standard deviations above the mean. If the standard deviation is 4, then a score of 5 is only one-half a standard deviation above the mean. Thus, standard deviation gives relative meaning to deviation units.

> Standard deviation is a linear measure of dispersion that gives relative meaning to the distance a score is from the mean; this occurs when the standard deviation unit is divided into the deviation of that score from the mean.

Since the variance and standard deviation are, by far, the most widely used and important measures of variability, we might comment briefly on them. Obviously, the more variable the scores of a distribution, the greater the measures of dispersion. Note that since the variance involves deviation scores, it is affected by every score in the distribution (rather than by just two, as is the range).

If we *add* a specified constant value to all scores of a distribution, we do not change the variance of the distribution. All we do is shift the entire distribution on the scale of measurement by the value of the constant.[5]

Suppose we *multiply* each score by a constant. Now, the distribution of scores generated by this multiplication will change in variability. The variance of the new distribution, in general, will be the square of the constant times the variance of the original distribution. In symbol form, if we represent the constant by C, the variance of the new distribution would be $C^2(S^2)$. Correspondingly, the standard deviation of the new distribution would be CS. Multiplying all scores in a distribution by a constant also multiplies the mean by that constant.

As an example of the above, consider the data in Table 2.2. For this set of scores the variance is 1.1 and the standard deviation is about 1.05. Now, if these scores were all multiplied by a constant value, say 2, the variance would increase to 4.4 (2 squared times 1.1); and the standard deviation would be 2.1 (2 times 1.05).

> If we multiply all the scores in a distribution by a constant, C, it has the effect of multiplying the variance by C^2 and the standard deviation by C.

The concept of variance is important in measurement from both a conceptual and a practical standpoint. Later in the text, we will discuss partitioning of variance according to sources, and quantitatively separating the variance into components ascribable to these sources. Other concepts, such as the reliability of measurement, introduced later, are embedded in the concept of variance. Many measurement procedures deal with the manipulation of the variance of one or more distributions.

Thus far we have mentioned three general characteristics that we use to describe a distribution: shape, location, and dispersion. Several measures of

---

[5]Mathematical proofs could be presented for the properties of the variance that we are introducing at this point; however, such proofs are not essential for the purposes of this text. For such mathematical developments, see, for example, Glass and Stanley, 1970, pp. 83–84.

central tendency and variability have been introduced. It is through these indices that we describe location and dispersion. Recall that measures of central tendency are points on the scale of measurement, and measures of variability are intervals (or their squares). The shape of a distribution can be determined by a histogram, or the shape of the distribution of a specific variable may be known, as will be described later.

z-Scores

Given a mean and a standard deviation, we can locate a score at a given number of standard deviations above or below the mean. For the X scores of Table 2.2, we found a mean of 3 and a standard deviation of 1.05, respectively. We then found that a score one standard deviation above the mean was 4.05; one-half standard deviation above the mean was 3.53, etc. Generally, we want to determine how far a given score is above the mean in standard deviation units. In other words, we have a given score that we want to interpret. To interpret a score in relation to other scores, we ask the question, How many standard deviation units is a given score from the mean? The answer to the question is called a z-score.

A z-score is the distance of a score from the mean, expressed in standard deviation units.

A z-score is simply the number of standard deviation units a given score is above or below the mean. It is found by the following formula:

$$z = \frac{X - \overline{X}}{S_x}.$$

(2.4)

In this formula, $X - \overline{X}$ is a deviation score, and dividing by S_x determines the number of standard deviation units above or below the mean. The algebraic sign of the deviation determines whether the score is above or below the mean. Consider the following example using two sets of scores: $S = 1, 2, 3, 4, 5$; and $M = 6, 7, 8, 9, 10$. The two sets of scores have the same shape and dispersion, but they differ in central tendency. Suppose a student has the score of 4 in spelling and 9 in mathematics. In which area, spelling or mathematics, did he excel? Converting the scores to standard deviation units: $(4 - 3) / 1.414 = .707$, and $(9 - 8) / 1.414 = .707$, we find that both performances resulted in the same relative position in their respective distributions; that is, in spelling and in mathematics, the student found himself .707 standard deviation units above the mean. The preceding comparison is possible because z-scores have a standard deviation of 1, and a mean of 0.

A group of scores transformed to *z*-scores will have a mean of
0 and standard deviation of 1.

The Normal Distribution

The normal distribution has considerable importance in psychological measurement. It is not a single distribution with a fixed scale of measurement, but is a family of distributions that assumes the general shape of a bell. We sometimes say that a variable, for example, mathematics achievement, is "normally distributed." This means that the shape of the distribution of mathematics achievement scores follows the normal curve. Normal distributions differ in variability; and, of course, location depends on the variable under consideration and its scale of measurement. Some examples of normal distributions are presented in Figure 2.5.

The unit normal distribution, or unit normal curve as it is called, has special characteristics. The unit normal curve is symmetrical about the mean, has a standard deviation of 1, and has an area under the curve of 1. The maximum height of the curve occurs at the mean of 0 and decreases in height for values of X farther from the mean. For values of X three standard deviations on either side of the mean, the curve approaches the base line, where it remains asymptotic to positive and negative infinity.

The relationship between variability and the area of the normal distribution is presented in Figure 2.6. The interval between the mean and one standard deviation on one side of the mean includes about 34 percent of the area. Thus, about 68 percent of the area is contained within plus or minus one standard deviation from the mean. Correspondingly, approximately 96 percent of the area under the curve is located within plus or minus two standard deviations from the mean. Approximately 99 percent of the area is located within plus or minus three standard deviations from the mean. Thus, knowledge of the scope and characteristics of the normal distribution relative to the area under the curve indicates that when scores are normally distributed, a score of plus or minus two standard deviations is a rare occurrence.

The student's first confrontation with standard deviation and descriptive

Figure 2.5   **Examples of "Normal" Distributions**

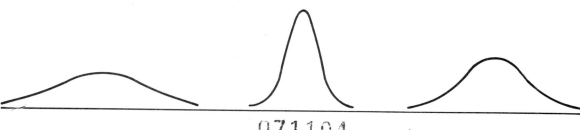

statistics can be esoteric. The difficulty arises because all of the statistical concepts just presented must be seen in relation to one another. For example, suppose a student's performance on a test of numerical ability resulted in a score of 70. In isolation, the score is meaningless. Suppose further, that on the same test, the mean for a larger, representative sample of college freshmen was 50 with a standard deviation of 10, and that the scores were approximately normally distributed. Relative to the mean alone, 70 has little meaning. Knowing that 70 is two standard deviations above the mean is practically meaningless until we know the characteristics of the normal curve. Then, a score located two standard deviations above the mean becomes relatively high, because it is higher than approximately 98 percent of all scores in the sample. Thus, mean, standard deviation, and the normal curve must be considered in relation to one another to make an interpretation of any score possible. (Further description of the unit normal curve will be presented in the next chapter.)

Covariation

Up to this point, we have limited our discussion to a single distribution. We have described the distribution and determined measures of central tendency and variability. Now, we turn our attention to the distribution of two variables, the bivariate distribution.

Recall that when we talked about a single variable, we plotted its histogram in a two-dimensional space on a flat plane. In discussing the bivariate distribution, we find it occurs in a three-dimensional space. Consider the two-variable situation presented in Table 2.5. Five individuals are measured on attributes X and Y. Figure 2.7 presents the distribution of the two variables. The individuals

Figure 2.6   **Area and Standard Deviation Intervals of the Normal Distribution**

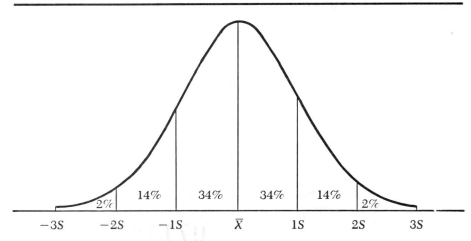

		14%	34%	34%	14%		
	2%					2%	
−3S	−2S	−1S	$\overline{X}$	1S	2S	3S

are located by coordinates defined by the measurement scales of the X and Y variables. For example, the coordinates for individual A locate that person at $X = 1$

Table 2.5   Scores for Five Individuals on Two Distinct Variables, X and Y

Individuals	X Score	Y Score	$(X - \overline{X})$	$(Y - \overline{Y})$
A	1	2	−2	−1
B	2	1	−1	−2
C	3	3	0	0
D	4	5	+1	+2
E	5	4	+2	+1

Figure 2.7   Plot of Bivariate Distribution Showing High Scores Related to High Scores and Low Scores Related to Low Scores

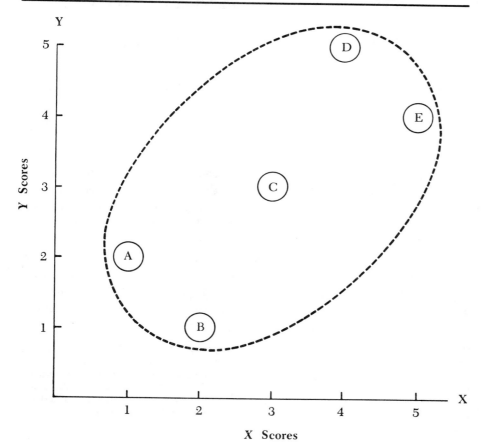

and $Y = 2$. Looking at Figure 2.7, we note a tendency for the bivariate distribution to be oriented in such a way that high scores on X are associated with high scores on Y, and low scores on X are associated with low scores on Y. For example, individuals D and E have positive deviation scores on both variable X and variable Y. Individuals A and B have negative deviation scores on both variable X and variable Y. If the individuals tend to be above or below the mean on both variables, we say there is a covariation in their scores. The covariance of X and Y is defined as:

$$\rho_{xy} = \frac{\Sigma(X - \overline{X})(Y - \overline{Y})}{N}. \tag{2.5}$$

The symbol, ρ_{xy}, is used to indicate covariance. Thus, *covariance is the average product of two sets of deviation scores.* Note that the deviation score for a given individual on X is multiplied by this same individual's deviation score on Y. Operationally, in determining covariance, we sum the products of the deviation scores, and divide by the number of observations on either variable.

Covariance is the average product of the deviation scores for two variables.

Covariance is a useful index of relationship, but it is not as easy to interpret as the correlation coefficient.

Correlation

One characteristic of covariance is that it exists in the units of the variables. If we are considering covariance between height and weight, with height measured in inches, this covariance would differ from the covariance between these two variables if height were measured in feet. In order to circumvent this characteristic and compare the degree of relationship between different pairs of variables, we standardize them, as we did with z-scores. To find z-scores we divided deviation scores by the standard deviation. In the case of covariance, we also divide by the standard deviation of each variable. When we do, we have a standardized measure of covariance called the *Pearson product-moment correlation coefficient*, identified by r. This coefficient is a standardized index of the relationship between two variables.[6]

[6]In this discussion for simplicity's sake, we will consider the relationship between two variables, that is, bivariate correlation. Actually, the concept of correlation can be extended to more than two variables. Multiple correlation involves the relationship between a single variable and a weighted linear combination of two or more variables. Canonical correlation involves the relationship between two groups of variables, each group containing two or more variables. The basic underlying reasoning is much the same; the computation and interpretation becomes increasingly complicated with more sophisticated correlation techniques.

Let us reconsider our previous discussion of the two variables, X and Y (illustrated by Figure 2.7). Each subject has an X score and a Y score; thus, we can think of the X, Y pairs as points on a graph. Such points may fall anywhere within the graph. It is conceivable that the points would fall along a straight line. Most likely, if we had a large number of pairs of scores, the points would not fall exactly on a straight line, but, depending on the extent of the relationship, cluster around a line. The plot of points, called a *scattergram*, would then have its boundaries defined by an ellipse (see Figure 2.8).

Another way to consider the correlation coefficient is that it reflects the degree to which the bivariate distribution (as Figure 2.7) forms a line, and also the orientation of the distribution of the two variables in the space. The coefficient, r, can take on values from -1.00 to $+1.00$. A positive 1.00 means that the bivariate distribution forms a perfect line, oriented so high scores on X are associated with high scores on Y, and low scores on X are associated with low scores on Y. Figure 2.9b presents this positive relationship—high scores associated with high scores and low scores with low scores. Conversely, a correlation coefficient of -1.00 also indicates a perfect linear relationship, but here high X scores relate to low Y scores, and low X scores relate to high Y scores. There is a perfect inverse, or negative relationship. Figure 2.9a presents this relationship.

It is extremely rare to find a perfect relationship between psychological measures. However, there are many cases where moderate relationships do exist. We might consider the relationship between IQ test and achievement test performance, in which a positive relationship is likely to be found. The positive, but modest, relationship simply means that high scores on the IQ test tend to go with high scores on the achievement test. If we have a relationship between two measures, such as IQ score and time required on a problem-solving task, the relationship is likely to be negative; that is, subjects with high IQ scores have short solution times, and subjects with low IQ scores have long solution times.

To summarize, we presented a conception of the bivariate distribution (Figure 2.7). This two-dimensional view of the bivariate distribution is known as a scattergram. Figure 2.8 presents scattergrams of varying positive and negative relationships. Figure 2.8 shows that if the correlation is nonzero, the points of the N individuals on the two variables will tend to form an ellipse, with the limiting case being a straight line—an r of plus or minus 1.00. As r goes from 0.00 to 1.00, the shape of the scattergram becomes increasingly linear (as shown in Figures 2.8a and 2.8e), which partially confirms the definition that r is an index of linear relationship between two variables.

> The Pearson product-moment correlation, r, is an index of linear relationship that varies between -1.00 and $+1.00$. The sign indicates whether the relationship is direct (positive) or inverse (negative); the index indicates the degree of linear relationship.

Figure 2.8   Diagrams Showing Scattergrams of Varying Relationships

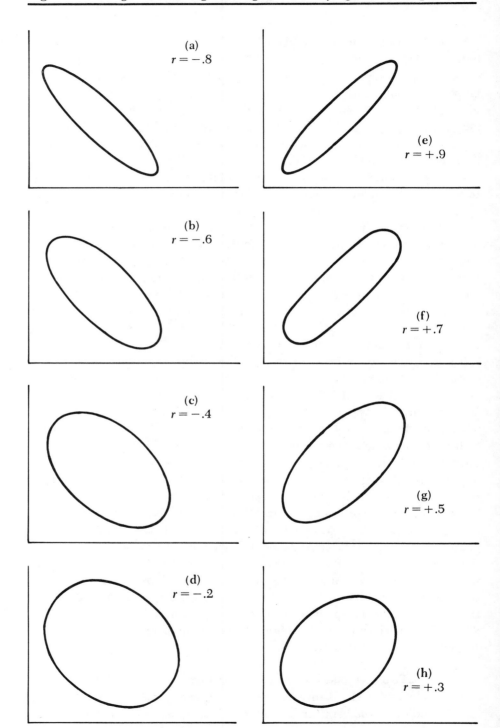

The correlation coefficient indicates the extent to which the points of the scattergram fit a straight line. Suppose a curvilinear relationship exists between two variables and r is computed (for example, the relationship between age and performance on a running task). In this case, r would be quite low, reflecting that the data would not fit a straight line. In this sense, r would be inappropriate because a straight line does not adequately represent the relationship between the variables. Assumptions about the underlying distribution of the variables may be introduced if, after r is computed, inferences are made regarding other indices.[7]

Computation of r_{yx}

Let us suppose that we have two continuous variables, X and Y, and that it is appropriate to compute the Pearson product-moment coefficient, r_{yx}.[8] There are several formulas available for computation of the coefficient—all of which give equivalent results. The following formulation, while nonefficient as a computational formula, has interesting conceptual properties:

Figure 2.9   Diagram Showing Negative and Positive Linear Relationships

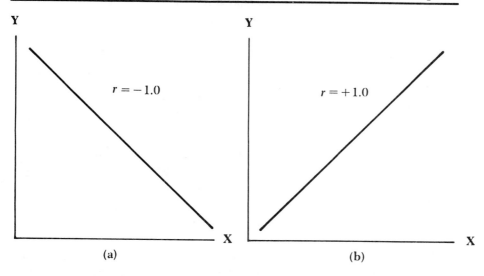

(a)   (b)

[7]As an example, the assumption that both variables are normally distributed is sometimes introduced. There is some controversy regarding this assumption, and it is made basically for the use of inferential statistics. For a detailed discussion of this assumption and its requirements, see, for example, Nunnally, 1967, pp. 125–126.

[8]The subscript yx in r_{yx} specifically indicates that we are correlating variables Y and X.

Table 2.6   Computational Example of the Product-Moment Correlation: Deviation Formula

Individual	X	Y	$X - \overline{X}$	$Y - \overline{Y}$	$(X - \overline{X})(Y - \overline{Y})$	$(X - \overline{X})^2$	$(Y - \overline{Y})^2$
A	1	2	−2	−1	2	4	1
B	2	1	−1	−2	2	1	4
C	3	3	0	0	0	0	0
D	4	5	1	2	2	1	4
E	5	4	2	1	2	4	1
					8	10	10

$$\frac{\Sigma(X - \overline{X})(Y - \overline{Y})}{N\sqrt{[\Sigma(X - \overline{X})^2/N][\Sigma(Y - \overline{Y})^2/N]}} = \frac{8}{5\sqrt{[10/5][10/5]}} = 8/10 = .8.$$

$$r_{yx} = \frac{\Sigma(X - \overline{X})(Y - \overline{Y})}{NS_xS_y} = \frac{\Sigma(X - \overline{X})(Y - \overline{Y})}{N\sqrt{[\Sigma(X - \overline{X})^2/N][\Sigma(Y - \overline{Y})^2/N]}}. \qquad (2.6)$$

What do we have in this formula? Recalling formula 2.5 for covariance, we see the average product of the deviation scores in the numerator of formula 2.6. Note that the retention of the algebraic sign of the deviation score is important. If high scores on one variable go with low scores on the other variable, the cross products will be negative. The denominator of the formula will always be positive, since standard deviations are always positive.

Another way of expressing formula 2.6 is as a standardized covariance. We see that each deviation score is divided by its respective standard deviation. Thus, formula 2.6 shows that all deviation scores have been transformed to z-scores, and formula 2.6 can be written:

$$r_{yx} = \Sigma z_x z_y / N. \qquad (2.7)$$

In formula 2.7, we see that the Pearson r, a standardized covariance, is simply the average product of the z-scores of the two variables under consideration.

> **The Pearson product-moment correlation, r, is the average product of the z-scores for two variables.**

Furthermore, when each individual's z-scores on X and Y are equal, formula 2.7 can be written: $\Sigma z^2/N$, which is the variance for z-scores—a value of 1.[9] When there is a perfect correspondence between two variables, formula 2.7

---

[9]A z-score is a deviation score and the mean z-score is 0. Thus, when a z-score is converted to a deviation score by subtracting 0, in essence, we retain the z-score. Therefore, applying the deviation formula for variance, the numerator is indeed the sum of the squared z-scores.

Table 2.7 Computational Example of the Product-Moment Correlation: Raw Score Formula

Individuals	X	Y	XY	X^2	Y^2
A	1	2	2	1	4
B	2	1	2	4	1
C	3	3	9	9	9
D	4	5	20	16	25
E	5	4	20	25	16
	15	15	53	55	55

$$\frac{N\Sigma XY - \Sigma X \Sigma Y}{\sqrt{[N\Sigma X^2 - (\Sigma X)^2][N\Sigma Y^2 - (\Sigma Y)^2]}} = \frac{5(53) - 15(15)}{\sqrt{[5(55) - 225][5(55) - 225]}}$$

$$= \frac{265 - 225}{\sqrt{50(50)}} = \frac{40}{50} = .8.$$

attains a value of 1. The computation of an imperfect relationship by formula 2.6 is presented in Table 2.6. We can also reduce formula 2.6 to the more convenient form:

$$r_{yx} = \frac{\Sigma(X - \overline{X})(Y - \overline{Y})}{\sqrt{[\Sigma(X - \overline{X})^2][\Sigma(Y - \overline{Y})^2]}}. \tag{2.8}$$

Let us consider a more functional variant of formula 2.8. A simple algebraic expansion of this formula results in the following computation version of the product-moment correlation:

$$r_{yx} = \frac{N\Sigma XY - \Sigma X \Sigma Y}{\sqrt{[N\Sigma X^2 - (\Sigma X)^2][N\Sigma Y^2 - (\Sigma Y)^2]}}, \tag{2.9}$$

where:

N = number of pairs of scores
ΣXY = sum of the cross products of the raw scores
ΣX = sum of the X scores
ΣY = sum of the Y scores
ΣX^2 = sum of the squared X scores
ΣY^2 = sum of the squared Y scores
$(\Sigma X)^2$ = sum of the X scores squared
$(\Sigma Y)^2$ = sum of the Y scores squared.

Utilizing this computational formula for the data in Table 2.6, we derive Table 2.7.

Thus, deviation and computational formulas give the same results. However, with large sets of test scores the computational formula, formula 2.9, is more suitable for use with calculators.

At this point, let us consider briefly the computational formula and what it contains relative to the variables. If two variables are unrelated, their sum of cross products is zero. Thus, the numerator of our formula goes to zero, and the correlation is zero. If one of the standard deviations is zero, one of the "variables" has been reduced to a constant, resulting in a denominator of zero. Consequently, the concept of correlation, under this condition, becomes meaningless.

Summary

In this chapter we have introduced basic statistical concepts and procedures related to measurement. The emphasis has been on the description of distributions singly in terms of measures of central tendency and measures of variability, and jointly in terms of correlation coefficients, describing the relationship between the two variables. It requires shape, location, and dispersion to describe a distribution adequately. The concept of variance of scores around the mean of the distribution is important in terms of the future uses we will make of it. In correlation we are interested in the concept of covariance, how the scores of two distributions covary together.

Suggested Readings

Bradley, J., & McClelland, J. *Basic statistical concepts.* Chicago: Scott Foresman, 1963, Chapters 1–6, 9, 10.

Ferguson, G. A. *Statistical analysis in psychology and education.* (3rd ed.) New York: McGraw-Hill, 1971, Chapters 1–4, 6, 7.

Popham, W. J. *Educational statistics: Use and interpretation.* New York: Harper & Row, 1967, Chapters 1–3, 5, 6.

Spence, J., et al. *Elementary statistics.* (2nd ed.) New York: Appleton-Century-Crofts, 1968, Chapters 5, 6, 10.

Individual Review Questions

ANSWERS

1. constant; variable
2. sex of the student; ability level
3. nominal

1. A characteristic that is the same for all subjects is called a _____, and a characteristic that takes on different values is called a _____.

2. In a study of elementary school mathematics instruction, which of the following would be considered organismic variables: sex of the student, instructional materials, class size, ability level, time for drill?

3. When numbers are used simply as labels indicating difference but not order, the scale of measurement is _____.

4. If $a = 4, b = 6, c = 8, d = 10$, and $b - a = d - c$, but $c \neq 2a$, we have a(n) _____ scale of measurement.

5. The categories "Democrat" or "Republican" do not imply order, therefore, their use constitutes a(n) _____ scale of measurement.

6. A five-point scale consisting of categories from "strongly agree" to "strongly disagree" would be considered a(n) _____ scale of measurement.

7. The measurement scale in the preceding question is a more "refined" scale than nominal, because it implies _____.

8. If $A = 5, B = 10, C = 15$; $B - A = C - B$ and $C = 3A$, we have a(n) _____ scale of measurement.

9. The number of students in the classes of a university is a *discrete/continuous* variable.

10. A graphic representation of a frequency distribution is a _____.

11. The distances between the points or categories of an ordinal scale are *equal/unequal*.

12. A measurement scale that contains an absolute zero, in addition to equal units, is a(n) _____ scale.

13. Measures of central tendency are _____ on the scale of measurement, in contrast to standard deviations, which are _____.

14. The point below which 50 percent of the scores in a distribution lie is called the _____.

15. The first computational step in determining the mean of a group of scores is to _____ all of the scores.

16. Considering measures of central tendency, extreme scores affect the _____, but not the _____.

17. When we subtract the mean from each score of a set of scores, the resulting scores are referred to as _____ scores.

18. The mean of a set of deviation scores is _____.

19. The average squared deviation about the mean is a measure of dispersion called the _____.

20. A linear measure of dispersion, the square root of the variance, is called the _____ _____.

21. What three characteristics are necessary for describing a distribution?

22.

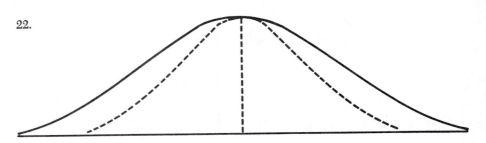

The two distributions shown have equal *means/variances/standard deviations/ medians*.

23. The interval on the scale of measurement over which the scores vary is the _____.

24. If a constant is added to all scores in a distribution, the *mean/variance* of the distribution would not be affected, but the *median/range* would be affected.

25. A *z*-score is a score given in _____ _____ units from the mean.

26. A negative *z*-score indicates that the score lies *above/below* the mean.

27. A distribution of *z*-scores has a mean of _____, and a standard deviation of _____.

28. The scale of measurement of the normal curve theoretically extends from minus _____ to plus _____.

29.

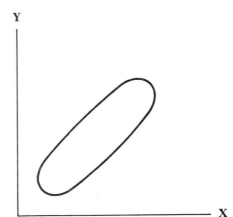

Given a scattergram with the points located within the ellipse shown, the correlation between X and Y would be approximately +1.00/−.7/0/+.2/+.7.

30.

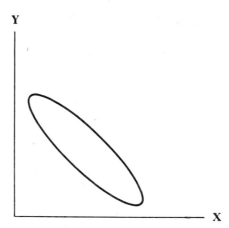

In a scattergram with the points located within the ellipse shown, the correlation between X and Y would be approximately $+.8/+.6/0/-.6/-.8$.

31.

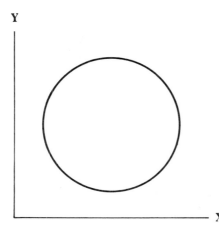

Points located in a circular scattergram as shown indicate a correlation between X and Y of approximately $+.5/+.2/0/-.2/-.5$.

32. Sixty-eight percent of the area of a normal curve is found within $\pm$ _____ standard deviation of the mean.

33. If we compute the average cross products of the deviation scores of two distributions, we have found the *correlation/covariance* between the variables of the two distributions.

34. The points of a scattergram representing a correlation of $+1.00$ or -1.00 would be located on a _____ _____.

35. If the sum of cross products between two variables is small relative to the variance of the distributions of the variables, the correlation will be *minimal/substantial.*

36. In computing a Pearson product-moment correlation coefficient, the numerator consists of the sum of the deviations of the ＿＿＿＿＿＿ ＿＿＿＿＿＿.

37. A negative correlation coefficient indicates a(n)＿＿＿＿＿＿ relationship between the variables.

38. Two variables, time required to perform a task and physical dexterity, are so related that those individuals with high dexterity can perform the task in the shortest time. The correlation between these two variables is *positive/negative.*

39. With nonzero correlation, the points of a scattergram tend to occupy a(n) ＿＿＿＿＿＿ shape.

40.

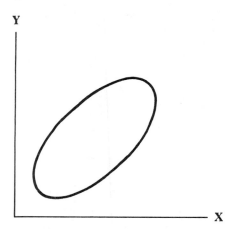

The scattergram shown would indicate a correlation between X and Y of approximately *+1.0/+.5/0/−.5/−1.0.*

41. The product-moment correlation between two variables can be expressed as the covariance divided by the product of the ＿＿＿＿＿＿ ＿＿＿＿＿＿ of the variables.

ANSWERS
35. minimal
36. cross products
37. inverse
38. negative
39. elliptical
40. +.5
41. standard deviations

2. (a) 2; (b) 3; (c) .67; (d) .82; (e) 1.22

Study Exercises

1. Distinguish between ratio, interval, and ordinal scales.
2. Consider the following set of numbers: $X = 1, 2, 3$.
   a. What is the mean?
   b. What is the range?
   c. What is the variance?
   d. What is the standard deviation?
   e. What z-value corresponds to an X of 3?

3. Suppose a student scores 63 on a test with a mean of 50 and a standard deviation of 10. How many standard deviations from the mean is the score?

4. Suppose a student scores two standard deviations below the mean on a test with $\bar{X} = 82$ and $S_x = 12$. What is the score?

5. Suppose that on a test with a mean of 76 and variance of 100 a student scores one and one-half standard deviations above the mean. What is the score?

6. A student scores 80 on a test with a mean of 50 and a standard deviation of 20. How many standard deviations from the mean is the score?

7. Consider the following set of numbers: $Y = 10, 20, 30$.
   a. What is the mean?
   b. What is the range?
   c. What is the variance?
   d. What is the standard deviation?
   e. What z-value corresponds to a Y of 30?

8. Using the sets of scores in problems 2 and 7:
   a. by what factor does the X variance differ from the Y variance?
   b. by what factor does the X standard deviation differ from the Y standard deviation?
   c. what effect does multiplying a set of numbers by a constant (C) have on the variance?
   d. what effect does multiplying a set of numbers by a constant (C) have on the standard deviation?

9. Consider the following sets of scores: $X = 1, 2, 3; Y = 1, 3, 2$.
   a. Using formula 2.8, compute r_{yx}.
   b. Using formula 2.9, compute r_{yx}.
   c. Plot the bivariate scatterplot of the X and Y variables.
   d. What is the meaning of r_{yx}?

10. The following (hypothetical) scores for 30 Ss are on variables X and Y: X being performance on a college freshman mathematics exam, and Y being performance on an exam in an introductory psychology course.

S No.	X	Y	S No.	X	Y	S No.	X	Y
1	104	71	11	139	96	21	140	89
2	99	68	12	95	90	22	118	77
3	107	51	13	107	72	23	92	52
4	72	89	14	93	81	24	105	60
5	109	90	15	102	88	25	113	81
6	119	80	16	84	63	26	110	79
7	135	93	17	79	65	27	133	95
8	79	55	18	138	94	28	113	75
9	92	69	19	136	90	29	108	81
10	100	67	20	75	55	30	88	63

ANSWERS

3. 1.3
4. 58
5. 91
6. 1.5
7. (a) 20; (b) 21; (c) 66.67; (d) 8.16; (e) 1.22
8. (a) 10²; (b) 10; (c) increases by a factor of C²; (d) increases by a factor of C
9. (a) 0.5; (b) 0.5; (d) a linear relationship between x and y
10. (a) mean = 106.13, variance = 378.38, standard deviation = 19.45; (b) 46; (d) .64

a. Compute the mean, variance, and standard deviation of the X distribution.
b. Determine the range of the Y distribution.
c. Construct a histogram for the X distribution.
d. Compute the Pearson product-moment correlation coefficient between X and Y.
e. In the context of the variables that X and Y represent, write a short statement interpreting the correlation coefficient.

11. What is the difference between covariance and the product-moment correlation coefficient?

12. Consider the following scores: $X = 1, 2, 3$; $Y = 3, 1, 2$.
    a. Compute r_{yx} using the deviation score formula 2.8.
    b. Compute r_{yx} using the computational formula 2.9.
    c. What does a negative r_{yx} imply?

Transformations 3

In the preceding chapter, we discussed distributions of scores and the statistics used to describe and relate such distributions. We dealt primarily with distributions of observed or raw scores from a group of subjects. When we attempt to interpret scores from different distributions and groups of individuals, it becomes apparent that we require some additional procedures to make the scores more readily comparable and interpretable. For example, suppose we know that Johnny has achieved scores of 82, 91, and 65 on performance tests A, B, and C, respectively. What do the scores mean in terms of relative performance?

In order to facilitate interpretation, the raw scores are transformed by adding or subtracting a constant, or by some combination of the four arithmetic operations. The score resulting from a given transformation often has a specific name. This chapter will consider some of the more common transformations.

One general class of transformed scores is called standard scores, which means simply that the scores have been transformed to have a given mean and standard deviation. The selection of a particular type of standard score, that is, one with a particular mean and standard deviation, is dictated by the use of the scores.

Linear Transformations

Initially, we will consider linear transformations. *Linear transformations preserve the relative differences between raw scores.*

z-Scores and the Unit Normal Curve

One of the more common and useful transformations is the z-score (previously discussed in Chapter 2). This distribution of transformed scores has a mean of 0 and a standard deviation of 1. The z-scores are found by formula 2.4:

$$z = \frac{X - \overline{X}}{S_x}.$$

In this formula, the transformation is made by subtracting the constant, $\overline{X}$, from the observed score, X, and dividing this difference by the constant value, S_x.

> **A z-score is simply the number of standard deviation units a given raw score is above or below the mean. For example, given a raw score of 70, a mean of 50, and a standard deviation of 10, the raw score of 70 will have a z-score of $+2$ (above the mean).**

Table 3.1 shows how a set of five raw scores (X), with $\overline{X} = 3$, and $S_x = 1.414$, was transformed to a set of z-scores (z). These transformed scores have a mean of 0 and a standard deviation of 1. Thus, an individual with an observed score at the mean has a z-score equal to 0, and positive and negative z-scores indicate only direction from (above or below) the mean.

> **When a set of raw scores with any mean and standard deviation is transformed into z-scores, the z-scores will have a mean of 0 and standard deviation of 1.**

Table 3.1 Computational Illustration of the Transformation to z-Scores

Individual	X	$X - \overline{X}$	$(X - \overline{X})^2$	$\dfrac{X - \overline{X}}{S_x}$	z	z^2
A	1	-2	4	$-2/1.414$	-1.414	2.00
B	2	-1	1	$-1/1.414$	-0.707	0.50
C	3	0	0	$0/1.414$	0.000	0.00
D	4	1	1	$1/1.414$	0.707	0.50
E	5	2	$\underline{4}$	$2/1.414$	1.414	$\underline{2.00}$
			10			5.00

$$S_x^2 = 10/5 = 2.0 \qquad S_z^2 = 5.00/5 = 1$$
$$S_x = 1.414 \qquad\qquad S_z = 1$$

Table 3.2 **Conversion of Raw Scores to z-Scores for Three Hypothetical Performance Tests**

Test	Raw score	Mean	Standard deviation	z-score
A	82	80	6.0	+0.33
B	91	96	3.0	−1.67
C	65	62	4.0	+0.75

For a better understanding of the function of z-scores, let us return to Johnny's scores of 82, 91, and 65. Suppose the means and standard deviations of the score distributions were as indicated in Table 3.2. The corresponding z-scores, also presented in this table, provide us with more information than we had in the raw scores. We see that Johnny's lowest obtained score of 65 was his best relative score (z-score of +0.75). Thus, the z-scores, with their common means and standard deviations (of 0 and 1), provide us with a method of comparing scores that the observed scores did not provide.

In order to discuss other transformations more meaningfully, we need to digress briefly here and further consider the unit normal curve or distribution. In the previous chapter, we introduced the normal curve and mentioned that it consists of a family of curves with an infinite number of members. We stated that shape, location, and variability define a distribution. Since it is impossible to construct tables for all combinations of means and variances for normal distributions, we consider the unit normal curve, which has a mean of 0, a standard deviation of 1, and an area of 1, to be the basic distribution.

The ordinates and areas of the unit normal curve appear in Appendix A. (The columns headed x/σ are standard scores, since $x = X - \overline{X}$, and $[X - \overline{X}]/\sigma =$ z-score; σ is another symbol for standard deviation.) The normal distribution is symmetrical around the mean; therefore, the areas on either side of an imaginary line through the mean and perpendicular to the base are equal. To find any point or score in the unit normal distribution, we must first convert the raw scores to z-scores. The area column of the table indicates the area under the unit normal curve between the mean and the given z-score. Thus, a z-score of +.32 indicates that a proportion of .1255 or 12.55 percent of the area of the curve lies between the mean and this z-score. Since the curve is symmetrical, 12.55 percent of the area of the curve also lies between a z-score of −.32 and the mean.

> To use the unit normal curve table, which has a mean of 0 and standard deviation of 1, we must first convert raw scores to z-scores, which also have a mean of 0 and standard deviation of 1.

43

By converting to z-scores, we can find the area between any two scores in a normal distribution. However, we must be careful to compute the area properly if the scores are on the same or opposite sides of the mean. Two examples should assist in clarifying the procedure.

Suppose we have a group of scores that we know is normally distributed. The mean of the distribution is 70, and the standard deviation is 6.0. What proportion of the area of this distribution lies between the scores of 73 and 78? Converting 73 and 78, we obtain z-scores of $+.50$ and $+1.33$, respectively. The corresponding area values from the table in Appendix A are .1915 for a z-score of $+.50$, and .4082 for a z-score of $+1.33$. These are the areas between the mean and the z-scores. Since both of these z-scores lie on the same side of the mean, we subtract the smaller from the larger area to determine the area between the two points. The proportion of area between the raw scores of 73 and 78 is therefore .2167, or approximately 22 percent of the distribution. This example is presented graphically in Figure 3.1.

Consider a second example. Suppose we have a group of 150 scores that is normally distributed, that has a mean of 85 and a standard deviation of 8. How many scores would be expected to fall between 83 and 91? First, we convert 83 and 91 to z-scores of $-.25$ and $+.75$, respectively. Using the table in Appendix A, we determine the area between the mean and z-scores to get .0987 for the z-score of $-.25$, and .2734 for the z-score of $+.75$. Since the scores lie on opposite sides

Figure 3.1   Area Between z-Scores of $+.50$ and $+1.33$ in a Normally Distributed Set of Scores

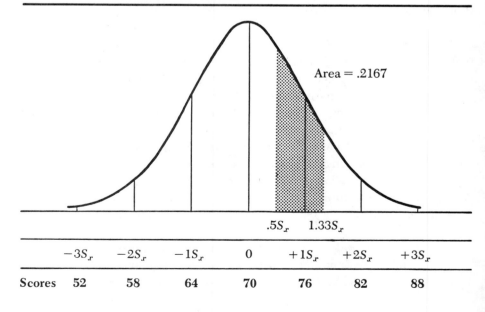

Area $= .2167$

$.5S_r$ $1.33S_r$

	$-3S_r$	$-2S_r$	$-1S_r$	0	$+1S_r$	$+2S_r$	$+3S_r$
Scores	52	58	64	70	76	82	88

of the mean, we add the areas, getting .3721 as the proportion of area included between the two points. To determine the number of scores we would expect to find between these two points, we multiply 150 (the total number of scores) by .3721 arriving at 55.8 or 56 scores. The distribution for area and for scores is presented in Figure 3.2.

The use of the unit normal distribution is not only convenient but essential. For example, suppose that an anxiety test was administered to an individual who subsequently received a score of 70. What can be said about the score? Under norm-referencing, a single score tells us nothing, but if we know that the mean and standard deviation were 50 and 10 respectively, we could tell that the score was two standard deviations above the mean. This additional information is still somewhat limited until we are informed that the anxiety scores were normally distributed. Now we can turn to Appendix A, and find that approximately 97.7 percent of all anxiety scores so distributed are below a score of 70.

> **The unit normal curve has a mean of 0, a standard deviation of 1, and an area of 1. The areas provided in Appendix A lie between the mean and the standard score.**

The unit normal distribution is convenient to use to interpret obtained scores. Tests of general and specific mental abilities, as well as performance scores on

Figure 3.2   Area Between z-Scores of $-.25$ and $+.75$ in a Normally Distributed Set of Scores

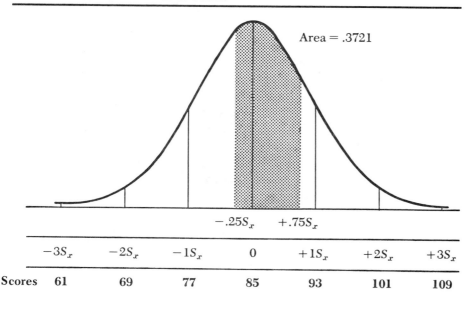

	$-.25S_x$	$+.75S_x$	

$-3S_x$	$-2S_x$	$-1S_x$	0	$+1S_x$	$+2S_x$	$+3S_x$
Scores 61	69	77	85	93	101	109

Area = .3721

achievement tests, commonly yield distributions of scores that very closely approximate the normal distribution. One rationale for the assumption that the scores are normally distributed evolves from test constructors selecting items of moderate difficulty. This practice results in scores that tend toward a normal distribution. As will be seen in greater detail in the next chapter, each obtained score has an error component, which is defined as random. This random component also should be normally distributed, and is a part of the obtained score.

T-Scores

The z-score, as a standard score, has two disadvantages. First, half the scores are negative, and second, scores are expressed as decimals. To eliminate these disadvantages, we can transform the z-scores to a set of scores with a different mean and standard deviation. One such transformation is the T-score transformation. Scores transformed to T-scores have a mean of 50 and a standard deviation of 10. This usually eliminates negative scores, since scores that are five standard deviations below the mean rarely occur. The decimals can be eliminated by rounding to the nearest integer. T-scores are easily computed by multiplying the z-score by 10 and adding 50. This transforming principle is the same regardless of the values we select for our mean and standard deviation. Thus, the generalized linear transformation is:

$$T = \left(\frac{X - \overline{X}}{S_x}\right)C_s + C_m, \tag{3.1}$$

where:

C_s = the constant value to be used for the new standard deviation
C_m = the constant value to be used for the new mean.

In Table 3.1, raw scores for five individuals were transformed to z-scores, which had a mean of 0 and a standard deviation of 1. Table 3.3 presents these z-scores transformed to T-scores with a mean of 50 and a standard deviation of 10. Thus, Table 3.3 confirms that when z-scores are multiplied by a constant and a second constant is added, the resulting set of scores has the multiplied constant as the standard deviation, and the added constant as the mean. In this example, $z(10) + 50 = T$, and the T-scores have a mean of 50 and a standard deviation of 10.

The T-score transformation is a linear transformation such that the distribution of scores has a mean of 50 and a standard deviation of 10.

Table 3.3   **Computational Illustration of *T*-Score Transformation**

Individual	X	z	z(10)	T	$T - \overline{T}$	$(T - \overline{T})^2$
A	1	−1.414	−14.14	35.86	−14.14	200
B	2	−0.707	−7.07	42.93	−7.07	50
C	3	0.000	0.00	50.00	0.00	00
D	4	0.707	7.07	57.07	7.07	50
E	5	1.414	14.14	64.14	14.14	200
	15			250.00		500

$$\overline{X} = \Sigma X/N = 15/5 = 3.$$
$$S_x^2 = 2.00.$$
$$\overline{T} = \Sigma T/N = 250/5 = 50.$$
$$S_T^2 = \Sigma(T - \overline{T})^2/N = 500/5 = 100.$$
$$S_T = 10.$$

Sten Scores

Sten scores are expressed in values of from 1 to 10. The name derives from "standard ten," indicating that the scores reflect ten standardized *categories*. The sten transformation is linear, and yields a distribution with a mean of 5.5 and a standard deviation of 2.0. Figure 3.3 presents a normally distributed set of scores and the corresponding sten categories. The Sixteen Personality Factor Test (16PF) is an example of a test utilizing a sten transformation.

Figure 3.3   **Normal Distribution of Scores in a Sten Transformation Showing Ten Classification Categories**

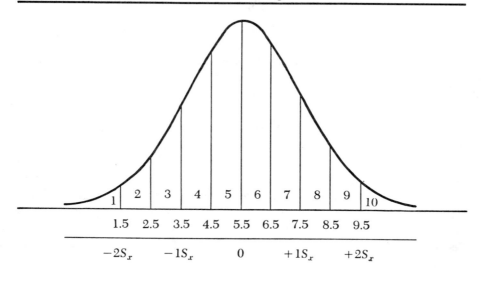

Scores from a sten transformation range from 1 (the lowest) to 10 (the highest), and are expressed to the nearest integer. The sten categories are all one-half standard deviation in width except the extreme categories of 10 and 1; these extreme categories include all raw scores two standard deviations or more above and below the mean, respectively. The sten score of 8 includes those raw scores one to one and one-half standard deviations above the mean, and the sten score of 9 includes those raw scores one and one-half to two standard deviations above the mean. Corresponding standard deviation units identify the lower sten categories. Sten scores of 4, 5, 6, and 7 reflect raw scores that are included between one standard deviation below and above the mean, and can arbitrarily be considered low average, average, and above average. Scores of 1, 2, 3, or 8, 9, and 10 are out of the average range. It is important to remember that these scores reflect quite large categories.

A sten score transformation is a linear transformation that has a mean of 5.5 and a standard deviation of 2.0. As such, the distribution of raw scores is divided into ten parts.

Stanine Scores

Stanine scores are expressed in values from 1 to 9. The name derives from "standard nine," indicating that the scores reflect nine standardized categories. The stanine transformation is linear, and gives a distribution with a mean of 5.0 and a standard deviation of 2.0. Figure 3.4 presents a normally distributed set of scores and the corresponding stanine categories. Stanine scores are particularly useful in interpreting achievement test results.

Scores from a stanine transformation range from 1 (the lowest) to 9 (the highest), and are expressed to the nearest integer. The stanine categories are all one-half standard deviation in width except the extreme categories of 9 and 1 that include all scores one and three-fourths standard deviations or more above or below the mean, respectively. The middle stanine category, 5, extends one-fourth standard deviation above and below the mean, the stanine score of 6 extends from one-fourth of a standard deviation to three-fourths of a standard deviation above the mean, the stanine score of 7 extends from three-fourths to one and one-fourth standard deviations above the mean, and the score of 8 extends from one and one-fourth to one and three-fourths standard deviations above the mean. Corresponding standard deviation units identify the lower stanine categories. Thus, stanine scores of 4, 5, and 6 can be considered in the average range, stanine scores of 7, 8, and 9 are above average, and stanine scores of 1, 2, and 3 are below average. Because broad classification categories are involved, the stanine transformation minimizes the tendency to pigeonhole a student with an exact score. We will see later that this procedure nicely circumvents measurement error by simply assigning a category or range of possible scores. Here again, no negative or decimal scores are involved after the transformation has been made.

> **A stanine score transformation is a linear transformation that has a mean of 5.0 and a standard deviation of 2.0. As such, the distribution of raw scores is divided into nine parts.**

Transformation of observed scores into both sten scores and stanine scores involves some loss of information. For example, all observed scores that transform into z-scores of -1.25 to $-.75$ are assigned the stanine score of 3. Unless the original scale of measurement had only nine different possible scores, some subjects having different observed scores will be assigned the same stanine score. The seriousness of the loss of information depends, at least in part, on the use to be made of the scores. It also depends, in part, on the reliability of the test, a concept to be discussed in succeeding chapters.

The student may feel that standard scores are used only when the variable is normally distributed. This is not necessarily so. Under a linear transformation, the distribution of standard scores will have the same shape as the original distribution of raw scores. That is, a normally distributed set of scores remains normal under a linear transformation. Also, a skewed distribution of scores remains skewed under a linear transformation.

Figure 3.4 **Normal Distribution of Scores in a Stanine Transformation Showing Nine Classification Categories**

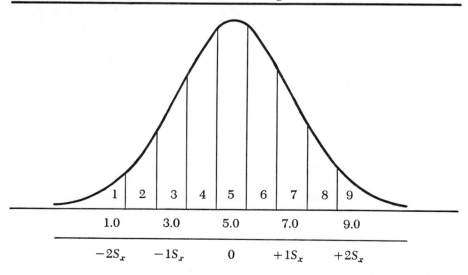

Under a linear transformation, the distribution of transformed scores will have the same shape as that of the original scores. That is, a linear transformation does not result in a normally distributed set of scores, unless the raw scores were normally distributed.

Area Transformations

If the shape of the distribution of the scores is changed as a result of the transformation, the resulting scores are obtained from an area transformation. An area transformation generally does not preserve the relative differences between raw scores.

Percentiles and Percentile Ranks

Teachers, guidance counselors, school psychologists, and others often find it necessary to interpret test scores to lay people who have little, if any, training in psychological measurement. Since it is difficult to use concepts like standard deviation to interpret test results, other methods can be used. One such method uses *percentiles* and *percentile ranks*.

A clear distinction must be made between percentile and percentile rank. A *percentile is a score point, a raw score, below which a given percentage of scores fall.* If 84 percent of the individuals in a group fall below the score of 115, then 115 is the 84th percentile.

A *percentile rank, as distinct from a percentile, is the value that undergoes the area transformation.* A percentile is a score point, while a percentile rank is the percentage of cases below that point. In the example in the preceding paragraph, the score of 155 is the 84th percentile, while the percentile rank of the score of 115 is 84. To communicate a test result, we simply say, "You scored at the 84th percentile. This means that 84 percent of the people in the group scored lower than you."

Table 3.4 provides an example of how to compute percentile ranks. Ten scores of five possible values (X) have varying frequencies of occurrence (f). A percentile rank is defined as the percentage of cases below the midpoint of a score interval. The interval for a score of 1 is from .5 to 1.5; thus, one-half of that score is located below the midpoint. In this example, a score of 1 has a percentile rank of 5. A score of 2 has a percentile rank of 20, and the 20th percentile is the score of 2. Percentile rank is computed by cumulating the frequency of the scores to the midpoint of the score interval (cf),[1] dividing this frequency by N, and multiplying by 100.

---

[1]The cumulative frequency to the midpoint of the interval, symbolized by cf, assumes that the frequencies in an interval are uniformly distributed.

Table 3.4   **Illustration of the Computation of Percentile Rank**

X	f	cf	cf/N	Percentile Rank
5	1	9.5	.95	95
4	2	8.0	.80	80
3	4	5.0	.50	50
2	2	2.0	.20	20
1	1	0.5	.05	5

A percentile is a score point below which a given percentage of scores fall. A percentile rank is a transformed value corresponding to the percentile point. In this context, a percentile is a value on the original scale of measurement, and a percentile rank is a value on a transformed scale.

The distribution of percentile ranks, the distribution of transformed scores, is rectangular (called a *uniform distribution*), since the interval between any two adjacent percentile ranks contains 1 percent of the area. Whenever we deal with a distribution of observed scores that is not rectangular, the transformation to percentile ranks results in a change in the relative distance between the scores. For example, if we transform a normally distributed set of raw scores into percentile ranks, it takes a smaller raw score interval to include 1 percent of the area near the middle of the distribution than it does at the extremes. Consider an illustration of this point. In a normally distributed set of scores, the difference between the percentile ranks of 50 and 55 is about .13 of one standard deviation. In contrast, the difference between the percentile ranks of 90 and 95 is approximately .36 of one standard deviation.

Consider an application of the above. One disadvantage of using percentiles and percentile ranks is that with normally distributed raw scores, raw score differences near the middle of the distribution result in larger differences in percentile ranks, while raw score differences near the extremes of the distribution result in smaller differences in percentile ranks. As an example, in Table 3.4, the one-point difference between the raw scores of 3 and 4 results in a difference in percentile rank of 30 points, while a one-point difference between the raw scores of 4 and 5 at the extremes of the distribution results in a difference in percentile rank of only 15 points.

Consider another example. Suppose an individual has English and Mathematics scores with z-values of 0 and .33, respectively. The individual would have percentile ranks of 50 and 63 for English and Mathematics, respectively, a difference in percentile ranks of 13 points for a difference in z-scores of .33. Similarly, if the same individual has Spelling and Science z-scores of 2.0 and 2.33, respectively, the difference in percentile ranks is only 1.29 points (percentile ranks are 97.72 and 99.01, respectively). Thus, a distortion occurs in the transformation from raw scores to percentile ranks; the relative difference between scores is not retained. As a result of this distortion, it is appropriate to ignore relatively large differences in percentile ranks in the middle of a normally distributed set of raw scores, and attend to relatively smaller differences in percentile ranks at the extremes of a normally distributed set of raw scores.

> **Percentile ranks are very convenient for easy interpretation of test scores, especially to lay people. However, two dangers exist for bell-shaped distributions: (1) large differences in percentile ranks in the middle of the distribution reflect small raw score differences; and (2) small differences in percentile ranks at the extremes of the distribution reflect large raw score differences.**

A second disadvantage of percentile ranks is that statistical or arithmetic computations on percentile ranks are inappropriate. For example, averaging the raw scores and finding the percentile rank of the average would produce a different result, except by chance, than averaging the percentile ranks because the relative difference between raw scores is not maintained in the transformation to percentile ranks.

> **Since percentile ranks do not retain the scale of the original measurement, we cannot apply arithmetic operations indiscriminately, and expect the results to be consistent with those obtained using the original scores.**

Percentile ranks are determined solely by the relation of the individual score to the distribution of scores under consideration. Percentile ranks should not be confused with the percentage of items correct. Rather, percentile ranks are associated with the number of people's scores below the midpoint of a given score. The median, by definition, is the 50th percentile, the point below which the scores of 50 percent of the *people* are located.

On occasion, we may encounter deciles, but these are only special cases of percentiles. The first decile is the 10th percentile, the second, the 20th percentile, etc. The ninth and highest decile is the 90th percentile. Quartiles are also special percentiles that divide the distribution into four equal areas. The first quartile is the 25th percentile, the second quartile, the 50th percentile (also the median and the fifth decile), and the third and highest quartile is the 75th percentile.

An important purpose of transforming distributions of test scores is to interpret the scores and ascribe some meaning to them. One way of interpreting test scores, for example, is to consider how others have performed on the test. For this, we turn to the use of norms. *Norms are summaries of statistics that describe the performance of subjects in a reference group on the test under consideration.*[2] Norms, then, consist of average or typical scores for subjects in a defined group. The normative population is the group for which the norms have been developed. Usually an entire population is not included, but a representative sample provides the information for computing the norms.

Norms

When interpreting test results, we would like some basis for uniform meaning from test to test. For example, if Susan attains a 95 on a reading achievement test and an 83 on an arithmetic achievement test, what does this mean? Often our measuring scales have a lack of uniform size within them, for a five-point increment on one part of the scale is not equivalent to the same increment on another part of the scale. Basically, an observed score can be given meaning by comparing it with the scores of some type of reference group. The use of norms enables us to use simple descriptive statistics, such as z-scores, to ascribe relative meaning to a score or scores.

In general, there are two procedures by which we can make normative comparisons. We can compare an individual's performance to that of his own group, a group of which he can logically and legitimately be considered a member. That is, we can determine his status within the group. Or we can classify an individual's performance in terms of the group in which it would fit best. Here we determine the group, rather than the status within the group. There are different types of norms within each of these general ways of making comparisons; we will now consider some of these types of norms.

> Norms are summaries of statistics used to compare an individual with a given group, or to a group of which he can logically be considered a member. The summary statistics are referred to as normative statistics, and the comparison group is referred to as the normative group.

Percentile Norms

One of the most widely used types of norms is the percentile norm. The basic meaning and construction of percentile ranks were discussed earlier in this chapter. Percentile norms provide the percent of scores in the normative group that fall below a given observed score. For example, if an individual attains an

---

[2]In this discussion, for simplicity, we will use the word *test* to mean some type of measuring instrument.

observed score of 65, and this score is the 43rd percentile in the normative group, it means that 43 percent of the normative group scored below this individual. This type of comparison clearly determines an individual's status within a defined group.

Percentile norms are widely applicable. The crux of their use is obtaining an appropriate normative group for the comparison. The selection of the normative group and the determination of its appropriateness are very important. Obviously, we need different normative groups for individuals of different ages, scholastic attainment, occupational goals, and the like. It makes little sense to compare the performance of graduate-school applicants with norms based on entering college freshmen. Clearly, when tests are used with varying groups, multiple sets of norms are required. Norms must be available for each distinct group for which the test is to be used, not only groups of different ages, but also groups with special goals or other characteristics. However, because of practical limits on the number of norms that can be reasonably acquired for unique or special test uses, it may be difficult to find an appropriate percentile norm.

A second problem in using percentile norms was discussed in connection with percentile ranks: typically, percentile ranks are distorted with the scale. Any user must consider this characteristic when interpreting percentile ranks.

> **Percentile norms provide the decided advantage of interpreting a score in terms of the percentage of scores below the midpoint of that score. However, since the percentile transformation does not retain the scale of the original raw scores, interpretive dangers associated with percentile ranks result.**

Standard Score Norms

Like percentile norms, standard score norms compare an individual's performance in terms of his status within a presumably appropriate reference group. Standard score norms can be in the form of z-scores, T-scores, stanines, or any accepted standard score form. As long as the transformation is linear, the characteristic of equal units is retained, if it existed in the original measurement scale, of course. So standard score norms, involving a linear transformation, have this advantage over, say, percentile norms. Multiple sets of norms are required for extensive use of a given test. In this respect, the requirement is the same as with any norms that provide an appropriate reference group in which we fit the individual's performance or determine his status.

Standard score norming procedures are valuable because they can be used to eliminate "undesirable" technical characteristics, such as negative scores. The descriptive information about the normative group contains the mean and standard deviation being used. It is the responsibility of the publisher (or constructor) of the norm to report this necessary information, and it is the responsibility of the norm user to become informed about it.

> **Standard score norms result from a linear transformation of the raw scores of some defined normative group. These transformed normative statistics provide specific interpretive advantages, such as eliminating negative scores, providing a given mean and standard deviation, etc. Standard scores have the advantage that any arithmetic operations carried out on raw scores can also be carried out on standard scores.**

Age Norms

Age norms are appropriate when we study a characteristic that demonstrates progressive changes with age. Age norms classify an individual's performance in terms of the group into which it best fits, the various groups being distinguished by age in this case. The norm for a given age is the average value of the characteristics for individuals of that age. It is only an average value, not an ideal value, nor, necessarily, an expected value, for all individuals in the age group. For example, weight is a characteristic that shows obvious changes with age in the early years of life. There are weight charts for boys, for instance, in which each weight can be interpreted as the average weight for a boy of a given age. Age norms are relatively familiar and, conceptually, they are quite simple.

However, age norms have definite disadvantages. With most psychological variables, there is a real question as to whether or not thinking of age as a uniform unit is reasonable. Does the difference in weight between years 7 and 8 equal that between years 14 and 15? As we go higher up the scale in years, it becomes apparent that we reach a point at which considering one year's growth as a unit is clearly inappropriate. Many variables diminish in their rate of change, and, in some cases, slowdowns occur abruptly at given points. If we were graphing such a variable, the curve would flatten or begin forming a *plateau* at this point. The lack of uniformity of the unit is most apparent at the extremes, but there may be no guarantee that the unit is consistent even in the middle range.

Diminished change or termination of change introduces a problem when we consider individuals who score much above the average. For example, what if we had a 13-year-old boy who weighed 255 pounds? The average man does not attain this weight, and there is no part in the weight curve with which to make the comparison. We might build an artificial curve, extrapolated on the basis of the maximum rate of change in the curve. However, this type of procedure is completely arbitrary and artificial, and does not correspond to reality. Such an extrapolation, for example, might be assigned a weight-age equivalent of 26 years, but it clearly does not correspond to the average weight of 26-year-olds. In fact, it does not correspond to the average weight at any age, and indicates only above-average weight at all ages.

Comparing the curves of age norms for different characteristics is extremely risky. The rate of change, as well as points of growth slowdown and termination, differs markedly from characteristic to characteristic. Some characteristics, such as performance on certain problem-solving tasks, show marked increase well into the 20s. Indeed, attempts at performance at lower ages may be inappropriate, and neither the curve nor, correspondingly, the norm exist at these ages.

In review, age norms are based on performance of the average individual at each age level. They are applicable for characteristics that change as a function of age during the period that such change is evident. They are most appropriate for the elementary school ages (and, possibly, junior and senior high school age ranges) for characteristics that change as a part of normal development. Of course, the problem of inequality of units across different ages exists, and information on the slowdown or termination of change for the characteristic under study is very important.

> **Age norms provide summary statistics that depict an individual's performance as representative of some age level. A disadvantage of age norms is that growth rate is not a constant factor, making some interpretations difficult. The advantage of age norms is the ease with which results can be communicated.**

Grade Norms

The general characteristics of grade norms are similar to those of age norms, except that the reference or normative groups are based on grade level instead of age. The average performance for students is determined for various grade levels. The difference between two grade levels usually is partitioned equally into ten parts. This, in essence, reflects considering a school year as consisting of ten months. The beginning of any grade is assigned the integer value of the grade; for example, 4.0 is the beginning of the fourth grade. If an individual scores at 5.6 in the grade norm of arithmetic achievement, her performance is comparable to that of the average of students at the sixth month of the fifth grade.

The limitations of grade norms are similar to those of age norms. The problem of uniform units across years exists. Grade norms are commonly used for performance in school subjects that have continuous instruction over a span of several grades. They are essentially meaningless for most high school subjects and for subjects that span only one grade. Interpolation of the norms for superior performance may give a result higher than the highest grade for which norms are meaningful.

Grade norms have the advantage of being convenient and relatively easy to determine. Their meaning is quite apparent, and, for this reason, they are easy to interpret. Their primary use occurs with academic and skills subjects taught in the elementary grades.

> **Grade norms provide summary statistics that depict an individual's performance as representative of some grade level. A disadvantage of grade norms is that growth rate is not a constant factor, making some intepretations difficult. The advantage of grade norms is the ease with which results can be communicated.**

Where Do Norms Come From?

Since norms provide reference groups for the interpretation of scores, it would be reasonable to ask about their source and how they are established. Norms for many psychological measures are empirically established at national, regional, and local levels.

Normative population, already introduced, is the larger group with which the individual is being compared, and is the source of the statistics we call norms. Often the normative population is so large that the entire population cannot be measured. Instead, a representative sample of the population is measured. This is the case, for example, with norms based on some national group. Sampling large populations, however, is often no easy task, and in some cases, adequate sampling of large populations is very difficult if not impossible to attain. Therefore, it is very important that an adequate description of both the sampling procedure and the sample obtained accompanies the norm, so the user has sufficient information on the reference group.

Although it may seem desirable intuitively to secure norms based on large groups, say national groups, it may not prove very useful. If we have a variable that is quite heterogeneous in the large population, the norms may not be relevant to any subpopulations. Combining heterogeneous groups may describe a "normal" individual that does not exist anywhere in the large population. Many areas of achievement and performance vary widely with regions of the country, type of schools, characteristics of subjects under consideration, etc. This variance may be due to any number of reasons, but whatever they are, the variance exists. Therefore, many test publishers provide regional norms and norms for various subgroups of the population. The sample used for norming purposes is often subdivided to obtain an adequate representation of specialized groups within the population. Generally, the more specific the norms, the more useful they become. It is possible, with adequate effort and resources, to construct local norms, and these can be very useful for many localized purposes.

Most norms are based on relatively large samples; many are based on hundreds or thousands of cases. This provides some stability for the statistics. However, "bigness" of sample is not equated necessarily with validity of the norms. More important than sample size is the adequacy or validity of the sampling plan in securing a sample that represents the population it is intended to represent. For example, a norm based on a large biased sample, selected because of easy availability of subjects, or containing an overrepresentation of a distinct subpopulation, would likely be misleading. The description of the sample usually contains the sample size. Whether this sample size is large or small, the sampling plan should be described also, and the publisher should demonstrate that his sample is representative of the population it claims to represent. In addition, a description of any sample subdivision is usually included; whether the subdivision is appropriate for the user's purposes can be determined from this description. There is, of course, a finite limitation to the detailed norms a test publisher can provide.

Any test user should not assume that the norms from one test battery to another are comparable. A grade placement of 4.3 on a given test does not mean that the individual would have received a grade placement of 4.3 on another test, if that test did not have the same normative group. If several tests were normed on the same group, population, or sample, the norms would be comparable, of course. However, this is likely to be the case only among the tests of a specific test battery, or in a localized situation in which several tests are given to the same group for the explicit purpose of securing comparable norms.

Norms may become obsolete; for many psychological variables, unless the norms are relatively current, they may be misleading. Many variables undergo change over time due to any number of factors. These are especially evident over extended periods, such as a decade. If a test is altered, it obviously requires a verification of the norms, and changes in the norms may be necessary. As changes occur in the existing population, the reference groups also change, and the norms become irrelevant.

In summary, we should avoid the use of unjustified "general" norms, and any norms, based on large or small reference groups, should be defined carefully. Local norms and self-developed special-group norms may be very helpful and well worth the development effort.

There are no predetermined standards of "pass" or "fail" for norms of psychological measures. Norms are for comparative purposes: comparing an individual's scores with those obtained by others. Norms do not represent perfect performance on the measure under consideration. They are transformed scores that provide relative rather than absolute information. Norms should generally not be viewed as standards, a not-uncommon misinterpretation when one is dealing with some educational variables. Norms are used for interpreting scores within the descriptive framework of the reference group.

Summary

In this chapter we have discussed the more common transformations on distributions of scores. Raw scores or observed scores are seldom interpreted readily in their original form. Transformations provide us a more meaningful context in which to secure the information contained in the score, and make appropriate interpretations. We have considered both linear transformations and area transformations.

Norms were discussed in this chapter since they are closely related to transformed scores. Norms themselves are the descriptive statistics of a defined reference group. The use of norms commonly involves some type of transformation to convert the raw scores into forms appropriate for comparison.

Suggested Readings

Helmstadter, G. *Principles of psychological measurement.* New York: Appleton-Century-Crofts, 1964, pp. 41–52.

Seashore, H. G. Methods of expressing test scores. *Test Service Bulletin,* January, 1955. New York: The Psychological Corporation.

Seashore, H. G., & Ricks, J. H., Jr. Norms must be relevant. *Test Service Bulletin,* May, 1950. New York: The Psychological Corporation.

Spence, J., et al. *Elementary statistics.* (2nd ed.) New York: Appleton-Century-Crofts, 1968, Chapters 4, 7.

Individual Review Questions

1. A distribution of observed scores is transformed to z-scores. An individual has a z-score of $+.3$. We know, therefore, that in the original distribution his score was *below/above* the mean.

2. An individual scores 78 in a distribution of scores with a mean of 70 and a standard deviation of 12. The individual's z-score is _____.

3. When using the table of areas of the unit normal curve provided, the area given is that contained between the _____ and the corresponding _____.

4. An individual scores one-half standard deviation above the mean on a test. The test scores are normally distributed. Therefore, approximately _____ percent of the test scores are below this individual's score.

ANSWERS
1. above
2. $+.67$
3. mean; z-score
4. 69

5. A distribution of 150 test scores is normal with a mean of 56 and a standard deviation of 4. Individual A scored 60 and Individual B scored 64 on the test. Approximately _____ scores would be expected to fall at or between the scores of these two individuals.

6. Susan scores 75 on a biology test with a mean of 69 and a standard deviation of 9, and 97 on a mathematics test with a mean of 88 and a standard deviation of 15. Her relative standing when compared with the class was higher on the *biology/mathematics* test.

7. The *T*-score distribution has a mean of _____ and a standard deviation of _____.

8. Any distribution of scores can be transformed into a set with a mean, *M*, and a standard deviation, *D*, by multiplying the *z*-scores by _____ and adding _____.

9. Given a *z*-score, to determine the corresponding *T*-score, we multiply the *z*-score by _____ and add _____.

10. In computing the area between two *z*-scores lying on the same side of the mean, we *add/subtract* the areas obtained from Appendix A.

11. If two *z*-scores are given, one positive and the other negative, to compute the area contained between the two scores, we *add/subtract* the areas obtained from Appendix A.

12. The sten scale contains _____ scores or units.

13. A distribution of stanine scores has a mean of _____ and a standard deviation of _____.

14. A distribution of sten scores has a mean of _____ and a standard deviation of _____.

15. With the exception of the extremes, each unit on the stanine scale has a length of *one/three-fourths/two-thirds/one-half/one-third/one-fourth* standard deviation unit.

16. The middle stanine score of 5 extends _____ standard deviation unit(s) on either side of the mean; therefore, it includes approximately _____ percent of the distribution's area.

17. A(n) *linear/area* transformation preserves the equality of the differences of the original scores.

18. The transformation to percentile ranks is a(n) *linear/area* transformation.

19. The interval between any two adjacent percentile ranks contains _____ percent of the area or scores of the distribution.

20. The median is the _____ percentile.

21. A set of test scores contains 200 scores and is normally distributed. The number of scores falling between the mean and the 55th percentile is _____ .

22. A score of 7 is one standard deviation above the mean in a _____ transformation.

23. A score of 8 is _____ standard deviations above the mean in a stanine transformation.

24. A score of 7.5 is one standard deviation above the mean in a _____ transformation.

25. A score of 3 is one standard deviation below the mean in a _____ transformation.

26. A sten score of 8.5 is the same as a stanine score of _____ .

27. Which score is higher: a sten score of 6 or a T-score of 50?

28. Which score is higher: a stanine score of 4 or a T-score of 30?

29. Which score is lower: a sten score of 8 or a T-score of 80?

30. Which is the lower score: the 30th percentile or a sten score of 3?

31. Which is the higher score: the 80th percentile or a T-score of 80?

32. A subject is told that he scores .8 of a standard deviation above the mean in a normal distribution of test scores. His obtained score is approximately the _____ percentile.

33. The best word to describe the shape of a distribution of percentile ranks is _____ .

34. The distribution of percentile ranks is *skewed/symmetrical*.

35. When transforming normally distributed scores to percentile ranks, it requires a *larger/smaller* interval on the original score of measurement to account for a given percentage of the area near the middle of the distribution than near the extremes.

36. In a percentile transformation from normally distributed scores, differences in percentile ranks near the middle of the distribution are *magnified/reduced*, and those near the extremes are *magnified/reduced*.

ANSWERS
19. 1
20. 50th
21. 10
22. stanine
23. 1.5
24. sten
25. stanine
26. 8
27. sten score of 6
28. stanine score of 4
29. sten score of 8
30. sten score of 3
31. T-score of 80
32. 79th
33. rectangular
34. symmetrical
35. smaller
36. magnified; reduced

61

37. Percentile ranks *do/do not* retain the unit of measurement of the observed scores.

38. In a normal distribution, it requires a *greater/lesser* raw score difference to move from a percentile rank of 60 to 63 than from a percentile rank of 91 to 94.

39. Which of these percentiles are also deciles? *15th/25th/30th/50th/75th*

40. Summary statistics that describe the performance of reference groups on a test are _____ _____.

41. Norms provide _____ rather than _____ information.

42. A fourth-grade student scores at the 75th percentile on the norms for his group on an achievement test. The test applies to several grades, each having its own norm group. If we compared his raw score to the percentile norms for fifth grade, we would expect it to be *higher/lower* than the 75th percentile.

43. A student scores at 6.3 grade norm on a standardized achievement test. His performance compares to the average of students at the _____ month of the _____ _____.

44. Seventh-grade norms are used inappropriately to interpret the test performance of a group of sixth graders. This inappropriate use would tend to *overestimate/underestimate* the performance of the sixth graders.

45. Age norms are most appropriate for students in the *elementary/secondary/college* age range.

46. A school principal has set as his goal that all students in the school will score at or above the median of the normative group. This is an example of misusing norms by using them as a _____.

ANSWERS
37. do not
38. lesser
39. 30th; 50th
40. normative statistics
41. relative; absolute
42. lower
43. third; sixth grade
44. underestimate
45. elementary
46. standard

1. (a) 2.30; (b) 92; (c) 118; (d) −1.2
2. (a) .84; (b) .98; (c) .99; (d) .16; (e) .31; (f) .09; (g) .24; (h) .01; (i) .02; (j) .64

Study Exercises

1. Given a set of scores with a mean of 100 and standard deviation of 10,
   a. what z-value corresponds to a score of 123?
   b. what score corresponds to a z-value of $-.80$?
   c. what score corresponds to a z-value of 1.80?
   d. what z-value corresponds to a score of 88?

2. Assuming a normally distributed set of scores with a mean of 0 and a standard deviation of 1,
   a. what proportion of the area is below $z = 1$?
   b. what proportion of the area is below $z = 2$?
   c. what proportion of the area is below $z = 2.2$?
   d. what proportion of the area is below $z = -1$?
   e. what proportion of the area is below $z = -.5$?
   f. what proportion of the area is between $z = 1$ and $z = 1.5$?

g. what proportion of the area is between $z = -.5$ and $z = -1.5$?

h. what proportion of the area is below $z = -2.2$?

i. what proportion of the area is between $z = 1.8$ and $z = 2.2$?

j. what proportion of the area is between $z = -1.6$ and $z = +.5$?

3. Assuming a normally distributed set of scores with a mean of 100 and a standard deviation of 10,

   a. what percentage of cases are below an X of 110?

   b. what percentage of cases are below an X of 120?

   c. what percentage of cases are between an X of 110 and an X of 120?

   d. what percentage of cases are below an X of 86?

   e. what percentage of cases are below an X of 100?

   f. what percentage of cases are between an X of 86 and an X of 100?

   g. what percentage of cases are between an X of 86 and an X of 125?

   h. what percentage of cases are below an X of 90?

   i. what percentage of cases are between an X of 90 and an X of 110?

4. Consider the following set of scores:

X	1	2	3	4	5
f	1	2	6	2	1

   a. Convert these scores to stanine scores.

   b. In what stanine is the score of 1?

   c. In what stanine is a score of 4?

   d. Show that the stanine scores have a mean of 5 and a standard deviation of 2.

5. Consider the scores in problem 4.

   a. Convert the scores to sten scores.

   b. In what sten is a score of 4?

   c. In what sten is the score of 5?

6. Consider the following scores:

X	6	4	3	2	1
f	1	1	5	2	1

   a. Convert the scores to percentile ranks.

   b. What happens to the differences in percentile ranks in the transformation from raw scores?

   c. The raw score difference between 1 and 2 has a _____ difference in percentile ranks than the raw score difference between 2 and 3.

   d. The one-point raw score difference between 1 and 2 has a _____ difference in percentile ranks than the two-point raw score difference between 4 and 6.

   e. For symmetrical bell-shaped distributions, small raw score differences in the middle of a distribution are transformed to _____ differences in percentile ranks. Large raw score differences at the extremes of the distribution are transformed to _____ differences in percentile ranks.

ANSWERS

3. (a) 84.13; (b) 97.72; (c) 13.59; (d) 8.08; (e) 50.00; (f) 41.92; (g) 91.30; (h) 15.87; (i) 68.26

4. (b) 1; (c) 7

5. (b) 7, or 8; (c) 9, or 10

6. (a) 95, 85, 55, 20, 5; (b) raw score differences are distorted; (c) smaller; (d) larger; (e) larger; smaller

4

Reliability

The preceding chapters introduced a definition of measurement and established the fundamental statistical principles necessary to consider more advanced concepts. This chapter will develop a theoretical definition of reliability, suggest the different meanings of reliability that are obtained with different empirical procedures, and develop the concept of error of measurement.

Obtained Scores and Their Variance Components

To discuss reliability, we must first accept the assumption that when we take a test, the score we obtain has a degree of error. On a number of test-taking occasions, we might not be precisely certain about an answer. For example, we may not be sure of the correct response among the multiple-choice alternatives, so we guess. The score we obtain might not reflect our true ability—be our true score. Theoretically, *the true score is defined as the mean score resulting from a large number of repeated measurements on parallel tests for the same individual.* As a result of our knowledge of test error, we generate the fundamental postulate of test theory:[1]

[1]The notations for this section are: X_{ij} is a test score for the ith individual on the jth test; X with no subscript is a test by itself; X_j is a score on the jth test; X_i is a score for the ith individual. The mean for the jth test is $\overline{X}_j$; the mean for the ith individual is $\overline{X}_i$. If two parallel tests are considered, the notations are X and X'. This chapter requires a basic knowledge of summation notation; Appendix B provides a review of the basic principles.

$$X_{ij} = T_{ij} + E_{ij}, \qquad\qquad (4.1)$$

where:

X_{ij} = an obtained score for the ith individual on the jth test

E_{ij} = an error component for the ith individual on the jth test

T_{ij} = true component for the ith individual on the jth test $(X_{ij} - E_{ij})$.

The focus of our attention is X_{ij} and E_{ij}, where X_{ij} is simply an obtained score. For the purpose of this discussion, E_{ij} will be defined as a nonsystematic random element.[2] As a random element, it has two characteristics that must be considered:

1. Mean error equals zero, which suggests that positive and negative error cancel each other over many measurements.

2. Error is uncorrelated, which suggests that error on one testing should not correlate with error on another testing, nor should error correlate with true score.

Having thus defined obtained and error scores, consider the N by n data matrix[3] of parallel tests on variables X_{ij} (where i indicates a row and j indicates a column) as presented in Table 4.1. The data matrix has N rows (N = number of individuals) and n columns (n = number of parallel tests). Thus, if $N = 500$ and $n = 100$, we have 100 parallel measurements for each of 500 people. Parallel measurements can be defined as *tests that measure the same thing*. Statistically, parallel tests or measurements have:

1. equal means,

2. equal variances and standard deviations, and

3. equal intercorrelations (when three or more tests exist).

Using the data matrix of Table 4.1, suppose we compute the variance of any column of the matrix, and then compute the variance of any row. What is the difference? The *column variance* is simply variance between people due to differences in their obtained scores on a single test, X. Since the obtained score, X, has been defined as the sum of the error and true components, the column variance includes these two factors. However, the *row variance* is quite different. Since all of the row measurements are parallel measures for the same individual, all X's in a row should be the same, and the row variance should be zero. However, because of the error component in each score, slight variation in the X's of a

---

[2]This is an oversimplified approach to the definition of error; nevertheless, it can be utilized to generate some practical principles of measurement.

[3]*Matrix* is used in this context as simply an N by n table. Since we are dealing with a data matrix, in this case, it means an organization of observed test scores with N people on one dimension and n tests on the other dimension. An entry X_{11}, in this matrix, is the score of the first individual on the first parallel test; X_{12} is the score of the first individual on the second parallel test; X_{21} is the score of the second individual on the first parallel test, etc.

Table 4.1   Data Matrix of n Parallel Tests for Each of N Individuals

Individuals	Parallel Tests					
	1	2	3	...	n	
1	X_{11}	X_{12}	X_{13}	...	X_{1n}	$T_1 = \sum\limits_{j=1}^{n} X_{1j}/n$
2	X_{21}	X_{22}	X_{23}	...	X_{2n}	$T_2 = \sum\limits_{j=1}^{n} X_{2j}/n$
3	X_{31}	X_{32}	X_{33}	...	X_{3n}	$T_3 = \sum\limits_{j=1}^{n} X_{3j}/n$
4	X_{41}	X_{42}	X_{43}	...	X_{4n}	$T_4 = \sum\limits_{j=1}^{n} X_{4j}/n$
.	.	.	.	...	.	.
.	.	.	.	...	.	.
.	.	.	.	...	.	.
N	X_{N1}	X_{N2}	X_{N3}	...	X_{Nn}	$T_N = \sum\limits_{j=1}^{n} X_{Nj}/n$

single individual occurs. This variation, due to the error component, is called *error variance*. Thus, we can symbolize the variance of rows and columns as:[4]

$$S^2_{row} = \sum_{j=1}^{n} \frac{(X_{ij} - \overline{X}_i)^2}{n} = S^2_{error}. \tag{4.2}$$

$$S^2_{column} = \sum_{i=1}^{N} \frac{(X_{ij} - \overline{X}_j)^2}{N} = S_x{}^2. \tag{4.3}$$

These two expressions of variance follow directly from the definition of variance. Let us summarize the characteristics and differences of these two variance components:

S^2_{row}
1. Sum is for the same person.
2. Sum is over different, but parallel, tests.
3. Deviation is about the individual's true score.
4. Any variance is due to error.

[4]The notation $\Sigma_{j=1}^{n}(X_{ij} - \overline{X}_i)^2/n$ means that we are focusing on the ith individual (any individual), and considering the squared differences on each of that individual's n tests ($j = 1, 2, \ldots, n$) taken about the individual's mean score. The notation $\Sigma_{i=1}^{N}(X_{ij} - \overline{X}_j)^2/N$ means that we are focusing on the jth test (any test), and considering the squared differences of the jth test of N people ($i = 1, 2, \ldots, N$) about the mean score for the jth test.

S^2_{column}
1. Sum is over different people.
2. Sum is for the same test.
3. Deviation is about the group mean.·
4. Variance is due to variation in X_i (the obtained scores of different individuals).

We can conceptualize three distributions in our matrix: a distribution of obtained scores (X), a distribution of true scores (T), and a distribution of error scores (E). For each of these distributions we would get three different types of variances: the variance of scores in any one of the n columns (called *obtained variance*), the variance of the column of true scores (T) on the extreme right (called *true variance*), and the variance of the scores in any one of the N rows (called *error variance*). Furthermore, these three types of variance can be due to individual differences plus error, to individual differences, and to error, respectively. If we were to superimpose the histograms of any row and column scores, we would get something like Figure 4.1.

In Figure 4.1, note that the mean for a column is less than that for a row. This indicates that the mean for the particular individual singled out is higher than the mean of all of the people on one of the parallel tests. This is an arbitrary choice on our part; we might have selected an individual who was below average. Additionally, the height of the histogram about $\overline{X}_{\text{row}}$ is less than $\overline{X}_{\text{column}}$ because we usually have fewer parallel tests than people taking them. Also, the rows vary

Figure 4.1 Histograms Contrasting Variation Due to Obtained Scores and Error Scores

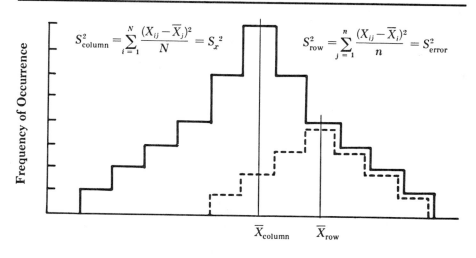

less than the columns, because error variance is generally a subset of the obtained variance. Thus, column variance is generally greater than row variance, because it includes individual differences in people tested, in addition to error variance.

Suppose the parallel tests of our matrix were highly reliable tests of musical ability administered to a group of college music majors. We would expect to find very little variance in any row (because the test is reliable, it has little variance due to error), or very little variance in any column (because both variance in individual differences and variance due to error are quite small).

Consider a different situation. Suppose we administered the highly reliable tests of musical ability to a cross section of college freshmen. We might still expect to find little variance in any row, but we might find great variance in the columns (because variance in individual differences has increased over the previous situation).

Finally, suppose the parallel tests of our matrix were very unreliable tests of musical ability administered to a cross section of college students. Here we might expect to find a larger variance in any row (because variance due to unreliability—error—is greater) and a larger variance in columns (because variance in both individual differences and error is large).

Having clarified the difference between variance due to individual differences plus unreliability (obtained variance), variance due to individual differences (true variance), and variance due to unreliability (error variance), let us recall the fundamental postulate in formula 4.1, $X_{ij} = T_{ij} + E_{ij}$, which simply states that any raw score contains an error component. The column mean subtracted from the raw scores gives the deviation scores. It follows that the deviation scores will also contain an error component, $x_{ij} = t_{ij} + e_{ij}$. Thus, for any test score, X_j (any of the parallel tests—the jth column), we can write the deviation score for any individual (any row—the ith row) as:

$$x_i = t_i + e_i. \tag{4.4}$$

Squaring both sides, we have:

$$x_i{}^2 = (t_i + e_i)^2 = t_i{}^2 + e_i{}^2 + 2t_ie_i.$$

Summing (the jth column for all individuals) and dividing both sides by N, we have:

$$\frac{\sum\limits_{i=1}^{N} x_i{}^2}{N} = \frac{\sum\limits_{i=1}^{N} t_i{}^2}{N} + \frac{\sum\limits_{i=1}^{N} e_i{}^2}{N} + \frac{2\sum\limits_{i=1}^{N} t_ie_i}{N}.$$

Symbolically this reduces to:

$$S_x^2 = S_t^2 + S_e^2 + \rho_{te}, \tag{4.5}$$

where:

ρ_{te} = covariance of the true and error components in deviation form.

Since our definition of error included the characteristic that true and error components do not covary (their covariance is zero), the last term, ρ_{te}, reduces to zero, and we see that:

$$S_x^2 = S_t^2 + S_e^2. \tag{4.6}$$

This is the mathematical development of the histograms illustrated in Figure 4.1, showing that obtained variance (column variance) was due to both true and error components. We can present formula 4.6 graphically (Figure 4.2) to show the obtained variance as the sum of the true and error components.

To summarize:

1. Variance obtained from the raw scores of a test is due to both true and error components.

2. Variance obtained from giving a parallel test over and over to the same individual is assumed to be due to the error component.

The obtained variance of a test can be partitioned into true and error components. The true component is due to systematic sources, such as individual differences in people; the error component is due to unsystematic sources, such as guessing, scoring errors, and recording errors.

Figure 4.2 Illustration of Obtained Variance as the Sum of True and Error Variance

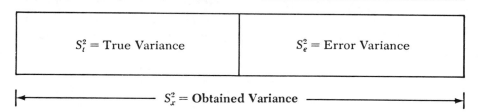

S_t^2 = True Variance	S_e^2 = Error Variance

S_x^2 = Obtained Variance

Reliability Theory

Reliability is concerned with consistency of measurement. That is, when we administer a test to a large group of people, we would like to feel that if that test or a parallel test is readministered, the scores will remain essentially the same. Additionally, we would like the correlation between test and retest, or between parallel tests, to approach unity. How can we develop this correlation?

The formula for the Pearson product-moment correlation (formula 2.6) is:

$$r_{yx} = \frac{\sum\limits_{i}^{N}(X_i - \overline{X})(Y_i - \overline{Y})}{NS_xS_y}.$$

Suppose we wish to correlate the N pairs of scores from any two parallel tests shown in Table 4.1. Substituting directly into the correlation formula and letting X_i and X_i' be the observed scores on the two parallel tests, we have

$$r_{xx'} = \frac{\sum x_i x_i'}{NS_xS_{x'}}, \tag{4.7}$$

where $x_i x_i'$ represents the scores of the parallel tests expressed as deviations from their means; and the subscript xx' in $r_{xx'}$ indicates the correlation of two parallel tests.

Substituting $t_i + e_i$ for x_i, and $t_i' + e_i'$ for x_i', we have

$$r_{xx'} = \frac{\sum\limits_{i=1}^{N}(t_i + e_i)(t_i' + e_i')}{NS_xS_{x'}}$$

$$= \frac{\sum\limits_{i=1}^{N} t_i t_i'}{NS_xS_{x'}} + \frac{\sum\limits_{i=1}^{N} t_i e_i'}{NS_xS_{x'}} + \frac{\sum\limits_{i=1}^{N} t_i' e_i}{NS_xS_{x'}} + \frac{\sum\limits_{i=1}^{N} e_i e_i'}{NS_xS_{x'}}. \tag{4.8}$$

However, error scores should not correlate, as shown in formula 4.5, which means that their covariance is zero. Therefore, the three terms on the right in formula 4.8, which involve covariance terms, should reduce to zero. Since true scores on parallel tests are identical for a given individual, $t_i(t_i') = t_i^2$, $S_x = S_{x'}$, and formula 4.8 reduces to:

$$r_{xx'} = \frac{\sum\limits_{i=1}^{N} t_i^2}{NS_x^2} = \frac{S_t^2}{S_x^2}. \tag{4.9}$$

What does formula 4.9 imply? In the previous section, we partitioned the obtained variance into true and error variance. Considering $r_{xx'}$ as an estimate of reliability, we see that it is the ratio of the true variance to the observed variance. Or, we can say that reliability according to formula 4.9 is simply the part of the obtained variance that is the true (or systematic) variance.

Consider an example: suppose we find that a given test has a reliability estimate of .93. What does this mean? The .93 indicates that the ratio of true variance to obtained variance is .93, or that 93 percent of the obtained variance is true variance. Thus, from our brief theoretical development, we find that a reliability coefficient expresses the proportion of obtained test variance that is true (or systematic) variance.

> **A reliability coefficient estimates the ratio of true variance to total variance. A reliability coefficient of .90 estimates that 90 percent of the obtained variance is true variance.**

Suppose someone tells us that the Wechsler Intelligence Scale for children has an estimated reliability of .93, with a standard deviation of 15. We can consider the following illustrative questions:

1. What is the obtained variance? $S_x^2 = 15^2 = 225$.
2. What percentage of the test variance is systematic variance? The estimated reliability of .93 indicates the proportion or ratio of systematic to obtained variance. Multiplying this by 100 gives the desired percentage: 93 percent.
3. What percentage of the test variance is error variance? Since systematic plus error variance equals total variance, 100 percent minus 93 percent = 7 percent.
4. What is the error variance? Since 225 is the total variance, and .07 is the proportion that is error, the actual error variance (S_e^2) is found by multiplying 225 by .07, which equals 15.75.

Or, if the California Test of Mental Maturity has an estimated parallel test reliability of .89, and a standard deviation of 16, we can ask these questions:

1. What is the proportion of error variance? .11.
2. What is the proportion of systematic variance? .89.
3. What is the true variance? $S_T^2 = .89 \times 256 = 227.84$.
4. What is the error variance? $S_e^2 = .11 \times 256 = 28.16$.
5. Confirm that true variance and error variance equal obtained variance. $S_x^2 = 227.84 + 28.16 = 256$.

To summarize: we have established a basic mathematical definition of reliability—the ratio of true variance to obtained variance.

Equivalence and Stability Reliability

We have stated that reliability is consistency of measurement, that it can be defined theoretically as that part of the total test variance that is systematic or nonerror variance, and that unreliability is that part of the total test variance due to error. While the theoretical definition of reliability is reasonably neat, the practical estimation of reliability is more complex. Different methods of empirically estimating reliability yield different coefficients. Indeed, there is no such thing as *the* reliability coefficient, just different methods with, in some cases, different meanings. Two of these different coefficients are referred to as the coefficient of equivalence and the coefficient of stability.

Suppose we administer a test to a group of people and, at a later time, readminister the test. Considered in the context of correlation, the relationship between the sets of scores is called test-retest reliability. With physical measures, we can test again and again to arrive at a consensus about scores. However, with psychological measures, the individual learns on each testing, and, therefore, changes with each measurement. When we remeasure a person, the trait under consideration has been changed, however slightly or extensively.

In order to circumvent, or at least to minimize, the effect of learning that results from test and retest, we change the test after each measurement, that is, we retest with a parallel test. The correlation between two parallel forms is called equivalence reliability. The problem with parallel forms is that although we can nicely approximate parallelism, we rarely, if ever, obtain it precisely. Thus, while test scores from both test-retest and parallel forms can be correlated to obtain reliability estimates, the two different procedures are measures of somewhat different constructs. With the test-retest approach, there is no change in the test, only an intervening time period. Thus, the test-retest form provides a measure of the *stability* of the trait under consideration. With parallel tests, we are concerned with the *equivalence* of the two or more parallel forms. Therefore, when actual coefficients are computed, they are often referred to as the *coefficient of stability* and the *coefficient of equivalence* for the test-retest and parallel test situations, respectively.

Let us consider again the matter of error. What is treated as error variance in the coefficient of stability? We can think of the total variance as a part that is stable or retained, a part that is unstable or changed, and a random component. True variance is the stable variance, and the unstable and random components are both treated as error.

What, then, is error variance in the coefficient of equivalence? Here we have two tests constructed to measure the same thing—to be parallel tests. Try as we may, however, we will never get the two tests exactly the same. Thus, the tests have components of variation that are equivalent, components that are nonequivalent or specific, and a random component. Here, the systematic or true variation is the equivalent component, and both the nonequivalent and random components are treated as error. Figure 4.3 summarizes these differences.

The upper left corner of Figure 4.3 represents the theoretical condition of the simultaneous dual administration of a test, say X. Since this condition cannot exist in practical situations, we must administer X and, at a later time, X again. As the intervening time increases, we get information about the relative stability of a given trait. As the reliability estimate approaches unity for increasingly longer periods of time, we become more confident about the stability of the trait

Figure 4.3 Diagram Depicting the Difference Between Equivalence and Stability Reliability

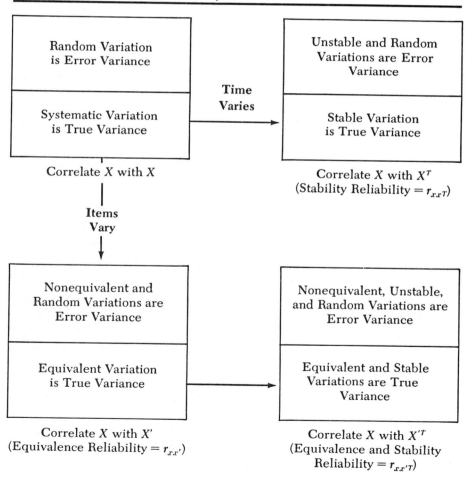

Random Variation is Error Variance

Systematic Variation is True Variance

Correlate X with X

Unstable and Random Variations are Error Variance

Stable Variation is True Variance

Correlate X with X^T
(Stability Reliability $= r_{xx^T}$)

Time Varies

Items Vary

Nonequivalent and Random Variations are Error Variance

Equivalent Variation is True Variance

Correlate X with X'
(Equivalence Reliability $= r_{xx'}$)

Nonequivalent, Unstable, and Random Variations are Error Variance

Equivalent and Stable Variations are True Variance

Correlate X with X'^T
(Equivalence and Stability Reliability $= r_{xx'^T}$)

Table 4.2 Correlation Coefficients Between Age-Level Standard Scores of Intelligence

						Years		
Av. of months	4, 5, & 6	10, 11, & 12	18, 21, & 24	27, 30, & 36	42, 48, & 54	5, 6, & 7	11, 12, & 13	14, 15, & 16
1, 2, & 3	.57	.28	−.04	−.09	−.21	−.13	−.02	−.01
4, 5, & 6		.52	.23	.10	−.16	−.07	−.08	−.04
10, 11, & 12			.60	.45	.27	.20	.30	.23
18, 21, & 24				.80	.49	.50	.43	.45
27, 30, & 36					.72	.70	.53	.46
42, 48, & 54						.82	.64	.70
Years								
5, 6, & 7							.85	.87
11, 12, & 13								.96

Adapted from Bayley, 1949.

in which we are interested. The upper right corner of Figure 4.3 represents this condition.

> **The coefficient of stability is the correlation between scores
> on a test given at two different times. Given a minimal amount
> of random variation, it indicates the degree to which the
> measured trait reflects stability.**

Table 4.2 contains a matrix of correlations between scores on a mental test with those on a test at a later age. The data of the matrix indicate that as individuals get older, the trait called "general intelligence" becomes increasingly stable, as evidenced by the increasing size of the correlation coefficients with age and between testings. The data of the matrix also indicate that the scores are unstable at earlier ages, as evidenced by the lower correlation coefficients. This is partially because we change what we call intelligence as the child is more able to deal with complex verbal materials. In other words, as we test older individuals, our tests of intelligence generally contain increasingly more verbal content.

Returning to Figure 4.3, let us consider equivalence reliability. In the lower left corner, we have the correlation of two parallel tests, X and X'. When correlating X with X', we find that the degree to which the two forms "measure the same thing" is reflected in the coefficient. It is apparent that test parallelism influences the degree of reliability. Indeed, the coefficient of equivalence is, in large measure, an index of the parallelism of two tests.

> The coefficient of equivalence is the correlation between scores on two parallel tests. Given a minimal amount of random variation, it indicates the degree to which parallelism was attained in the two tests.

We see that while parallel forms reliability estimation reflects information about form equivalence, test-retest estimation reflects information about the stability of a trait over time. Clearly, stability and equivalence reliability estimates are indices with different meanings, and to use the term *reliability* indiscriminately for both is to invite inaccuracy in communication.

In the lower right corner of Figure 4.3, lasting general variance, treated as systematic variance, is called equivalence and stability reliability.

Having discussed equivalence reliability, stability reliability, and equivalence and stability reliability, what would a coefficient of .90 for each tell us? An equivalence coefficient of .90 indicates that approximately 90 percent of the variance of X is equivalent to the variance of X'. An equivalence coefficient of .90 also tells us that 10 percent of the variance is nonequivalent and/or random variation. A stability coefficient of .90, however, indicates that on later testing, 90 percent of the variance of X remained stable. A stability coefficient of .90 also tells us that 10 percent of the variance was random, and/or due to instability of the trait. A coefficient of equivalence and stability of .90 indicates that 90 percent of the test variance is equivalent and stable, whereas 10 percent can be attributed to random error, trait instability, or nonequivalence of forms. While these sources of residual variation are of academic interest, of greatest importance for the beginning student is the distinction between equivalence and stability reliability. A third distinct type of reliability coefficient (to be discussed in the next chapter) is called *internal consistency reliability*.

In the first section of this chapter, we developed the principle that the total variance could be partitioned into true and error variance. Next, we saw that reliable variance was true variance, and that reliability could be defined as the proportion of the total variance that was true. Finally, in this section, we would like to focus on error variance, the nonreliable component, and develop the concept of standard error of measurement.

Given the unreliability of a test, the informed test interpreter should recognize that he must assume some error for any test score. He also knows that for a given test, the higher the reliability estimate, the lower the error; and, conversely, the lower the reliability estimate, the higher the error. For example, Figure 4.4 illustrates some examples of the correspondence between the reliability estimate

Standard Error of Measurement

and the components of variance. It indicates that with higher reliability there is a decrease in error variance. For the examples in Figure 4.4, if S_x equals 16, S_x^2 or the obtained variance is 256, and the error variance would be 153.6, 102.4, and 51.2 ($256 \times .60, 256 \times .40$, and $256 \times .20$) for tests A, B, and C, respectively.

In Table 4.1 at the beginning of the chapter, the n columns of that matrix represented parallel tests and gave us the obtained variance. Since the tests were parallel, all column variances should have been equal. The N rows gave us N estimates of error variation for each individual. These N estimates of error variation did not have to be equal; however, the average of the error variances provided us with a common estimate of error variation. In discussing reliability, when we found the percent of error variation, it was this averaged error variation over the N people that was specified. For example, if a test with a variance of 256 had a reliability of .90, we said that $1 - r_{xx'}$, or .10, was the proportion of error variance. Also, $S_x^2(1 - r_{xx'})$, or 25.6, would be the error variance ($256 \times .10 = 25.6$). This value, 25.6, was the average error variation for all N individuals in the data matrix.

From this information, we can now establish that the standard deviation of the error distribution can be found from the following formula:

$$S_e = S_x \sqrt{1 - r_{xx'}}. \tag{4.10}$$

This standard deviation is called the *standard error of measurement*. Table 4.3 presents the standard errors of measurement for different standard deviations and reliability coefficients.

Figure 4.4   Graphic Representation of the Relationship of Reliability to Error Variance

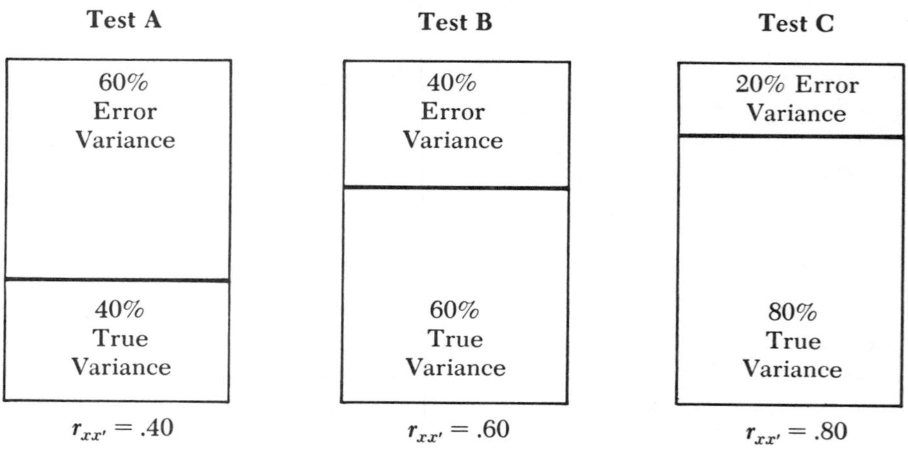

Test A	Test B	Test C
60% Error Variance	40% Error Variance	20% Error Variance
40% True Variance	60% True Variance	80% True Variance
$r_{xx'} = .40$	$r_{xx'} = .60$	$r_{xx'} = .80$

Table 4.3   **Standard Errors of Measurement for Given Values
of Reliability Coefficients and Standard Deviations**

S_x	Reliability Coefficient					
	.95	.90	.85	.80	.75	.70
30	6.7	9.5	11.6	13.4	15.0	16.4
28	6.3	8.9	10.8	12.5	14.0	15.3
26	5.8	8.2	10.1	11.6	13.0	14.2
24	5.4	7.6	9.3	10.7	12.0	13.1
22	4.9	7.0	8.5	9.8	11.0	12.0
20	4.5	6.3	7.7	8.9	10.0	11.0
18	4.0	5.7	7.0	8.0	9.0	9.9
16	3.6	5.1	6.2	7.2	8.0	8.8
14	3.1	4.4	5.4	6.3	7.0	7.7
12	2.7	3.8	4.6	5.4	6.0	6.6
10	2.2	3.2	3.9	4.5	5.0	5.5
8	1.8	2.5	3.1	3.6	4.0	4.4
6	1.3	1.9	2.3	2.7	3.0	3.3
4	.9	1.3	1.5	1.8	2.0	2.2
2	.4	.6	.8	.9	1.0	1.1

This table is based on the formula $S_e = S_x \sqrt{(1 - r_{xx'})}$. For most purposes the result will be sufficiently accurate if the table is entered with the reliability and standard deviation values nearest those given in the test manual. Be sure the standard deviation and the reliability coefficient are for the same group of people.

Source: Doppelt, 1956.

> **The standard error of measurement, $S_e = S_x \sqrt{1 - r_{xx'}}$, is the
> average of the standard deviations we would obtain if each of N
> individuals were measured on n different, but parallel, tests.**

The standard error of measurement is extremely important in assisting in test interpretation. Suppose a student takes the California Test of Mental Maturity (CTMM) on which he scores 116. The test manual informs us that the obtained standard deviation is 16, $r_{xx'}$ is .91, and S_e is 4.8. What kind of interpretation can we make? Suppose, for the purpose of illustration, that 100 parallel tests existed, were administered to this same student, and yielded a mean score of 118, which is also the student's true score (any row of Table 4.1). Administering the 100 parallel tests to N individuals would give us N estimates of error variance. The average of these individual variances due to error is the error variance. This average estimate of the error distribution is the smaller histogram in Figure 4.1. Since that initial discussion, we have established that the error variance can be found mathematically by finding $S_x^2(1 - r_{xx'})$. Also, the standard deviation, called the standard error of measurement, is determined by formula 4.10. In this hypothetical situation, the standard deviation is 4.8, and we expect the error to be normally distributed, as previously defined.

From our discussion of the normal distribution, we know that 68 percent of the cases fall within one standard deviation of the mean (in this case, $T \pm 1S_e = 118 \pm 4.8 = 113.2\text{--}122.8$). The problem is, however, that we never know the true score, T, and cannot give 100 parallel tests to the same person. However, when we give a test once to a person with a true score of 118, the probability is .68 that the test score comes from the range 113.2–122.8, because 68 percent of the area in the normal curve is between $\overline{X} \pm$ one standard deviation. Suppose we test the individual and acquire an X in this range, say 116. The $116 \pm 1S_e$ (111.2–120.8) spans his true score of 118. If we were to give the test again, the probability would be .68 that X would be in the range $T \pm 1S_e$, in this case, the interval 113.2–122.8. If, on this second testing, the score fell out of the range, say it was 113, the interval 108.2–117.8 would fail to span T. If this procedure were repeated over and over for all of the scores in Figure 4.5, roughly 68 percent of the intervals $X \pm 1S_e$ would span the individual's true score. Figure 4.5 is a

Figure 4.5   Plot of Error Variation Occurring from the Administration of 100 Parallel Tests to an Individual with a True Score of 118

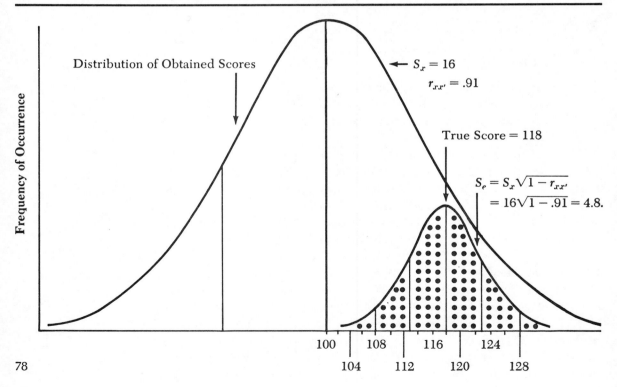

graphic representation of this procedure. The large distribution represents a distribution of obtained scores, which in this case has a standard deviation of 16. The smaller distribution represents a hypothetical distribution of 100 scores from 100 parallel tests administered to the same individual. The mean of these 100 scores is the individual's true score, in this case 118.

What can we make of all this? We can see that, given an obtained score for an individual, we can determine the interval $X \pm 1S_e$ spanning one standard error on either side of the obtained score. We sometimes say that we are 68 percent confident that the interval spans the true score. Returning to our subject's CTMM score of 116, we can say that we are 68 percent confident that the interval spans his true score ($116 \pm 4.8 = 111.2–120.8$).

What would happen for a test of higher reliability, say $r_{xx'} = .96$? We know .96 is more reliable than .91; the error of measurement is $16\sqrt{1 - .96} = 3.2$. Holding all other factors constant, we find that increasing reliability reduces the size of the interval necessary for a specified confidence level. With a reliability of .96, the interval ($116 \pm 3.2 = 112.8–119.2$) has a probability of .68 of spanning the true score. Thus, we can see that the higher the reliability, the lower the error of measurement, and the more confidence we can place in the accuracy of our test score. Accuracy of the test score in this context means a smaller error of measurement and a corresponding smaller interval necessary for spanning the true score with a given probability.

Summary

We noted in the preceding section that as the reliability increases, the magnitude of the errors decreases. However, even with relatively high reliability coefficients, say around .90, substantial errors can still occur. When interpreting an individual's score, one should give close consideration to the standard error of measurement. On the other hand, when comparing tests, the reliability coefficient will often be most important. Very often measures are expressed in different units and are not directly comparable. In such situations, the coefficient of reliability is the applicable basis for comparing the tests. Assuming other things equal, the test with the higher reliability is desired, since it more consistently places the individual accurately within the group.

Situations do exist in which we are specifically interested in both stability and equivalence reliability. We may be interested in concept mastery where this mastery is evidenced by a marked change in performance. If change in attitude or change in an underlying trait is of primary interest, it may be necessary to accept low stability reliability and high equivalence reliability in order to meet the objectives of the testing.

In this chapter we have discussed the concept of reliability and what it means in terms of the scores on a test. We saw that equivalence and stability of test scores are considerations of reliability. The separation of these concepts, and their meaning relative to reliability was presented. Additional procedures for empirically estimating reliability are presented in the next chapter.

Suggested Readings

Brown, F. *Principles of educational and psychological testing.* Hinsdale, Ill.: Dryden Press, 1970, Chapter 3.

Ebel, R. *Measuring educational achievement.* Englewood Cliffs: Prentice-Hall, 1965, Chapter 10.

Guilford, J. *Psychometric methods.* (2nd ed.) New York: McGraw-Hill, 1954, pp. 349–354.

Gulliksen, H. *Theory of mental tests.* New York: Wiley, 1950, Chapter 2.

Helmstadter, G. *Principles of psychological measurement.* New York: Appleton-Century-Crofts, 1964, pp. 33–41, 58–66.

Hoyt, C. Reliability. In C. W. Harris (Ed.), *Encyclopedia of educational research.* New York: Macmillan, 1960, pp. 1144–1147.

Nunnally, J. *Psychometric theory.* New York: McGraw-Hill, 1967, Chapters 6, 7.

Individual Review Questions

1. When considering reliability, an observed test score conceptually consists of the _____ and the _____ components.

2. If we (theoretically) computed the mean score of a large number of repeated measurements on parallel tests for a given individual, this mean score would be the individual's _____ score.

3. A given individual (theoretically) is administered a large number of repeated measurements. The variability of the scores is due to _____.

4. A statistical characteristic of three or more parallel measurements is equality of _____, _____, and _____.

5. The covariance of true and error components is *one/substantial/minimal/zero.*

6. An observed test score is made up of the *product/sum/ratio* of the true and error components.

7. When administering a test to a large number of individuals, the obtained variance in the test scores consists of true variance and _____ variance.

8. In a summary word, reliability is concerned with the _____ of measurement.

ANSWERS

1. true; error (any order)
2. true
3. error, or specificity
4. means; variances, or standard deviations; intercorrelations (any order)
5. zero
6. sum
7. error
8. consistency

9. Specifically, reliability has different meanings under varying conditions. With a test-retest situation, reliability is a measure of _____ of measurement.

10. With the coefficient of stability, consistency is defined as being over _____.

11. With the parallel forms test situation, reliability is a measure of _____.

12. With the coefficient of equivalence, consistency is defined as being over _____.

13. On parallel tests, the *observed/true/error* scores are theoretically equal for a given individual.

14. If we correlate the scores on a test with those of a parallel test, the correlation coefficient, considered an estimate of reliability, is the ratio of _____ variance to _____ variance.

15. Reliability is classically defined as the correlation between _____ forms. This is an index of _____ reliability.

16. Reliability is theoretically defined as the ratio of _____ variance to obtained variance.

17. A reliability coefficient indicates the _____ of systematic variation in a test.

18. If a test has a reliability estimate of .85, this would indicate that _____ percent of the observed variance is true variance.

19. If the estimated reliability of a test is .79, the proportion of observed variance that is error variance is _____.

20. A test has a reliability of .4. The ratio of true variance to obtained variance in this case is approximately *2 to 5/5 to 2/1 to 4/4 to 6.*

21. If the estimated reliability of a test is .76 and the standard deviation of the observed scores is 10, the error variance is _____.

22. Low correlation coefficients between scores on repeated testings indicate that the trait measured by the test is _____.

23. Performance on similar tests of intelligence tend to become more *stable/unstable* with increasing age.

24. Computing the correlation between two parallel tests provides the coefficient of *equivalence/stability,* while computing the correlation between two administrations of the same test provides the coefficient of *equivalence/stability.*

25. The standard error of measurement is the _____ _____ of the theoretical distribution of _____ scores.

ANSWERS
9. stability
10. time
11. equivalence
12. items
13. true
14. true; observed
15. parallel; equivalence
16. true, or systematic
17. proportion
18. 85
19. .21
20. 2 to 5
21. 24
22. unstable
23. stable
24. equivalence; stability
25. standard deviation; error

26. If test scores contain no true variance, the reliability of the test is _____.

27. As the correlation between two parallel tests increases, the standard error of measurement will *increase/decrease.*

28. The relationship between the reliability coefficients and the standard error of measurement is *direct/inverse.*

29. Suppose we had a large number of the scores on the same test for a given individual (theoretical, but not practically possible), and we constructed an interval of ± one standard deviation around each score. Assuming the scores to be normally distributed, we would expect _____ percent of the intervals to span the individual's true score.

30. In practice, we have one score for a given individual, and can construct a single interval around it. Therefore, instead of actually having a percentage of intervals spanning the true score, we say that the single interval has a _____ of including the true score.

31. An interval ± 1.96 standard deviations on either side of an observed score is constructed. Assuming the scores to be normally distributed, this interval has a probability of _____ of including the true score.

32. As reliability increases, the size of the interval required to span the true score with a given probability *increases/decreases.*

33. In order to determine the standard error of measurement, in addition to the reliability coefficient, it is necessary to know the *mean/shape/standard deviation* of the distribution of observed scores.

34. The reliability coefficient of a test is .84, and the variance of the observed scores is 100. With these results, the standard error of measurement is _____.

35. Two tests have identical reliability coefficients. The test with the greater observed variance will have the *larger/smaller* standard error of measurement.

36. The primary difference between a coefficient of stability and a coefficient of equivalence is in the *computation/interpretation.*

37. The threat of "learning from the test" or possible practice effects is greater with the coefficient of *stability/equivalence.*

38. The coefficient of equivalence is an index indicating the extent to which *individuals/testing conditions/test forms* are comparable.

39. If someone concluded that there had been marked change in a trait from one testing to a subsequent testing, he would likely be basing his conclusion on a *high/low* coefficient of *stability/equivalence.*

ANSWERS
26. zero
27. decrease
28. inverse
29. 68
30. probability
31. .95
32. decreases
33. standard deviation
34. 4
35. larger
36. interpretation
37. stability
38. test forms
39. low; stability

Study Exercises

1. Suppose $S_e = 3$ and $S_t = 4$, what is S_x?
2. Suppose $S_x^2 = 25$ and $S_t = 5$, what is S_e?
3. Suppose $S_x = 4$ and $S_e = 3$, what is $r_{xx'}$?
4. Suppose $S_t = 3$ and $S_x^2 = 10$, what is $r_{xx'}$?
5. Suppose $S_x = 15$ and $S_e = 5$, what is $r_{xx'}$?
6. Suppose $r_{xx'} = .90$ and $S_x = 10$, what is S_t?
7. Suppose $r_{xx'} = .90$ and $S_t^2 = 225$, what is S_e^2?
8. Suppose $S_t = 12$ and $S_e^2 = 9$, what is $r_{xx'}$?
9. Suppose $r_{xx'} = .91$ and $S_x = 15$, what is S_e?
10. Suppose $r_{xx'} = .84$ and $S_x = 16$, what is S_e?
11. Suppose $S_t = 9$ and $S_x^2 = 98$, what is $r_{xx'}$?
12. Suppose $r_{xx'} = .90$ and $S_t = 4$, what is S_e^2?
13. Suppose $r_{xx'} = .60$ and $S_e^2 = 20$, what is S_x?
14. Suppose $S_e = 5$ and $S_t^2 = 144$, what is S_x?
15. Suppose $r_{xx'} = .64$ and $S_x^2 = 169$, what is S_e?
16. Suppose an individual received an obtained score of 109 on a test with a standard error of measurement of 5. What limits would you set so you would be 68 percent confident that you spanned the true score?
17. Suppose an individual received an obtained score of 109 on a test with a standard deviation of 16 and an error of measurement of 5. What is $r_{xx'}$?
18. For the data in problem 16, what limits would you set so you would be 95 percent confident that you spanned the true score?
19. Suppose an individual receives a score of 110 on a test with $r_{xx'} = .91$, and $S_x = 15$. What interval will span the true score with a .68 probability?
20. If the test for the individual in problem 19 had a reliability of .84, what interval would span the true score with a .68 probability?
21. Suppose an individual received an obtained score of 112 on the test in problem 9. What limits would you set so you would be 68 percent confident that you spanned the true score?
22. Suppose an individual received an obtained score of 118 on the test in problem 9. What limits would you set so that you would be 95 percent confident that you spanned the true score?
23. Suppose an individual with a true score of 113 takes a test with $r_{xx'} = .91$ and $S_x = 15$. What is the probability that this individual could score as high as 118? 123?
24. Suppose an individual received an obtained score of 115 on a test with a mean of 100 and standard deviation of 15. Interpret the score if $r_{xx'} = .91$.
25. For a given test, what is the relationship between reliability and error of measurement?
26. An individual scores 115 on a test with a mean of 100 and a standard deviation of 15. The test has an equivalence reliability of .91 and a stability reliability of .84 (over six months).
    a. Upon immediate retesting with a parallel test, what will the error of measurement be?
    b. Given this error of measurement, what interval has a .68 probability of spanning this individual's true score?
    c. Suppose the individual is tested again in six months. What interval has a .95 probability of spanning the true score?

ANSWERS
1. 5.0
2. 0.0
3. .44
4. .90
5. .89
6. $\sqrt{90}$, or 9.49
7. 25
8. .94
9. 4.5
10. 6.4
11. .83
12. 1.78
13. 7.07
14. 13
15. 7.8
16. 104–114
17. .90
18. 99.2–118.8
19. 105.5–114.5
20. 104–116
21. 107.5–116.5
22. 109.18–126.82
23. $p < .14$; $p < .02$
24. inverse relationship
25. inverse relationship
26. (a) 4.5; (b) 110.5–119.5; (c) 103.24–126.76

5   Reliability Estimation

In the preceding chapter, we developed a mathematical model which defined reliability as the proportion of nonerror variance in a test score. Also, we noted that reliability has different meanings depending on the empirical operations used in its estimation. In this chapter, we will consider the factors that influence reliability, and the procedures by which we estimate reliability empirically, including the important topic of internal consistency reliability.

Classically, a reliability estimate is computed from the correlation between two equivalent measurements. As a correlation coefficient, its maximum value is one. A reliability coefficient of one is assumed to indicate no measurement error in either of the two scores. Negative reliability coefficients are empirically possible, but theoretically meaningless. A correlation coefficient of zero indicates no relationships between the measures, thus signifying a complete lack of systematic variation. If the coefficient is zero, the score distributions of both measurements are assumed to be due to error.

The two measures correlated to obtain a reliability estimate may be two parallel forms of the test administered to the same group of subjects (coefficient of equivalence), or it may be the same test administered to the same group of subjects on two different occasions (coefficient of stability). In this context, we have used the symbols $r_{xx'}$ to designate equivalence reliability, and $r_{xx}r$ to designate stability reliability. Also, since we will be focusing on factors that influence the magnitude of reliability estimates, we shall use the symbols $r_{oo'}$ and $r_{nn'}$ to represent the *original* and the *new* estimates respectively. Also, we will use the symbols S_{e_o} and S_{e_n} to represent the old and new standard errors of measurement respectively—that is, before and after certain factors are introduced.

As indicated previously, all things being equal, we generally prefer the more reliable test. In order to enhance test reliability, it is important to know what factors affect reliability. There are several factors that should be considered.

Factors Influencing Reliability Estimates

Test Length

Suppose you are with a friend on a rifle range and want to determine if he is a good marksman. You would not come to any conclusion about his marksmanship after only one shot, or even two. Rather you would like to have a number of trials before you come to a conclusion—you would like a long test on which to base a judgment. You feel intuitively that with a number of trials you get a better picture of his true score; that is, you are reducing the possibility of error and enhancing the reliability of your inference. The same principle holds in psychological measurement: all other things equal, a longer test of the same item type will tend to be more reliable.

Suppose a classroom teacher gave a 20-item spelling examination. A reliability estimate is computed, and found to be .60. What might be done to increase this reliability? The answer is, of course, to increase, possibly double or triple, the length of the test *with the same kind of items.* This last point is of extreme importance. If you were trying to ascertain if your friend is a good marksman with just three trials, you would not ask him to shoot the rifle one trial, drive a golf ball one trial, and serve a tennis ball on the other trial. Rather, you would have him fire the rifle three times, and base your conclusion on these three similar trials. Analogously, if you wish to increase the reliability of a spelling test, you must increase the test with spelling items. Increasing the test with mathematics items will not increase your ability to discern if a student can spell. The Spearman-Brown prophecy formula estimates the increase in reliability with an increase in test length, when the items are of a similar nature:

$$r_{nn'} = \frac{K r_{oo'}}{1 + (K - 1) r_{oo'}}, \tag{5.1}$$

where:

$r_{nn'}$ = reliability of the new test of increased length
K = the factor by which the test has been increased to attain the new length
$r_{oo'}$ = reliability of the original test.

In formula 5.1, K reflects the increase or decrease in the length of the test. K is greater than 1 when the test is increased in length. As an example, $K = 2$ if the test is doubled in length; $K = 3$ if the test is tripled in length; and, for an increase from 20 to 30 items, $K = 1.5$. Values of K less than 1 will generally result in decreasing estimates of reliability.

In the spelling test situation just mentioned, suppose the teacher had sufficient time to give a 40-item test, doubling a 20-item test with a reliability of .60 ($r_{oo'}$). The computation of the Spearman-Brown formula would estimate the increase in reliability for the test of doubled length ($K = 2$) as:

$$\frac{2(.60)}{1.0 + (2 - 1).60} = \frac{1.20}{1.60} = \frac{3}{4} = .75.$$

The Spearman-Brown formula predicts that if a 20-item test with a reliability of .60 is increased to 40 similar items, the reliability of the 40-item test should be about .75, an increase in reliability of .15.

Suppose, instead of 40 items, our teacher decides to use a 60-item test of similar content. This is an increase of 40 items over the 20-item test, tripling the length. The Spearman-Brown formula can be computed in either of two ways:

1. as an increase from 20 to 60 similar items ($K = 3$):

$$\frac{3(.60)}{1.0 + (3 - 1).60} = \frac{1.80}{2.20} = .82, \text{ or}$$

2. as an increase from 40 to 60 items ($K = 1.5$):

$$\frac{1.5(.75)}{1.0 + (1.5 - 1).75} = \frac{1.13}{1.38} = .82.$$

The second computation is based on our previously gained knowledge that a 40-item test had an $r_{xx'} = .75$. Inspecting the reliability coefficients, note that while the initial 20-item increase resulted in an increase in systematic variance of .15 (from .60 to .75), the second increase of 20 items resulted in an increase in reliability of .07 (from .75 to .82). Keeping the amount of increase constant (in this case 20 items) resulted in decreasing gains in reliability as overall test length increased.

From the previous examples, it is possible to plot a graph of increase in reliability with increased test length to assist in understanding the effect of test length on reliability. Figure 5.1 presents a plot of test length (K) against reliability. An additional estimate of reliability is included for a test of 80 items, $r_{nn'} = .86$. Figure 5.1 reveals that although increasing the length of a test with similar items results in increased reliability, the increases get systematically smaller as K increases over the original length of the test. While lengthening a test with similar items increases reliability, unlimited lengthening of a test results in minimal increases in reliability for larger values of K.

> **As test length is increased with similar items, reliability increases. However, with each new length increment, the increased effect on reliability is less than for the previous increment.**

Thus, all other factors being equal, if a short, moderately reliable test is increased in length with similar items, the lengthened test will have higher reliability. With increased length, the error variance increases more slowly than the true variance; error variance and true variance increase by factors of K and K^2, respectively.

As an example, suppose a 10-item test has a variance of 144 and a reliability of .60. The true variance is 86.40 (.60 $\times$ 144), and the error variance is 57.60 (.40 $\times$ 144). If we triple the test length, the error variance will increase by a factor of three ($K = 3$) to 172.80 (57.60 $\times$ 3). The true variance will increase by a factor of nine ($K^2 = 9$) to 777.60. Figure 5.2 diagrams this example. Since the total variance of the increased test is the sum of the true and error variance, the total test variance will be 950.40. Also, since reliability is the proportion of true variance in a test (777.60/950.40), the reliability for the 30-item test will be .818. Our calculations can be checked by simply substituting the appropriate

Figure 5.1 Increase in Reliability with Increased Test Length

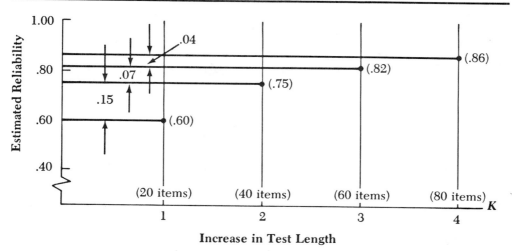

Increase in Test Length

information into the Spearman-Brown formula. A 10-item test with reliability of .60, when increased to 30 similar items, yields the following reliability estimate:

$$\frac{3(.60)}{1 + (3 - 1).60} = \frac{1.80}{2.20} = .818.$$

Figure 5.2   Diagram of Increased Variance Components Resulting from Increasing Test Length ($K = 3$) with Similar Types of Items

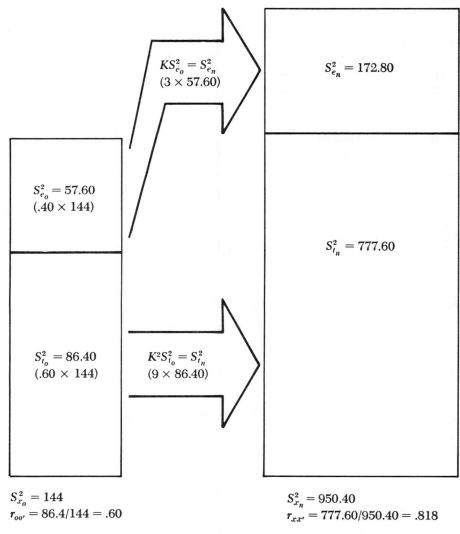

$KS^2_{e_o} = S^2_{e_n}$
(3×57.60)

$S^2_{e_n} = 172.80$

$S^2_{e_o} = 57.60$
$(.40 \times 144)$

$S^2_{t_n} = 777.60$

$S^2_{t_o} = 86.40$
$(.60 \times 144)$

$K^2 S^2_{t_o} = S^2_{t_n}$
(9×86.40)

$S^2_{x_o} = 144$
$r_{oo'} = 86.4/144 = .60$

$S^2_{x_n} = 950.40$
$r_{xx'} = 777.60/950.40 = .818$

$S^2_{x_o}$, $S^2_{t_o}$, and $S^2_{e_o}$ are the variances of obtained, true, and error scores, respectively, for the original test.
$S^2_{x_n}$, $S^2_{t_n}$, and $S^2_{e_n}$ are the variances of obtained, true, and error scores, respectively, for the new or lengthened test.

Thus, we can compute the effect of increased test length on reliability with the Spearman-Brown formula, or from our knowledge that error and true variance increase by factors of K and K^2, respectively.

> **Increasing test length by a factor of K has the effect of increasing true variance by a factor of K^2 and error variance by a factor of K.**

What implication does this have for the standard error of measurement? First, since the error variance increases by a factor of K with an increase of similar items, the standard error of measurement will increase by a factor of $\sqrt{K}$. That is,

$$S^2_{e_n} = KS^2_{e_o};\qquad\qquad(5.2)$$

therefore,

$$S_{e_n} = \sqrt{K}S_{e_o}.\qquad\qquad(5.3)$$

> **As a test is increased in length with similar items, the standard error of measurement increases by a factor of the square root of K.**

Consider the above illustration from a different vantage point. Lengthening the test with similar items increases the obtained, true, and error variances. For example, note that in Figure 5.2 the variances of the original and lengthened tests were 144 and 950.40, respectively. Therefore, the standard deviations of the raw scores are 12.00 and 30.83, respectively. The standard deviations of the error scores, the standard errors of measurement, are 7.60 and 13.15 for the original and lengthened tests, respectively. The ratio of the standard error of measurement to the standard deviation of obtained scores is smaller for the lengthened test ($13.15/30.83 = .43$) than it is for the original test ($7.60/12.00 = .63$). This suggests that the standard error of measurement increases with an increase in test length; however, it is smaller relative to the standard deviation of the obtained test scores.

Range of Talent

Another factor that influences the magnitude of the reliability coefficient and the standard error of measurement is the range of abilities of the group being tested. Increasing the range of abilities in a group systematically increases true variance and, hence, reliability. In general, reliability coefficients will be higher when the group dispersion is greater, and will be lower when the group dispersion is less. However, the standard error of measurement remains relatively constant under changes in group dispersion. Why is this the case?

Consider a situation in which parallel tests, X and X', are administered to a group of fifth-grade students. The test has a standard deviation of 10 and a reliability of .60 for the fifth-grade group. Later, the test is also given to a group of sixth graders; the standard deviation for the fifth- and sixth-grade groups combined is 15. Figure 5.3 illustrates this example.

Suppose that an individual, A, in the fifth-grade distribution took the test over and over again. Her error of measurement would not be influenced by additions to the group. That is, the error of measurement for individual A would be constant whether she was a member of the fifth-grade distribution, or of the fifth- and sixth-grade distribution. The standard error of measurement becomes the average

Figure 5.3   Scatterplot of the Distribution of Fifth-Grade Students with that of Fifth- and Sixth-Grade Students Combined

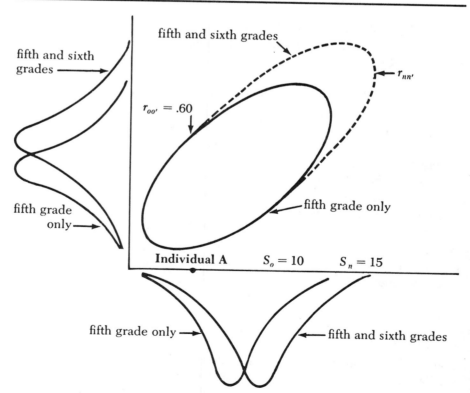

of the standard errors for all individuals. As such, it tends to be constant no matter what group membership we impose. It follows from the error of measurement formulas of the previous chapter that:

$$S_o \sqrt{1 - r_{oo'}} = S_n \sqrt{1 - r_{nn'}}, \tag{5.4}$$

where:

S_o and $r_{oo'}$ = the standard deviation and reliability for the original group
S_n and $r_{nn'}$ = the standard deviation and reliability for the new group.

Solving for $r_{nn'}$ we have:

$$r_{nn'} = 1 - \frac{S_o^2}{S_n^2}(1 - r_{oo'}). \tag{5.5}$$

Consider again the situation of the fifth- and sixth-grade scores. We had an original standard deviation and reliability estimate of 10 and .60 respectively; we want to know the reliability estimate, $r_{nn'}$, if the standard deviation is increased to 15. By formula 5.5 above, we have

$$r_{nn'} = 1 - \frac{100}{225}(1 - .60) = 1 - .18 = .82.$$

We see that as the range of talent increased ($S_o = 10$ to $S_n = 15$), the reliability estimate increased from .60 to .82.

Consider another example. Suppose a mathematics test is given to a large group of undergraduates for whom the standard deviation is 12 and the reliability estimate is .85. Later, the test is given to a group of mathematics majors for whom the standard deviation is 10. What will be the estimated reliability for the restricted range of talent?

$$r_{nn'} = 1 - \frac{144}{100}(1 - .85) = 1 - .22 = .78.$$

Thus, as the range of talent is restricted, the estimated reliability decreases. In summary, as the range of talent increases, the estimated test reliability increases, because the error variance remains constant, while variance due to individual differences (true variance) increases. Also, since the error variance remains relatively constant from one group to the next, the standard error of measurement remains relatively constant under changes in range of talent.

As the range of talent in a group systematically increases, the reliability of the test increases; as the range decreases, the reliability of the test will also decrease. Also, as the range of talent in a group increases or decreases, the standard error of measurement remains relatively constant.

Similarity of Item Content

Before we proceed further, we must develop the principle of composite variance. As an example, suppose we gave two tests, X and X', to a group of individuals. Suppose the variance of test X and also of test X' was 2, and the correlation between the test scores, $r_{xx'}$, was 0.8. Now we create a new score, a composite of the sum of the scores on tests X and X'. What would be the variance of this composite score? Table 5.1 presents the data for this example (with $X + X'$ denoting the composite scores, and $x + x'$ denoting the composite scores minus the mean of the composite scores). As shown in the table, the variance of the composite scores, $S_{x+x'}^2$, is 7.2. The variance of the two original scores, $S_x{}^2 + S_{x'}{}^2$, add to 4. We find that the variance of the composite scores is greater than the sum of the variances of the original scores: 7.2 is greater than 4. The variance for the two-test composite scores can be found by:

$$S_{x+x'}^2 = S_x{}^2 + S_{x'}{}^2 + 2r_{xx'}S_x S_{x'}. \tag{5.6}$$

For this example, we find the composite variance to be:

$$2 + 2 + 2(.8)\sqrt{2}\sqrt{2} = 7.2.$$

Generalizing, any composite variance will have n variance terms, where n is the number of tests in the composite; and $n(n-1)$ covariance terms.

> **The composite variance for n tests can be found by adding the n test variance terms and the $n(n-1)$ test covariance terms.**

Consider composite variance in terms of test items. Here two sources influence the composite variance: (1) the item variance for each of the tests, and (2) the covariance (similarity) between the tests. What effect does covariance have on reliability? Suppose we have a 10-item test on which we wish to maximize the reliability. The variance of the 10-item test can be thought of as a 10-variable composite. This composite will have 100 terms: 10 variance terms, and 90 covariance terms, all of which must be as large as possible to maximize total test dispersion. To maximize the influence of the 90 covariance terms, we want

Table 5.1 Computation of Composite Variance

X	X'	$X + X'$	$x + x'$	$(x + x')^2$
1	2	3	−3	9
2	1	3	−3	9
3	3	6	0	0
4	5	9	3	9
5	4	9	3	9
				36

$$S^2_{x+x'} = 36/5 = 7.2.$$

$r_{xx'}S_xS_{x'}$ to be as large as possible, and one way to do this is to get $r_{xx'}$ as close to one as possible. How do we increase $r_{xx'}$? We use similar items that tend to correlate highly with each other. When $r_{xx'}$ is zero or close to zero, the composite variance is small, since all covariance entries are zero or near zero.

Another way to think of this problem is in terms of the classical definition of reliability. Since reliability is the proportion of systematic (true) variance in a test, anything that systematically increases dispersion will increase reliability. How does this relate to similarity of content? The answer lies in the covariance terms (see formula 5.6). Since similar items have nonzero correlations, the total test variance consists of the variances and covariances of the items. Dissimilar items, by definition, have zero intercorrelations, and in this situation the total test variance consists only of the item variances, since the covariance terms are zero. Thus, other factors being equal, a given number of similar items will have greater systematic dispersion (and, hence, greater reliability) than an equal number of dissimilar items.

> Other factors constant, as the intercorrelation of the test items increases (as items measure similar concepts), the reliability of the total test increases. As the intercorrelation of the items decreases (as items measure different concepts), the total test variance decreases.

Item Difficulty

We have observed that test length, range of talent, and item similarity have different effects on reliability and the standard error of measurement. A fourth factor influencing reliability is the level of difficulty of the items. The level of difficulty, p, is *the proportion of those taking the test that answer a particular item correctly.* If a test is very easy or very difficult, we get either very large or very small proportions of people answering the individual items correctly.

Either way the result is a skewed distribution with very little dispersion. Without dispersion, the items do not correlate, and we fail to attain maximum reliability.

Before proceeding further, let us introduce a simplified method of computing item variance. The computational formula for variance, formula 2.3, presented in Chapter 2, is:

$$S_x^2 = \frac{\Sigma X^2 - (\Sigma X)^2/N}{N}.$$

Instead of using formula 2.3, the variance of items scored 1 or 0 (either correct or incorrect) can be found by simply multiplying the proportion answering the item correctly (passing the item), p_x, by the proportion not answering correctly (failing the item), q_x. Since the answer must be either correct or incorrect, q_x is equal to $1 - p_x$. Thus, S_x^2 can be computed more simply:

$$S_x^2 = p_x(1 - p_x) = p_x q_x. \tag{5.7}$$

Table 5.2 presents the computation of the variance of a dichotomously scored item using the computational formula and formula 5.7. This table shows that item variance can be computed by using formula 2.3 or by obtaining the $p_x q_x$ value.

To illustrate the effect of difficulty level on test reliability, formula 5.6 for composite variance is:

$$S_{x+x'}^2 = S_x^2 + S_{x'}^2 + 2r_{xx'}S_x S_{x'},$$

which now can be written in terms of p and q, given any two items, X and X':

$$S_{x+x'}^2 = p_x q_x + p_{x'} q_{x'} + 2r_{xx'}\sqrt{p_x q_x}\sqrt{p_{x'} q_{x'}}. \tag{5.8}$$

When an item is of moderate difficulty, .50, the item variance is maximized at .25. For a dichotomously scored item, maximum variance occurs when subjects are

Table 5.2 **Computation of Variance for a Dichotomous Variable**

X	X^2	
1	1	$\dfrac{\Sigma X^2 - (\Sigma X)^2/N}{N} = \dfrac{3 - (9/5)}{5} = \dfrac{3 - 1.8}{5}$
0	0	
1	1	$= \dfrac{1.2}{5} = .24.$
1	1	
0	0	$p_x = 3/5;\ q_x = 2/5$
3	3	$p_x q_x = 3/5(2/5) = 6/25 = .24.$

Table 5.3   **Variances of Items for
Varying Difficulty Levels**

p_x	q_x	$p_x q_x = S_x{}^2$	
1.0	.0	.00	
.8	.2	.16	
.6	.4	.24	
.5	.5	.25	←Maximum
.4	.6	.24	variance
.2	.8	.16	
.0	1.0	.00	

sorted into two equal groups. Table 5.3 presents the variances of items of varying difficulty levels. If all items are of 50 percent difficulty, and if $r_{xx'}$ has been maximized by selecting similar items, we are systematically maximizing test variance and, hence, test reliability. From formula 5.8, we see that two things, difficulty level and similarity of item content, determine the test dispersion. Since both of these are systematic sources of variance, maximizing both results in high reliability.

One of the interesting characteristics of item difficulty is that items with difficulty levels in the range .4 to .6 have a variance of .24 to .25. Items with difficulty levels in the range .3 to .7 have variances of .21 to .25. Thus, selecting items of moderate difficulty tends to maximize dispersion systematically. It is only with extremely difficult or easy items (where $p < .2$ or $p > .8$) that dispersion is minimized. However, the selection of moderately difficult items does not guarantee high item intercorrelation. Moderate item difficulty is a necessary, but not sufficient, condition for high item intercorrelation. For example, we might have a spelling item and a mathematics item, both of moderate difficulty, both approaching maximum dispersion individually. However, the two items may have a very low correlation; and, therefore, the right term of formula 5.8, $2r_{xx'}\sqrt{p_x q_x}\sqrt{p_{x'} q_{x'}}$, approaches zero, and $S_x{}^2$ is not maximized.

Table 5.4 presents an illustration in which item difficulty is the same, but item intercorrelation differs. We might have the responses shown to two items, A and B, by four individuals in each case (1 indicates a correct response; 0, an incorrect response).

In both cases item difficulty is the same; namely, .50. Item intercorrelation in Case 1 is 0.0; in Case 2 it is 1.00. Note that $S_{x+x'}^2$ for Case 1 is .50 and for Case 2 it is 1.00. While difficulty level was held constant, where similarity of item content was greatest, test variance was greatest.

Since all moderately difficult items tend to approach maximum dispersion, similarity of item content becomes most important. Similarity of item content becomes a more crucial factor in the maximization of reliability than does diffi-

Table 5.4   Illustration of the Effect of Differing Item Intercorrelations on Composite Variance

Case 1		Case 2	
A	B	A	B
1	0	1	1
1	1	1	1
0	0	0	0
0	1	0	0

culty level. (Difficulty level and similarity of content will be more thoroughly considered in the later discussion of item analysis.)

> **When a test is constructed of items such that 50 percent of those taking the test correctly answer each item, the item variance is maximized. If items are extremely easy or extremely difficult, item variance approaches zero.**

In summary, we can say that four important factors affecting reliability estimation are:

1. *Increased test length*—the longer the test of similar items, the higher the reliability estimate.
2. *Increased range of talent*—the greater the dispersion due to individual differences, the higher the reliability estimate.
3. *Increased similarity of item content*—the more similar the items are in content, the greater the intercorrelations, and the higher the reliability estimate. Items similar in content have higher correlations; items of dissimilar content have lower or zero correlations.
4. *Selection of items of moderate difficulty level* maximizes total test dispersion. The higher the item dispersion, the higher an item correlates with other items. Selection of items around moderate difficulty levels is a necessary, but not sufficient, condition for high item intercorrelations.

Empirical Methods for Estimating Reliability

In the previous chapter, we discussed the test-retest and parallel forms methods of estimating reliability to indicate that the two different procedures resulted in coefficients that measured different constructs, namely, stability and equivalence. Now that we have discussed the Spearman-Brown formula (5.1), we are free to introduce other methods for estimating reliability as well as the coefficient of internal consistency, which is an index of yet another construct.

Table 5.5 **Hypothetical Data Matrix for a
4-Item Test Administered to Six Subjects**

Individuals	Items				Total scores (X)
	1	2	3	4	
1	+	0	0	0	1
2	+	+	+	+	4
3	+	0	+	0	2
4	+	+	0	+	3
5	+	0	0	+	2
6	0	0	0	0	0

Split-Half Reliability

Test-retest reliability and parallel forms reliability require two administrations of the test under consideration. It is desirable in some situations to obtain a reliability estimate from a single administration of a test. As an illustration, consider a 4-item test administered to a group of six individuals. Their pattern of correct (+) and incorrect (0) responses in a 6 by 4 data matrix is shown in Table 5.5.

How can we get a reliability estimate from this single administration of the test? One method that has been used is to split the test into two parallel forms of two items each. For the matrix of Table 5.5, three such splits could be made: items 1 and 4 against 2 and 3; items 1 and 2 against 3 and 4; and finally, items 1 and 3 against 2 and 4. The last split, called the odd-even split, is generally preferred, because such factors as speed, practice, fatigue, etc. tend to be more evenly distributed over the two forms with this split of the items. For example, as the individual becomes fatigued, if odd items are in one form and even items in another, the fatigue factor tends to occur evenly in both forms. Also, if an individual fails to complete the test, this factor tends to appear in both forms.

One method of obtaining an equivalence reliability estimate for the matrix of Table 5.5 is to use an odd-even split and correlate the halves. Suppose we get a correlation of .32 between the half tests. Is this the reliability of the 4-item test? No, it is the parallel forms reliability (where parallelism is assumed) of a 2-item test. However, we want to estimate the reliability of the 4-item test. From our knowledge of the effect of test length on reliability, with $K = 2$, we can take the reliability of the 2-item test and estimate the reliability for the 4-item test by using the Spearman-Brown formula. This results in a reliability estimate of

$$\frac{2(.32)}{1 + (2 - 1).32} = \frac{.64}{1.32} = .48.$$

Thus, we see that while the estimated reliability for a 2-item test is .32, we really gave a 4-item test for which we find an estimated reliability of .48. This procedure is referred to as split-half reliability estimation.

Internal Consistency Reliability

We have seen that one way to compute a reliability estimate from a single form is to split the test into halves, correlate the half tests, and then estimate the reliability of the full-length test using the Spearman-Brown formula. This seems to be a reasonably satisfactory method for estimating reliability, except for the disconcerting fact that a number of other splits are possible—any one of which, under the right circumstances, might be defended. The obvious way to eliminate this problem is to compute all of the possible splits, correct them with the Spearman-Brown formula, and then obtain the average reliability estimate. However, for a large test, this is an overwhelming task unless some shortcut is available. Several people (Kuder & Richardson, 1937; Hoyt, 1941; Cronbach, 1951) independently attacked and resolved this problem by producing abbreviated methods for finding the mean of all possible split-half estimates. The most appropriate method, given the background we have developed, is the KR-20 formula, developed by Kuder and Richardson:

$$r_{20} = \frac{n}{n-1} \left(1 - \frac{\sum\limits_{i=1}^{n} p_i q_i}{S_x^2} \right), \tag{5.9}$$

where:

$\quad n$ = number of items

$\quad p_i$ = proportion passing an item

$\quad q_i$ = proportion failing an item.

Using the matrix of Table 5.5 and the KR-20 formula, the mean of all possible split halves is computed:

$$\frac{4}{3}\left(1 - \frac{30/36}{10/6}\right) = \frac{4}{3}\left(1 - \frac{.83}{1.67}\right) = .67.$$

The corrected reliability estimates for the front-back, odd-even, and inner-outer splits are .86, .48, and .67, respectively. Thus, the arithmetic mean of these three estimates is .67, giving the same result as the formula.

Having determined the mean of all possible split halves, both arithmetically and by formula 5.9, we might ask if this method of estimating reliability has

Table 5.6   Three Possible Splits for a 4-Item Matrix
of Dissimilar Content

Individuals	Items			
	S_1	S_2	M_1	M_2
1	S_{11}	S_{12}	M_{11}	M_{12}
2	S_{21}	S_{22}	M_{21}	M_{22}
.	.	.	.	.
.	.	.	.	.
.	.	.	.	.
N	S_{N1}	S_{N2}	M_{N1}	M_{N2}

Split 1	Split 2	Split 3
Odd—Even	Inside—Outside	Front—Back
$S_1 M_1 - S_2 M_2$	$S_2 M_1 - S_1 M_2$	$S_1 S_2 - M_1 M_2$

measured a different construct than either equivalence or stability reliability. The answer, of course, is yes. The mean of all possible split halves is a measure of *internal consistency reliability*. Internal consistency means the degree to which the items intercorrelate, or the degree to which the items measure the same trait(s). To the degree that different traits are measured by different items, or that the item intercorrelations are not reasonably constant, the KR-20 coefficient is lowered.

> **The coefficient of internal consistency is the mean of all possible split-half reliability estimates. It reflects the degree to which the item content is similar. When other factors are constant, comparison of items of similar content gives higher internal consistency estimates than comparison of items of dissimilar content.**

Let us consider a different illustration of internal consistency. Suppose a 4-item test, Test A, is constructed with the first two items being spelling questions, and the final two, arithmetic questions. A second test, Test B, composed of four spelling items, is also constructed. No matter how Test B with all spelling items is split, the forms created by the splits will be parallel, and the parallel forms reliability should be relatively constant. However, if we split the items of Test A, two splits will yield parallel forms with both a spelling and mathematics item in each form, but the front-back split will have the two spelling items in one form and the two mathematics items in the other. Table 5.6 depicts this situation. This is clearly a nonparallel situation that will tend to yield a low reliability estimate. It follows that when the three reliability coefficients, two high and one low, are averaged, the result will be a lower KR-20 coefficient because of the dissimilar content of the test material. Thus, items of similar content result in relatively similar splits, whereas items of dissimilar content result in some bad splits, and, hence, in lowered reliability coefficients. If the item content is similar, the correlations tend to be high and constant, and the test tends to be internally consistent.

We can conclude that using the KR-20 formula is appropriate when the content of the test items is similar. As a measure of internal consistency, the KR-20 formula is widely accepted and almost synonymous with reliability. In an effort to simplify its computation, Kuder and Richardson (1937) assumed that the difficulty levels of the items were the same. When this assumption is made, KR-20 reduces to the following formula, called KR-21:

$$r_{21} = \frac{n}{n-1}\left(1 - \frac{\overline{X}(n - \overline{X})}{nS_x^2}\right), \qquad (5.10)$$

where:

$\overline{X}$ = the mean score of the group on the test

n = the number of items on the test.

The KR-21 formula is one of the easiest of all possible methods for computing reliability estimates. It requires only a set of scores, and the additional assumption that $p_1 = p_2 = p_3 = \ldots = p_n$, that is, that the difficulty levels of the items are equal. When this assumption is met, the coefficient from KR-20 equals that from KR-21; when it is not met, KR-21 will give a reliability estimate less than that secured from KR-20. Consider the data matrix of Table 5.5. In this matrix the item difficulties are not the same, and the reliability for these data computed by KR-21 gives an estimate of:

$$\frac{4}{3}\left(1 - \frac{2(4 - 2)}{4(1.67)}\right) = .53.$$

Thus, we note that the KR-21 estimate of .53 is less than the KR-20 estimate of .67 secured earlier, because the assumption of equal item difficulty was not met.

Difference Reliability

Often in interpreting test results, it becomes necessary to determine, for a given individual, which of two abilities is greater. For example, often tests measuring two different abilities are administered to the same individual. Because of the measurement error associated with each test, it is possible for the person to be equally competent on both abilities, yet not obtain exactly the same scores. Since slight differences can be due to random fluctuation, we need to determine when score differences are great enough to be considered nonchance. Suppose we administer a test battery and find that a given individual has a z-score of 1.2 on science, and 1.4 on mathematics. Can we say that ability in science is lower? This is a difference reliability problem, and requires development of a new standard deviation—the standard error of the difference.

To develop the standard error of the difference, we postulate the existence of two parallel tests that measure the same ability. An individual is administered the two tests, and the difference is computed. Theoretically, the scores should be identical, but due to measurement error, we might find a slight difference. Now, think of the individual taking the pairs of tests over and over, say 100 times. Each time we compute the difference between scores, and we build a distribution of these 100 chance differences. Sometimes the difference is positive (the first test score is higher), and sometimes it is negative (the second test score is higher). Most of the time the difference approaches zero, and the mean difference is zero. These chance differences are normally distributed, and have a standard deviation:[1]

$$S_{e_1-e_2} = S_x\sqrt{2 - r_{11'} - r_{22'}}, \tag{5.11}$$

where:

$\quad S_{e_1-e_2}$ = the standard deviation of chance differences from testing on two parallel forms

$\quad S_x$ = the subtest standard deviation

$\quad r_{11'}$ = the reliability of the first parallel form

$\quad r_{22'}$ = the reliability of the second parallel form.

Using the previous example, an individual obtains a z-score of 1.2 on science and 1.4 on mathematics. Suppose we also know that the reliabilities of the tests are .91 for science, and .93 for mathematics. The standard error of the distribution of chance differences would be:

$$S_{e_1-e_2} = 1\sqrt{2 - .91 - .93} = 1\sqrt{.16} = .4.$$

Thus, on the distribution of chance differences, .4 is one standard deviation above the mean difference of zero. Since the observed difference $(1.4 - 1.2 = .2)$ is one-half standard deviation from the mean, it could easily have occurred by chance. Therefore, we cannot suggest that the scores measuring one ability were higher than the other except by chance.

[1]For a more complete discussion, see Magnusson, 1966, pp. 90–98.

Consider another example. Suppose that on the XYZ test of mental ability an individual obtains a T-score of 55 on ability $X(r_{xx'} = .89)$, and a T-score of 68 on ability $Y(r_{yy'} = .86)$. Can we say that our friend's true score is higher on ability Y than on X—can the difference between the T-scores of 13 points be considered nonchance? Utilizing formula 5.11 and recalling that T-scores have a standard deviation of 10, we find the error of the difference is

$$S_{e_1 - e_2} = 10\sqrt{2 - .89 - .86} = 5.$$

We observe that on a distribution of chance difference with zero mean and standard deviation of 5, a difference of 13 points is 2.6 standard deviations from the mean. Thus, we can be quite certain that our friend has a greater than chance facility on ability Y than on X.

Having discussed the theory and computation of the standard error of the difference, we consider the reliability of the difference. The formula for difference reliability is:

$$r_{\text{diff}} = \frac{r_{11} + r_{22} - 2r_{12}}{2 - 2r_{12}}. \tag{5.12}$$

What are the factors that maximize the difference reliabilities? From formula 5.12 it is apparent that difference reliability will be low when: (1) the subtest reliabilities are small, and (2) the subtest intercorrelations are large. Put another way, the conditions that maximize difference reliability are:

1. that the subtests measure well—the reliabilities are high, and
2. that the subtests measure different abilities—the subtest intercorrelations are low.

For us to determine if two abilities of an individual are different, the tests must measure different abilities. A survey of some of the less well developed tests presently in use quickly reveals that the opposite conditions exist; that is, many tests purport to measure different abilities, but actually do not. Also, a number of the marketed tests attempt to define many shorter subtests rather than a few longer ones. As a result, the shorter tests have much lower reliabilities. Thus, knowing how to determine when a difference is nonchance can be an asset to the individual doing test interpretations.

Summary

This chapter and the immediately preceding one have dealt in detail with the reliability of measurement. Reliability deals with consistency and precision. How consistently will our instrument measure? How consistently will results be reproduced if we measure the same individuals again? What is the equivalence between the results of the two measurement occasions? When we have obtained a score, how precise is it? These are the considerations of reliability.

In summary, we have considered the effect of test length and range of talent on reliability estimation. With other factors remaining constant, reliability estimates increase with increased test length and with increases in range of talent; reliability decreases as the test is shortened and as the range of talent decreases. In addition to these factors, unreliability can be minimized by clarifying test instructions, and by reducing scoring errors. Opportunity for extensive guessing at item responses tends to decrease reliability. As an example, guessing can be controlled by using multiple-choice rather than true-false questions, by increasing the number of options in the former, and by increasing the attractiveness of these options. In general, we can suggest that careful attention to the details of test-item construction should result in an increase in reliability. (Item construction is discussed in greater detail in Chapter 11.)

In addition to factors that influence reliability estimates, we considered split-half and internal consistency estimates of reliability. A split-half estimate was computed by splitting the test into halves, correlating the half-test scores, and correcting for length using the Spearman-Brown formula. The mean of all possible split halves is a measure of internal consistency, that is, the degree to which the items measure a single psychological trait. Internal consistency estimates, formulas KR-20 and KR-21, were introduced, and their similarities and differences discussed.

Thus far, we have considered the consistency of the test items in assessing the qualities they were designed to measure. We have not dealt with the question of what the test actually measures. What is being measured deals with validity, which will be discussed in subsequent chapters.

Suggested Readings

Brown, F. *Principles of educational and psychological testing.* Hinsdale, Ill.: Dryden Press, 1970, Chapter 4.

Ebel, R. *Measuring educational achievement.* Englewood Cliffs: Prentice-Hall, 1965, Chapter 10.

Guilford, J. P. *Psychometric methods.* (2nd ed.) New York: McGraw-Hill, 1954, Chapters 13, 14.

Helmstadter, G. *Principles of psychological measurement.* New York: Appleton-Century-Crofts, 1964, pp. 62–86.

Magnusson, D. *Test theory.* Reading, Mass.: Addison-Wesley, 1966, Chapters 7, 9.

Wesman, A. G. *Reliability and confidence.* Test Service Bulletin No. 44. New York: Psychological Corporation, 1952.

Individual Review Questions

1. A reliability coefficient of 1.00 between two equivalent measures indicates no measurement _____ in either of the two measures.

2. A reliability coefficient of 0 between two equivalent measures indicates that the distributions of scores on both tests consist entirely of _____.

3. Increasing the length of a test with similar items has the effect of _____ reliability.

4. Increasing the length of a test with entirely different types of items has the effect of _____ _____ reliability.

5. The formula used to estimate the increase in reliability with increased test length is known as the _____ _____ formula.

6. A test of 20 items has an estimated reliability of .60. Later, the test is increased with 20 additional similar items. The reliability will _____.

7. A test of 30 items has an estimated reliability of .50. A test composed of 60 similar items should have an estimated reliability of _____.

8. As a 15-item test is increased in length to 60 similar items, each successive set of 15 items results in increased reliability, but at a _____ rate.

9. A 60-item test has an estimated reliability of .80. If this test is divided into two shorter tests, the reliability of each subtest will be _____ than .80.

10. A 30-item test with an estimated reliability of .60 is increased in length by adding 30 similar items. The reliability of the 60-item test will _____ and the standard error of measurement will _____.

11. In general, as a test is increased in length with similar items, the standard error of measurement will _____.

12. For a test of fixed length, as the reliability increases, the standard error of measurement _____.

13. For a test of fixed length, the relationship between reliability and the standard error of measurement is _____.

14. Reliability and the standard error of measurement are both a _____ of test length.

15. As a test is lengthened from 30 to 60 items (with similar items), the error variance increases by a factor of _____, while the true variance increases by a factor of _____.

ANSWERS
1. error
2. error
3. increasing
4. not increasing, or not changing
5. Spearman-Brown
6. increase
7. .67
8. decreasing
9. less
10. increase; increase
11. increase
12. decreases
13. inverse
14. function
15. K; K^2

16. As a test is lengthened from 30 to 60 items (with similar items), the standard error of measurement will increase by a factor of _____.

17. A 20-item test with a standard error of measurement of 2 is increased to 80 items (with similar items). The standard error of measurement of the 80-item test will be approximately _____.

18. As range of talent increases, the variability of the distribution of scores _____.

19. The development of the range of talent formula is based on the assumption that when the range of talent is increased, the _____ variance remains constant.

20. As the range of talent decreases from one testing situation to the next, the standard error of measurement _____ _____.

21. In a test, the standard deviation of obtained scores is 15, and the estimated reliability is .91. Later, the test is used again, and the standard deviation of the obtained scores is 11. The standard error of measurement in the second use will be approximately _____.

22. As range of talent decreases, the reliability _____, and the standard error of measurement remains constant.

23. Increasing the range of talent is simply another way of saying that the _____ variance is being increased.

24. Individual differences are _____ when there is a decrease in the range of talent.

25. When a test is increased in length with _____ items, the standard error of measurement is increased.

26. The difficulty level of an item is defined as the _____ of people answering it correctly, or passing it.

27. Generally, a test composed of similar items of _____ difficulty level will be more reliable than a test composed of similar, but _____, items.

28. To have maximum dispersion, an item must have a difficulty level of _____.

29. To say that an item has a variance of .25 suggests that the item has sorted the people into _____ equal groups.

30. If an item given to 100 people has a difficulty level of .2, the item has a variance of _____. This suggests that the item sorts people into two groups: one group consisting of _____ people, who passed the item, and another consisting of _____ people, who failed the item.

31. A test constructed from 20 similar items of moderate difficulty will have a greater _____ than 20 items of similar content, which are very easy.

32. In general, a test consisting of all easy or all difficult items will result in a score distribution that is highly _____, while a test comprised of all moderately difficult items will be _____ shaped.

33. If a test consists of items, all of which have difficulty levels close to zero, the distribution of scores will have very _____ variance.

34. When using the split-half approach to determine test reliability, in essence, we split the test into two _____ forms.

35. The KR-20 estimate is a shortcut procedure for finding the _____ of all possible split halves.

36. In contrast to the coefficient of stability, the KR-20 estimate is a measure of _____ consistency.

37. A high index of internal consistency indicates that the item content of the test is very _____.

38. When item content is extremely varied, the KR-20 estimate will tend to be _____.

39. The KR-21 formula can be used as a substitute for the KR-20 formula, if the assumption of equal item _____ can be met.

40. If the assumption of equal item difficulty is not met, the KR-21 reliability estimate will be _____ than the KR-20 estimate.

41. If the assumption of equal item difficulty is met, the KR-21 reliability estimate will be _____ _____ the KR-20 estimate.

42. The degree to which the items of a test all measure the same psychological trait is the meaning of the _____ consistency of a test.

43. When two parallel forms are correlated, a coefficient of _____ is obtained.

44. When the test-retest correlation is computed, a coefficient of _____ is obtained.

45. When a split-half reliability estimate is computed, a coefficient of _____ is obtained; however, the mean of all possible split halves is a coefficient of _____ _____.

46. A split-half estimate is obtained by correlating the scores from the half tests, and correcting with the _____ _____ formula.

ANSWERS

31. variance, or dispersion
32. skewed; bell
33. little, or small
34. parallel, or equivalent
35. mean
36. internal
37. similar, or homogeneous
38. low, or suppressed
39. difficulty
40. less
41. equal to
42. internal
43. equivalence
44. stability
45. equivalence; internal consistency
46. Spearman-Brown

47. When the Spearman-Brown correction is used with the split-half method for estimating reliability, K is equal to _____.

Study Exercises

1. Suppose that a teacher gives a 15-item test that has an estimated parallel forms reliability of .40. What would be the estimated reliability of a 30-item test consisting of the original 15 items plus 15 additional similar items?

2. Suppose you have a test of 30 items with a standard deviation of 10 and a reliability estimate of .60. What will be the estimated reliability of a test with 60 similar items? What will be the standard error of measurement of the 60-item test?

3. Suppose a single item has an estimated reliability of .15. What will be the estimated reliability of a test consisting of 80 similar items?

4. Suppose a 90-item test has a standard deviation of 15 and a reliability estimate of .95. What will be the estimated reliability of half the test? What will be the standard error of measurement for a 45-item test?

5. Suppose a 60-item test has a reliability estimate of .80. What will be the average estimate of a single item?

6. A test is given to a group of students for which the standard deviation is 10, and $r_{xx'}$ is .60. Later, additional students take the test, and the standard deviation for the combined groups is 13. Will the estimated reliability for the combined groups increase or decrease? The standard error of measurement? What will be the estimated reliability for the combined groups? The standard error of measurement?

7. A music aptitude test is given to a large number of music majors. The standard deviation for this group is 5, and the estimated reliability is .60. Later, a representative group of students is given the test, and the standard deviation for the two groups combined is 9. What will be the estimated reliability for the combined groups? The standard error of measurement?

8. Suppose a spatial visualization test is given to a large group of representative students. The standard deviation is 10, with an estimated reliability of .90. Later, the test is used with a group of engineering students. The standard deviation for the engineering students is 8. What will be the estimated reliability for the engineering students? The standard error of measurement?

9. Consider the following data matrix.

Items

$$\begin{array}{c}\text{People}\end{array}\begin{bmatrix} + & + & + & + \\ + & + & + & 0 \\ + & + & 0 & 0 \\ + & 0 & 0 & 0 \\ 0 & 0 & 0 & 0 \\ + & + & + & + \\ 0 & 0 & 0 & 0 \end{bmatrix}$$

a. Compute the odd-even reliability estimate. The standard error of measurement.
b. Compute the KR-20 reliability estimate. The standard error of measurement.
c. Compute the KR-21 reliability estimate. The standard error of measurement.
d. How does KR-20 compare in magnitude with KR-21? Why?

ANSWERS

47. 2

1. .57
2. .75; 8.9
3. .93
4. .90; 2.37
5. .06
6. increase; the standard error of measurement remains the same; .76; 6.3
7. .88; 3.1
8. .84, 3.16
9. (a) .92; .45 (b) .87; .58 (c) .81; .70 (d) lower; because the assumption that $p_1 = p_2 = p_3 = p_4$ is not met

107

10. Suppose a test with a variance of 64 has a reliability of .6. Assuming the test is doubled in length with similar items, what will be the new variance? The new standard error of measurement?

11. What happens to test reliability when you lengthen a test? To standard error of measurement?

12. What happens to test reliability when you increase the group dispersion? To standard error of measurement?

13. A teacher constructs a test, A, and a parallel form, B. The variances for A and B are both 10, and the parallel forms reliability is .60. What will be the estimated reliability of A and B combined? What will be the obtained variance of the combined test?

14. What do we mean when we say KR-20 and KR-21 are "internal consistency" estimates?

15. Consider the following data matrix.

Items

$$\text{People} \begin{bmatrix} + & 0 & + \\ 0 & + & 0 \\ 0 & 0 & 0 \\ + & + & + \end{bmatrix}$$

a. Compute the KR-20 reliability estimate. The standard error of measurement.
b. Compute the KR-21 reliability estimate.
c. How does KR-20 compare in magnitude with KR-21? Why?

16. Show that the average item intercorrelation of problem 15, when inserted in the Spearman-Brown formula with $K = 3$, has a stepped-up estimate of .60.

17. What implication does problem 16 have for the notion of internal consistency?

ANSWERS

10. 204.8; 7.16

11. increases; increases by a factor of $\sqrt{K}$

12. increases; remains the same

13. .75; 32

14. They are indices of the degree to which items measure similar content.

15. (a) .60; .71 (b) .60 (c) they are equal; because the assumption that $p_1 = p_2 = p_3$ is met

16. $r_{12} = 0$, $r_{13} = 1$, $r_{23} = 0$, $r_{ij} = .33$; $3(.33)/$ $1 + (3 - 1).33 = .60$

17. the higher the average item intercorrelation, the higher the KR-20 estimate

Criterion Validity

6

Test reliability and validity have been called the *sine qua non* of psychological measurement. In the previous two chapters, we discussed reliability and methods for its estimation, indicating that they could all be summarized as methods for estimating "consistency." Furthermore, we noted that the empirical estimation of reliability yielded at least three different kinds of consistency coefficients: stability, equivalence, and internal consistency. Thus, reliability has different meanings depending on the operations performed during estimation. So it is with validity. Validity is generally defined as *the degree to which a test measures what it is intended to measure.* However, differing testing purposes and methods of validation also result in variations that further complicate test validation.

In discussing reliability, it became evident that a test did not have a single reliability index. Rather, the estimated reliability of the test depended on the group to which the test was administered, how the test was administered, and how the reliability was computed. So it is with validity. A test does not have a single validity coefficient. It is incorrect to speak of *the* validity of a test. A test has as many validities as it has purposes. It may be valid for one purpose, but not another. Indeed, it would be more appropriate to suggest that we are not validating the test, but rather the inferences we wish to make from our knowledge of the test results.

To the less experienced student, the meaningful assimilation of the many different methods of validating a test can be overwhelming. Rozeboom (1966,

p. 187) suggests that the different adjectives used to describe validity coefficients (for example, content validity, predictive validity, factorial validity, intrinsic validity, etc.) simply reflect the method used to validate the test. While this statement facilitates an understanding of the validity problem, it alone does not provide the conceptual structure necessary to integrate, yet differentiate, these different methods.

A more complete discussion of the validity problem is provided by the American Psychological Association's "Technical Recommendations for Psychological Tests and Diagnostic Techniques" (1954) and *Standards for Educational and Psychological Tests and Manuals* (1966). These reports have been instrumental in clarifying the validity problem, and in establishing the parsimonious classifications of criterion, content, and construct validity. Prior to these reports, there had been a number of papers on validity, but these recommendations formalized and integrated previous activity.

Gulliksen's (1950, p. 88) study of validity defined it traditionally as how well a test predicts some specified criterion (with *criterion* defined as *quantified performance on a task*). However, the formalization of construct validity in the "Technical Recommendations" added a new dimension to validity. These two dimensions of validity are reflected in two questions, which assist in clarifying the concepts of validity:

1. How well does the test predict a criterion performance in which we are interested?
2. What behavioral content or psychological constructs does the test measure?

The purposes served by measurement in dealing with these questions are very different. In the first question, *the focus is on the criterion,* and we seek to establish a relationship between the test performance and the criterion performance. The second question, on the other hand, *focuses on the test,* and inquires about the abilities or behavioral domains it samples. This chapter will deal with the first question—criterion validity; the next chapter will deal with the second question—content and construct validity.

> Purpose determines the method of validation used on a particular problem. The problem will require either that you predict some criterion performance, or that you investigate the content or constructs that a test actually measures.

Criterion Validity

Whenever we consider validation of a particular test, we must clarify the *purpose* for which the test is being used. Statements about test validity must always be made in the context of some purpose.

Tests can be used for a variety of purposes, such as selecting people for a particular program, position, or task. Examples might include the selection of students for a graduate program, applicants for a training position, or workers for an assembly line. In many situations, actual trial periods in a program, position, or task are impractical or impossible, and psychological measurements can aid in personnel selection. Of course, this assumes that the psychological measure used is a valid replacement for the trial period. In most cases the relationship between performance on the test and in the trial period is a matter of degree. Thus, another point about psychological measurements is that their validity is always *a matter of degree*, rather than an all-or-nothing property (Nunnally, 1967, p. 75). Since validity is a matter of degree, whether a test is "valid enough" can only be resolved in the context of a specific situation. Always, however, the information yielded by a test gives clues that assist in a particular decision.

Finally, there is *the decision*. Once purpose and degree of validity have been specified, there is the matter of the particular decision to be made. If the useful information acquired from the test offsets factors of cost, inconvenience, time, etc., the test is valid enough.

> **Validity is concerned with the degree to which a test measures what it is supposed to measure. However, the purpose for giving a test and the decisions to be made determine when a test is valid enough.**

The Criterion

Generally, criterion validity is established through the use of a coefficient of correlation. This coefficient is an index of the relationship between a test performance and some quantifiable or dichotomized *criterion behavior*. The criterion behavior is generally the performance we wish to predict. Some examples of criterion performances are: college grade point average, passing or failing some course of study, or success as a secretary. In the last case, success can be defined by supervisor ratings of secretarial skills.

Criterion validity can also be thought of as a "test-substitution" situation. For example, a company might establish a relationship between a test and secretarial performance. Table 6.1 provides an example of such a situation. Once the test-criterion relationship is established, the inference can be made that high scores on the test can be substituted for the criterion, and the test scores can be used to assist in making decisions about the hiring of secretaries.

Although the above relationship can be shown to hold, inferences about individuals are not without error. Table 6.1 indicates that, because validity is a matter of degree, there is only a *tendency* for high scores to be associated with high ratings. Inferences about individuals may result in selection of some poor

111

Table 6.1 Percent of Stenographers in Each
Third on SET-Clerical Test Who
Earned Various Proficiency Ratings

SET-Clerical Test Score	Proficiency Rating		
	Low	Average	High
Upper Third	18	33	50
Middle Third	29	36	28
Lowest Third	53	31	22
Total Percent	100	100	100
No. of Stenographers	17	39	18

Source: Doppelt, 1953.

secretaries and rejection of some good ones. However, the alternative would be to train more people than are necessary and retain only the best. The testing alternative can result in less of a financial expenditure, and avoid the wasted effort and anguish of a training program in which many do not succeed. Each alternative has its strengths, and as the test-criterion correlation coefficient increases, the testing alternative becomes more tenable. At any rate, an understanding of criterion validity requires that the *criterion* be operationalized. The criterion, then, is some quantified index of performance on a task for which a test-performance substitution is desired.

> **In criterion validation, the criterion is a quantified index of performance on some task for which a test-performance substitution is desired. This test-performance substitution is increasingly justified as the test-performance correlation coefficient increases.**

Validity Coefficients

A validity coefficient is often expressed as a product-moment correlation or some index of relationship. An example of a validity coefficient might be the correlation between college entrance examination scores and the criterion of college grade point average. This correlation is often reported to be about .55. One of the conclusions reached after studying various types of validity coefficients is that they tend to be quite low. Why do entrance examinations correlate only about .55 with grade point average? To answer this, one must ask, What contributes to college grade point averages? Very quickly, we recognize that grade point average is a function of such factors as academic ability, study habits, motivation, error, and the like. The entrance examination score tends to sample only one of these components—academic ability. The correlation between grade point average and entrance examination scores will increase as the test reflects more of the factors involved in the variability of grade point average. The test with the higher criterion-test correlation will be the one that best samples the many factors involved in the criterion performance.

> Suppose some criterion performance, some task, requires abilities A, B, and C. The test that has high criterion validity will also sample abilities A, B, and C.

How, then, do we select tests to be used in criterion validity studies? First, we can analyze the criterion and the tests for their similarity. This amounts to doing an a priori analysis of both. Second, we can study the literature to determine if other similar studies have identified relationships. Finally, we can undertake our own empirical search for criterion correlates. Ultimately, a test will likely be selected on the basis of a combination of all these considerations.

Criterion Validity as Predictable Variation

A criterion validity coefficient is the correlation between a given test and some criterion performance. Other things being equal, the test having the higher correlation with the criterion is the more useful. Furthermore, the test with the higher product-moment correlation coefficient allows us to *predict* the criterion performance better.

Consider the matter of prediction. A squared validity coefficient reflects the proportion of predictable variance in a test. That is,

$$r_{yx}{}^2 = S_{y'}{}^2/S_y{}^2, \tag{6.1}$$

where:

$S_{y'}{}^2 = $ predictable variance
$S_y{}^2 = $ total test variance.

But what is meant by predictable variance?

Figure 6.1 presents a scattergram of twelve pairs of X and Y scores. For this fictitious validation group data, suppose the criterion, Y, was a set of supervisor ratings of secretarial skills, and the X variable was scores on a secretarial skills test. Given the data in Figure 6.1, what supervisor rating would be expected for a person who applied for a secretarial position, and who scored 5 on the secretarial skills test? A study of the data reveals that the four people who scored 5 on the secretarial skills test received average supervisor ratings of 2.5 (average of the Y scores of 2, 2, 3, and 3). Therefore, we say that the *predicted score* for an individual who had a secretarial skills test score of 5 is 2.5. The predicted Y score, designated Y', for an individual with a given X score can be defined as the average Y score for people in the validation group who had that given X score. The predicted Y score for individuals who received X scores of 3 and 1 would be 2 and 1.5, respectively.

In addition to the scattergram, Figure 6.1 presents the X, Y, and Y' (predicted Y scores) for the 12 individuals in the validation group. Variances for each of the sets of scores are: $S_x^2 = 2$, $S_y^2 = .5$, and $S_{y'}^2 = .167$. The product-moment correlation between X and Y is .58.

Consider formula 6.1 again. The squared correlation between the two variables, X and Y, gives us the proportion of predictable criterion variance. Thus, from Figure 6.1, we see that

$$r_{yx}^2(.58^2) = S_{y'}^2/S_y^2 = .167/.5 = .334.$$

That is, the squared correlation coefficient between the test and the criterion will indicate the proportion of variance in the criterion distribution that is predictable

Figure 6.1   Diagram Showing the Predicted Y Scores for Twelve People

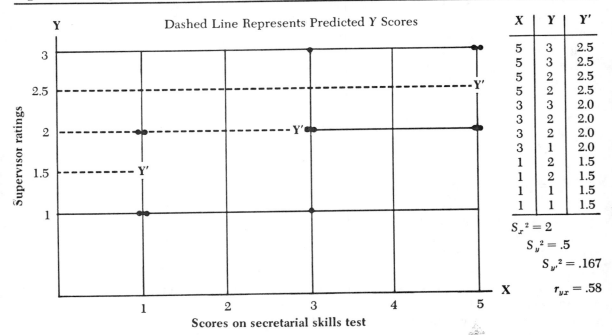

X	Y	Y'
5	3	2.5
5	3	2.5
5	2	2.5
5	2	2.5
3	3	2.0
3	2	2.0
3	2	2.0
3	1	2.0
1	2	1.5
1	2	1.5
1	1	1.5
1	1	1.5

$S_x^2 = 2$

$S_y^2 = .5$

$S_{y'}^2 = .167$

$r_{yx} = .58$

variance, when a linear relationship between the predictor and criterion can be assumed.

> **A predicted criterion score for an individual with a given test score (predictor) can be computed by finding the mean of the criterion scores of other people who have the same test score.**

Given the notion of predictable variance, the variance of the criterion variable can be partitioned into two independent components: one, the predictable component; the other, the unpredictable component. The squared correlation coefficient, r_{yx}^2, gives us the proportion of predictable criterion variance. The proportion that cannot be predicted by the test variance then becomes $1 - r_{yx}^2$. Intuitively, these relationships make sense. If $r = 0$, there is no predictable variance; further, the test variable would have no validity, since it predicts no variance in the criterion variable. If $r = +1.00$ or -1.00, there would be no unpredictable variance, and all the variance of the criterion variable is accounted for by the variance of the test or predictor.

Consider an example of the criterion validation of a test. In a midwestern college of engineering, a program of counseling for engineering freshmen was undertaken (partially reported by Ritter, 1954). As part of the program, entrance examination scores and grade point averages at the end of the freshman year were routinely gathered. In his office, the director of the program had a huge board representing the plot of grade point averages against examination scores. Each time the grade point average scores were available, a colored maptack was positioned on the plot at the intersection of the grade point average and entrance examination score for each individual. Different classes were represented by maptacks of varying colors, and when a class graduated, its group of tacks was removed. Additionally, all individuals with freshman grade point averages of less than "C" were identified and represented by red tacks. In this way, a constant check on the criterion validity of the entrance examination was maintained. Figure 6.2 presents a fictitious plot of these scores.

In addition to checking on the validity of the entrance examination, the scatterplot also assisted in counseling. When necessary, marginal students entering the college could be shown the previous performances of students with similar entrance examination scores. By seeing how other people with similar entrance examination scores had fared, potential students could get a clue about the probability of their own success in that specific engineering college. Consider individual A in Figure 6.2. It is clear that A has about one chance in two of succeeding (attaining a grade point average of C or greater) in engineering, while individual C has little or no chance of failing. In the past, about one in two

115

students with A's entrance score successfully completed the program, while practically all students with C's entrance score were successful.

In addition to the individual information given by the test-criterion relationship, the scatterplot also provided the admissions committee of the college with information about the selection of students, and the proportion of failing students at various cutting points. In this case, the cutting point is the entrance examination score below which prospective students will generally be denied admission to the program. From Figure 6.2 it is apparent that as the cutting point is lowered, the proportion of failing students will tend to increase. Inferences from the above data assume that year-to-year fluctuation is nonsystematic. When that assumption is not met, the criterion validity of the test is in doubt.

In the above example, the entrance examination validation was related to a specific purpose. Clearly, the cost of the testing is justified when a college

Figure 6.2   Plot of Entrance Examination Scores Against Grade Point Average

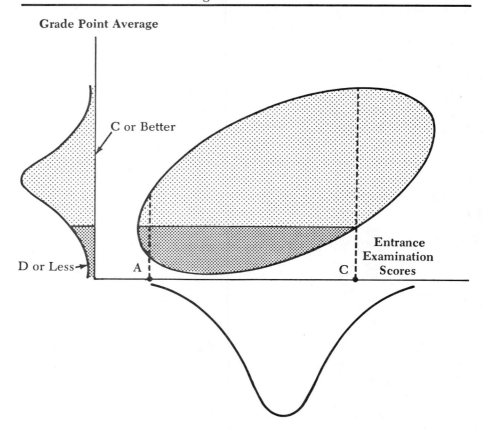

official uses test information to confirm his tentative decision to accept an applicant into a college. The cost of the test is also justified when an individual uses test information to confirm his tentative decision to go to college. It is also justified when an individual who has a very low probability of success in engineering uses the test information to make the decision to seek success in a field more compatible with his abilities—money for college can be more wisely invested, and much agony can be averted.

Expectancy Tables

Another way of considering the criterion validity problem is through expectancy tables. Criterion validity coefficients can change quickly with a change in the task (criterion), or with a change in the group of people involved. Thus, in practice, criterion validity is often established with a small number of individuals on very specific tasks. Expectancy tables can be used for this purpose.

To build an expectancy table, criterion-test categories are established, similar to those shown in Figure 6.3. Here, five grade categories and nine score categories have been established. Next, the test-criterion relationships are tallied (14 people had grades of B and test scores of 60–69). Finally, these tallies are summed and converted to percentages. These sums and percentages are presented in Table 6.2. From Table 6.2 we can find the possibility of obtaining any given grade for a test score category.

Expectancy tables can provide a simple, but practical method for establishing

Figure 6.3 **Expectancy Grid Showing how Students' Grades in Rhetoric and Previously Earned Scores on the *DAT Sentences Test* Are Tallied in Appropriate Cells**

Scores on D.A.T. Sentences Test	Grades in Rhetoric					Totals
	F	D	C	B	A	
80 – 89					/ 1	1
70–79				/ 1	//// 4	5
60–69			/// 3	++++ ++++ //// 14	++++ 5	22
50–59			++++ //// 9	++++ /// 8	++++ / 6	23
40–49		/// 3	++++ ++++ /// 13	++++ / 6		22
30–39	/ 1	/// 3	++++ //// 9	/// 3		16
20–29	/ 1	//// 4	/// 3			8
10–19		// 2				2
0–9		/ 1				1
	2	13	37	32	16	100

Data from Kansas State Teachers College; grade of F = failure, no grade of E given; N = 100 freshman girls; mean test score = 48.58, S = 15.2, r = .71.
Source: Doppelt, 1949.

Table 6.2   Expectancy Table Prepared from Figure 6.3

Total No.	Number receiving each grade					Test Scores	Percent receiving each grade					Total Percent
	F	D	C	B	A		F	D	C	B	A	
1					1	80 − 89					100	100
5				1	4	70–79				20	80	100
22			3	14	5	60–69			14	63	23	100
23			9	8	6	50–59			39	35	26	100
22		3	13	6		40–49		14	59	27		100
16	1	3	9	3		30–39	6	19	56	19		100
8	1	4	3			20–29	13	50	37			100
2		2				10–19		100				100
1		1				0–9		100				100
100	2	13	37	32	16							

Source: Doppelt, 1949.

the test-criterion relationships for a specific group and task. It is a practical method for studying criterion validity. Additionally, a product-moment correlation coefficient can be computed to establish a criterion validity coefficient.

Selection Ratio

Once the purpose for which a test is to be used and the degree of validity have been specified, the decision situation determines whether the test is valid enough. One factor that enters into this decision is the selection ratio. Consider the expectancy table (Table 6.2). While there is only a modest relationship between the test scores and grades, only superior performances would result if one could limit selection to those with scores of 70 or higher. That is, if the ratio of people selected to people applying is very small, selecting only people with high test scores results in selection of people who generally exhibit a higher criterion performance. The selection ratio is the ratio of people to be selected to the total pool of people applying. A very small selection ratio can make a test with a low validity coefficient a very effective test. Thus, the selection ratio is extremely important in the decision process.

Summarizing, establishing criterion validity is a complex problem. It requires specifying the purpose for testing, and establishing the relationship between the test and the criterion; and it is a function of the selection ratio. In any given situation, all these factors, along with many others, must be considered. Further, population change, selection ratio change, etc. will determine whether or not a test is valid enough. A test can have criterion validity in one setting, but not in another.

In the previous chapter, we discussed the effects of test length, range of talent, item intercorrelations, and item difficulty on test reliability. However, validity is not necessarily affected in the same manner as reliability. In this section we shall discuss the effects of test reliability, item intercorrelation, range of talent, and test length on criterion validity.

Factors Influencing Criterion Validity

Effects of Test Reliability

In our discussion of test reliability, we partitioned the total test variance into true and error components. Error variance was defined as random variation, and, as such, was not expected to correlate with anything. But, if a test is to have criterion validity, at least some of its variance must be reliable. Since error variance is nonsystematic, it must be the systematic or reliable variation of a test in which the valid variance is embedded. We say *reliability is a necessary, but not a sufficient, condition for test validity.* A test must be reliable to be valid, but reliability does not insure criterion validity. For example, a highly reliable test of the ability to drive a golf ball probably has no criterion validity for the task of selecting managerial personnel.

> **Reliability is a necessary, but not sufficient, condition for criterion validity.**

In order to place the true and valid components of a test in perspective, let us review some basic measurement principles, and show their interrelationships. First, the reliability coefficient $(r_{xx'})$ *directly* determines the proportion of the total test variance that is true. Second, the validity coefficient (r_{yx}) *squared* yields the proportion of total test variance that is predictable or valid.

Consider an example using these two principles of reliability and validity. Given a test with a reliability estimate of .81 and a validity coefficient of .60, we square the validity coefficient, and find that 36 percent of the total test variance is predictable. Since 81 percent of the test variation is reliable and 36 percent is predictable, it follows that 45 percent of the test variance is reliably measured, but is not valid with respect to the criterion. We use the term *specific variance* to define reliably measured test variance that fails to correlate with the criterion. A pictorial partitioning of the variance for this example is presented in Figure 6.4.

If we know the obtained variance of the test scores (which can be computed if the scores are known) and the validity coefficient, we can actually compute the predictable or valid variance. Suppose, in the above example, the obtained variance is 200. Since the validity coefficient is .60, the predictable variance can be determined by multiplying .36 (the validity coefficient squared) by 200. This gives a predictable variance of 72.

What can we conclude about the relationship of the validity coefficient to the reliability coefficient? When all of the true variance is specific variance, the validity coefficient is zero. On the other hand, if a test has no specific variance, all of the true variance would be valid or predictable. The reliability coefficient indicates the proportion of test variance that is true, and the *square* of the validity coefficient indicates the proportion of obtained variance that is predictable. The valid or predictable variance must be contained in the true variance. Thus, if *all* true variance were valid, the *square* of the validity coefficient would equal the reliability coefficient (not its square).

Figure 6.5 illustrates this relationship. In examples *a, b,* and *c,* all tests have reliability estimates of .81. Recall that when $r_{xx'} = .81$, 81 percent of the test variance is systematic or true variance; so 19 percent is error. However, the test-criterion validities are .50, .70, and .90 for *a, b,* and *c,* respectively. In example *a,* the validity coefficient, .50, squared, indicates that 25 percent of the test variation is predictable or valid variance. The specific variance, 56 percent, is found by subtracting the predictable variance from the true variance (systematic) component. In example *b,* the validity coefficient of .70, squared, indicates that 49 percent of the test variation is predictable or valid variance, and the specific variance is 32 percent. Note that with reliability held constant, as test validity

Figure 6.4   **Illustration of the Interrelationships of True, Error, Predictable, and Specific Variance Components**

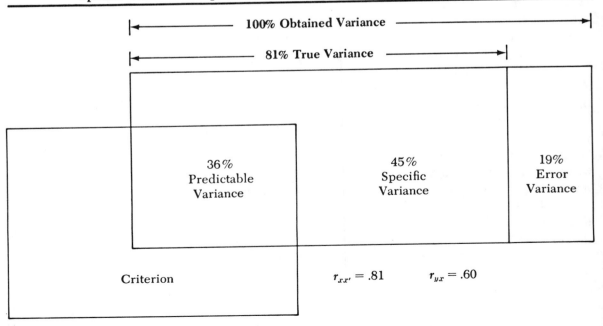

increases, the specific variance decreases. Finally, in example *c*, when the validity coefficient is the square root of the reliability (.90), the specific variance is zero. Therefore, the maximum value of the validity coefficient is the square root of the reliability coefficient. We can express this as:

$$\text{Max } r_{yx} = \sqrt{r_{xx'}}. \tag{6.2}$$

A test can have a validity coefficient as high as the square root of its reliability.

Suppose a test has an estimated reliability of .84. What would be the percentage of specific variance if $r_{yx} = .60$? Utilizing our knowledge of variance components, we know that 84 percent of the variance is true, and 36 percent ($.60^2 \times 100$) of the variance is predictable; therefore, 48 percent of the variance is specific. Similarly, if estimated reliability is .64, and $r_{yx} = .70$, only 15 percent of the variance would be specific. If we had the same reliability estimate, and $r_{yx} = .80$,

Figure 6.5 Illustration of the Relationship Between Reliability and the Magnitude of the Validity Coefficient

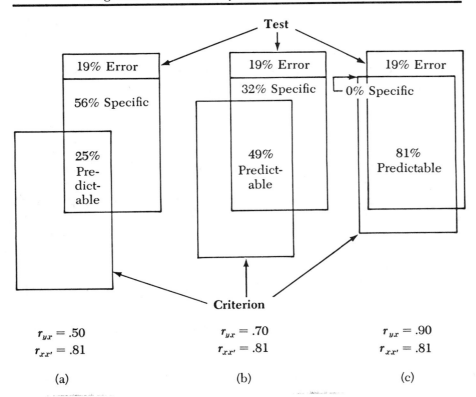

$r_{yx} = .50$ $r_{yx} = .70$ $r_{yx} = .90$
$r_{xx'} = .81$ $r_{xx'} = .81$ $r_{xx'} = .81$

(a) (b) (c)

there would be no specific variance. In this last case, the validity coefficient would have reached its maximum value.

These examples show that as a test becomes increasingly reliable, it has the potential for a higher validity coefficient. Unreliability restricts the test from doing a "better" job of predicting a criterion; thus, unreliability also reduces or attenuates the validity of the test. Measurement error tends to attenuate correlations (that is, makes them closer to zero). A *correction for attenuation* is sometimes required when estimating the validity coefficient. This correction indicates what the criterion validity coefficient would be if the test and/or criterion were perfectly reliable.

We can correct for attenuation under two conditions: (1) if one variable is perfectly reliable, and (2) if both variables (predictor and criterion) are perfectly reliable. Consider the first condition. Suppose we have the reliability estimate for X as $r_{xx'}$, and the correlation between X and Y as r_{yx}. Then, assuming that X is perfectly reliable, we can make a new estimate of the validity coefficient, $r_{t_x y}$, with the partial correction for attenuation as:

$$r_{t_x y} = r_{yx} / \sqrt{r_{xx'}}, \tag{6.3}$$

where:

$r_{t_x y}$ = the correlation of "true" scores on X with "obtained" scores on Y.

We can illustrate the use of formula 6.3 by the following example. Suppose a test correlates .60 with a criterion, and the test has an estimated reliability of .64. If we assume the test reliability to be 1.0, we can estimate the new validity coefficient:

$$r_{t_x y} = .60 / \sqrt{.64} = .60/.8 = .75.$$

Thus, we can conclude that as the test is made increasingly reliable, its validity with this particular criterion will approach .75.

Consider a situation in which both the test and criterion are perfectly reliable (that is, reliability coefficients are 1.00). Let $r_{yy'}$ be the reliability estimate of the criterion, with the remaining notations the same as formula 6.3. The new estimate of the validity coefficient with the complete correction for attenuation is given by:

$$r_{t_x t_y} = r_{yx} / \sqrt{r_{xx'}} \sqrt{r_{yy'}}, \tag{6.4}$$

where:

$r_{t_x t_y}$ = the correlation of true scores on X (perfectly reliable X scores) with true scores on Y (perfectly reliable Y scores).

We can again consider an example. Suppose a test has a reliability of .49, the criterion has a reliability of .81, and the correlation between test and criterion is .45. The validity estimate, corrected for attenuation, would be:

$$r_{t_x t_y} = .45/\sqrt{.49}\sqrt{.81} = .71.$$

This example shows that unreliability in the measures tends to decrease validity. As the test and criterion become increasingly reliable, we would expect the validity estimate to move from .45 toward .71, when both the test and criterion are perfectly reliable.

> As test and criterion measures increase in reliability, the validity
> of the test increases, but not necessarily markedly. The correc-
> tion for attenuation, $r_{t_x t_y}$, estimates the correlation between
> the true scores of the test and the criterion.

The correction for attenuation enables us to estimate validity, if our measurement instruments were perfectly reliable. It provides information about how much the validity of a test can be increased if reliability is increased. In essence, it estimates the relationship between "true" test and criterion scores. Because of the assumption of perfect reliability, the correction for attenuation must be cautiously interpreted. If an improper estimate of reliability is made, or if the estimate is unstable due to some technical reason (such as very few observations), the correction can be in error. Empirical evidence of such erroneous corrections is given by the fact that corrected estimates can exceed 1.00. Of course, this is a theoretical impossibility since valid variance would then exceed obtained variance. The correction for attenuation can be particularly helpful when working with short, modestly reliable tests. Such situations are common in early stages of test development, especially in basic research studies for which necessary measuring instruments must be developed.

Let us summarize our discussion of the effects of reliability on criterion validity. First, we have generated several methods for studying the effects of reliability on criterion validity. In all of the methods studied, increased reliability resulted in modest increases in criterion validity. Thus far, our examples have been restricted to the criterion validity situation. More generally, however, it can be suggested that increased reliability is a necessary, but not sufficient, condition for test validity. That is, a test must be reliable to be valid, but reliability does not guarantee validity.

Effects of Test Length

Since criterion validity is modestly affected by reliability, and since reliability is rather drastically affected by test length, it is reasonable to question the effects of test length on validity. Figure 6.6 presents a plot of test length against criterion validity for tests having validity coefficients of .20, .40, and .60. It can be inferred from studying the plot that, other factors constant, lengthening a test with similar items results in a modest increase in criterion validity.

Increasing the length of a test with similar items tends to increase validity, but only to a modest extent.

Effects of Item Intercorrelation

In Chapter 5, we noted that one of the factors influencing reliability was the degree of item intercorrelation (high item similarity). Indeed, internal consistency reliability can be shown to be the average item intercorrelation of a test inserted into the Spearman-Brown formula and stepped up N times. The higher the average item intercorrelation, the higher the computed reliability estimate using formula KR-20, an index of internal consistency reliability.

Loevinger (1954) has indicated that this increase in item intercorrelations generally lowers criterion validity. Why is this so? Suppose we have a criterion

Figure 6.6   **Increases in Validity with Increased Test Length**

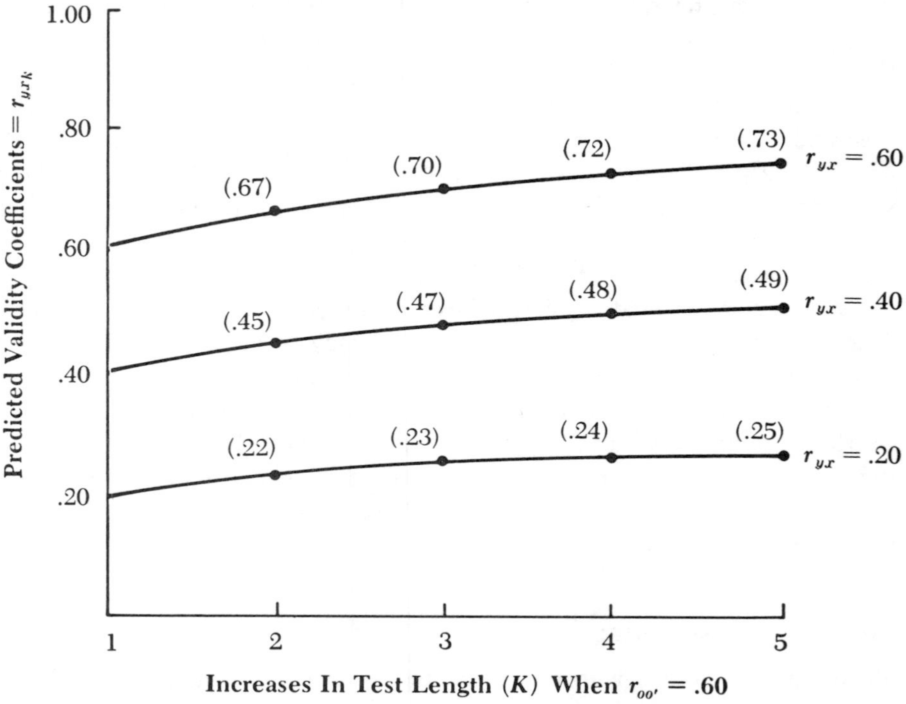

performance that calls for three separate abilities: A, B, and C. High criterion validity requires not a one-ability test with high internal consistency, but rather a test with low internal consistency, because three abilities are being sampled. Thus, we see that maximizing internal consistency reliability has little effect on validity when predicting a complex criterion. Loevinger has called this phenomenon the *attenuation paradox*.

> **Given a complex criterion, a test with low item intercorrelations —measuring many different abilities—will generally have a higher criterion validity than a test that measures only one of these abilities.**

The attenuation paradox can be dealt with in a number of ways. First, we can develop single-score tests that measure a number of different abilities. This type is referred to as an *omnibus test*. Because the omnibus test has many different kinds of items and abilities represented, it generally correlates well with many criterion performances. As an example, a given test might include numerical, verbal, spatial, and reasoning items. While the test will generally correlate with a large number of tasks, the single-score format does not readily allow us to determine which ability or combination of abilities is involved in the criterion performances (since the various abilities are not "separated out" of the test score).

A second approach to the attenuation paradox is to develop a multiscore test with items of a given type sorted in subtests of similar items. Since a number of different subtest scores are included in the total test score, the opportunity for the subtest scores to correlate with many different criterion performances is still possible. Additionally, the separate validity coefficients (one for each subtest) give more analytical information about the criterion performances. For example, suppose we are trying to predict success in a course in psychological measurement. Suppose, also, that no spatial ability is required in this performance, but that twice as much numerical ability is required as vocabulary and reasoning ability. To predict a student's success in the course, we could combine and weight each person's subtest scores: $Xc = 2Xn + 1Xv + 1Xr + 0Xs$, where Xc is course grade point average, Xn is numerical subtest score, Xv is vocabulary subtest score, Xr is reasoning subtest score, and Xs is spatial subtest score. Indeed, this composite score should have more criterion validity than any subtest by itself, or by the simple addition of the subtests into an unweighted composite. The procedure of weighting more than a single score is referred to as *multiple correlation;* it will not be considered in this text.

Figure 6.7 summarizes the effects of test intercorrelations on criterion validity. Figure 6.7*a* illustrates the situation where subtest A, with a correlation of .5, predicts 25 percent of the criterion variance. An entirely different set of abilities

Figure 6.7 Illustration of the Effect of Subtest Similarity on Criterion Validity

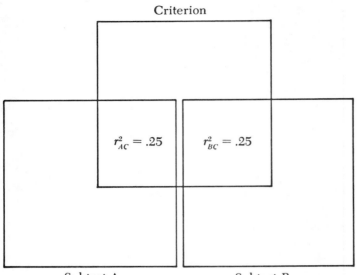

	X_C	X_A	X_B
X_C	1.0	.5	.5
X_A		1.0	.0
X_B			1.0

Test-Criterion Correlations

(a) **Low Subtest Similarity**

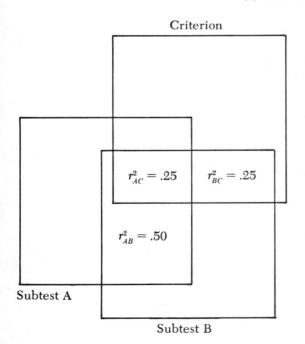

	X_C	X_A	X_B
X_C	1.0	.5	.5
X_A		1.0	.707
X_B			1.0

Test-Criterion Correlations

(b) **High Subtest Similarity**

is sampled with subtest B, and the correlation between the two subtests is zero (the similarity of items on subtest A with items on subtest B is low). Now, subtest B may or may not predict an entirely new source of criterion variance. Let us suppose it does predict, and the correlation between subtest B and the criterion is also .5. Thus, 50 percent of the criterion variance can be predicted with subtests A and B combined. But, if subtest B does not correlate with the criterion, no increase in criterion validity will be observed with the addition of that subtest.

Now, consider the case where subtest B is added, but the items of subtest A correlate highly with the items of subtest B (item similarity is high). Figure 6.7*b* presents the situation where subtests A and B each correlate .5 with the criterion, but have a subtest intercorrelation of .707. In this situation, the two subtests predict a substantial portion of the criterion variance; but, because of their relatively high intercorrelation, the two subtests account for less of the criterion variance than they would have had the subtest intercorrelation been lower.

This example illustrates the more general principle that tests with lower item correlations can have higher criterion validity coefficients than tests with higher item intercorrelations. It should be understood, however, that low item intercorrelations alone do not guarantee that all items will correlate with the criterion.

> **Generally, tests with lower item intercorrelations can have higher criterion validity coefficients than tests with higher item intercorrelations.**

Effects of Range of Talent

In Chapter 5, we found that a restriction in range of talent resulted in a restriction of the true variation. The principle developed was that as test dispersion decreased, so did test reliability. So it is with test validity, since the valid variance is a subset of the true variance. To the degree that a correlation exists between a test and a criterion, that correlation will decrease if the variance of either the predictor or criterion decreases. Conversely, the correlation will increase if the variance of either the predictor or criterion increases.

> **A restriction in the range of either the predictor or the criterion variables results in a change in the validity coefficient. Decreases or increases in dispersion result in decreases or increases in the validity coefficient, respectively.**

In summary, this chapter developed the basic principles of criterion validity. Criterion validity can be considered as the ratio of valid or predictable variance to obtained variance. The square of the criterion validity coefficient equals this

Summary

proportion of predictable variance. Predictable variance is a component of true variance. We can correct the validity estimate for attenuation, that is, correct it for the unreliability of the measures. Also, to maximize criterion validity, we often need to measure different abilities reliably. Increased range of talent increases criterion validity. Finally, the selection of predictors with low inter-correlations and high criterion validity coefficients maximizes prediction when more than one predictor is used.

Given an understanding of basic principles, we can see that criterion validity is embedded in a complex decision process in which selection ratio, cost of testing, and degree of validity are all relevant factors. The question of whether a test is valid enough can only be answered in the context of this network of factors.

This chapter has shown that criterion validity is generally concerned with the prediction of some performance in a practical setting. It should be obvious that the purpose for testing dictates the importance of the criterion validation. However, there are situations in psychology where there is no criterion, and in such cases, we need to focus on what the test itself actually measures rather than the criterion. The next chapter will consider validity from that perspective.

Suggested Readings

Anastasi, A. The concept of validity in the interpretation of test scores. *Educational and Psychological Measurement*, 1950, 10, 67–78.

Brown, F. *Principles of educational and psychological testing*. Hinsdale, Ill.: Dryden Press, 1970, Chapter 5.

Cattell, R. Validity and reliability: A proposed more basic set of concepts. *Journal of Educational Psychology*, 1964, 55, 1–22.

Cronbach, L. Validity. In C. W. Harris (Ed.), *Encyclopedia of educational research*. New York: Macmillan, 1960, pp. 1551–1555.

Cronbach, L. Test validation. In R. Thorndike (Ed.), *Educational measurement*. (2nd ed.) Washington, D.C.: American Council on Education, 1971, pp. 443–507.

Ebel, R. Must all tests be valid? *American Psychologist*, 1961, 16, 640–647.

Kaufman, A. *Restriction of range: Questions and answers*. Test Service Bulletin No. 59. New York: The Psychological Corporation, 1972.

Individual Review Questions

ANSWERS
1. validity; reliability
2. test; criterion

1. Test *reliability/validity* deals with the extent to which a test measures what it is supposed to measure, while test *reliability/validity* is concerned with the test's consistency of measurement.

2. The criterion validity coefficient is an index of the relationship between the _____ and a measure of _____ behavior.

3. Establishing criterion validity requires reference to performance on a criterion that is *external/internal* to the test.

4. The _____ of the correlation coefficient between scores on a test and scores on a criterion indicates the proportion of predictable variance between the two measures.

5. Performance on a reading test and corresponding reading scores in class correlate approximately .2. We would consider the reading test to predict _____ percent of reading score variance.

6. The correlation coefficient between a test and a criterion is .7. The proportion of predictable variance between the test and criterion is _____.

7. The proportion of nonpredictable test variance, in terms of the correlation coefficient, is given by _____.

8. A correlation of .50 between a test and a criterion would indicate that (*.25/.50/ .75/1.00*) of the test variance is nonpredictable.

9. The nonpredictable test variance *is/is not* correlated with the variance of the criterion measure.

10. A set of test scores has a variance of 75, and the scores correlate .6 with a criterion measure. The proportion of predictable variance is _____.

11. The placement of students into college prep, vocational, and general high school tracks, based on an achievement and interest inventory, assumes that the inventory has _____ validity.

12. As a criterion validity coefficient increases, we would expect the predictable criterion variance to *decrease/increase*.

13. As the criterion validity coefficient decreases, the _____ variance increases.

14. Establishing a criterion validity coefficient is a(n) *empirical/judgmental* process.

15. A test with a reliability estimate of .70 correlates .80 with a criterion variable. Therefore, _____ percent of the test variance is reliably measured, but not valid with respect to this particular criterion.

16. A test has an estimated reliability of .60, and a criterion validity coefficient of .50. Therefore, _____ percent of the variance is specific variance.

17. A predictor variable and a criterion variable have reliability estimates of .64 and .36, respectively. The variables correlate .40. Applying a correction for attenuation under the condition that both predictor and criterion are perfectly reliable would give a new estimate of the validity coefficient of _____.

ANSWERS
3. external
4. square
5. 4
6. .49
7. $1 - r_{yz}^2$
8. .75
9. is not
10. .36
11. criterion
12. increase
13. nonpredictable, or specific
14. empirical
15. 6
16. 35
17. .83

18. Suppose that all the true variance of a predictor is predictable variance. The square of the *reliability/validity* coefficient would then equal the *reliability/validity* coefficient.

19. The maximum value of the validity coefficient of a test relative to the reliability is the _____ _____ of the reliability coefficient.

20. The estimated reliability of a test is .81. The maximum value for the validity coefficient of this test is _____.

21. Unreliability in a test tends to *decrease/increase* the validity of the test.

22. A test developer is working with "experimental" tests that have reliability coefficients around .50. He is attempting to estimate test validity with selected criterion measures. In this situation he *would/would not* likely use the correction for attenuation in estimating validity.

23. We know that reliability is rather markedly affected by test length. Corresponding increases in test length have a rather *marked/modest* effect on the criterion validity of a test (assuming similarity of items).

24. A test has an estimated validity of .63. Increasing the test length to four times its original length would result in a _____ increase in validity.

25. A test with low item intercorrelations will generally have *higher/lower* criterion validity than a test that has high item intercorrelations.

26. Increasing internal consistency reliability by adding similar items while not increasing criterion validity is known as the _____ paradox.

27. A test consists of several subtests, each designed to measure a single ability. A composite score for the entire test would tend to have *greater/lesser* criterion validity than the score for any single subtest.

28. A decrease in the variance of either (or both) the predictor or criterion tends to *decrease/increase* the validity.

29. The ratio of _____ variance to obtained variance is equal to the square of the validity coefficient.

30. An art aptitude test is used to predict the course grades in an introduction to art history. The validity coefficient is found to be .35. Later, the validity coefficient is computed for art majors in an advanced course. The validity coefficient will probably be _____ for the art majors.

31. An omnibus test generally has higher criterion validity than an internally consistent test, because the items of an omnibus test can correlate with _____ sources of criterion variance.

ANSWERS
18. validity; reliability
19. square root
20. .9
21. decrease
22. would
23. modest
24. modest
25. higher
26. attenuation
27. greater
28. decrease
29. predictable
30. lower
31. several

32. The statement that reliability is a necessary, but not sufficient, condition for validity means that _____ reliability does not insure a valid test.

33. Criterion validity can be improved by lengthening a test with similar items or with dissimilar items. Generally speaking, lengthening a test with similar items results in a _____ increase in criterion validity, while lengthening a test with dissimilar items can result in _____ increases in criterion validity coefficients.

34. Lengthening a test with similar items results in increased reliability, but in only modest increases in criterion validity. Lengthening a test with dissimilar items results in little or no increase in reliability, but can result in higher criterion validity. This phenomenon, in which increased reliability results in modest increases in criterion validity, is referred to as the _____ _____.

35. A test can correlate as high as the square root of the _____.

36. The statement that reliability is a necessary, but not sufficient, condition for criterion validity implies that a _____ test may not necessarily be a _____ one.

37. The correction for attenuation, $r_{t_x t_y}$, approximates the criterion validity of a test if both the test and criterion were _____ reliable.

38. Generally speaking, a *longer/shorter* test is more reliable.

39. Generally speaking, lengthening a test with similar items markedly increases _____, and results in a modest increase in criterion _____.

40. Generally speaking, increasing a test with dissimilar items results in _____ increase in test reliability, and can result in a _____ increase in criterion validity.

41. A single-score test comprised of many items of differing content is called an _____ test.

42. The predictable variance of a criterion is 50 and the obtained variance is 100. The criterion validity of the test is the _____ _____ of .50.

43. A squared criterion validity coefficient indicates the proportion of _____ variance in a criterion.

44. Two tests, A and B, each correlate .60 with a criterion. Assuming that tests A and B are uncorrelated, each test predicts _____ percent of the criterion variance, and together they predict _____ percent of the criterion variance.

45. A test with lower item intercorrelations generally has higher _____ validity coefficients than a test with higher item correlations.

ANSWERS
32. high
33. modest; greater
34. attenuation paradox
35. reliability
36. reliable; valid
37. perfectly
38. longer
39. reliability; validity
40. little, or no; marked
41. omnibus
42. square root
43. predictable
44. 36; 72
45. criterion

46. A criterion has an obtained variance of 144 and the criterion validity coefficient is .707. The predictable variance of the criterion is _____.

47. A test has a reliability of .81; this means that the criterion validity coefficient of this test can be, but need not be, as high as _____.

48. As range of talent decreases, reliability _____ and criterion validity _____.

Study Exercises

1. A test correlates .6 with a criterion job performance. What proportion of the job performance variation is predictable?
2. A test has a reliability estimate of .6, and a criterion validity coefficient of .8. What is wrong?
3. Suppose a test, X, correlates .5 with a criterion, Y. A second test, uncorrelated with X, also correlates .5 with Y. How much of the Y variance is predictable from the two tests?
4. A test predicts 25 percent of the variance of grade point average. What is the correlation between test and grade point average?
5. A test has a criterion validity coefficient of .7, and the criterion has a reliability of .9. What is the proportion of
   a. true variance?
   b. predictable variance?
   c. specific variance?
6. A test has a criterion validity coefficient of .5. The reliability of the criterion and the test are .64 and .81, respectively.
   a. What would be the magnitude of the validity coefficient given a perfectly reliable criterion?
   b. What would be the magnitude of the validity coefficient given a perfectly reliable predictor?
   c. What would be the magnitude of the validity coefficient given a perfectly reliable predictor and criterion?
7. Test A has an equivalence reliability estimate of .90, and a stability estimate (over three years) of .64. How high can the test, administered in the beginning of the freshman year in college, correlate with grade point average three years later?
8. Test A correlates .5 with a given task, while Test B correlates .4 with that same task. Assuming that Tests A and B are uncorrelated, how much task variance will Tests A and B predict?
9. A test has a criterion validity coefficient of .5. If the test and criterion have estimated reliabilities of .84 and .64, respectively,
   a. what is $r_{t_z y}$?
   b. what is $r_{t_z t_y}$?
10. A test has a criterion validity coefficient of .4, and estimated reliability of .84, when used on a group with a variance of 169. Will the criterion validity coefficient, when used on a group with a standard deviation of 10 be higher or lower than .4?

ANSWERS

46. 72
47. .9, or $\sqrt{.81}$
48. decreases; decreases

1. .36
2. The predictable or valid variance (.64) is greater than the reliable variance (.60).
3. 50 percent
4. .5
5. (a) .90; (b) .49; (c) .41
6. (a) .63; (b) .56; (c) .69
7. .80
8. 41 percent
9. (a) .55; (b) .68
10. lower

Content and Construct Validity 7

In the last chapter we defined validity as the degree to which a test measures what it is supposed to measure. Furthermore, we attempted to impose some structure to the validity problem by focusing on the purpose of testing. The purpose, we said, defines what the test is supposed to measure, and, to a degree, dictates the method of validation.

Cattell (1964) suggests that test validation appears on a continuum from practical to conceptual validity. On the practical end of the continuum, the focus is on the criterion; on the conceptual end, the focus is on the test. The preceding chapter dealt with the practical problem of substituting a test for a task, criterion validity. This chapter will focus on the test, and inquire into the concepts it measures.

To investigate what concepts a test measures, we need to understand the aspects of test validation referred to as *content validity* and *construct validity*. With content validity, the concepts to be measured are specified by the test developer, and are generally the principles embedded in an achievement test. For example, a unit test in psychological measurement might focus on reliability and the standard error of measurement. In this case, the purpose of testing is to assess prior learning in the area being measured, and the content and format of the test reflect that purpose.

When a test is used to assess prior learning, we generally are concerned with the content validation of the concepts or principles embedded in an achievement test.

With the construct validity of a test, on the other hand, the unobservable constructs measured by the test must be inferred from observed behavior. These theoretical constructs are specified by the theory used to construct that test. For example, suppose someone wants to develop a test of "joviality." The initial step would be to define what is meant by joviality. To develop this definition, the test developer would consider behaviors manifested by persons considered jovial. This process would lead to a definition of joviality in terms of specific behaviors and their associated constructs.[1] We might say that a mini-theory about joviality has been developed, or at least is implicit in the definition. When the test is constructed and completed, it should reflect the mini-theory and the behaviors and constructs embedded in that theory.

Generally, the purpose of testing is prediction, and a particular theory about human behavior is used as the basis for developing the test. While the constructs measured by the test are specified by the theory, as the construct validity is investigated, the theory may be confirmed.

Consider an example of the theory-confirming characteristics of construct validity. Suppose a particular theory of intelligence is used to develop an intelligence test. The test should reflect that theory, and as the validation is undertaken, the theory may be confirmed and clarified. That is, as the test predicts behavior and relates to other measures, we gain information about intelligence as a theoretical construct. Thus, test validation is theory confirming. From our discussion thus far, we find that construct validation is probably more important to the theoretical psychologist, while criterion and content validation are probably more important to the practical psychologist.

When a test is used to assess traits or constructs, we generally are concerned with the validation of the constructs embedded in the test. Construct validation generally requires the confirmation of the theory that specified the constructs.

While the focus on concepts measured by the test is common to both content and construct validity, the purpose of testing may be different. To some extent, this difference can be used to distinguish between content and construct validity. While the distinction is not a simple one, keeping in mind the purpose of testing will help to clarify the difference between content and construct validity.

[1]An extension of this logic could result in specification of the constructs associated with these behaviors. This point will be clarified later in the chapter.

When the purpose of testing is to assess the degree of learning associated with a unit of instruction, the test is called *an achievement test*. The content of the unit of instruction to be measured is referred to as the *domain of content*. For example, a domain of content could refer to all the concepts or principles associated with ninth-grade algebra. If a test had as its domain of content the concepts or principles in psychological measurement, the purpose for testing requires construction of a test that will sample this specific domain of content.

Content Validity

Consider a different example: suppose we wish to evaluate the numerical reasoning ability of a group of college students. This numerical ability can be defined as the ability to add, subtract, multiply, and divide. In the strictest sense, this is not an end-of-course achievement test, since the test is used to evaluate present numerical ability. However, this purpose also requires the sampling of the defined domain of content.

> **When the content validity of a test is established, the varying purposes all dictate that a domain of content be sampled.**

In the examples just cited, since there is no criterion against which the test can be validated, the test must stand by itself as a valid instrument—it must represent some defined domain of content. One way the test is validated is to define the domain of content, to do a logical analysis of the domain, and to select a pool of items with proper statistical characteristics to represent the concepts in the domain.

Thus, content validation results from the specification and the logical analysis of a given content domain. Consider this statement from the APA's "Technical Recommendations" (1954) on content validation:

> Content validity is evaluated by showing how well the content of a test samples the class of situations or subject matter about which conclusions are to be drawn. Content validity is especially important in the case of achievement and proficiency measures [p. 13].

As an illustration, how could the content validation of an achievement test in spelling be undertaken? The content domain might be specified by selecting a dictionary. Next, a logical analysis of the domain is undertaken to determine the proportion of nouns, verbs, adverbs, and adjectives. A representative number of each of these items is sampled and administered as a preliminary test. The test is scored, and the scores collected and analyzed. From these data, each item is studied to determine its difficulty, and how well it distinguishes good from bad spellers. Finally, a test representing the domain is developed from those items with statistically adequate properties. When the test is completed, it should give a valid and reliable measure of a given person's performance. The validity of the test is embedded in the concepts that the items measure, and the degree to which they sample the conceptual structure of the domain.

Unfortunately, content validation of most achievement tests is not as straightforward as that of a spelling test. Specification of the domain of content and item development is considerably more complex. An achievement test manual describes this for a subtest on vocabulary:

> The items in the test consist of a word in context followed by four possible definitions. Stimulus words were chosen from the Thorndike and Rinsland word lists, as were words constituting the definitions. Nouns, verbs, and adjectives were given approximately equal representation, with a few adverbs at each grade level. . . . The first and most important basis for deciding whether to include a particular item in the final form of the tests was an analysis of the mental processes required of the pupil to select the correct response to the item. . . . Tryout data were then consulted to determine whether it was in the acceptable range of difficulty for each grade and whether it showed satisfactory discrimination between different levels of development [Lindquist & Hieronymus, 1964, p. 27].

From this description of the content validation of an achievement test, we see that the domain of content, along with the procedure for logical analysis, is specified. Statistical analysis is undertaken to select items of appropriate discriminability and difficulty level.

The steps in content validation of a test are: specification of a domain of content, logical analysis of the domain, and statistical analysis of a pool of tryout items from which the final test is constructed.

Selecting a valid achievement test requires determination of whether the domain of content specified by the test developer conforms to the content specified by whatever instruction underlies the achievement. In other words, are the concepts embedded in the test representative of the concepts taught in a given class or school? For example, the incongruity between test structure and school objectives was obvious when modern mathematics was introduced into the schools. Students from schools in which traditional mathematics was taught tended to fare badly on tests that focused on concepts of modern mathematics. Similarly, tests representing traditional concepts of mathematics were not valid where schools stressed modern mathematics curricula.

Summarizing our discussion of content validation, this method of validation generally occurs in the absence of some specific criterion performance, when the purpose of testing is the assessment of prior learning. When this is the case, the concepts associated with the unit of instruction are embedded in the content of the test, and the test becomes a valid measure of that unit. Content validation requires that the focus be on the concepts the test measures. In contrast, with criterion validation, some external measure—the criterion—is of greater interest than the performance measured by the test itself.

Construct Validity

Reviewing again, validity is the extent to which a test measures what it is supposed to measure. Furthermore, when a test is used as a substitute measure for some external performance, we speak of it as *criterion validity*. When the purpose of testing is to assess a unit of instruction or sample a domain of content, we are generally concerned with the *content validity* of the test. However, if the purpose of the test is to validate a theory or assess human traits, the *construct validity* of the test is of major importance. All of these methods can be associated with the validation of any test—or with the validating inferences made from any test.

Construct validity is emphasized when tests are used for scientific inquiry, and when we wish to confirm the measurement of human traits. To clarify this distinction, the APA's "Technical Recommendations" (1954) says about construct validity:

> Construct validity is evaluated by investigating what qualities a test measures, i.e., by demonstrating that certain explanatory constructs account to some degree for performance on the test [p. 14].

This statement refers to the qualities, concepts, or constructs that a test measures. In this context, qualities, concepts, and constructs are synonymous with human traits. Construct validity can be used to confirm which psychological traits a test measures. These traits might reflect the intellectual, interest, or personality characteristics of an individual.

This statement also suggests that construct validity is concerned with the degree to which these traits account for performance on a test. Here the focus is on scientific inquiry. That is, we ask the questions: What accounts for the variation in test performance? Why do some people score high and some score low? In short, we inquire into constructs that account for human behavior. As such, we use the tests as instruments of scientific inquiry.

Summarizing, it should be clear that most tests measure certain psychological traits. Construct validity is concerned with whether or not the test measures the traits it is supposed to measure. Also, some psychologists inquire into problems of human behavior. These psychologists develop theories about human behavior, and test their theories using psychological measurements. In this way, construct validity is also related to the use of tests to confirm theories.

> Construct validity is concerned with the traits embedded in a test; that is, the degree to which certain constructs account for performance on a test.

The Logic of Construct Validation

Both of the above uses of tests require a rather complex system of logic. The remainder of this chapter will be used to develop this logic. First, we will consider the logic of construct validation when tests are used as instruments of psychological theory. Then, we will consider the logic of construct validation when we attempt to confirm that a test is a measure of some psychological trait. Construct validity is a highly complex subject, but the discussion that follows should provide the basic concepts for the beginning student.

Tests as Instruments for Theory Development

We have emphasized that construct validation is important in scientific inquiry; that is, we can use tests for theory development. But what is a theory? How do tests fit into theory development? In order to clarify these questions, we shall develop the logic behind a mini-theory, and attempt to show how psychological measurements relate to the development of this theory.

In order to understand our mini-theory, consider the following philosophical position: Bolles (1967, Ch. 1) suggests that the purpose of science is to predict behavior and develop generalizable relations from if-then observations (if a situation occurs, then a given response follows). Furthermore, he suggests that when the if-then relationships occur close together in time, in temporal contiguity, we can infer that the situation might well have caused the response. For example, the cause of pain in the thumb is inferred to be from a blow by a hammer. However, when the observed situation and response are not in temporal contiguity, sometimes the causal inference is in error.

Consider an example of how a causal inference might be in error. Suppose we observe that when teachers' salaries are increased, beer consumption goes up. Suppose also that a near-linear relationship seems to exist: low salaries—low consumption, and high salaries—high consumption. Can we infer that the increase in teachers' salaries was the cause of the increase in beer consumption? On the contrary, such an assumption would probably be erroneous because a third variable, economic conditions, affects both teachers' salaries and beer consumption.

Why was one inference correct and the other incorrect? When conditions are such that the researcher manipulates the situation and quickly observes the response, we are more confident in our inference that one caused the other.

Such is the case with the hammer and the thumb. With the example of increased salaries and beer consumption, the situation and response did not occur in temporal contiguity, nor were the situation and response systematically manipulated. In that case, the chances for erroneous inference were greatly increased.

Thus, we can conclude that observations tell us how and when something happens. Why something happens is always an inference. Explanation occurs when a phenomenon is recognized as an example of a principle with which we are familiar, and when a theory, encompassing previously demonstrated principles, is repeatedly confirmed. Thus, in the preceding example, the theory that increased teacher salaries resulted in increased beer consumption might be disconfirmed when a sudden deterioration in economic conditions results in decreased beer consumption, although teachers' salaries remain high temporarily.

Theory development requires: (1) a number of terms; (2) a number of rules relating the terms, called *syntax;* and (3) definitions of the terms or their relations to empirical events, called *semantics.* Suppose, for example, that we wish to investigate some factors that influence—account for variation in—examination performance. After studying the problem, we hypothesize that intelligence and motivation are multiplicatively related to examination performance. Symbolically, we write:

$$_sE_r = {_sR_r} \times {_sD_r},$$

where:

$_sE_r$ = tendency to perform
$_sR_r$ = intelligence
$_sD_r$ = motivational state.

First, note that we can operationally define and manipulate the motivational state by varying the announcement about the examination. For the same test, we might announce a major examination to one group and a minor quiz to another. Second, intelligence might be defined from a previously administered test score. Third, response might be defined as performance on the examination. Now, the various elements of our formula are all represented, and we can study the effect of motivational state on examination performance for individuals of various ability levels. We have operationally defined all the terms in our mini-theory, and we have specified the relationship between the terms. All of the elements of a testable theory are present.

How does theory construction relate to construct validity? The response on the intelligence test might be simply used to predict the examination performance. This use of the test-criterion relationship is an example of criterion validity. Given a positive relationship between the test and the criterion, the inference can be made that bright people score higher on examinations. However, the above inference is only one aspect of a much more complex situation. Our mini-theory was set up to study the relationship of intelligence *and* motivation to examination performance. Construct validation can also be used to study that multiplicative relationship.

Recall that our mini-theory defined a multiplicative relationship between $_sR_r$ and $_sD_r$. Thus, we can multiply the scores of the individuals on the operationally defined variables, and predict examination performance. If the multiplicatively combined scores predict performance better than either variable, alone or in another combination, our theory is confirmed. In this way, tests can be used as instruments of psychological theory. Further, if the theory is confirmed, the tests as measures of the constructs are also partially confirmed.

We have suggested that explanation occurs when a phenomenon is recognized as an example of a principle with which we are familiar. Explanation also occurs when a theory, encompassing previously demonstrated principles, is repeatedly confirmed. Our example showed how a mini-theory might be used to predict and explain human behavior through the use of hypothetical constructs. The example then illustrated how we might use these constructs to predict behavior and to develop principles generalizable from if-then relationships.

If our theory were confirmed in a still different setting, we would become more confident about its generalizability, and feel that we understand the relationship between intelligence and motivational state; that is, in many situations, bright, motivated people should outperform dull, motivated people, etc. We would expect, relatively, very low performance from dull, unmotivated individuals. We can theorize that motivational state and intelligence have the status of explanatory constructs, because they account for variation in a wide range of performances.

The preceding discussion allows us to summarize what Cronbach and Meehl (1955) have suggested is the logic of construct validation. First, to define something is to specify the interlocking system of constructs that we have called syntax. For example, research indicates that intelligence can be defined as the ability to educe relationships. It is defined this way in the hierarchical structure of human abilities—in the context of a system of constructs. Second, relationships can be defined between observables and observables (that is, two things observed), observables and constructs (one thing observed, the second a trait), or constructs and constructs (both are traits). This enables us to anchor our unobservable constructs to observables, in order to keep the theory testable. Constructs must be recognized here as existing only in theory to explain human behavior. Finally, Cronbach and Meehl suggest that to understand "why" or to "learn about something" is to clarify both the constructs and the relationships between the constructs. They suggest that construct validity is evaluated by "determining what psychological constructs account for test performance [p. 282]," and that investigating a test's construct validity is not essentially different from the general scientific procedures for developing and confirming a theory (p. 300).

> **Theory development requires the operational definition of constructs (semantics) and the specification of the relationship between constructs (syntax). Construct validation procedures can be used to clarify constructs and test the basic theory.**

Acceptance and understanding of construct validation in measurement requires acceptance and understanding of the philosophy of science presented, and of the use of constructs in a theory. If one rejects the philosophy of science or the concept of a construct, he cannot accept the notion of construct validation. There are many in psychology who will accept these ideas, and perhaps an equal number who will not, but that is another issue. Our discussion centers on construct validity as a part of test validation.

Tests as Measures of Psychological Constructs

We have indicated that construct validity is of particular importance when we are testing a theory. Construct validity is also important when it is used to confirm a test as a measure of a construct. The distinction between these two is very fine. Indeed, except for instructional purposes, the distinction should probably not be made. It appears that when a theory is confirmed, so is the test as a measure of a given construct. Likewise, when a test is confirmed as a measure of a construct, so is the theory underlying the test development.

However, the use to which a test is put may emphasize whether we are more interested in the theoretical bases of a test or in its validity as a measure of a construct. In this section we shall consider a different focus to the construct validation of a test—the confirmation of the test as a measure of a construct. As with the previous section, the theory-testing aspects of the test development are implicit.

We previously indicated that explanation occurs when a phenomenon is recognized as an example of a principle with which we are familiar. In the testing situation, the stimuli (test items) are operationally fixed, and widely variant responses can occur for different people. In order to relate the test to the response —to explain the variation—we postulate explanatory constructs to account for performance on the test. As an example, if the stimulus content is numerical and the responses vary, we infer that high-scoring people are better in numerical ability than are low-scoring people. Numerical ability is an inferred construct used to account for performance on the test. When we observe people with high and low scores getting high and low grades in arithmetic, respectively, we confirm our theory of numerical ability, and suggest that we can explain why the variation in grades occurs. At this point, you should be able to distinguish between construct validity (numerical ability as an explanatory construct) and criterion validity (the correlation of the test with the criterion). Numerical ability is a construct that has explanatory value because the phenomenon (that performance varies with ability) is recognized as a familiar principle from which inferences can be made. That is, students who scored high or low on tests of arithmetic were inferred to have high or low numerical ability, and were predicted to have high or low mathematics grade point averages, respectively.

How do we know that a test measures numerical ability? What methods are used for clarifying just what construct or ability a given test measures? Indeed, there is no one method for arriving at a conclusion about what construct a test measures. However, a number of methods are used quite commonly.

Probably the most common way of validating a test as a measure of a construct is through correlational analysis. Tests that measure the same trait should tend to correlate with one another. Similarly, tests of different traits should tend to have low or zero correlations with one another.

The logic of simple correlational analysis is very straightforward. Tests that have *face validity*—that is, they appear to measure numerical ability—are correlated with other tests that do or do not appear to measure that ability. If tests that appear to measure numerical ability correlate highly with one another and have low correlations with tests of other abilities, their construct validity is confirmed. We can also say that correlations between like tests of the same trait should converge, while correlations of tests of different traits should diverge.

> **Correlation analysis can be used in establishing the construct validity of a test. Scores on tests measuring the same construct tend to be correlated; tests not measuring common constructs tend to have low, or no, correlation between their scores.**

Campbell and Fiske (1959) have developed correlational analysis into what they call convergent and discriminant validation by the multitrait-multimethod matrix. Test variances converge increasingly as the test correlations increase, and diverge increasingly as the correlations approach zero. Table 7.1 presents this matrix. By measuring several traits using several methods, the correlations can be organized to show convergence and divergence among the tests. The diagonal numbers outside the triangles in parentheses contain reliability coefficients. The diagonal numbers outside the triangles in brackets are the convergent validity coefficients (same traits–different methods). What is the difference

Table 7.1   A Multitrait-Multimethod Matrix

Traits	Method 1 A$_1$	B$_1$	C$_1$	Method 2 A$_2$	B$_2$	C$_2$	Method 3 A$_3$	B$_3$	C$_3$
Method 1									
A$_1$	(.89)								
B$_1$	.51	(.89)							
C$_1$	.38	.37	(.76)						
Method 2									
A$_2$	[.57]	.22	.09	(.93)					
B$_2$	.22	[.57]	.10	.68	(.94)				
C$_2$	.11	.11	[.46]	.59	.58	(.84)			
Method 3									
A$_3$	[.56]	.22	.11	[.67]	.42	.33	(.94)		
B$_3$	.23	[.58]	.12	.43	[.66]	.34	.67	(.92)	
C$_3$	.11	.11	[.45]	.34	.32	[.58]	.58	.60	(.85)

Source: Campbell & Fiske, 1959, p. 82. Copyright 1959 by the American Psychological Association. Reprinted by permission.

between the coefficients in solid as opposed to broken triangles? Coefficients in solid triangles represent different traits but similar methods of measurement, while those in broken triangles reflect measures of differing traits using differing methods.

Consider an example. The first measure of trait A correlates .57 with the second measure of trait A. Also, from the variance interpretation of correlation, 32 percent (.57 squared) of the variation of trait A$_1$ is predicted from trait A$_2$. From the pattern of correlations, it is possible to confirm the constructs using the multitrait-multimethod matrix.

As an example of the use of the multitrait-multimethod matrix, suppose a researcher had constructed a test that his theory suggests is a unique measure of numerical ability. To validate the Unique Numerical Ability Test, he must demonstrate that his test correlates with two other numerical ability tests, and is not measuring, say abstract reasoning, or general reasoning abilities. Thus, three traits, numerical reasoning, abstract reasoning, and general reasoning, might be sampled (Traits A_1, B_1, C_1). Also, each trait might be sampled by one of three different methods: multiple-choice test, completion test, and a performance test (Methods 1, 2, and 3). A total of nine tests are administered. These tests are appropriately arranged in the matrix, and studied for their convergent and divergent properties. If the three numerical tests correlate highly with one another, but not with the tests of other traits, the construct validity of the Unique Numerical Ability Test would appear to be established.

In the above illustration, the focus of the validation procedure is on confirming the test as a measure of a trait or construct. Nevertheless, by this procedure the theory underlying the development of the Unique Numerical Ability Test is also confirmed. As before, it is impossible to discriminate completely between the theory-confirming and the construct-confirming properties of construct validation procedures. However, again, we have illustrated the proposition that with construct validation, we are validating the theory underlying the test.

> **Construct validation procedures postulate explanatory constructs to account for variation in a given task. To the degree that these constructs have operational meaning and do account for the variation, the construct validity of the test is confirmed.**

Thus, with construct validity, we have been investigating the constructs or abilities a test measures. In practice, a test is related to some psychological construct, say anxiety. When an individual scores high or low on that test, a psychologist can infer that the individual is high or low in anxiety. To the degree that the test has validated a psychological theory, the psychologist's inference has been validated. To validate the inferences made from a test, the psychologist must understand the theory underlying test development. As the psychologist increases her knowledge of the theoretical and empirical bases of a test, she can increase her confidence in the validity of her inferences.

> **Purpose determines whether we should be primarily concerned with criterion, content, or construct validity. When the purpose for testing dictates that we inquire into the traits accounting for test variation, we are primarily concerned with construct validity.**

Summary

Let us review validity. Validity is concerned with what a test is supposed to measure; that is, validity is determined by the purpose for which the test is to be used.

Since there are so many uses to which a test can be put, there are as many different situations for which a test can be validated. Also, each of these many situations requires a different method of validation; these different methods of test validation can be grouped into the categories of criterion, content, or construct validation.

We suggested previously that when the purpose for testing required prediction of criterion scores, criterion validation was appropriate. Criterion validity can be established by expectancy tables and simple correlation.

When the purpose for testing is to assess prior learning, content validity is important. In this chapter we have emphasized the purposes and methods that can be used to establish content validity. One method by which we establish content validity is through a logical analysis of the domain of content to be covered by the test.

Finally, in this chapter, construct validity has been considered. When the purpose of testing dictates the validation of a test as a measure of a specific psychological trait, construct validity is important. Different situations or purposes require validation of different tests as measures of a trait, and different methods are used in securing that validation; the multitrait-multimethod matrix is one such method. We also pointed out that when a test is validated as a measure of a trait, the theory on which the trait is based is also validated. In this sense, construct validation is a theory-testing or theory-confirming procedure.

It is important for the student to recognize that criterion, content, and construct validation are different facets of test validation. Each time a test is developed and put into use, criterion, content, and construct validation may be undertaken to validate the test. Furthermore, the purpose of the testing requires a focus on one, some, or all of these types of validation.

Suggested Readings

Bolles, R. *Theory of motivation.* New York: Harper & Row, 1967, Chapter 1.

Cronbach, L., & Meehl, P. Construct validity in psychological tests. *Psychological Bulletin,* 1955, 52, 281–302.

Loevinger, J. Objective tests as instruments of psychological theory. *Psychological Reports,* 1957, 3, 635–694.

Peak, H. Problems of objective observation. In L. Festinger & D. Katz (Eds.), *Research methods in the behavioral sciences.* New York: Dryden Press, 1953, pp. 243–299.

McCorquodale, K., & Meehl, P. On a distinction between hypothetical constructs and intervening variables. *Psychological Review,* 1948, 55, 95–107.

Stevens, S. Psychology and the science of science. *Psychological Bulletin,* 1939, 36, 221–263.

Individual Review Questions

1. When a theory includes an unobservable process in the prediction of human behavior, a test that reflects the process has *construct/content/criterion* validity.

2. If the test described in question 1 increases prediction, and this is our major purpose, we say the test has *construct/content/criterion* validity.

3. An increase in the criterion validity of a test, through its use as a measure of a construct, _____ the theory underlying the development of the test.

4. When a test is sampled from a specified domain, we say it has _____ validity.

5. When the concepts to be measured are specified by an underlying theory and the test development proceeds on this basis, we are concerned with _____ validity.

6. Once a construct, such as numerical ability, has been clearly defined, a test constructor samples from the _____ of content in order to establish content validity.

7. Criterion, content, and construct test validation can be identified as parts of the total _____ of any test.

8. When a test has as its major purpose the prediction of some performance, _____ validity is of major concern.

9. When a test is used to sample school achievement in a specific area, _____ validity is of major concern.

10. When a test is constructed to measure a specific human ability, we say _____ validity is of major concern.

11. When content validity is established, a domain of content is _____.

12. A test stands by itself as a measure of a given domain when _____ validity is established.

13. Before a domain can be sampled, a(n) _____ analysis of the domain of content is generally undertaken.

14. Content validity is especially important in validating a test of *intelligence/achievement/creativity*.

15. Construct validity is especially important in _____ a test of human abilities.

16. Content validation occurs through a(n) _____ analysis of the domain of content under consideration.

17. Suppose a theory postulates an additive relation between two constructs. We refer to this relation as _____.

18. A construct is hypothesized as a(n) *explanatory/stimulus* variable.

19. Construct validity not only involves the operational meaning of constructs, but also the extent to which such constructs predict criterion _____.

20. To keep a theory testable, the constructs must be anchored to _____.

21. The extent to which a test can be used as a measure of some external performance is *construct/content/criterion* validity.

22. A test is used to support or refute a theory. Such use of a test involves *construct/content/criterion* validity.

23. Operationally defining the situation and response is the part of theory construction known as _____.

24. A test is constructed such that the stimulus material involves the manipulation of spatial concepts. In this situation spatial perception is a(n) _____ _____.

25. For the test in the preceding question, the extent to which performance on the test correlates with later performance in three-dimensional map construction indicates the degree of *construct/content/criterion* validity of the test.

26. A construct reflects a process that *is/is not* directly observable.

27. If the purpose of the test is the assessment of human abilities, we are probably most interested in _____ validity.

28. We wish to use a test to screen individuals to be selected for a particular job. We are probably most interested in _____ validity.

29. If the purpose of the test is the prediction of some future performance, we are probably most interested in _____ validity.

30. Content validity is appropriate for any occasion in which the purpose for testing dictates that a specified _____ of content is to be sampled.

31. If the purpose of testing concerns the development of a psychological theory, we are probably most interested in _____ validity.

32. We wish to use a test to determine the learning that has occurred in a seminar in labor relations. We are probably most interested in the _____ validity of the test.

ANSWERS
17. syntax
18. explanatory
19. variance
20. observables
21. criterion
22. construct
23. semantics
24. inferred construct
25. criterion
26. is not
27. construct
28. criterion
29. criterion
30. domain
31. construct
32. content

33. Any time the construct validity of a test is established, a psychological theory has been _____, at least implicitly.

34. When the purpose of testing dictates concern about the concepts or principles embedded in the test, we are probably not interested in _____ validity.

35. Criterion validity is probably most important when the purpose of testing dictates the prediction of *past/present/future* performance.

36. Content validity is probably most important when the purpose of testing dictates the assessment of *past/present/future* learning.

37. Any time a test is used to confirm a psychological theory, the test itself is confirmed as a measure of a particular psychological _____.

38. Different validation procedures dictate different methods of validation. The method for establishing the content validity of a test is through a _____ analysis of the domain of content.

39. One method for establishing the construct validity of a test is through the use of a _____ _____ matrix.

40. A researcher is interested in doing a study on the development of "self-concept" in various ethnic groups. To select tests to be used in the project, he is probably most interested in _____ validity.

41. An industrial psychologist wishes to increase the productivity of sales personnel coming into his organization. If he is most interested in the personality characteristics of personnel with high and low sales records, he is probably most interested in the _____ validity of the tests. However, if he is simply interested in selecting people with the possibility of increasing sales, he is probably most interested in the _____ validity of the tests.

42. A test is selected and used as a measure of creativity. Later, the test is found to have a substantial correlation with the creative output of a large number of professional artists. We say the test has been confirmed as an explanatory _____, while confirming the _____ on which the test was developed.

ANSWERS
33. confirmed
34. criterion
35. future
36. past
37. construct
38. logical
39. multitrait-multimethod
40. construct
41. construct; criterion
42. construct; theory

Study Exercises

1. Discuss the proposition that with content and construct validity, the focus is on the test, while with criterion validity, the focus is on the criterion.
2. Distinguish between content, construct, and criterion validation procedures.
3. If a national test publisher were developing a general test in mathematics for high school seniors, what types of validity would be of major concern? What might the publisher do to establish the validity of the test?

4. If a national test publisher were developing a test of general mental ability for an adult population, how would construct, content, and criterion validation procedures be utilized? What norming procedures would be utilized, and how do normative considerations enter into the validity picture?

5. For each of the following statements, which might be found in test manuals, indicate the type of validity implied.
   a. Achievement scale A is based on widely used texts in introductory calculus.
   b. Scores on mechanics aptitude test B correlate .60 with supervisor's ratings after three months on the job.
   c. Scores on numerical ability scale D correlate from .45 to .85 with five recognized measures in numerical and spatial performance.

6. Discuss the proposition that test reliability is a necessary, but not sufficient, condition for test validity.

7. What is the mathematical relationship between test reliability and a test validity coefficient?

8. In what way is the notion of internal consistency reliability similar to that of construct validity?

9. Suppose the ABC Achievement Test includes a subtest in mathematics. Also, the Smart Intelligence Test includes a numerical ability subtest. In what ways will these subtests be similar? Different? What dictates the validation procedures associated with each of these two subtests?

10. Obtain the manuals of two or three psychological tests that are designed to measure one or more constructs. Determine what evidence is presented on the validity of the tests. How adequate is the evidence on the validity for each test?

ANSWERS

5. (a) content; (b) criterion; (c) construct

7. Max $r_{yx} = \sqrt{r_{xx'}}$, or $r_{yz} = \sqrt{r_{xx'}}$

8

Factor Analysis:
A Procedure for Identifying
Psychological Constructs

The preceding chapter gave an overview of content and construct validity; these two methods of test validation focused on the concepts measured by the test. Also, in that chapter we examined some of the methods available for establishing the content or construct validity of a test. Another method used to confirm what content or constructs a test measures is *factor analysis*. This chapter will clarify the basic principles and research results associated with this method.

In this chapter, the centroid factoring of a matrix of test intercorrelations is partially illustrated. We do not intend to teach the centroid factoring procedure; in fact, the procedure has generally been superceded by other, more sophisticated methods. Rather, we intend to use this rather straightforward procedure to demonstrate the methods and results associated with factor analysis. After completing the chapter, the student should be able to read a factor matrix and indicate how factor analytic results have influenced the theory and practice of psychological measurement.

Basic Principles   In order to develop the principles of factor analysis, we will use a single illustrative example. We will assume that four tests have been given to a large number of individuals, and that all possible correlation coefficients among these four

Table 8.1 Matrix of Intercorrelations of Four Variables

	(a)						(b)			
	1	2	3	4			1	2	3	4
1	.81	.00	.72	.18		1	$h_1{}^2$	r_{12}	r_{13}	r_{14}
2	.00	.64	.08	.64		2	r_{21}	$h_2{}^2$	r_{23}	r_{24}
3	.72	.08	.65	.24		3	r_{31}	r_{32}	$h_3{}^2$	r_{34}
4	.18	.64	.24	.68		4	r_{41}	r_{42}	r_{43}	$h_4{}^2$

r_{ij}'s are correlation coefficients
$h_i{}^2$ are communality estimates

tests have been computed. That is, we have correlations between tests 1 and 2, 1 and 3, 1 and 4, 2 and 3, 2 and 4, and 3 and 4. These six correlations can be displayed in a 4 by 4 matrix of test intercorrelations, which is simply a table with correlation coefficients in the off-diagonal cells.[1] The content of the two matrices in Table 8.1 will be the basis for our discussion of factor analysis.

The matrix of intercorrelations for our example, shown in Table 8.1a, contains two types of entries, *communality estimates*, and correlation coefficients. Table 8.1b diagrams these two types of entries. Note that the communality estimates are in the diagonal cells, and the correlation coefficients are in the off-diagonal cells. (We will clarify the meaning of the communality estimates later in the chapter.)

In Table 8.1, the correlation between tests 1 and 2 is .00, between tests 1 and 3 is .72, etc. Note that the matrix is symmetrical about the main diagonal; that is, the correlation between tests 1 and 2 is also the correlation between tests 2 and 1, that is $r_{12} = r_{21}$, $r_{13} = r_{31}$, etc.

Before we proceed further, let us study the pattern of correlations in Table 8.1a. This pattern reveals that tests 1 and 3 correlate highly, and, therefore, share the measurement of a more or less common (meaning *joint*, or *common-to-both*) trait. Also, tests 2 and 4 correlate highly, and appear to be sharing in the measurement of a second trait. Thus, the pattern of high and low correlations in Table 8.1a suggests that two traits are being assessed by the four measures: tests 1 and 3 are assessing one trait, and tests 2 and 4 are assessing a second trait. Factor analysis of this matrix should confirm that two traits are being measured by the tests just cited.

---

[1]An *n* by *n* matrix of test intercorrelations can be classified according to two types of cells, r_{ii} and r_{ij}. The r_{ii} cells contain, among other things, the self-correlation of the *i*th test, while the r_{ij} cells contain the correlations between the *i*th and *j*th tests. The *n* cells containing the r_{ii} coefficients are referred to as the *diagonal* cells, or the *main diagonal*, while the $n(n - 1)$ cells in which the r_{ij} coefficients are located are referred to as the *off-diagonal* cells.

Centroid Factoring

It should be made clear that factor analysis, as presented in this illustration, usually starts with a matrix of test intercorrelations. The procedure, generally based on the patterns of test intercorrelations, is designed to identify the traits being measured by the tests in the matrix. High intercorrelations indicate that tests converge or share in the measurement of some common trait or traits, while low intercorrelations indicate divergence or the absence of some common trait.

Table 8.2 illustrates the calculation of the first factor using the centroid method.[2] This simple procedure yields four factor *loadings,* the a_{iI}'s. The subscript i indicates the ith test, while Roman numeral I indicates the first factor. These loadings are correlation coefficients between the four tests and the first centroid factor. The loadings can also be thought of as validity coefficients—the correlation of a test with the first factor. The principle of squaring the validity coefficient can be used to indicate the proportion of test variance predictable from or due to each factor. For example, the loading of .67 for test 1 indicates that 45 percent (.67 squared) of the variance in test 1 is predictable from, or due to, the first factor.

Table 8.2   Calculation of the Loadings for the First Centroid Factor

	1	2	3	4	
1	.81	.00	.72	.18	
2	.00	.64	.08	.64	
3	.72	.08	.65	.24	
4	.18	.64	.24	.68	
C_i	1.71	1.36	1.69	1.74	$\Sigma C_i = 6.50$
$\div$	2.55	2.55	2.55	2.55	$\sqrt{6.50} = 2.55$
a_{iI}	.67	.53	.66	.68	

Step 1. Insert estimates of the test communality into the main diagonal of the matrix of test intercorrelations. A number of such estimates can be used (e.g., reliability estimates, or the highest row correlation). (For this example, the actual value is known and used.)

Step 2. Add each column of the matrix (C_i).

Step 3. Sum the column sums from Step 2 $(\Sigma C_i = 6.50)$.

Step 4. Obtain the square root of $\Sigma C_i (\sqrt{\Sigma C_i} = 2.55)$.

Step 5. Divide the $\sqrt{\Sigma C_i}$ value into each column sum to obtain the factor loadings, a_{iI}. The a_{iI} are the loadings of the test on the first centroid factor.

[2]*Centroid,* in this context, means a *geometric average* or *centrally located factor.*

A loading is a product-moment correlation between a test and a perfectly reliable measure of a given factor. Since a loading is a validity coefficient, the squared product-moment correlation indicates the proportion of test variance due to that particular factor.

Now that the loadings for the first factor (I_c) have been computed (.67, .53, .66, and .68), loadings for a second factor (II_c) can also be computed. However, extraction of the loadings for the second centroid factor requires a somewhat tedious and complex procedure that is beyond the scope of this elementary discussion.[3] Thus, we shall simply provide the loadings for the second centroid factor. The centroid factor matrix in Table 8.3 gives the loadings of the four tests on both the first and second centroid factors, I_c and II_c. The loadings in the first column are those computed in Table 8.2. The loadings in the second column are simply given. Note that the factor matrix is arranged so the rows correspond to tests and the columns to factors.

To demonstrate that the loadings of the centroid factor in Table 8.3 have been derived from the correlation matrix of Table 8.1, the following formula may be used:

$$r_{ij} = a_{i\mathrm{I}}a_{j\mathrm{I}} + a_{i\mathrm{II}}a_{j\mathrm{II}} + \ldots + a_{im}a_{jm}, \tag{8.1}$$

where:

m = the number of factors
$a_{i\mathrm{I}}$ = the loading of test i on factor I.

Formula 8.1 indicates that the correlation between any two tests can be obtained by multiplying the loadings of the two tests on each factor and summing over all factors. From the centroid factor matrix in Table 8.3 and formula 8.1, we find the following correlations among the four tests:

$$r_{12} = .67(.53) + (-.60).59 = .00$$

$$r_{13} = .67(.66) + (-.60)(-.46) = .72$$

$$r_{14} = .67(.68) + (-.60).47 = .18$$

$$r_{23} = .53(.66) + .59(-.46) = .08$$

$$r_{24} = .53(.68) + .59(.47) = .64$$

$$r_{34} = .66(.68) + (-.46).47 = .24$$

[3]For the reader with a greater interest in the computational procedures involved in centroid factoring, see Guilford, 1954, pp. 470–538.

Table 8.3 Schematic Diagram of Correlation Matrix and Associated Factor Matrices

Correlation Matrix					Centroid Factor Matrix			Rotated Factor Matrix	
	1	2	3	4		I_c	II_c	I	II
1	.81	.00	.72	.18	Centroid	1	.67 −.60	1	.90 .00
2	.00	.64	.08	.64	Factoring	2	.53 .59	2	.00 .80
3	.72	.08	.65	.24		3	.66 −.46	3	.80 .10
4	.18	.64	.24	.68		4	.68 .47	4	.20 .80

Between the Correlation Matrix and Centroid Factor Matrix: an arrow (→). Between Centroid Factor Matrix and Rotated Factor Matrix: "Rotational Transformation" with an arrow (→). Before Centroid Factor Matrix: "Centroid Factoring".

The correlation between two tests is determined by summing the products of the loadings of the two tests over all factors.

From this illustration, one very important point can be made. The loadings from the 4 by 2 centroid factor matrix can be used to reproduce the correlation matrix. Therefore, the loadings from only two factors were necessary to reproduce the off-diagonal correlation coefficients. In other words, *only two traits were needed to account for the correlations among the variables.* This is the problem in factor analysis—to find the minimum number of factors, and their consequent loadings, necessary to reproduce the off-diagonal elements of the correlation matrix.

The problem in factor analysis is to find the minimum number of factors necessary to reproduce the off-diagonal elements of the correlation matrix.

The Rotation Problem in Factor Analysis

Two of the more technical aspects of the factor analytic method are the communality and rotation problems. Because of the relative complexity of these problems and the introductory nature of this text, these topics will be discussed at a very elementary level.

Before proceeding further, a brief recapitulation of the factoring procedure may be in order. This review should help to put the communality problem, the factoring procedure, and the rotation problem in perspective. First, we began with a matrix of test intercorrelations. Next, we inserted communality estimates into the main diagonal of the correlation matrix and extracted enough factors to reproduce the off-diagonal elements of the correlation matrix. For the example being discussed in this chapter, communalities were inserted into the main diagonal of the 4 by 4 matrix of test intercorrelations and two centroid factors were extracted. Then, formula 8.1 was used to confirm the fact that two factors were enough to account for all of the intercorrelations in the 4 by 4 matrix. Table 8.3 presents a schematic diagram illustrating the 4 by 4 matrix of test intercorrelations and the associated 4 by 2 centroid factor matrix.

Since the centroid factoring has resulted in a matrix capable of reproducing the off-diagonal elements of the correlation matrix, factoring can be terminated. However, often an additional transformation of the centroid factor matrix is undertaken. This second transformation is referred to as *rotation* in factor analysis. The schematic diagram of Table 8.3 also shows the rotated factor matrix, which is simply a rotational transformation of the centroid factor matrix. When formula 8.1 is applied to the rotated factor matrix, the loadings of that matrix will also reproduce the off-diagonal elements of the correlation matrix.

After the centroid factoring has been completed, this centroid factor matrix can be transformed, rotated, into a new factor matrix also capable of reproducing the off-diagonal elements of the correlation matrix.

Thus far, our discussion of factor analysis has introduced the three different matrices of Table 8.3: a correlation matrix, a centroid factor matrix, and a rotated factor matrix. Recall that the factoring of the correlation matrix was undertaken to obtain a more parsimonious description of the tests in the correlation matrix; both of our factor matrices attain that end. Indeed, an infinite number of factor matrices could be generated that would reproduce the off-diagonal elements of the correlation matrix. However, only a few of these many matrices would be psychologically meaningful.

Considerable controversy has arisen over the rotation problem in factor analysis. Those psychologists who rotate the centroid factor matrix suggest that the procedure clarifies the meaning of the factors, while those who do not rotate (or rotate only while maintaining the first factor) point to the meaningfulness of the unrotated factors. It seems that the decision to rotate or not to rotate is highly related to the question of test validity. That is, the major research hypothesis or the purpose underlying testing largely determines the decision to rotate or not to rotate. Generally speaking, nonrotational procedures are followed in situations in which the research hypothesis focuses on the psychological meaning of the first centroid factor. For example, we shall see later that in the case of intelligence tests, this focus on the first factor has assisted attempts to find the common feature or element among intelligence tests. By way of contrast, rotational procedures are associated with research hypotheses that focus on the psychological meaning of the groupings of tests embedded in the matrix of test intercorrelations. In the discussion to follow, we shall focus on the rotated and

Reading a Factor Matrix

155

unrotated factor matrices for information about the construct validity of specific tests. More important, however, we shall set the stage for a discussion of existing theories of intelligence and their methodological foundations. A knowledge of these theories will do much to increase student understanding of the theory and practice of intelligence testing.

Types of Factors

What are the various types of factors and how are they related to factoring procedures? First, recall that a factor matrix is arranged so the rows correspond to tests and the columns to factors. The loadings in the factor matrix are correlation coefficients between tests and factors (think of the correlation as being between the test and a perfectly reliable measure of the factor). These loadings can be squared to obtain the proportion of variance in the test that can be predicted from the perfectly reliable measure of the factor. Squared loadings indicate the proportion of predictable variance in the test that can be accounted for by that factor.

Now, consider the centroid factor matrix of Table 8.3. Note that the first centroid factor, I_c, has moderate to high loadings for all tests. A factor that has moderate to high loadings for all tests is referred to as a *general factor*. The squared loadings for each test indicate the substantial involvement of that factor in all tests. The general factor is usually found as the first factor in the unrotated centroid factor matrix, and can be used to identify the common element involved in all of the tests.

Factor II_c has a different pattern; it has both high positive and high negative loadings, and is referred to as a *bipolar factor*. It can be thought of as representing a psychological continuum with tests of high positive loadings on one end of the continuum and high negative loadings on the other. Extroversion-introversion is an example of a bipolar psychological continuum. The second factor in an unrotated centroid factor matrix is usually a bipolar factor.

A third type of factor is the *group factor,* one in which a group of tests has high loadings, but at least one test has a near-zero or zero loading. That is, a group of tests, but not all tests, has substantial variance accounted for by that factor. Group factors often emerge from the transformation of the centroid factor matrix into the rotated factor matrix.

> **A general factor has substantial loadings on all tests. A bipolar factor has both high positive and high negative loadings. A group factor has high loadings on most of the tests, but has at least one zero loading.**

Table 8.4 **Squared Factor Loadings for the Unrotated and Rotated Factor Matrices**

I_c	II_c	I	II
.45	.36	.81	.00
.28	.35	.00	.64
.44	.21	.64	.01
.46	.22	.04	.64
1.63	1.14	1.49	1.29
58.8%	41.2%	53.6%	46.4%
(a)		(b)	

Previously, we suggested that the decision to rotate or not to rotate the factor matrix was a function of the purpose of the research hypothesis under consideration. Now, we have defined three types of factors: general, bipolar, and group factors. A study of Table 8.3 reveals that the centroid factor matrix contains the general and bipolar factors, and the rotated matrix contains two group factors. Thus, we see that the general factor emerges directly from the centroid factoring procedure; the rotational transformation breaks down the general factor, and can result in a matrix of group factors.

Variance Due to a Factor

Now, let us consider how to determine the percentage of variance due to a given factor. Table 8.4 presents the matrix of squared loadings associated with each factor of the centroid factor and rotated factor matrices of Table 8.3. We noted previously that the loadings in these matrices can be squared to determine the proportion of predictable variance due to a given factor.

To determine the proportion of variance due to each factor, the squared loadings are summed for each factor. For example, these sums are 1.63 and 1.14 for the centroid matrix, and 1.49 and 1.29 for the rotated matrix. Next, the variances for the factors are combined to obtain the total variance due to the two factors (2.77 and 2.78 for the centroid and rotated factors, respectively). Then, to obtain the proportion of variance due to a particular factor, the total variance due to both factors is divided into the variance due to any one factor. This gives the proportion of variance due to a given factor. For factor I_c, it is 58.8 percent ($1.63/2.77 \times 100$) of the variance due to the general factor. The variance due to the first and second factors of the rotated factor matrix are 53.6 and 46.4 percent, respectively ($1.49/2.78 \times 100$; $1.29/2.78 \times 100$).

In addition to illustrating the procedure involved in determining the percentage of variance due to each factor, this example also illustrates that the rotational transformation breaks down the general factor. That is, the general factor accounts for 58.8 percent of the variance, while the first factor in the rotated matrix accounts for only 53.6 percent of the common factor variance.

Communality of a Test

At this point it is appropriate to reintroduce communality. Communality is the proportion of the variance of a test due to all of the factors. The values in the main diagonal of Table 8.1 can be checked against the proportions of variance of Table 8.4. The communalities can be found by summing the rows of Table 8.4. More generally, the communality of the ith test, h_i^2, is given by:

$$h_i^2 = \sum_{j=1}^{m} a_{ij}^2, \tag{8.2}$$

where:

m = the number of factors.

As an example, the communality of test 2 in Table 8.3 is found by:

$$h_2^2 = (.53)^2 + (.59)^2 = .2809 + .3481 = .6290,$$

with the .53 and .59 factor loadings coming from the centroid factor matrix.

The communality problem in factor analysis is associated with the number of factors problem. As the communalities are adjusted, the number of factors necessary to reproduce the correlation coefficients in the off-diagonal cells can vary. Further consideration of the communality problem is beyond the scope of this elementary text.

The communality of a test, h^2, is the proportion of variance shared by that test and all of the factors.

A Concrete Example

Let us consider an example of the interpretation of a rotated factor matrix. Table 8.5 presents a 16 by 5 factor matrix of cognitive tests. In the study from which the matrix was taken, eight cognitive abilities were selected for investigation. Sixteen tests, two for each ability, were administered to each of 94 individ-

Table 8.5 A Sixteen by Five Factor Matrix of Cognitive Tests

	Test No.	I Plan- ning	II Vocab- ulary	III Span Memory	IV Rote Memory	V Reason- ing
Object-number	1		−.30		.79	
First and last names	2				.82	
Vocabulary	3		.87			
Advanced vocabulary	4		.91			
Logical reasoning	5		.32			.64
Nonsense syllogisms	6					.75
Auditory number span	7			.90		
Auditory letter span	8			.88		
Ship destination	9	.55				.56
Necessary arithmetic operations	10					.69
Finding A's	11	.41			.31	
Number comparisons	12	.56				
Locations	13	.44				.62
Letter sets	14	.50				
Map planning	15	.63				
Maze tracing speed test	16	.77				

Loading less than .30 arbitrarily omitted.

uals. The matrix provides clues about the factorial or construct validity of the tests. As an example, consider the analysis of the components of variance of the tests shown in Figure 8.1. For the Object-number test, we find a split-half reliability of .73, indicating that about 73 percent of the total variation is reliable, and about 27 percent is error. Furthermore, by squaring the loading of .79 on factor IV, we find that about 62.41 percent of the test variation appears to be associated with a rote memory factor, and about 9 percent with the verbal comprehension factor. With about 73 percent of the variation reliable, and about 71.41 percent due to rote memory and verbal comprehension, about 1.59 percent of the variance $(73 - 71.41)$ is specific variance. Specific variance is the difference between true variance and variance due to the factors; it is reliable variance that cannot be attributed to any factor in the matrix, and it is specific to that test.

Naming the Factors

One final aspect associated with reading a factor matrix is naming the factors. Naming factors varies in difficulty according to the study being conducted. In many cases, naming factors is very straightforward; in others it is very difficult. In the well-researched areas of intelligence, personality, and interests, major

Figure 8.1 **Analysis of the Components of Test Variance for Object-Number and Vocabulary Scores**

Variable 1 Object-Number

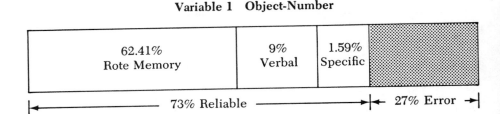

Variable 3 Vocabulary

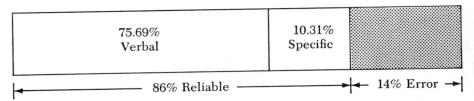

factors are easily identifiable, while in less-researched areas or with more obscure factors in major areas, naming factors becomes more difficult. For the beginning student, the major factors associated with the main domains of human abilities are quite readily identifiable. It is these factors, and the way they are identified, that should interest the beginning student.

Factors are identified by studying the pattern of loadings associated with the various factors. The squares of these loadings indicate the proportion of variance due to a particular factor, and tests with unusually high loadings give clues as to the nature of the factor or dimension of ability under investigation. Factorial research over the years has identified tests, called *reference tests*, that have high loadings on particular factors. These reference tests can be used in factorial studies to assist in factor identification (French, Ekstrom, & Price, 1963).

Table 8.5 illustrates how factors might be named. Factor I is studied for patterns of loadings. Tests 15 and 16 have the highest loadings, .63 and .77, respectively. Since these tests have been defined by French, Ekstrom, and Price (1963, pp. 43–44) as reference tests for a Planning factor, factor I is identified as such. Similarly, tests 3 and 4 have been identified as reference tests for a Vocabulary factor. The remaining factors can be named from the pattern of loadings for various tests that have been identified as reference tests for various factors by prior research.

Exploratory studies using factor analysis do not always yield such easily definable factors. Also, factor names vary according to the biases of a particular researcher. Nevertheless, the pattern of loadings leads to factor labels. Again, for the beginning student, the extremely well researched domains of human abilities have identified major factors with relatively little disagreement over the nature of most of the factors. With a reasonable amount of study, the student will quickly become familiar with the major dimensions of ability: Verbal, Performance, Vocabulary, Numerical, Reasoning, etc. Generally, as human abilities research progresses, more factors become identifiable. However, if concentrating on factorial research, the reader will find many areas where factors are less well defined. Nevertheless, as these factors are labeled, the pattern of loadings allows the investigator to make inferences about the name of the factor under investigation.

Factor analysis is one method by which we can determine the internal structure of tests of human abilities. This section will present the results of research designed to clarify the structure of human abilities.

Factor Analysis and Human Abilities

Hierarchical Factor Theory

At the turn of the century, Spearman (1904) developed a theory of intelligence based on his efforts to factor a matrix of test intercorrelations. From the pattern of positive intercorrelations, he originally hypothesized a single intellective factor that was referred to as "g," and defined as the ability to educe relationships. The Spearman-Burt-Vernon tradition evolved when it was observed that the "g" factor by itself could not account for all the test intercorrelations. That is, a single factor would not reproduce the correlations in the correlation matrix (see formula 8.1). In this tradition, Burt (1949) observed that a slight rotation of two or three factors could be undertaken to arrive at a general factor and one or two major group factors. Table 8.6 presents such a pattern. The + sign indicates a high correlation. Factor I is the general factor, and factors II and III are major group factors. As a result of Burt's research, a hierarchical structure of human abilities was formulated. Vernon (1950) describes this predominantly British theory of intelligence in considerable detail.

Hierarchical theory is committed to the general ("g") factor. This factor is believed to reflect a predominantly inherited trait. When older children who have had the benefit of academic preparation are administered a battery of cognitive tests, the factor matrix, in addition to "g," generally yields a verbal-educational (v:ed) factor and a spatial-mechanical (k:m) major group factor.

Table 8.6   **Factor Pattern Showing General
and Major Group Factors**

	I	II	III
1	+	+	0
2	+	+	0
3	+	+	0
4	+	+	+
5	+	0	+
6	+	0	+
7	+	0	+

Table 8.7 Simple Summation and Group Factor Analyses of Tests Given to 1,000 Army Recruits

Tests	Unrotated Centroid Factors					Rotated Group Factors					
	I_c	II_c	III_c	IV_c	h^2	"g"	$k{:}m$	ed	v	n	h^2
Progressive Matrices	.77	+.23	+.10	−.16	.68	.79	.17				.65
Dominoes (non-verbal)	.80	+.09	+.19	−.12	.70	.87					.75
Group Test 70, Pt. I	.74	+.16	+.03	−.08	.58	.78	.13				.62
Squares	.63	+.35	.00	+.01	.52	.59	.44				.54
Assembly	.37	+.54	−.15	+.28	.52	.24	.89				.85
Bennett Mechanical	.69	+.33	−.17	+.07	.62	.66	.31				.54
Verbal	.88	−.24	−.26	−.14	.92	.79		.29	.45		.90
Dictation	.79	−.42	−.25	−.11	.88	.62		.54	.48		.90
A.T.S. Spelling	.81	−.32	−.20	−.11	.80	.68		.41	.43		.82
Instructions	.89	−.06	+.11	−.15	.82	.87		.23	.09		.82
Arithmetic, Pt. I	.84	−.29	+.22	+.23	.89	.72		.49		.39	.91
Arithmetic, Pt. II	.86	−.16	+.12	+.13	.80	.80		.38		.16	.82
A.T.S. Arithmetic	.84	−.21	+.26	+.14	.84	.77		.36		.32	.82
Variance percent	59.8	8.5	3.1	2.2	73.5	52.5	8.7	8.4		6.9	76.5

Source: Vernon, *The Structure of Human Abilities*, 1950, p. 23, by permission of Methuen and Co., Ltd., publishers.

The verbal-educational factor can be further reduced to verbal (v) and numerical (n) minor group factors. Similarly, the spatial-mechanical group factor can be reduced to less academic, but still cognitive, factors. These major and minor group factors are recognized as learned abilities. When a battery of tests is administered to young children or to a generally unschooled population, the major group factors appear to be less distinct. Table 8.7 presents a factor matrix conforming to hierarchical factor theory.

Table 8.7 confirms the similarity between the first centroid factor and the "g" factor loadings. The first factor was rotated just enough to maintain "g," and yet clarify the major and minor group factors. From their moderate or high loadings on certain tests, the second and third factors can be recognized as the spatial-mechanical ($k{:}m$) and verbal-educational ($v{:}ed$) major group factors, respectively. Those tests that load on the spatial-mechanical group factor are less culture-bound than the culturally biased verbal and numerical tests that load on the $v{:}ed$ group factor. Also, the minor numerical and verbal group factors are identified. Figure 8.2 illustrates the hierarchical structure of human abilities, showing how the "g" factor, major group factors, minor group factors, and specific group factors evolve.

To better understand Figure 8.2, think of the variance of any given intelligence test. According to hierarchical theory, some of the variance of a test is due to a general intellective factor, some is due to a major group factor, and the remaining variance to some other minor source. Figure 8.2 represents these constructs according to their decreasing ability to account for variance. The unrotated factors of Table 8.7 confirm this decreasing ability to account for variance; that is, from left to right, the factor loadings tend to decrease.

The hierarchical structure of human abilities gives us a better understanding

Figure 8.2   Diagram Illustrating Hierarchical Structure of Human Abilities

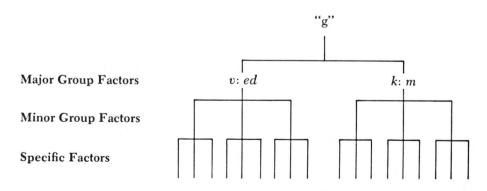

Source: Vernon, *The Structure of Human Abilities*, 1950, p. 22, by permission of Methuen and Co., Ltd., publishers.

of the problems associated with the measurement of intelligence. There is a commitment to "g," because it generally accounts for more than 50 percent of the common factor variance. That is, to know about "g" is to have a major source of information about an individual. Tests of the major and minor group factors provide additional information.

Primary Mental Abilities Theory

While Burt was clarifying the general factor theory by adding the group factors to Spearman's "g" factor, Thurstone set about obtaining multiple factors of more nearly equal variance. Thurstone's (1936) multiple factor approach was designed to break down the general factor through rotation. The rotated factor matrix of Table 8.3 reflects the type of factor upon which Thurstone concentrated his interpretive efforts. As a result of this type of analysis, Thurstone (1936) identified the following primary mental abilities:

V—Verbal Relations
P—Perceptual Speed
I—Induction
N—Number
M—Memory
D—Deduction
W—Word Fluency
S—Visualizing

The primary mental abilities research of Thurstone subsequently led to the development of multiple-score tests. Essentially, the primary mental abilities or multiple-score approach to testing yields more information about an individual than does the single-score, "g" factor approach. Ultimately, it is the purpose for which the test is used that dictates whether a multiple-score or a single-score test is used. Usually, when time is a factor, the shorter single-score test is used instead of the longer multiple-score test.

As more and more information was gathered about the criterion validity of the various primary mental ability tests, it became apparent that some of the primaries had more generalized criterion validity; that is, they correlated with more things in life. As a result, most present-day multiple-score tests include some combination of the following four primaries:

Verbal (or Vocabulary)
Number (or Numerical)
Reasoning (Inductive and Deductive)
Spatial (or Visualization)

Present-day single-score tests also utilize some combination of items that reflect the content of the above four primaries. Usually, vocabulary and numerical

Table 8.8 **Median Correlations of Differential Aptitude Tests with School Marks**

	English	Mathematics	Science	Social Studies
Verbal reasoning	.49	.33	.54	.48
Numerical computation	.48	.47	.52	.46
Abstract reasoning	.32	.32	.42	.32
Space	.26	.26	.34	.24
Mechanical comprehension	.21	.19	.40	.21
Clerical speed and accuracy	.22	.16	.24	.21
Spelling	.44	.28	.36	.36
Sentences (English usage)	.50	.32	.45	.43

Source: Vernon, *The Structure of Human Abilities*, 1950, p. 169, by permission of Methuen and Co., Ltd., publishers.

items receive greater emphasis because of their higher criterion validity, since highly valued occupations in our society require proficiency in vocabulary and arithmetic. Certainly, the greatest effect of Thurstone's work has been the development of multiple-score aptitude and intelligence tests.

One of the more successful multiple-score tests is the Differential Aptitude Test (DAT). Although the DAT is not strictly based on Thurstone's work, the subtests do reflect his primary abilities to a degree. Table 8.8 presents the median correlations of the DAT with various academic criterion performances. Table 8.8 also offers an opportunity to distinguish between construct and criterion validity. The rows indicate the abilities or constructs the DAT purports to measure, while the columns present the criterion validity coefficients of the tests with the various courses. Table 8.8 also partially confirms the generally higher criterion validity of the verbal and numerical tests.

Finally, Thurstone's work stimulated a logical analysis of tests according to *content, process,* and *form.* By content, we refer to the figural, symbolic, or semantic nature of the test materials. By process, we might refer to whether reasoning, memory, or perception is required by the test. By form, we refer to the structure of the test items, whether they are classificational or relational in nature. The analysis of tests according to content, process, and form can be illustrated by a 3 by 3 by 2 taxonomic model, as shown in Figure 8.3. It has 18 cells, and provides the logical basis for classifying 18 different types of tests.[4] An example might be a perception test using symbolic content with classificational forms. The model is an excellent example of what we meant by logical analysis in our previous discussion of content validity, because it provides a scheme for classifying the content of tests on the three attributes or dimensions.

[4]This example is designed to be illustrative only; a more complete discussion is provided in Guilford, 1959b.

Over the years, arguments over the appropriateness of hierarchical or multiple-group factor theory have been rampant, and no clear-cut resolution is in sight. We can state that tests based on hierarchical factor theory are more appropriate for some purposes, while tests based on multiple-group factor theory may be more appropriate for another purpose. What is of concern here, however, is test validation. Depending on purpose, a test based on one theory may be more valid than a test based on another theory.

Summarizing, we can see that factor analysis has resulted in two extensive research traditions. Both traditions have contributed substantially to the theory and practice of intelligence testing. That is, depending on the testing situation, one might use a unifactor or a multiple-factor intelligence test. As an example, using the prediction of academic success as a goal, it is apparent that Thurstone's Vocabulary and Numerical Reasoning factors generally correlate significantly higher with grade point average than a single factor based on "g" alone. Conversely, there are other situations where tests from the "g" factor tradition are more appropriate than are those reflecting primary mental abilities theory.

Figure 8.3 Illustrative Taxonomic Model for Various Types of Tests

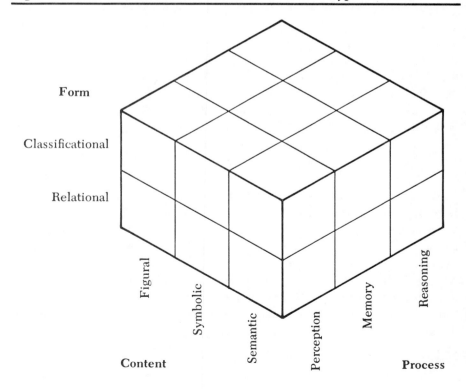

Summary

Some principles and basic concepts of factor analysis have been discussed in this chapter. Factor analysis is of particular importance to construct validity, since it provides a procedure for the identification of psychological constructs or traits. Factor analysis can be based on the intercorrelations of psychological data. The data, generally consisting of several different test scores, are analyzed through their intercorrelations, and a number of factors (usually less than the number of tests) are identified. This reduction to a few factors tends to simplify the description of the original test data.

As a procedure, however, factor analysis has not reached the ultimate in conceptual precision. It is one thing to perform a factor analysis, and identify a number of factors. It may be a more difficult task to interpret the nature of the factors implied by groupings of the tests, and to designate satisfactorily the meanings and labels for such factors. Nevertheless, factor analysis has become a very useful and legitimate procedure for studying the underlying constructs in psychological data, and for developing and testing psychological theories.

Suggested Readings

Adcock, C. *Factorial analysis for non-mathematicians.* London: Cambridge University Press, 1954.

Guilford, J. *Psychometric methods.* 2nd ed. New York: McGraw-Hill, 1954, Chapter 16.

Kerlinger, F. *Foundations of behavioral research.* 2nd ed. New York: Holt, Rinehart & Winston, 1973, Chapter 37.

Thomson, G. *The factorial analysis of human ability.* Boston: Houghton-Mifflin, 1969.

Individual Review Questions

1. In factor analysis, the variance among the variables that is due to the factors is called the _____.

2. The correlation coefficient between a test and a factor is called a _____.

3. A squared factor loading indicates the _____ of test variation due to that factor.

4. In reflecting the extent to which a test is related to, or is representative of, a factor, a loading can be considered a _____ _____.

5. Considering the communality of a given variable, it is the *product/sum/difference* of the variance components the variable has in common with the factors.

6. In order to determine operationally the communality of a given test, we would sum the _____ _____ for that test over all factors.

ANSWERS
1. communality
2. loading
3. proportion
4. validity coefficient
5. sum
6. squared loadings

7. Suppose a test has loadings of .6 and .7 on factors I and II respectively. The communality of the test is _____.

8. Suppose test A has loadings of .6 and .7 on factors I and II, respectively, while test B has loadings of .8 and .2 on factors I and II, respectively. The correlation between tests A and B will be _____.

9. From the information secured in a factor analysis, the correlation between two variables can be determined by summing the _____ of the loadings of the two variables over all factors.

10. A factor analysis involving several variables results in two factors. Variable A has loadings of .6 and .2 on factors I and II, respectively, and variable B has loadings of .9 and .3 on the same two factors in that order. The correlation between variables A and B is _____.

11. A matrix of correlation coefficients consisting of factor loadings is called a _____ matrix.

12. Factor A has loadings in excess of .5 with all the tests of a test battery. Factor A is a _____ factor.

13. Factor C has loadings of .80, .52, and −.73 with three of the n tests. With this pattern of loadings, factor C is a _____ factor $(3 < n)$.

14. Factor E has high positive loadings with three tests of a battery, and zero loadings with the remaining tests. Therefore, factor E is a _____ factor.

15. A factor matrix is rotated and test A is found to have a .65 loading on factor I and a .40 loading on factor II. Test A has a split-half reliability of .75. Therefore, _____ percent of the variance of test A is reliable, and _____ percent and _____ percent of the total variance are associated with factors I and II, respectively, leaving a specific variance of _____ percent.

16. In the preceding question, _____ percent of the variance of test A is error variance.

17. The difference between true variance and communality is the _____ variance.

18. Spearman's theory of intelligence postulated a single intellective factor referred to as _____, which represents the _____ factor.

19. The general factor in hierarchical theory is considered predominantly as a(n) *inherited/learned* trait.

20. Thurstone's multiple factor approach to intelligence theory was designed to reduce the general factor through _____ into several _____ _____.

21. A factor pattern for four factors and six tests is as follows, with + indicating a substantial loading.

Factors

	I	II	III	IV
1	+	+	0	−
2	+	+	+	0
3	+	+	+	0
4	0	+	+	0
5	0	+	+	0
6	0	+	0	+

With this type of pattern, factor I is a _____ factor, factor II a _____ factor, factor III a _____ factor, and factor IV a _____ factor.

22. When a logical analysis of test materials is being conducted and the materials are classified according to their symbolic, figural, or semantic nature, the analyzer is concerned with the *content/process/form* of the materials.

Consider the following factor matrix.

	I_c	II_c	$r_{xx'}$
1	.7	−.6	.90
2	.6	.4	.80
3	.7	−.5	.83
4	.6	.5	.83
5	.5	.4	.88

23. The above matrix is a(n) _____ factor matrix. The first factor is a _____ factor, while the second factor is a _____ factor.

24. The correlation between variables 1 and 2 in this problem is _____.

25. The communality of variable 3 is _____, while its specific variance is _____.

26. The percentage of variance due to the first and second factors, respectively, is _____ and _____.

27. In the above problem, suppose a criterion has loadings of .5 and .6 on the first and second factors, respectively. The correlation between variable 5 and the criterion will be _____, and the variable with the highest criterion validity coefficient will be variable _____.

28. The specific variance of variable 5 is _____.

29. The correlation between variables 4 and 5 is _____.

30. The proportion of variance due to the general factor for variable 4 is _____, while the proportion of variance due to the bipolar factor is _____.

31. The correlation between variables 3 and 5 is _____.

ANSWERS
21. group; general; group; bipolar
22. content
23. unrotated, or centroid; general; bipolar
24. .18
25. .74; .09
26. 62.3%; 37.7%
27. .49; 4
28. .47
29. .50
30. .36; .25
31. .15

169

Study Exercises

1. Consider the following correlation matrix:

	1	2	3	4	$r_{xx'}$
1	1.0	.56	.07	.00	.86
2		1.0	.22	.18	.91
3			1.0	.63	.89
4				1.0	.89

    a. How much of the variance of variable 1 is predictable from variable 2?
    b. How many clusters of tests are represented by the intercorrelations?
    c. What tests are in each of the above clusters?
    d. How much of the variance of variable 1 is specific (relative to variable 2)?

2. Consider the following factor matrix:

	I	II	$r_{xx'}$
1	.7	.0	.86
2	.8	.2	.91
3	.1	.7	.89
4	.0	.9	.89

    a. Reproduce all the correlations between the four variables.
    b. What is the communality of variable 2?
    c. Distinguish between group, general, and specific factors.
    d. Is factor I a group, general, or specific factor?
    e. What is the specific variance of variable 3?
    f. What percentage of the common factor variance is due to factors I and II, respectively?

3. Consider the following factor matrix from Lawley and Maxwell (1963, p. 61):

Tests	Factors		
	I	II	III
1. Comprehension	.86	−.11	.11
2. Arithmetic	.78	.55	.00
3. Similarities	.83	.07	.13
4. Vocabulary	.81	−.02	.22
5. Digit Span	.60	.21	.11
6. Picture Completion	.66	.06	.47
7. Picture Arrangement	.70	.09	.40
8. Block Design	.55	.40	.51
9. Object Assembly	.58	.10	.63
10. Coding	.68	.20	.34

    a. Does the factor matrix support the verbal-performance distinction?
    b. What type of factor is I?
    c. What type of factor is III?
    d. Which test is the least well defined factorially?
    e. Which two tests have the highest intercorrelation?

4. Given that tests 1, 3, and 8 have estimated reliabilities of .85, draw a schematic indicating proportions of true, specific, and error variance. Indicate proportions of variance due to factors I, II, and III, respectively.

ANSWERS

1. (a) .31; (b) two; (c) 1 = 1, 2; II = 3, 4; (d) .55

2. (a) See the matrix of problem 1. (b) .68; (d) group; (e) .39; (f) 46%; 54%

3. (a) yes, it tends to; (b) general-verbal; (c) group-performance; (d) test 5; (e) tests 1 and 4, $r_{14} = .723$

4. Proportions of variance due to factors for the three tests are:

	I	II	III
1	.74	.01	.01
3	.69	.01	.02
8	.30	.16	.26

5. Below are the unrotated and rotated factor matrices. Show that rotation has "broken down" the general factor.

$$
\begin{array}{cc}
\mathbf{I}_c & \mathbf{II}_c \\
\begin{bmatrix} .46 \\ .68 \\ .62 \\ .67 \end{bmatrix} & \begin{bmatrix} .53 \\ .48 \\ -.42 \\ -.58 \end{bmatrix}
\end{array}
\qquad
\begin{array}{cc}
\mathbf{I} & \mathbf{II} \\
\begin{bmatrix} .7 \\ .8 \\ .1 \\ .0 \end{bmatrix} & \begin{bmatrix} .0 \\ .2 \\ .7 \\ .9 \end{bmatrix}
\end{array}
$$

6. Consider the following factor matrix:

	I	II	$r_{xx'}$
1	.8	.0	.90
2	.5	.5	.89
3	.1	.8	.86

a. What are the correlations between tests 1, 2, and 3?
b. What is the communality of test 1, test 2, and test 3?
c. What is the specific variance of test 1, test 2, and test 3?
d. How much of the common factor variance is due to factor I and factor II, respectively?

ANSWERS

5. There is less variance accounted for by factor I (46%) than is accounted for by factor $\mathbf{I}_c$ (59.5%).

6. (a) $r_{12} = .40$, $r_{13} = .08$, $r_{23} = .45$; (b) .64, .50, .65; (c) .26, .39, .21; (d) 50.28%, 49.72%

9 Measurement of Human Abilities

In previous chapters, we established some basic principles of psychological measurement. In this chapter, we will consider the uses of tests in the context of these principles. This chapter will illustrate both theoretical and practical uses of ability measurements, and clarify the constructs generally represented by tests of this type.

The Role of Measurement in Theory

What role does measurement play in psychological theory? Previously, we defined a construct as an explanatory variable in human behavior reflecting a process that is not directly observable.[1] An example of a construct is intelligence, which, as inferred from Raven's Matrices, reflects the ability to see relationships. Similarly, the construct drive may be inferred from a score on, say, the Taylor Manifest Anxiety Scale (TMAS). Suppose we multiply our two constructs, intelligence and drive, to develop a third construct that we will call tendency to perform. We are assuming a multiplicative relationship between the constructs, and we would expect the highly motivated and intelligent individual to have a high response tendency, while anyone with zero drive would tend not to respond at all. While this is quite a crude theory, it does provide a beginning for considering relationships between the constructs.

[1]For a more complete discussion of this topic, see McCorquodale and Meehl, 1948.

172

Consider this example in a practical setting. Suppose we wished to predict success in academic work. We might use our theory to predict the grade point average (GPA) of a large number of students. First, we can determine if intelligence and/or drive are related to GPA. Next, we can attempt to determine whether the constructs are additively or multiplicatively related. Thus, we see the role of measurement in the validation of a theory—how we can use test scores to predict and, to a degree, to explain human behavior.

While this theoretical approach can assist our understanding of behavior, a more complete understanding is reached through the integration of research in learning and human abilities. We turn our focus now to the influence of learning on human abilities.

In Chapter 4 we focused on the principle of stability reliability. Each score consists of a stable and an unstable part, and test variance was partitioned into stable, unstable, and random components. Table 4.2 showed that as individuals approach maturity, their scores become increasingly stable. So it is with the primary mental abilities.[2] As an individual approaches maturity, his primary abilities stabilize. Figure 9.1 plots stability factors against age to illustrate this effect. To what do we owe this increasing stability?

From research on human abilities, we find that as children increase in age and amount of schooling, primary abilities are more easily defined. Factor analytic research indicates that in cultures where formal schooling is nonexistent, not mandatory, or terminates early, the primary factors are not as distinct, or fail to emerge. The inference is that the primaries are at least partly a function of formal school experiences.

Flavell (1963, p. 86) outlines Piaget's taxonomy of the developmental periods through which the individual passes: the sensorimotor period (birth to 2 years); the concrete operations period, composed of two subperiods: the preoperational (2 to 7 years), and the concrete operations (7 to 11 years); and the formal operations period (11 to 15 years). Cognitive development can be traced from simple discrimination and generalization in the sensorimotor stage to highly abstract and internalized thought in the formal operations stage. In the concrete operations stage, an individual first relies heavily on external objects to assist his reasoning (for example, using fingers to assist in counting). The ability to deal with abstractions is very primitive. Later, after more experience, the individual approaches the formal operations stage of internalized abstract reasoning.

Piaget, along with Vernon and others, suggests that learning is vital to this cognitive development. Also, the relative stability of the primary abilities (Figure 9.1) occurs at about the time that internalization or the formal operations stage is complete, that is, around age 15. Thus, development of cognitive ability occurs

[2]Primary mental abilities were introduced and discussed in Chapter 8.

sequentially in the sensorimotor, concrete operations, and formal operations periods.

Let us be more specific about the growth of cognitive abilities. But, what is meant by cognitive ability? First, a cognitive ability is inferred from performance. When someone performs well in mathematics, we say he has high numerical ability. Objectively, abilities are behavior descriptions. When considered from this point of view, abilities are related to content areas. Numerical ability differs from spatial ability by the nature of the stimulus content. We can look at human abilities in terms of stimulus content and the resulting behavior description. This method is reflected in the symbolic, figural, and semantic content of Figure 8.3 in the previous chapter, and is reflected in Guilford's (1959b) theory of human abilities.

Additionally, when we consider an ability from the point of view of process, we refer to such distinctions as memory, reasoning, and perception. But, is the process that intervenes between numerical content and response the same as that which intervenes between spatial content and response? Such an answer can only come from testable theories and research. It should be obvious that

Figure 9.1   Estimated Curves for the Development of Specific Primary Mental Abilities

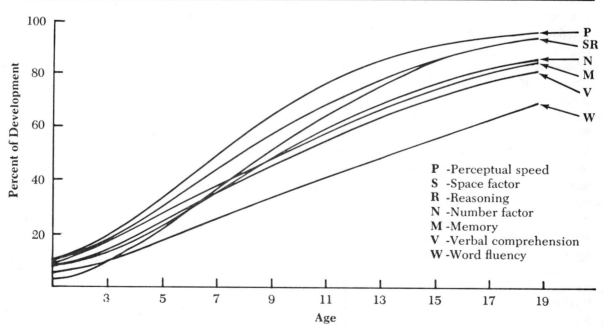

P -Perceptual speed
S -Space factor
R -Reasoning
N -Number factor
M -Memory
V -Verbal comprehension
W -Word fluency

Source: Thurstone, 1955.

both content and process are involved in the definition of an ability; however, the study of process is generally incomplete. Let us see how such study is related to measurement.

Learning psychologists refer to the unit of learning as *a habit*. A habit is inferred from behavior, and becomes highly stable with reinforced practice. Habits and abilities are similar in that they are a function of stimulus content, are inferred from behavior, and reflect a mediating process.

Furthermore, learning-to-learn research has identified the learning set as a more generalizable habit or nonspecific transfer mechanism. For example, when an individual practices making the same (or a similar) response to the same (or similar) stimulus content, we say he develops habit—he learns. Also, if he makes the same response to varying stimulus content, we say he develops a learning set—he learns to learn. He learns to employ strategies, and in a novel situation, these strategies result in appropriate novel responses.

At a less experimental level, we can illustrate how the learning set phenomenon appears to operate in the classroom setting. Consider the teacher who has her students learn multiplication by rote, and then gives a series of story problems for a test. Because of the lack of similarity between the training and the test, students generally perform badly on the test. On the other hand, suppose she teaches by rote, by successive addition, by story problem, and then gives a number of real problems requiring multiplication. Because the students in the second illustration have had practice in several differing modes, some of them should perform better on a test than those receiving the single mode of rote instruction. Thus, in this situation, learning set research has provided us with knowledge of the process that appears to bridge the gap between learning and human abilities research.

While it is apparent that learning affects test scores, the crucial link—the definitive experiment—between learning set and human abilities research has not been completed. Ferguson (1970) implies, and we agree, that further learning set research will provide this definitive link in process research. In any event, research in human learning, development, and measurement is highly interrelated, and measurement plays an essential role in this research.

The notion of a construct as an explanatory variable in human behavior has contemporary meaning. Our discussion thus far has been designed to clarify that meaning, and to integrate it into the logic of theory construction and construct validation. Let us accept the notion that intelligence is a construct. When a test that exemplifies one theory of intelligence is compared with tests used to investigate other theories, the result is a number of tests that vary somewhat in

The Role of Measurement in Practice

175

what they measure. For example, a test of intelligence exemplifying hierarchical theory is not exactly the same as a test exemplifying primary mental abilities theory. Consequently, different intelligence tests tend to be similar, yet different. Focusing on this difference, we find that intelligence tests can be classified on a continuum, one end of which is anchored in school-learned concepts.

As an example of the continuum, Cattell (1968) has referred to crystallized and fluid abilities. He suggests that fluid abilities tend to be inherited, while crystallized abilities tend to be learned. Thus, a nature-nurture continuum is implied. Cronbach (1960, p. 235) also refers to a continuum: one end with a maximum educational loading, the other with a minimum educational loading. Also, Mehrens and Lehmann (1969, p. 72) suggest a specific-to-global continuum. These continua are not exactly the same; however, they assist in organizing tests and test score variation. In the discussion that follows, we shall refer to an intelligence continuum that will have Raven's Progressive Matrices (RPM) and the School and College Ability Test (SCAT) positioned near the extremes to reflect relatively greater hereditary and environmental involvement, respectively.

Raven's Progressive Matrices

According to the hierarchical theory of intelligence, the first factor to be extracted from a matrix of intelligence test intercorrelations is a general factor, "g," or the ability to see relationships. It would appear that "g," as a construct, reflects a process highly related to inductive reasoning. The second factor, according to hierarchical theory, is a factor associated with the verbal and performance characteristics of the task. The last factors extracted are minor group factors that are associated with the specific content of the tests. According to Vernon (1950, p. 27), the "g" factor, major group factors, and minor group factors account for decreasing proportions of variation. Furthermore, the role of heredity is greater in the "g" factor, while the minor group factors tend to be learned.

Figure 9.2 presents a sample item representative of those found in Raven's Progressive Matrices. Sixty matrices of increasing difficulty level are included in the test for which normative data on a cross section of British subjects are available. Table 8.7 in the preceding chapter indicates that the Raven's test has a loading of .79 on the "g" factor, and very low loadings on the major and minor group factors. This "g" factor loading indicates that approximately 62 percent of the variance of the test is accounted for by the first factor. The essentially zero loadings on all other factors also indicate that this test is relatively homogeneous in content. Also, since the Raven's test is representative of "g," it is also assumed to have a high hereditary component.

Since the Raven's test minimizes verbal abilities, it can be used without instructions or with only minimal assistance. Because of this characteristic, it can also be used in conjunction with tests of educational achievement to identify students with good reasoning ability who score badly on tests measuring learned academic concepts. In this context, the concept of an underachiever was developed (Thorndike, 1963). To identify an underachiever, a bivariate plot of the Raven's test against a test of educational achievement can be drawn. Achievement scores can be predicted from Raven's scores, and underachievers can be identified. For individuals so identified, remedial treatment in weak areas can be prescribed.

Figure 9.2 Sample Item Illustrating Those Found in Raven's Progressive Matrices Test

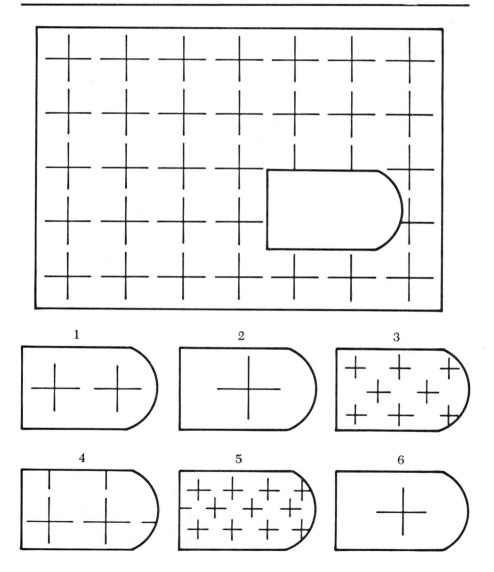

Since the Raven's test has minimal cultural content, it is a reasonable test for use with culturally disadvantaged groups. While the test is not completely devoid of learned concepts, its use to identify reasoning ability is more defensible than use of tests that have a maximum educational loading. Such tests have a built-in bias.

While the homogeneous "g" factor content of the Raven's test makes it useful in the above setting, the homogeneous content imposes limitations on the criterion validity of the test. Recall that criterion validity is generally higher when item intercorrelations are low—when different abilities are incorporated into the test. Since the Raven's test tends to focus on a single construct, the items will tend to have high correlation, and the test will generally have a lower criterion validity. We can suggest that the Raven's test has high construct validity, but will probably be somewhat restricted in criterion validity. Also, to the degree that the criterion is culturally biased, the test will probably not correlate as highly with the criterion performance as a test that reflects those biases. Nevertheless, its highly specialized characteristics make it useful in a variety of specialized settings.

School and College Ability Test

In his original work, Thurstone (1936) suggested eight primary mental abilities (see Chapter 8). Later, as additional tests were added, additional factors were defined. However, just a few of these many factors have had significant practical applications. Vernon (1950, p. 171), in reviewing the work of the primary ability theorists, suggested that the verbal, reasoning, numerical, and spatial primaries should provide a common base for British-American research activity. Similarly, McNemar (1964) pointed to the proliferation of primary factors, and suggested that only numerical and verbal factors provide significant information above and beyond a measure of general mental ability. Many criterion validity studies support these statements, and, as a result, many intelligence tests constructed in this country include only vocabulary and quantitative (or numerical) information.[3] The School and College Ability Test (SCAT) was selected for inclusion in this discussion because of the test's commitment to the measurement of school-learned abilities. Thus, it tends to be opposite the Raven's test on the intelligence continuum. Consider the following statement from the SCAT (1957) technical manual:

[3]The term *verbal*, in psychological measurement, is often synonymous with the term *vocabulary*. However, sometimes the meaning of *verbal* is more general and refers also to language concepts. When verbal is used in conjunction with the hierarchical theory of intelligence, the "language concepts" definition is appropriate; when referring to primary abilities, the term usually is synonymous with "vocabulary"; and when referring to a test, either definition might be appropriate. A "verbal" test might be a vocabulary test, or might focus on more general language concepts.

In considering the general purpose of the SCAT series . . . , the Advisory Committee recommended strongly that the new tests should measure "school-learned abilities" directly, rather than psychological characteristics or traits which afford indirect measurement of capacity for school learning [p. 5].

The manual suggests that the best single predictor of next year's academic performance is how well an individual succeeds this year. Thus, the test samples this year's learning to predict next year's performance. While criterion validity appears to be of secondary importance to construct validity for the Raven's test, what is important for the SCAT is the correlation with academic grade point average. Since verbal and mathematical materials are necessary to affect criterion validity, content validity is also of importance.

An updated version of the test is SCAT Series II (1967). The *Handbook* indicates that the relatively homogeneous content of the verbal and quantitative subtests yields internal consistency estimates of between .87 and .92 for these separate subtests. Also, the two subtests yield intercorrelations ranging from .68 at grade 5 to .76 at grade 12. The reasonably high reliabilities and somewhat lower inter-correlation between subtests also support the verbal-quantitative distinction. Figure 9.3 presents this distinction in graphic form. The squared correlation between the two different variables ($.68^2 = .46$) indicates that about 46 percent of the variance is due to some factor common to the two tests, perhaps "g." Accordingly, the mathematical and verbal subtests each yield 44 percent specific variation. Forty-four percent of the variation of the mathematical subtest is reliably measured and distinct from that of the verbal subtest. This empirical relationship between subtests provides additional support for the specifications of a mathematical and a verbal construct.

The validity of a test is defined as the extent to which a test measures what it is supposed to measure. According to the SCAT Series II *Handbook* (1967, p. 41),

Figure 9.3   Graphic Representation of the Variance Components of the SCAT for Fifth-Grade Students

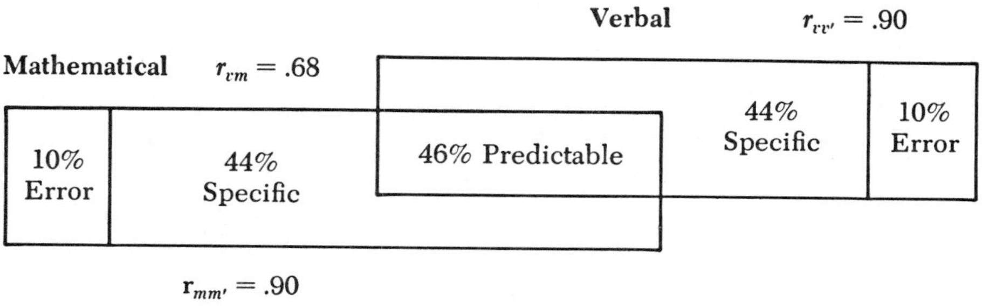

Data source: *SCAT Series II Handbook,* 1967, p. 42.

Table 9.1 Average Correlations Between SCAT Series II Scores and Academic Performance

	Grade 5			Grade 8			Grade 11			Grade 12		
	Avg. r	Avg. r ±1 S.D.	Number of Schools	Avg. r	Avg. r ±1 S.D.	Number of Schools	Avg. r	Avg. r ±1 S.D.	Number of Schools	Avg. r	Avg. r ±1 S.D.	Number of Schools
SCAT Series II-V vs. English Comp. grade	.54	(.23–.76)	5	.52	(.21–.73)	8	.50	(.42–.57)	2	.41	(.18–.59)	8
SCAT Series II-V vs. English grade[*]	.69	(.54–.78)	5	.52	(.29–.69)	8	.52	(.34–.66)	7	.46	(.27–.60)	23
SCAT Series II-M vs. Mathematics grade	.58	(.41–.71)	9	.61	(.41–.76)	12	.65	(.63–.68)	3	.43	(.30–.54)	7
SCAT Series II-T vs. Grade Point Average	.68	(.58–.76)	5	.59	(.30–.77)	11	.65	(.32–.84)	8	.59	(.45–.70)	26

[*]English Composition and English Literature combined.
Source: SCAT Series II Handbook, 1967, p. 42.

SCAT measures the ability to succeed in future academic work. Thus, the most important aspect of the test validation is criterion validity, the criterion being a measure of academic success, such as grade point average. Table 9.1 presents the average correlation of SCAT subtests with school grades. The correlation of .68 between the composite test score (T) and grades indicates that the test accounts for as much as 46 percent of the criterion variation, and attests to the success of SCAT in meeting its major goal—the prediction of academic success. Also, the stability reliability of the test over the period in question must be at least .46. That is, the stable variation from the time of testing until the time at which the criterion data are gathered is 46 percent of the total test variation.

Since the focus of the SCAT is on the measurement of school-learned abilities, it is apparent why this test was selected to be opposite the Raven's test on the intelligence continuum. It would be incorrect to infer that all variation in the Raven's test is due to inherited abilities, or that all variation in the SCAT is due to learned abilities. While all systematic variation in the Raven's test is not due to heredity, a relative emphasis is implied.

California Test of Mental Maturity

A third group test of general ability, which lies somewhere between the Raven's and the SCAT on the intelligence test continuum and offers considerable contrast to them, is the California Test of Mental Maturity (CTMM). We previously discussed the importance of the verbal, reasoning, numerical, and spatial factors. The CTMM tends to measure these factors. While not factorially defined, the content of the CTMM is similar to the content of the corresponding primaries.

The CTMM includes four relatively independent subtests that have been rescaled to have a mean of 100 and a standard deviation of 16. The four subtest scores can be displayed graphically to yield an ability profile. An ability profile is a graphical representation of a set of scores so organized that the relative positions of the scores can be identified. Of course, this requires a linear transformation of the scores common to all of the subtests. The test profile can be utilized to indicate an individual's ability scores in terms of elevation and configuration. Elevation indicates whether abilities tend to be high, medium, or low. Configuration indicates whether an individual scores high on one subtest and low on another. Figure 9.4 presents the profile of three individuals: A, B, and C. Individuals A and B differ in elevation; B and C differ in configuration.

While the CTMM can be scored to reflect the verbal, numerical, reasoning, and spatial primaries, it actually consists of seven subtests: a single verbal test, and two spatial, two reasoning, and two numerical tests. These seven subtests can be combined to yield various types of measures. In Table 9.2, the seven subtests are variously grouped to yield six measures: spatial relationships, logical

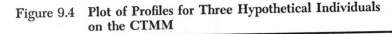

Figure 9.4 **Plot of Profiles for Three Hypothetical Individuals on the CTMM**

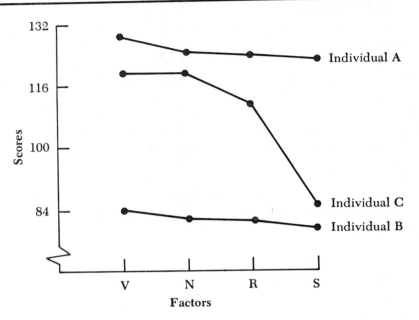

reasoning, numerical reasoning, verbal concepts, language ability, and non-language ability. The entries on the diagonal in this table are split-half reliability estimates. The underlying theoretical structure for the first four factors in Table 9.2 comes from primary mental abilities theory. The language and nonlanguage measures tend to reflect the verbal-performance distinction. Of the seven sub-tests in the CTMM, the three subtests that are highly influenced by schooling form the language group: Inference, Numerical Quantity, and Verbal Concepts. The four subtests less systematically influenced by schooling form the nonlanguage grouping: Sensing Right and Left, Manipulation of Areas, Similarities, and

Table 9.2 **Intercorrelation of Various Subtest Groupings for the CTMM**

	SR	LR	NR	VC	Lang.	Nonlang.
Spatial Relationships	.86	.26	.32	.17	.21	.72
Logical Reasoning		.86	.49	.38	.59	.55
Numerical Reasoning			.89	.46	.53	.58
Verbal Concepts				.90	.85	.35
Language ability					.94	.52
Nonlanguage ability						.87

Source: *California Test of Mental Maturity Manual,* 1957, pp. 5, 6.

Number Series. The nonlanguage subtests are embedded in pictorial or numerical content for which reading is minimized. Figure 9.5 shows the test profile of the CTMM with this grouping of the subtests.

Consider Table 9.2 again. Since both spatial relationships subtests are included in the nonlanguage grouping, the relatively high correlation of .72 between spatial and nonlanguage scores results. Similarly, the fact that no spatial relationships subtests are included in the language grouping accounts for the low correlation of .21 between the spatial and language scores. The 4 percent predictable variance can be explained by the common element of reasoning required in each.

The logical reasoning factor consists of two subtests, one pictorial (Similarities) and one verbal (Inference). The pictorial subtest is included in the nonlanguage score, while the verbal subtest is included in the language score. Thus, we see why logical reasoning correlates with both the language and nonlanguage scores. Numerical reasoning consists of the Number Series and Numerical Quantity

Figure 9.5   Breakdown of the Subtests of the CTMM into Primary Abilities, Language, and Nonlanguage Scores

			Examinee's Score	
Factor	Test	Possible Score	Language	Non-language
Spatial Relationships	1. Sensing Right and Left	20		☐
	2. Manipulation of Areas	15		☐
	Total (1 + 2) ☐	35		
Logical Reasoning	3. Similarities	15		☐
	4. Inference	15	☐	
	Total (3 + 4) ☐	30		
Numerical Reasoning	5. Number Series	15		☐
	6. Numerical Quantity	15	☐	
	Total (5 + 6) ☐	30		
Verbal Concepts	7. Verbal Concepts	50	☐	
	Total (7) ☐	50	—	
	Language Data	80	☐	
	Mental Age			
	Non-Language Data	65		☐
	Chronological Age (Average Grade Placement Equivalent)		☐	
	Intell. (M.A.) Grade Placement		☐	

From: California Short-Form Test of Mental Maturity, Advanced (Grades 10 to Adult), '57 S-Form.

(story) subtests that are divided to obtain nonlanguage and language scores, respectively. Additionally, the Verbal Concepts subtest, which is highly affected by culture and education, is part of the language score.

Consider the split-half reliability estimates in the diagonals of the matrix in Table 9.2. First, it should be noted that these estimates are based on data gathered from grades 9 through 12. For any one of these grades, group dispersion would probably be lower, resulting in slightly lower coefficients due to the restricted range of talent (see Chapter 5). Also, the reliability estimate of the language score is relatively higher than the estimates of its component scores. As the Inference, Numerical Quantity, and Verbal Concepts subtests are combined, to the degree that the items correlate, the lengthened test increases in reliability. This also occurs for the nonlanguage score. The low intercorrelation (.52) between the language and nonlanguage scores, along with relatively high reliability estimates, provides support for the grouping of the subtests into these two categories.

The practical uses of the CTMM are numerous. First, a profile of scores can be plotted to indicate strengths and weakness in individual or group abilities. The test can be used as a screening device to identify exceptional children. Next, one might look at differences in language and nonlanguage scores for diagnostic clues for a given individual. The nonlanguage section can serve a useful purpose when it is desirable to have a score that is less influenced by cultural biases than a highly verbal test. Finally, all scores on the test can be used to provide clues about academic and vocational success.

Two other tests are exceptionally noteworthy for prediction of academic and vocational success. These differential aptitude tests are briefly considered later in the chapter.

Distinctions Between Types of Tests

In Chapters 6 and 7, criterion, content, and construct validity were discussed as aspects of the total validation of any test. Now, we shall distinguish between achievement, ability, and aptitude tests by focusing on test validity.

Recall that the purpose of testing dictates which aspect(s) of validity is of greatest importance. It follows that if the primary purpose of testing is to assess learning, content validity is of primary consideration, and tests are referred to as achievement tests. When the primary purpose of testing is to predict human behavior, criterion validity is of major importance, and the tests are often called aptitude tests. When the primary purpose of testing is to assess present abilities, construct validity is of major importance, and the tests are called ability tests, intelligence tests, etc. Since all tests reflect at least a degree of learning, they are, in some sense, achievement tests. Correspondingly, since all tests tend to reflect constructs of varying degrees of sophistication, they are, to some degree, ability tests. Finally, to the degree that tests are used to predict behavior, they are aptitude tests. Thus, the distinction between achievement, ability, or aptitude tests is highly related to the primary purpose for which the test was developed. Figure 9.6 depicts the difference between achievement, ability, and aptitude tests.

To emphasize the relationship of the purpose to the type of test, while the *same item* can often be used in a test of achievement, ability, or aptitude, it is the format of the test, and some slightly differing content, that classifies it as an achievement, ability, or aptitude test. As an example, an intelligence test might include items representing various cognitive abilities that yield a single measure of general ability. An achievement test, however, has the same or similar items organized into subtests, their content usually reflecting the school curriculum. While achievement, ability, and aptitude tests do measure slightly different content, the similarity in content is much greater than the difference. The greatest

Figure 9.6 Diagram Depicting Differences Between Achievement, Ability, and Aptitude Tests, as a Function of the Major Purpose for which Each Was Designed

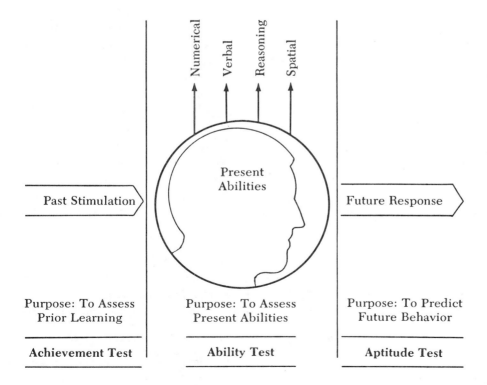

185

distinction between the tests is not in differing content and process, but rather in the purpose to which the test is put, and the format this purpose dictates. Having given some consideration previously to ability tests, let us now consider those tests whose major purpose lies in prediction of future performance.

> When the major purpose for which the test was designed is the assessment of prior learning, content validity is of major importance, and the tests are referred to as achievement tests.
>
> When the major purpose for which the test was designed is the assessment of psychological abilities, construct validity is of major importance, and the tests are typically referred to as ability tests.
>
> When the major purpose for which the test was designed is the prediction of behavior, criterion validity is of greatest importance, and the tests are typically referred to as aptitude tests.

Tests of Differential Aptitudes

The Differential Aptitude Test (DAT) consists of eight subtests: Verbal, Spelling, Sentences, Numerical, Abstract Reasoning, Spatial, Mechanical, and Clerical. While the names and content of the subtests are generally patterned after primary mental abilities research, additional information can be gleaned from hierarchical abilities research. Note that the first five subtests above are related to the verbal-educational major group factor. Similarly, the Spatial, Mechanical, and Clerical subtests, by the nature of their content, tend to be related to the spatial-mechanical group factor. Thus, the test content has a slightly greater involvement with the verbal-educational factors. Figure 9.7 depicts this interpretation of the construct validity of the DAT.[4] Since the DAT is used primarily for counseling high school students, the above "mix" is highly appropriate. The emphasis on school-learned abilities is useful for predicting success in college. Similarly, the Spatial, Mechanical, and Clerical subtests give information about important, less verbal primaries. This nonlanguage information is valuable in counseling people into technical curricula or jobs.

By way of contrast, the General Aptitude Test Battery (GATB) is a differential aptitude test that has a greater involvement with the spatial-mechanical abilities. The GATB consists of the following nine subtests: General, Verbal, Numerical, Spatial, Form Perception, Clerical Perception, Motor Coordination, Finger Dexterity, and Manual Dexterity. The GATB test was developed for use by the

---

[4]While this interpretation clarifies the construct validity of the DAT, it must be emphasized that the DAT is organized into a number of relatively large factors in the Thurstone tradition rather than in scales of graduated importance as in hierarchical theory. The diagram indicates only the greater "verbal" involvement of the DAT.

United States Employment Service in assisting people to find jobs. It was also influenced by Thurstone's work on primary mental abilities. In terms of our knowledge of the hierarchical model, three subtests might be classified as verbal-educational, while the remaining six subtests are spatial-mechanical. Thus, a greater spatial-mechanical component is found in the subtests of the GATB, and a greater verbal-educational component in the DAT. Table 9.3 presents a matrix of correlations of the DAT and GATB subtests. The intercorrelations of the DAT and GATB subtests indicate that, while the general and verbal scales of the GATB correlate moderately with all subtests of the DAT except clerical, the perception and performance subtests (P, Q, F, K, and M) are relatively specific. The global nature of the GATB-G subtest as an index of intelligence is roughly confirmed by the consistently high correlations with the other seven DAT subtests.

Summarizing our discussion of tests of differential aptitudes, the major focus of these tests is to predict future performance. We considered two such tests: the DAT is a highly verbal test designed to counsel college-bound high school graduates; the GATB is a more performance-oriented test designed to assist adults in job placement. Thus, the purpose for the test exerts a great deal of influence over the type and the character of the subtests.

Figure 9.7   Schematic Representation of the Content of the DAT from the Viewpoint of Hierarchical Theory

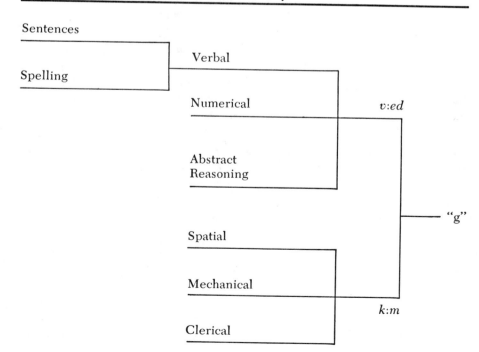

Table 9.3 Correlations Between DAT and GATB Subtests

DAT Subtests	GATB Subtests								
	General (G)	Verbal (V)	Numerical (N)	Spatial (S)	Form Perception (P)	Clerical Perception (Q)	Motor Coordination (F)	Finger Dexterity (K)	Manual Dexterity (M)
Verbal	.78/.72	.72/.68	.54/.49	.54/.47	.21/.21	.41/.24	.29/.08	.20/.17	−.03/−.04
Numerical	.66/.53	.52/.33	.62/.51	.32/.28	.01/.03	.22/.22	.27/−.04	.13/.25	.05/.20
Abstract Reasoning	.68/.57	.48/.30	.45/.38	.56/.52	.14/.25	.26/.18	.21/−.03	.17/.18	.00/.05
Spatial	.59/.52	.49/.29	.24/.26	.72/.66	.21/.44	.22/.20	.19/.15	.35/.30	.11/.18
Mechanical	.62/.43	.56/.25	.25/.26	.68/.41	.13/.16	.09/.04	.24/.01	.39/.16	.08/.23
Clerical	.25/.15	.18/.05	.33/.34	.07/.06	.46/.43	.53/.59	.61/.38	.27/.27	.46/.29
Spelling	.66/.59	.66/.59	.57/.59	.21/.21	.03/.12	.51/.52	.32/.18	.08/.18	.10/.16
Sentences	.74/.62	.75/.68	.56/.43	.36/.26	.05/.10	.33/.28	.33/.16	.17/.11	.12/.03

Values to the left of the diagonal are for males, and those to the right of the diagonal are for females.

Source: Bennett, Seashore, & Wesman, 1959, p. 73. Reproduced by permission. Copyright 1947, 1952, © 1959 by The Psychological Corporation, New York, N.Y. All rights reserved.

Individual Tests of General Mental Ability

The Stanford-Binet Test

Around the turn of the century, Alfred Binet set about studying a wide variety of tasks in an effort to develop an intelligence test that would discriminate "bright" from "dull" children. While many of his contemporaries were investigating simple sensory relationships, Binet began to focus on tasks that required more complex cognitive functioning. Binet and Simon (1916, p. 192) defined intelligence as "the capacity to judge well, to reason well, and to comprehend well." In 1904, Binet was commissioned by Paris school officials to develop a test that could be used to discriminate mental retardates from normal children. Today, based upon this earlier effort, we have the much-modified Stanford-Binet test (S-B), which was developed in this country. This section will describe the construction of the earlier test, and thus indicate some of the principles underlying the development of this well-known "standard" of intelligence testing.

Several criteria were associated with the selection of items for the Binet test. First, items were selected that met the stated definition of intelligence. To the degree that the items had comprehending, judging, and reasoning in common, the items should develop low but significant correlations. The low correlations would indicate that the items were measuring different functions to a large extent, but still retained a common "general" function.

Another criterion for selecting Binet items was that, to a point, older people have a greater tendency to pass a given item than younger people. Thus, groups of items could be developed that were appropriate for a typical chronological age. In other words, theoretically there should exist items that *no* typical 8-year-old children can pass, about *50 percent* of typical 9-year-old children can pass, and that *all* typical 10-year-old children pass. These items, geared to a particular chronological age (CA), are used to specify a corresponding mental age (MA). If the items are well selected, all typical 8-year-old children will fail the item, while all typical 10-year-old children will pass the item. Thus, the S-B can be compared to a stairway in which each of the steps is a mental age level.

In the construction of the later versions of the S-B, there were six items, and 2 months of mental age for each item at each mental age level. The individual with a mental age of 9, regardless of chronological age, should tend to pass items through mental age level 9. Also, she should tend to fail all items at the 10-year age level. The highest mental age level at or below which all items are passed is referred to as the *basal age,* while the first level at which the individual fails all items is referred to as the *ceiling.* In scoring the test, an individual is given credit for all months of mental age below her basal age, and generally does not receive credit for months of mental age above her ceiling. Figure 9.8 depicts the

Figure 9.8   A Pictorial Representation of an Individual's Performance on the Stanford-Binet Test (MA of 9 years, 6 months)

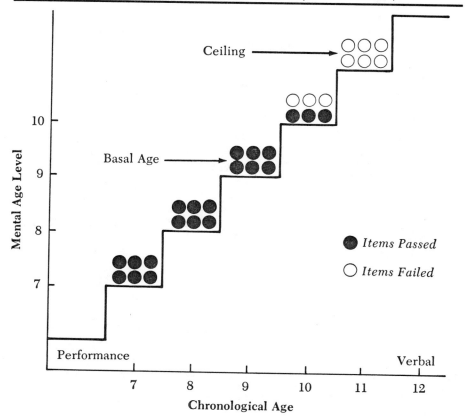

performance of an individual who passed all items through mental age 9, and only three of six items in mental age 10. She failed all items at mental age 11. Thus, with a basal age of 9 and ceiling of 11, her mental age is established as 9 years, 6 months.

One of the results of the empirical approach used in the development of the S-B is that different abilities are measured at different age levels. A small child does not comprehend, judge, and reason in the same mode as an adult. Thus, the abilities identified by the S-B vary through sensorimotor, performance, and verbal abilities. A factor analytic study of longitudinal test data by Hofstaetter (1954) confirms that what is measured by intelligence tests changes from early childhood to the mature adult level. Figure 9.9 presents the results of this study. The very young child is tested on his ability to make sensorimotor discriminations. Later, reasoning is sampled by rather concrete performance-type tasks. Finally, in the maturing adult, the focus is on verbal ability. Thus, the instability found in early intelligence scores as shown in Table 4.2, can be attributed, at least in part, to a changing definition of intelligence. The verbal-performance distinction on the baseline of Figure 9.8 reflects this changing definition.

Figure 9.9   **Plot of the Factors to Show the Changing Sources of Variation in the Composition of Mental Tests**

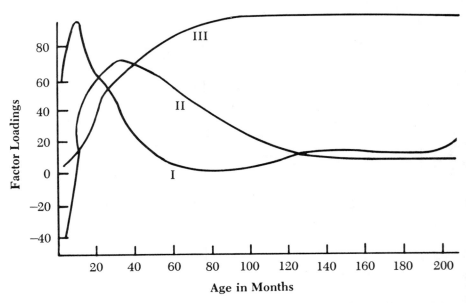

Source: Hofstaetter, 1954, p. 161. Reprinted by permission of the author and *The Journal of Genetic Psychology.* This interpretation of the factors is ours. Hofstaetter referred to the factors as: Sensorimotor Alertness (I), Persistence (II), and Provisional Action (Abstract Behavior) (III).

Let us review a number of the characterizations associated with the development of the S-B test.

1. The S-B test can be conceptualized as a stairway with each step representing a different mental age.

2. Items were selected for each age level by difficulty and discriminability. Difficulty means that items were found that individuals from a given chronological age level could pass. Discriminability means that while the items are about right for one level, they are too difficult for the adjacent lower level, and too easy for the adjacent higher level.

3. Items were selected that measure the cognitive processes of comprehending, reasoning, and judging well. Items that appeared to meet this definition, that had low, but positive, intercorrelation, and that met the above criteria for establishing a mental age level were selected for use. Items that have low positive intercorrelations contain a "general" factor, yet measure other complex functions.

4. While the S-B test samples similar, yet different, abilities at each age level, slightly different abilities are sampled across different age levels. At the older levels, the focus of measurement is on school-learned "verbal" abilities, as opposed to "performance" abilities at the younger level.

The Intelligence Quotient. After the Binet test was brought to this country, an additional index for quantifying test performance was soon developed. This index has come to be known as the *intelligence quotient* or IQ. More specifically, this index is referred to as a *ratio IQ*, since the ratio of mental age to chronological age reflects a unique way of reporting test performance. The average 9-year-old should have a mental age of 9 years. If so, the ratio of MA/CA, multiplied by 100 is 100. The 12-year-old (CA) with average intelligence (MA = 12) also has an intelligence quotient of 100. Thus, the individual whose mental age development lags behind his chronological age would have an intelligence quotient of less than 100, and correspondingly, the individual with a mental age exceeding chronological age would have an intelligence quotient in excess of 100. Thus,

$$IQ = \frac{\text{Mental Age (Months)}}{\text{Chronological Age (Months)}} \times 100. \qquad (9.1)$$

In Figure 9.8, the child passed all items through mental age level 9, and three items from mental age level 10. While her chronological age (9 years) was 108 months, her mental age was 114 months. Therefore, her ratio IQ is 106.

While the ratio IQ is a useful index for comparing performances across age levels, certain problems were recognized quickly. While chronological age continues to increase, studies of the development of mental age show a "plateauing" around ages 14 to 18. The point at which a given individual's plateau is reached is obviously a function of many factors, such as early childhood experiences, genetic factors, and amount of schooling. The fact remains that IQ computed by the above method would decrease after about age 18, despite a relative stability in items answered correctly—the mental age.

Piaget suggests that as an individual progresses through school, he increasingly develops the ability to internalize abstract symbols. In the S-B, these symbols are used to determine if the individual judges well, reasons well, and comprehends well. When individuals leave school, they begin to internalize other, less formal concepts—they concentrate on their jobs. For many people, this means the end of formal verbal and numerical training, and their scores begin to plateau or even drop slightly. It follows that the IQ score of an 18-year-old is a function of both how fast or slow he learned (genetic factors), the kinds of training received (environment), and the interaction of the two. What is important here is that the *average* human appears to develop in mental age until approximately age 18, which, not surprisingly, is roughly the time the average member of our society terminates his schooling. Thus, the educational enterprise can be thought of as a period in which learning sets reflecting cultural abstractions are internalized. As the child gets older, the learning sets become more highly specialized and internalized. Also, an increasing cultural bias is reflected in the internalization of verbal and numerical content. Finally, our measures of intelligence increasingly reflect these learned cultural abstractions. This is more obvious for tests at the environmental extreme of the intelligence continuum than at the hereditary extreme.

Cattell's (1968) suggestion that there are two components in the spectrum of intelligence tests is particularly appropriate here. He distinguished between *crystallized* and *fluid* intelligence, and suggested that they reflect essentially learned and inherited abilities, respectively. When the crystallized or learned abilities of adults are studied, the pattern indicates that these learning sets are relatively stable over time (Figure 9.10b). On the other hand, when the primarily inherited or fluid abilities are tested over time, a relative increase and then a decline with age is observed (Figure 9.10a). In the traditional intelligence test, the crystallized and fluid components are confounded, or mixed together, resulting in a measure that shows an apparent growth and then a decline in intelligence (Figure 9.10c). Thus, the ratio IQ becomes increasingly inappropriate as an individual's CA begins to exceed the point at which the MA begins to plateau or even to decline. This CA is about 20 years, according to the Cattell data.

Consider another example. An individual with an MA of 20 years and a CA of 18 years would have a ratio IQ of about 110. The same individual, assuming stability in the MA, would have a ratio IQ of 100 at a CA of 20, and at CA 22, his ratio IQ would be 91, despite the fact that no change in performance occurred.

It becomes obvious that a better index is required, especially for young adults. This index was furnished with the development of the Wechsler Adult Intelligence Scale (Wechsler, 1955, pp. 2–3), and is referred to as the *deviation IQ*. In discussing transformations in Chapter 3, we suggested that to change a set of scores with a given mean and standard deviation to a set with a new mean and new standard deviation, we simply multiplied the z-scores by the desired new standard deviation, and added the desired new mean. This principle was used to develop the deviation IQ.

Figure 9.10 **Patterns for Fluid and Crystallized General Ability Performance for Various Ages**

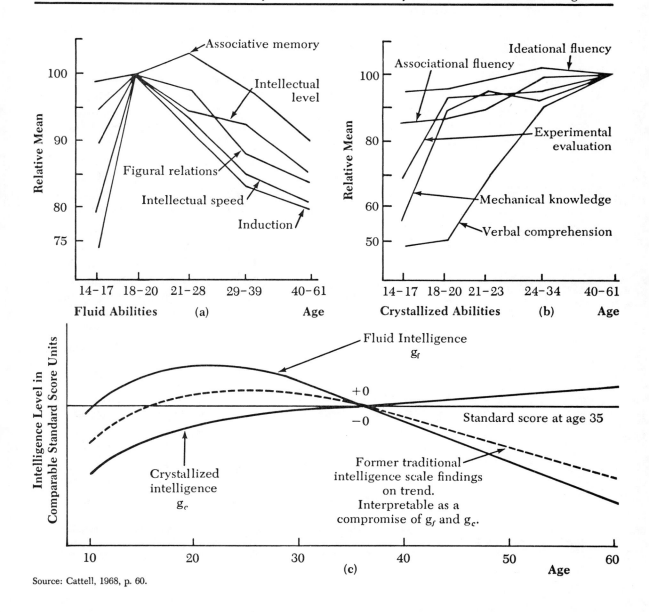

Source: Cattell, 1968, p. 60.

We have observed that mental age is relatively stable over large periods of time after about chronological age 18. If all individuals of age 18 to 25 are considered as a reference group with a defined mean and standard deviation, it is possible to convert their scores to z-scores, multiply these scores by 15, and add 100.[5] The result is a norm group for which the mean is 100 and the standard deviation is 15. Thus, an individual is compared with only those people in the norm group who tend to exhibit a somewhat similar degree of stability. Also, as individuals age, their performances are contrasted with individuals undergoing somewhat similar experiences and with a similar age. The concept of deviation IQ appears to be much more appropriate for adult use for these reasons.

Dispersion and Error of Measurement in the S-B Test. In Chapter 5 we discussed the coefficient of equivalence as an index of the degree of similarity between parallel forms of a test. The S-B test has several forms, and it is appropriate to consider the scatter or dispersion in the bivariate plot of two forms. Figure 9.11 presents the plot of scores for forms L and M of the S-B test.

In Chapters 4 and 5, a theory of test scores was developed in which the standard error of measurement was the average of the standard errors over all individuals. Thus, it was assumed that the errors of measurement were constant for all individuals at all mental ability levels. However, Figure 9.11 shows that while measurement error is relatively constant over the ability midrange, it is larger at the higher levels and smaller at the lower levels. Cronbach (1960, p. 175) suggests that this error is about 2.5 points at the lower level (below 70), 5.0 points through the midrange, and about 6.0 points at the upper levels (above 130). Thus, practitioners using the S-B for individuals from the lower ranges can place greater confidence in it, and can expect the interval necessary to span the true score to be smaller than for individuals at the upper levels. Given a score of 70, we can expect that in two of three testings, the range 67.5 to 72.5 (one standard error of 2.5 on either side of the observed score) will span the true score.

To summarize:

1. The ratio IQ is defined as the ratio of mental age to chronological age, multiplied by 100. The fact that mental age increases in proportionately smaller amounts, while chronological age is constantly increasing, makes the ratio IQ inappropriate for adults.

2. The deviation IQ is found by defining a given age group, converting the scores to z-scores, multiplying by the standard deviation (16 for the S-B), and adding 100. In this way, the individuals in a given group are compared only with those

---

[5]The selection of 15 for a standard deviation and 100 as a mean is, to a large extent, arbitrary. However, it is obvious that the selection of a mean of 100 was influenced by the ratio IQ of 100, both representing "average" performance of some defined group. The standard deviation selected is usually 15 (or 16 in the case of the S-B).

of a somewhat similar chronological age. In terms of the S-B, all individuals in a given range have their scores converted to a standard deviation of 16 and a mean of 100. Thus, despite the fact that the original means and standard deviations differ, after transformation, all groups have means of 100 and standard deviations of 16.

3. When a plot of the bivariate distribution of forms L and M of the S-B is made (Figure 9.11), the measurement error is unequal across the range of general adults. Individuals who score about two standard deviations below the mean seem to manifest very small measurement error. Conversely, individuals who score about two standard deviations above the mean manifest greater measurement error.

4. In addition to the fluctuation in the size of the error of measurement, the distribution of error appears to be skewed toward the mean of the ability continuum. This phenomenon can be explained partially by the regression effect.

Figure 9.11 **IQ's Obtained by 7-year-olds When Tested on Two Forms of the Stanford-Binet**

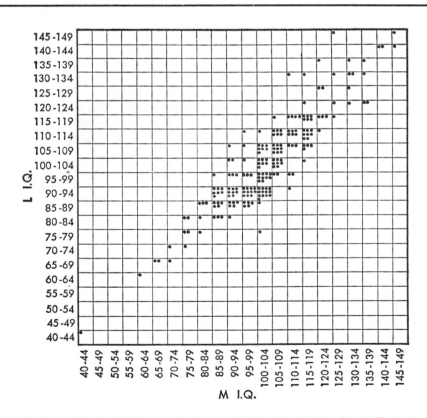

Source: L. Terman & M. Merrill, *Measuring Intelligence*, p. 11. Copyright 1960, Houghton Mifflin Co., Boston. Reprinted by permission of the publisher.

Individuals who score two standard deviations above or below the mean on the original test can be considered to have error in their favor or against them, respectively. On the second administration, due to the random nature of error, the scores will appear closer to the mean. This is the regression effect; that is, a tendency of extreme scores to regress toward the mean on retesting.

The Wechsler Scales

Earlier in this chapter, we discussed group tests that consisted of a number of relatively homogeneous subtests, and indicated how various group tests were designed to reflect psychological theories of intelligence. The Stanford-Binet test is an individualized intelligence test that yields a single global measure. However, we pointed out the verbal-performance distinction by indicating that the Stanford-Binet test became less performance-oriented and more verbally oriented as subjects approached maturity. With the Wechsler Scales, we have individualized instruments that yield both a verbal and a performance score at all levels. There are presently three such scales, one for adults and two for children. In our discussion, we will consider only the Wechsler Adult Intelligence Scale (WAIS). This section will illustrate the exemplary norming procedure, and focus on the construct validity of the test.

Norms for the Wechsler Scales.[6] The normative group on which the WAIS was based was designed to represent as closely as possible the U.S. adult population. The WAIS normative group consisted of a nationwide sample of 1,700 adults. Based on the 1950 census, 18 testing centers were established throughout the United States. A stratified sampling plan was adopted, and the following stratification variables were incorporated into that plan:

1. Age: Norms were developed for each of seven age groups from 16 to 24 years. (Recall the earlier discussion of deviation IQ.)

2. Sex: Equal numbers of men and women were included in each age group.

3. Geographic region: The country was divided into the four major divisions specified in the census report, and subjects were sampled in proportion to their population.

4. Urban-rural residence: An urban area was defined as a community of greater than 2,500 inhabitants. Subjects were sampled in proportion to those listed in the population census reports.

[6]This material was abstracted from Wechsler, 1955, pp. 5–11.

5. Race (white-nonwhite): The sample included whites and nonwhites in proportion to the census reports.

6. Occupation: The sample included subjects from 13 job classifications according to their proportion in the census reports.

7. Education: Subjects were sampled according to five education levels, and in proportion to their incidence in the census reports.

Thus, the norming of the WAIS was a highly technical and well-developed effort. Every attempt was made to make the normative group representative of the population.

Rationale and Subtests. The WAIS test was an extension and modification of the previously developed Wechsler-Bellevue Scales. The WAIS was developed to provide a technically more appropriate and better-normed clinical instrument. As such, the following subtests were grouped and included as verbal or performance scales:

Verbal Scale

1. *Information:* This test covers a wide range of items of a highly general nature. The items reflect the type of content that most individuals in our culture have had the opportunity to assimilate. It is expected that the range of assimilated information reflects a given individual's intellectual capabilities.

2. *Comprehension:* This test consists of problem situations and is designed to elicit comprehension, evaluation, and practical problem-solving activity.

3. *Arithmetic:* This test covers arithmetic skills that are of elementary school level. Arithmetic items are widely used in tests of general ability, and are typically referred to as quantitative or numerical ability items.

4. *Similarities:* The subject is required to indicate how a pair of words are similar. Thus, the focus is on specifying relationships between verbally oriented materials.

5. *Digit Span:* The subject is required to repeat three to nine digits forward and two to eight digits backward. The test is similar to what factor analytic studies have identified as Span Memory. While memory factors fail to correlate with other primaries and thus are poor indicators of intelligence, the inability to retain digits for short periods assists in clinical diagnosis.

6. *Vocabulary:* This subtest consists of 40 items of increasing difficulty in which the S must define the word meaning. This subtest corresponds to the verbal primary identified by Thurstone.

Performance Scale

7. *Digit Symbol:* This is a code-substitution subtest in which the S is shown

nine divided boxes. In the upper half of the box is a digit, in the lower half a symbol. The S is required to respond to given digits with the appropriate symbol.

8. *Picture Completion:* This is a sequence of cards in which the S must respond to incomplete detail in the picture.

9. *Block Design:* This subtest consists of nine colored cubes with which the S copies ten given designs. Two sides of each cube are red, two sides are white, and two sides are diagonally divided into both red and white.

10. *Picture Arrangement:* This is a picture-story sequence. A series of dis-arranged pictures is presented to the S who is required to order them into a sequence to tell a story.

11. *Object Assembly:* The S is required to reconstruct complete figures from figures that have been cut into several parts.

It was Wechsler who pioneered the deviation IQ concept. As a result, the WAIS yields Full Scale, Performance, and Verbal scores, which are linearly transformed (as discussed in Chapter 3) to yield means of 100 and standard deviations of 15. The shorter subtests are transformed to yield scores with means of 10 and standard deviations of 3. This transformation allows direct comparison from one subtest score to the next. Table 9.4 presents the matrix of WAIS subtest intercorrelations for 200 males and females, age 18–19. Reliability estimates are shown in the diagonal entries.

A brief study of the subtest intercorrelations of the WAIS quickly reveals that some subtest intercorrelations are extraordinarily high. The result, of course, challenges the relative independence of the scales. Looking at the subtest correlations and reliabilities, we ascertain that while 59 percent of the variation in verbal scores can be predicted from performance scores, the high subtest reliabilities allow for significant components of specific variation. In this case, the specific variation is estimated to be 37 and 34 percent for the Verbal and Performance scales, respectively. Thus, we have a modest degree of specific variation upon which to base our inferences about differences in verbal and performance abilities. A similar analysis can be undertaken to determine if any pair of WAIS subtests have significant sources of specific variation.

What basic abilities, then, does the WAIS measure? A factor analytic study of the WAIS should shed some light on the problem.[7] Table 9.5 presents a factor matrix of the WAIS subtests. A study of the factor matrix indicates that the first factor is a general-verbal factor. That is, all tests with a higher verbal saturation have a relatively high loading on that factor. The second factor is a group-performance factor. The inclusion of the Digit Symbol subtest in the performance scale is not confirmed. The validity of the verbal-performance distinction is at

[7]Numerous factor analyses of the Wechsler Scales have been done; see, for example, Davis, 1956. The factors found in some studies have been quite different from the subtests as organized.

Table 9.4 Matrix of Intercorrelations

	Information	Comprehension	Arithmetic	Similarities	Digit Span	Vocabulary	Digit Symbol	Picture Completion	Block Design	Picture Arrangement	Object Assembly	Verbal Score	Performance Score
Information	.91	.71	.64	.76	.54	.81	.65	.64	.60	.59	.54	.83	.75
Comprehension	.71	.79	.59	.65	.48	.71	.54	.53	.47	.49	.42	.74	.61
Arithmetic	.64	.59	.79	.62	.52	.64	.50	.50	.52	.44	.45	.71	.60
Similarities	.76	.65	.62	.87	.55	.78	.56	.63	.55	.56	.50	.80	.69
Digit Span	.54	.48	.52	.55	.71	.60	.50	.45	.41	.37	.39	.62	.53
Vocabulary	.81	.71	.64	.78	.60	.94	.64	.62	.56	.55	.48	.86	.70
Digit Symbol	.65	.54	.50	.56	.50	.64	.92	.45	.52	.51	.47	.68	.57
Picture Completion	.64	.53	.50	.63	.45	.62	.45	.82	.69	.60	.62	.67	.72
Block Design	.60	.47	.52	.55	.41	.56	.52	.69	.86	.59	.69	.62	.77
Picture Arrangement	.59	.49	.44	.56	.37	.55	.51	.60	.59	.66	.58	.60	.69
Object Assembly	.54	.42	.45	.50	.39	.48	.47	.62	.69	.58	.65	.55	.72
Verbal Score	.83	.74	.71	.80	.62	.86	.68	.67	.62	.60	.55	.96	.77
Performance Score	.75	.61	.60	.69	.53	.70	.57	.72	.77	.69	.72	.77	.93

Source: Wechsler, 1955, p. 15. Reproduced by permission. Copyright © 1955 by The Psychological Corporation, New York, N.Y. All rights reserved.

Table 9.5 **Factor Matrix for the WAIS**

	I	II
1 Information	.77	.45
2 Comprehension	.78	.27
3 Arithmetic	.72	.31
4 Similarities	.76	.40
5 Digit Span	.72	.18
6 Vocabulary	.84	.36
7 Digit Symbol	.65	.37
8 Picture Completion	.42	.74
9 Block Design	.33	.82
10 Picture Arrangement	.36	.72
11 Object Assembly	.23	.84

This analysis is based on the extraction of two factors from the matrix of Table 9.4.

least partially upheld. The correlation of .77 between the Verbal and Performance scores in Table 9.4 also confirms this distinction.

Often, after administering the WAIS, we wish to determine the difference between the true scores on the subtests. We must decide whether the differences between obtained subtest scores are greater than can be attributed to chance. In other words, how large an obtained score difference between the subtests on the verbal and performance scales must there be before we could infer that there was a difference in the true scores? Using the standard error of difference formula (5.11), we find that the standard error of the difference is approximately 5 points ($15 \sqrt{2 - .96 - .93} = 4.95 \cong 5$). Using the standard normal curve (Appendix A), it requires 1.96 standard deviation units on either side of the mean to include 95 percent of the area. Including 95 percent of the area leaves 2.5 percent in each tail, or 5 percent (5 out of 100). Multiplying 4.95 by 1.96, we get 9.7, so a difference as large as 9.7 could occur by chance only 5 times in 100. This probability of .05 is a commonly used level below which we conclude that the difference did not occur by chance. Thus, a difference of 9.7 or greater between the observed scores would justify the inference of a difference in verbal and performance abilities. That is, we infer that the *true* verbal and performance scores are not the same.

One of the uses of the WAIS is to interpret the profiles resulting from the subtest scores. Any attempt to provide a profile interpretation should begin with determining which subtests are amenable to profile analysis, that is, which subtests have high reliabilities and low intercorrelations. Such a procedure, in combination with difference reliability estimation, eliminates much subjectivity in test interpretation. Thus, we see that questions of reliability, validity, and interpretation are inextricably bound to fundamental psychometric principles.

This chapter has considered the measurement of human abilities from both a theoretical and a practical point of view. We have seen that the measurement of achievement, ability, and aptitude is closely related to the purpose for which the test was designed. Selected ability tests and their relationships to corresponding theories of intelligence were discussed. The S-B and the WAIS were briefly discussed as individual intelligence tests.

This chapter provided a background, both theoretical and practical, on the measurement of human abilities. As specific tests were helpful in illustrating or supporting theory, identifying problems, or providing continuity in the chapter, they were introduced. Of course, any discussion of intelligence testing would be incomplete without the basic testing work of Binet. The student should view this chapter as background to enhance his knowledge of ability measurement in a general way. Numerous other tests could have been discussed to illustrate the various concepts. However, the chapter was not designed to compare tests for test selection. Appropriate references for test selection are generally available in libraries and testing centers.[8]

Summary

Suggested Readings

Bayley, N. Mental development. In C. W. Harris (Ed.), *Encyclopedia of educational research.* New York: Macmillan, 1960, pp. 817–823.

Cattell, R. Are IQ tests intelligent? *Psychology Today,* 1968, March, 56–62.

Harris, C. W. Intelligence. In C. W. Harris (Ed.), *Encyclopedia of educational research.* New York: Macmillan, 1960, pp. 715–718.

Hunt, J. McV. *Intelligence and experience.* New York: Ronald Press, 1961.

McNemar, Q. Lost: Our intelligence? Why? *American Psychologist,* 1964, 9, 871–882.

Mehrens, W., & Lehmann, I. *Standardized tests in education.* New York: Holt, Rinehart & Winston, 1969.

Vernon, P. E. Ability factors and environmental influences. *American Psychologist,* 1965, 20, 723–733.

Wesman, A. Intelligent testing. *American Psychologist,* 1968, 23, 267–274.

Individual Review Questions

1. As individuals approach adulthood, scores on measures of primary mental abilities tend to become increasingly *stable/unstable* with age and experience.

2. According to Piaget's periods of development, the period from 2 years to about 11 years of age is the _____ _____ stage.

ANSWERS
1. stable
2. concrete operations

[8]See, for example, Buros, 1965, and later Mental Measurements Yearbooks.

3. The relative stabilization of the primary mental abilities occurs during Piaget's _____ _____ period.

4. A student is judged to have well-developed writing ability. This ability is_____ from performance on writing tasks.

5. When we infer that an individual has a given ability, our inference is made from _____.

6. An individual approaches the golf ball with an open stance every time he hits the ball from the tee or fairway. This individual has developed a _____.

7. A student begins the solution of problems, whether in mathematics, chemistry, or other content areas, by ordering the given factors and identifying the unknowns. This individual has developed a _____ _____.

8. A distinction between habit and learning set is: for a habit, the individual develops the same response to *different/same* stimuli; while with a learning set, the same response is developed toward *different/same* stimuli.

9. Instructors are attempting to develop within their students a similar approach to solving varying problems. The instructors are attempting to develop a *habit/learning set.*

10. A learning set is an *observable/unobservable* process.

11. With reference to Cattell's continuum of abilities, the ability to apply a learned, logical procedure for the solution of problems is a *crystallized/fluid* ability.

12. In the theory of hierarchical structure, the minor group factors would tend to be *inherited/learned.*

13. Normative data on the Raven's Matrices test indicate that the test has a high loading on the *"g" factor/major group factors/minor group factors.*

14. Performance on the Raven's Matrices test is influenced highly by a *hereditary/learned* component.

15. A student scores poorly on English achievement tests but performs relatively high on the Raven's Matrices test. Such an individual is said to be a(n) _____.

16. The homogeneous content of the Raven's Matrices test tends to *decrease/increase* the criterion validity of the test, and *decrease/increase* the KR-20 reliability estimate.

17. If we were interested in measuring school-learned abilities, the *Raven's Matrices/SCAT* would be our more likely choice of test.

ANSWERS
3. formal operations
4. inferred
5. behavior
6. habit
7. learning set
8. same; different
9. learning set
10. unobservable
11. crystallized
12. learned
13. "g" factor
14. hereditary
15. underachiever
16. decrease; increase
17. SCAT

18. Raven's Matrices test appears to exemplify what Cattell calls *crystallized/fluid* ability, while the CTMM appears to exemplify what is referred to as *crystallized/fluid* ability.

19. Crystallized abilities tend to have a larger _____ component than fluid abilities.

20. Fluid abilities tend to have a larger _____ component than crystallized abilities.

21. For the Raven's Matrices test, as a measure of "g," we would place more importance on *construct/criterion* validity.

22. A test with heterogeneous content can have high criterion _____, and *high/low* internal consistency reliability.

23. A test with homogeneous content can have low criterion validity and *high/low* internal consistency reliability.

24. The intercorrelations of the verbal and mathematical subtest scores of SCAT tend to *decrease/increase* with the increasing age of students being tested.

25. As intercorrelations between subtest scores decrease, we would infer that the primary mental abilities they measure are becoming *less/more* distinct.

26. The correlation between verbal and quantitative subtests for a given group is .60. Therefore, we can infer that the common factor(s) accounts for _____ percent of the variance.

27. A *high/low* correlation between two subtest scores would support the theory of distinct constructs, reflected by performance on the subtests.

28. When considering the major purpose for which SCAT was designed, *construct/criterion* validity is of more importance.

29. A necessary condition for profile analysis is high subtest reliability and _____ subtest correlations. This increases the difference _____ of any two tests.

30. A person taking several different IQ tests can get slightly varying scores because the tests are based on different _____ of intelligence, and because there is an error of _____.

31. The conditions for profile analysis are *high/low* subtest reliabilities, and *high/low* subtest intercorrelations.

32. The above question suggests that the subtests must measure consistently (reliability), and they must measure _____ abilities.

ANSWERS
18. fluid; crystallized
19. learned, or environmental
20. hereditary
21. construct
22. validity; low
23. high
24. decrease
25. more
26. 36
27. low
28. criterion
29. low; reliability
30. theories, or conceptions, or definitions; measurement
31. high; low
32. different

33. A bright person with a bad environmental background might be expected to score slightly *higher/lower* on tests of crystallized intelligence, and slightly *higher/lower* on tests of fluid intelligence.

34. In the CTMM we would expect relatively *high/low* correlation between scores on the language subtest and the spatial reasoning subtest.

35. If we rated the Raven's test, CTMM, and SCAT on a continuum of influence of school learning, the order of the tests from high to low influence would be _____, _____, _____.

36.

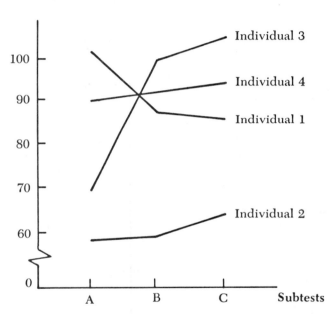

In the profiles shown, Individuals 4 and 2 differ most in *configuration/elevation*, and Individuals 3 and 1 differ most in *configuration/elevation*.

37. In the profiles in question 36, Individuals 2 and 3 differ in *elevation/configuration/ both elevation and configuration*.

38. We would expect that scores on a high level word-meaning subtest would be *markedly/minimally* affected by the formal education of the individual.

39. A teacher is selecting tests to assess achievement in mathematics. The validity of major concern is *construct/content/criterion* validity.

40. A psychologist is testing a group of delinquent underachievers in order to determine their psychological abilities. The validity of major concern is *construct/content/ criterion* validity.

41. Criterion validity assumes major importance when dealing with *ability/achievement/aptitude* tests.

42. The major distinction between tests of ability, achievement, and aptitude comes in the *content/process/purpose* of the test.

43. The content of the DAT is highly *perceptual/verbal* in orientation.

44. If we were making a selection between the DAT and the GATB test batteries, and desired the one least influenced by previous formal education, we would select the _____.

45. The perception and performance subtest scores of the GATB tend to have *high/low* correlations with those of the verbal subtests of the DAT.

46. A counselor at a vocational placement service is to choose between the DAT and the GATB for use with his clients. His most likely choice would be the _____.

47. In the initial selection of Binet test items, performance on a group of items *was/was not* assumed to be dependent on the age of the individual being tested.

48. An individual taking a Binet test passed all the items through mental age 7, passed some of the items for mental ages 8 and 9, and passed no items for mental age 10. For this individual 7 is the _____ age, while 10 is the _____.

49. When using the Stanford-Binet with older children or young adults, the items tend to emphasize *sensorimotor/spatial/verbal* ability.

50. The index of intelligence known as the intelligence quotient, associated with the Binet test, is the ratio of _____ age to _____ age, multiplied by 100.

51. As an individual reaches young adulthood and formal verbal training is terminated, the IQ determined from a Stanford-Binet test would tend to *decrease/increase*.

52. The mental age of the average individual, as indicated by the Stanford-Binet test, tends to stabilize or plateau at about age _____.

53. Performance on tests near the hereditary end of the intelligence continuum would tend to be *less/more* influenced by cultural factors than those near the environmental end.

54. Using Cattell's components in the intelligence spectrum, we would say that crystallized intelligence is to learned abilities as _____ intelligence is to inherited abilities.

55. According to Cattell, as an individual grows older, we would expect the *crystallized/fluid* abilities to show the greater stability.

ANSWERS
41. aptitude
42. purpose
43. verbal
44. GATB
45. low
46. GATB
47. was
48. basal; ceiling
49. verbal
50. mental; chronological
51. decrease
52. 18
53. less
54. fluid
55. crystallized

56. Measurement error in the Stanford-Binet test tends to *decrease/increase* with higher levels of performance.

57. On the WAIS, the deviation IQ transforms all scores to a reference or score distribution with a mean of _____ and a standard deviation of _____.

58. The WAIS was based on a stratified sampling plan for U.S. adults that included seven stratifying variables in the _____ group.

59. The WAIS has eleven subtests grouped into the dichotomy of verbal and _____ scales. The arithmetic subtest is grouped with the _____ scale.

60. Although the Full Scale, Performance, and Verbal scores of the WAIS are transformed to deviation IQ's, the scores on the 11 subtests are transformed to distributions of scores with a mean of _____ and a standard deviation of _____.

61. The factor loading of .37 between the Digit Symbol subtest of the WAIS and the second factor, called a group-performance factor, *supports/fails to support* the contention that the Digit Symbol subtest is primarily a performance rather than a verbal subtest.

62. When attempting to assess prior learning, one is dealing with an *ability/achievement* test.

63. When assessing psychological constructs, one is dealing with an *ability/achievement* test.

64. The primary difference between tests of achievement, aptitude, and ability lies not in their items, but in the _____ for which they were designed.

65. When attempting to predict a specific future performance, one deals with an *achievement/aptitude/ability* test.

Study Exercises

1. Distinguish between intelligence as an entity and intelligence as a construct.
2. Distinguish between a habit and a learning set.
3. Distinguish between crystallized and fluid intelligence.
4. How are the Raven's Progressive Matrices and the School and College Abilities Test related to Cattell's conception of intelligence?
5. Contrast the difference in growth curves for crystallized and fluid intelligence.
6. In terms of the crystallized and fluid distinction, explain why research with the typical American IQ test shows a decline in intelligence at about age 18.
7. Contrast the roles of heredity and environment on tests of crystallized and fluid abilities.
8. Distinguish between verbal and performance abilities. Between language and non-language abilities.
9. Distinguish between achievement, ability, and aptitude tests.

10. Using the factor matrix in Table 9.5:
   a. which of the tests appear to be highly verbal tests?
   b. which of the tests appear to be performance tests?
   c. does the matrix confirm the grouping of the Digit Symbol test as a performance ability?
   d. what is $r_{3,6}$? $r_{9,11}$? $r_{3,9}$? $r_{6,11}$? Given the above r's, do the verbal tests correlate highly with each other? Do the performance tests correlate highly with each other? Is the correlation between verbal and performance tests as high as the correlation between the two verbal tests, and between the two performance tests?

11. Consider the matrices in Tables 9.4 and 9.5.
   a. How much of the Verbal score variation is predictable from the Performance scores?
   b. How much of the Verbal and Performance scores variance is specific? Systematic?
   c. How can you explain the high intercorrelation of Verbal-Performance scores?
   d. Does the WAIS appear to have a larger Verbal or Performance component? Is this consistent with what we would expect to find for a test that purports to measure adult intelligence?
   e. Suppose you did a factor analysis on the Wechsler Preschool and Primary Scales of Intelligence. Would you expect to find a larger Verbal or a larger Performance component? Why?

12. Although the subtests of the WAIS are of different lengths and variability, why is it possible to compare, say, arithmetic subtest scores with verbal scores?

13. Distinguish between ratio and deviation IQ measures. What are the strengths of the deviation IQ?

14. Refer to the matrix in Table 9.3 and Figure 9.7.
   a. Which of the DAT subtests are verbal- and which are performance-oriented? Do the verbal tests of the DAT correlate highly with the verbal tests of the GATB?
   b. Do the verbal tests of the DAT correlate with the performance tests of the GATB?
   c. Does the matrix of Table 9.3 support a verbal-performance dichotomy?

ANSWERS

10. (a) Tests 1 through 6;
   (b) Tests 8 through 11;
   (c) it tends not to;
   (d) $r_{3,6} = .72$, $r_{9,11} = .76$, $r_{3,9} = .49$, $r_{6,11} = .50$; yes; yes; no

11. (a) .59;
   (b) specific verbal = .37, specific performance = .34, systematic verbal = .96, systematic performance = .93;
   (c) the influence of a general factor; (d) larger Verbal component; yes;
   (e) larger Performance component; because intelligence of younger children is generally assessed by studying their performance on nonverbal tasks

14. (a) Verbal subtests: Verbal, Numerical, Abstract Reasoning, Spelling, and Sentences; Performance subtests: Spatial, Mechanical, and Clerical; yes, they tend to correlate;
   (b) the DAT-Verbal subtests tend to have lower correlations with GATB-Performance than with GATB-Verbal;
   (c) yes, it tends to

10 Measurement of Interests and Personality

In the previous chapter, we discussed the tests concerned with the measurement of cognitive abilities. Such tests, to a large extent, are what we have previously referred to as aptitude, ability, or achievement tests. On the other hand, interests and personality characteristics are usually considered to be noncognitive. We characterize such behavior as noncognitive because it is not as clearly a process of perceiving or knowing as the behavior classified as cognitive. In the fields of education and psychology, noncognitive measures are important relative to such questions as: Why do students with high academic ability perform badly in school? What clues can be provided about the interest patterns of a given student? What information can be secured about the personality characteristics of an individual? This chapter will review some of the major interest and personality inventories, and provide basic information about these tests. With this basic information, teachers, counselors, and psychologists can begin to grapple with questions similar to those above.

Measuring Noncognitive Characteristics

There are several problems associated with the measurement of noncognitive characteristics. One is definition. For example, what do we mean by the terms *personality* and *interests*? How are they similar, and how are they different? As we discuss interest and personality measures, we shall attempt to clarify these definitions.

Another problem associated with the measurement of noncognitive characteristics is faking. Interest and personality measures are, for the most part, self-report inventories and, as such, can be falsified. An individual is asked to respond to an item by indicating his preference for activity A or B, for example. Obviously, he can respond by indicating the alternative that is not his preference. Evidence of susceptibility to faking has been found by administering the same measures to subjects on two different occasions, and varying the instructions. On one occasion, the Ss are told to be frank and truthful in their responses, and on the other, they are instructed to respond in what they perceive to be the most socially acceptable manner. In such studies, the median score generally shifts between the two testings.

Suppose that the subjects do fake responses to a personality inventory. Nunnally (1970, p. 369) raised the question of whether this has any effect on the validity of the measures. One possible result of faking could be a shift in the distribution of scores from a distribution of hypothetically valid scores to some other distribution. The means would be somewhat different, and the shape of the distribution might be changed slightly. However, since scores are interpreted in a relative sense, this shift of means might be of little or no consequence. That is, there might be a general tendency for Ss to retain the same rank-order positions in the distributions.

Reliability is also important, as it might be lowered because of faking. Although reliability coefficients of personality and attitude inventories often appear low, this can result from an inadequate number of items. By increasing the number of items, the reliability of personality measures can be increased to a satisfactory point. Nevertheless, it must be recognized that faking is a possibility, and may exist in certain situations.

In an earlier chapter, we mentioned response set, a tendency for an individual to respond in a given way to a group of items. Response set may be a problem in personality and attitude measurement. We may have an individual who tends to respond "yes" or to agree with any difficult or controversial issue. This responding tendency has been called *acquiescence*. Some individuals may tend to be overly cautious, and others to respond in an extreme manner. Royer (1965) evaluated studies related to response sets.

Holtzman (1964) identified one of the problems in personality assessment as separating personality variance from method variance. That is, the traits that emerge are not independent of the methods used to measure them. For instruments administered on a one-to-one basis, the examiner himself becomes a part of the instrument and the interaction between examiner and S becomes a source of variation. Campbell and Fiske (1959) have suggested ways to separate the relative contributions of content and methods. Nevertheless, the problem remains that the measurement of a given personality trait is a function of both the method used and the characteristic assessed.

Other problems are also associated with personality and attitude measures. Measurements may be bound to a given country, culture, or society. There also are moral questions raised with personality assessment, such as invasion of privacy, aftereffects of stressful situations, and confidentiality of information. If such problems arise, they must be given consideration in the specific situation.

Because we cannot neatly resolve these problems at this time is no reason to discontinue the use of the inventories we presently have. Indeed, it is essential that we continue to use and refine our measures in an attempt to resolve the problems. If one understands that a trait does not exist independent of its measurement, one will realize that it is only through striving for more measurement sophistication that clarity can be brought to the study of noncognitive human behavior. That is, the scientific study of noncognitive characteristics can proceed only as rapidly as the measurements of these characteristics are developed.

One purpose of this chapter is to introduce the interesting problem of personality assessment. We will focus on two rather distinct areas of noncognitive measurement: the assessment of interests, and the assessment of personality. Before going into detail about specific instruments, we will consider the reliability and validity of noncognitive measurements.

Reliability and Validity

The reliability and validity of noncognitive measurements are more complex than those of cognitive-ability measurements. In cognitive-ability measurements, the score is a function of ability level, which places somewhat of an upper limit on the score. That is, we test for *maximum* performance. While it is possible for the bright person to fake a low score, it is doubtful whether a low-ability individual could fake a high score. With noncognitive measures, however, we attempt to test an individual's *typical* performance.

In our study of reliability, we distinguished between equivalence, stability, and internal consistency reliability. However, with noncognitive measures, internal consistency reliability becomes a goal to be attained, for internal consistency is a necessary condition for the reliable measurement of a given trait. Also, we may find (or desire to find) less stability reliability than with cognitive-ability measurements. Indeed, if a patient is undergoing therapy, it may be desirable to find that a certain trait is not highly stable, especially when therapy is attempting to change or eliminate the trait. Noncognitive traits tend to stabilize at a slightly slower rate than most cognitive-ability measures.

High equivalence or internal consistency reliability is desirable for noncognitive measures. Stability of the trait being measured may or may not be desirable depending upon the situation.

The validity of noncognitive tests is still concerned with content, criterion, and construct validity. Since the investigation of the noncognitive-behavioral domain is limited by lack of sophistication in measurements, construct validity is highly important. That is, the more clarity brought to the traits being measured, the more sophisticated and definitive can be our theories.

One of the ways of studying noncognitive measures is in terms of the primary focus of validation. That is, Was the test developed using content, criterion, or construct validation procedures? Criterion-oriented personality and interest inventories exemplify criterion validation procedures, while tests constructed to have highly homogeneous (internally consistent) sets of items exemplify, in part, construct validation procedures.

The specific validation procedure used with a noncognitive test in large part focuses on the nature and the possible use of the test. Construct validity takes on particular importance in situations where we are attempting to define and clarify the traits under study.

From an empirical point of view, either of the above methods of validation is about equally effective. Eventually, as a result of research and innovation, all noncognitive measures should reflect an increased degree of content, criterion, and construct validity. Presently, however, they fall short of cognitive measures in all aspects of validity. Nevertheless, in some settings, noncognitive measures can provide a valuable supplement to a cognitive-ability battery. In this chapter, we shall consider both interest and personality measures by focusing on tests that exemplify various construction and validation procedures. After considering the initial origins of the inventories, the focus will be on any communality of traits they might possess.

An interest can be defined as *an attitude or valence toward an activity*. From this definition, it is clear that an interest is a motivational variable. A variety of inventories, utilizing different methods of validation, have been developed to survey human interests. Strong (1966) developed the Vocational Interest Blank (SVIB) using strictly empirical methods. His interest in prediction of behavior led to *criterion keying*. That is, he developed scoring keys related to a wide variety of occupations. SVIB items were included in an occupational scale when people in that occupation responded differently than people not in the occupation. By way of contrast, Kuder (1960) developed the Kuder Preference Record–Vocational by selecting items that reflect interest traits. Operating from a more theory-oriented position, he developed what can be called *homogeneous* or *trait keying*.

Interest Inventories

Kuder selected items on the basis of their intercorrelations with other items. Thus, a homogeneous set of items (items having high correlations) can be said to reflect a common interest trait.

Thus, while the SVIB and the Kuder-Vocational focused on different approaches in their development, some interesting questions contrasting the two instruments can be raised. Which is better, a test focusing on criterion validation or a test focusing on trait validation? Can a test in which criterion validity is inferred from trait patterns be as effective as one using criterion keying? What interest traits can be inferred from a test developed using criterion keying? These are questions that can be important to the practitioner. However, before we give further consideration to these questions, let us consider the characteristics of the SVIB and Kuder-Vocational tests.

Strong Vocational Interest Blank

The total validation of any good inventory requires content, criterion, and construct validation. When an interest inventory is developed, interest categories are identified, and content validation of these categories is undertaken. Next, response to items or total test score is correlated with some criterion. As an example, items that reflect business interests are studied to determine how businessmen respond. Of special interest are the differences in responses between businessmen and nonbusinessmen on specific items. If an item is expected to reflect a scientific interest, it is studied to determine if scientists respond one way while nonscientists respond another. Still later, perhaps, the test items are correlated or factor analyzed to determine homogeneous sets of items. In this way, homogeneity or internal consistency is established, and the process of identifying constructs is begun.

The SVIB was developed by focusing on criterion validation procedures. The inventory consists of 399 items, divided into eight parts. The first five parts, consisting of 280 items, require the subjects to respond L, I, or D (for like, indifferent, or dislike). The sixth part requires the ranking of preferences for various activities; for example, of the ten activities, select the three best liked and the three least liked. Part 7 requires expression of preferences for paired items, and Part 8 requires responding "yes" or "no" to various statements of self-characteristics.

The items of the SVIB were selected by identifying those items that discriminate between various occupations, and weighting the items to develop the occupational and nonoccupational keys. The weighting procedure is an attempt to include in the scoring those items most relevant to the occupation under consideration. The scoring key for a given occupation was developed by comparing the responses of a group of men engaged in the occupation with those of a group of men-in-general. The percentages of men-in-general responding in a given way

Table 10.1   Criterion Weighting of the Strong Vocational Interest Blank—Engineer Scale

First Ten Items on Vocational Interest Blank	Percentage of Men Giving Each Response among:						Differences in Percentage between Engineers and "Men-in-General"			Scoring Weights for Engineer Scale		
	"Men-in-General"			Engineers								
	L	I	D	L	I	D	L	I	D	L	I	D
Actor (not movie)	21	32	47	9	31	60	−12	−1	+13	−1	0	1
Advertiser	33	38	29	14	37	49	−19	−1	+20	−2	0	2
Architect	37	40	23	58	32	10	+21	−8	−13	2	−1	−1
Army officer	22	29	49	31	33	36	+9	+4	−13	1	0	−1
Artist	24	40	36	28	39	33	+4	−1	−3	0	0	0
Astronomer	26	44	30	38	44	18	+12	0	−12	1	0	−1
Athletic director	26	41	33	15	51	34	−11	+10	+1	−1	1	0
Auctioneer	8	27	65	1	16	83	−7	−11	+18	−1	−1	2
Author of novel	32	38	30	22	44	34	−10	+6	+4	−1	1	0
Author of technical book	31	41	28	59	32	9	+28	−9	−19	3	−1	−2

to the items are compared with the percentages of responses of men in the occupation under consideration. Table 10.1 considers engineers, and gives an example of the criterion weighting of the first ten items of the SVIB. As indicated by the right three columns, various options are weighted differently. For example, a response of I to item 1 does not add to the score for the Engineer Scale. Thus, the SVIB Engineer Scale items were selected by identifying those items that discriminated between men-in-general and engineers. Liking acting or advertising results in negative scoring weights on the Engineer Scale, while liking to be an architect or army officer results in positive scoring weights. The magnitude of the weight is a function of the item's discriminability—the correlation of the item with the dichotomous engineer or men-in-general criterion.

> In criterion-keyed scoring of an interest inventory, such as the SVIB, the responses of those Ss in a given group, such as an occupation, are compared to responses of Ss not in the group. Responses to items are weighted according to the difference in response of the two groups. The specific weight assigned to an item response depends on the extent to which the item discriminates between the two groups.

The SVIB occupational items were selected by utilizing approximately 300 successful men in each criterion (occupation) group. After establishing that an

Figure 10.1 SVIB-SCII Profile for Occupational Scales

Occupational Scales

Code	Scale	Sex Norm	Std Score Very Dissimilar	Dissimilar	Ave	Similar	Very Similar
RC	FARMER	m					
RC	INSTRUM. ASSEMBL.	f					
RCE	VOC. AGRIC. TCHR.	m					
REC	DIETITIAN	m					
RES	POLICE OFFICER	m					
RSE	HWY. PATROL OFF.	m					
RE	ARMY OFFICER	f					
RS	PHYS. ED. TEACHER	f					
R	SKILLED CRAFTS	m					
RI	FORESTER	m					
RI	RAD. TECH. (X-RAY)	f					
RI	MERCH. MAR. OFF.	m					
RI	NAVY OFFICER	m					
RI	NURSE, REGISTERED	m					
RI	VETERINARIAN	m	15	25	35 45	55	
RIC	CARTOGRAPHER	m					
RIC	ARMY OFFICER	m					
RIE	AIR FORCE OFFICER	m					
RIA	OCCUP. THERAPIST	f					
IR	ENGINEER	f					
IR	ENGINEER	m					
IR	CHEMIST	f					
IR	PHYSICAL SCIENTIST	m					
IR	MEDICAL TECH.	f					
IR	PHARMACIST	m					
IR	DENTIST	f					
IR	DENTIST	m	15	25	35 45	55	
IR	DENTAL HYGIENIST	f					
IRS	PHYS. THERAPIST	f					
IRS	PHYSICIAN	m					
IRS	MATH-SCI. TEACHER	f					
ICR	MATH-SCI. TEACHER	m					
IC	DIETITIAN	f					
IRC	MEDICAL TECH.						
IRC	OPTOMETRIST	m					
IRC	COMPUTER PROGR.	f					
IRC	COMPUTER PROGR.	m					
I	MATHEMATICIAN	f					
I	MATHEMATICIAN	m	15	25	35 45	55	
I	PHYSICIST	f					
I	BIOLOGIST	m					
I	VETERINARIAN	f					
I	OPTOMETRIST	f					
I	PHYSICIAN	f					
I	SOCIAL SCIENTIST	m					
IA	COLLEGE PROFESSOR	f					
IA	COLLEGE PROFESSOR	m					
IS	SPEECH PATHOL.	f					
IS	SPEECH PATHOL.	m					
IAS	PSYCHOLOGIST	f					
IAS	PSYCHOLOGIST	m	15	25	35 45	55	
IA	LANGUAGE INTERPR.	f					
ARI	ARCHITECT	m					
A	ADVERTISING EXEC.	f					
A	ARTIST	f					
A	ARTIST	m					
A	ART TEACHER	f					
A	PHOTOGRAPHER	m					
A	MUSICIAN	f					
A	MUSICIAN	m					
A	ENTERTAINER	f					
AE	INT. DECORATOR	f					

Code	Scale	Sex Norm	Std Score Very Dissimilar	Dissimilar	Ave	Similar	Very Similar
AE	INT. DECORATOR	m					
AE	ADVERTISING EXEC.	m					
A	LANGUAGE TEACHER	f					
A	LIBRARIAN	f					
A	LIBRARIAN	m					
A	REPORTER	f					
A	REPORTER	m					
AS	ENGLISH TEACHER	f					
AS	ENGLISH TEACHER	m					
SI	NURSE, REGISTERED	f					
SIR	PHYS. THERAPIST	m					
SRC	NURSE, LIC. PRACT.	m					
S	SOCIAL WORKER	f					
S	SOCIAL WORKER	m					
S	PRIEST	m	15	25	35 45	55	
S	DIR., CHRISTIAN ED.	f					
SE	YWCA STAFF	f					
SIE	MINISTER	m					
SEA	ELEM. TEACHER	m					
SC	ELEM. TEACHER	f					
SCE	SCH. SUPERINTEND.	m					
SCE	PUBLIC ADMINISTR.	m					
SCE	GUIDANCE COUNS.	m					
SER	RECREATION LEADER	f					
SEC	RECREATION LEADER	m					
SEC	GUIDANCE COUNS.	f					
SEC	SOC. SCI. TEACHER	f	15	25	35 45	55	
SEC	SOC. SCI. TEACHER	m					
SEC	PERSONNEL DIR.	m					
ESC	DEPT. STORE MGR.	m					
ESC	HOME ECON. TCHR.	f					
ESA	FLIGHT ATTENDANT	f					
ES	CH. OF COMM. EXEC.	m					
ES	SALES MANAGER	m					
ES	LIFE INS. AGENT	m					
E	LIFE INS. AGENT	f					
E	LAWYER	f					
E	LAWYER	m	15	25	35 45	55	
EI	COMPUTER SALES	m					
EI	INVESTM. FUND MGR.	m					
EIC	PHARMACIST	m					
EC	BUYER	f					
ECS	BUYER	m					
ECS	CREDIT MANAGER	m					
ECS	FUNERAL DIRECTOR	m					
ECR	REALTOR	m					
ERC	AGRIBUSINESS MGR.	m					
ERC	PURCHASING AGENT	m					
ESR	CHIROPRACTOR	m					
CE	ACCOUNTANT	m					
CE	BANKER	f	15	25	35 45	55	
CE	BANKER	m					
CE	CREDIT MANAGER	f					
CE	DEPT. STORE SALES	f					
CE	BUSINESS ED. TCHR.	f					
CES	BUSINESS ED. TCHR.	m					
CSE	EXEC. HOUSEKEEPER	f					
C	ACCOUNTANT	f					
C	SECRETARY	f					
CR	DENTAL ASSISTANT	f					
CRI	NURSE, LIC. PRACT.	f					
CRE	BEAUTICIAN	f					

item differentiated the criterion group from men-in-general, the scale was linearly transformed to a *T*-score scale with a mean of 50 and a standard deviation of 10. The various criterion groups were used as norming groups for this rescaling. Thus, a score of 55 on the Engineer Scale indicates an inventoried interest score one-half standard deviation above the mean of the norm group, consisting of approximately 300 engineers.

In 1974, the Strong-Campbell Interest Inventory (SCII) was published, presenting scores on various occupational scales in profile form. The Occupational Scales profile is shown in Figure 10.1. Each scale was developed by testing 200–300 happily employed males or females in the occupation and isolating the items answered differently than the general sample. The scales have been normed by converting the scores of the occupational sample to *T*-scores. An individual scoring between 26 and 44 scores in the "average" range, and has responded as the general sample. As an individual deviates farther from the "average," his responses become either increasingly similar or dissimilar to those of the occupational group, depending upon the direction of the score. These categories are indicated along with the standard score (*T*-score) obtained. Profiles are separated for males and females. The scoring on a given scale is based on an empirical comparison with the appropriate reference group. That is, the scoring is based on the observed responses of a specific group, not on internal logic or a priori argument.

The Strong-Campbell Interest Inventory also has other scales different from the Occupational Scales. An example is the Basic Interest Scales. These are homogeneous scales, constructed by grouping together items with high intercorrelations. These scales were normed on a general sample of 600 men and women. The scales are grouped into six "themes" with one to five scales in a theme. As an example, science and mathematics appear in the same theme while art and writing appear in another theme. The other kinds of scales will not be discussed in detail here.

> **The SVIB provides numerous scoring options to determine occupational interests, basic interests, and interests related to selected characteristics. Scoring is based strictly on an empirical comparison of an individual's responses to those of a designated reference group.**

Given the method of criterion keying, just how effective is the SVIB (or the SVIB-SCII) in predicting success in various occupations? First of all, the evidence seems to indicate that interest inventories can provide a valuable supplement to ability measures. While the criterion coefficients are generally low to modest, the score obviously fulfills a function as a motivational variable. Strong (1955) found correlations of .3 with job satisfaction ratings after 18 years, and specialized

Figure 10.2   Kuder Preference Record–Vocational, Profile Sheet

NAME _____   AGE ____ SEX ____ GROUP _____ DATE OF TEST _____

Print   Last   First   Initial   M or F

PROFILE SECTION

BOYS and GIRLS

GRADES 9–12

DIRECTIONS FOR PROFILING

1. Copy the V-Score from the back page of the answer section in the box at the right.

   If your V-Score is 37 or less, there is some reason for doubting the value of your answers, and your other scores may not be very accurate. *If your V-Score is 45 or more*, you may not have understood the directions, since 44 is the highest possible score. *If your score is not between 38 and 44, inclusive, you should see your adviser. He will probably recommend that you read the directions again, and then that you fill out the blank a second time, being careful to follow the directions exactly and to give sincere replies.*

   If your V-Score is between 38 and 44, inclusive, go ahead with the following directions.

2. Copy the scores 0 through 9 in the spaces at the top of the profile chart. Under "OUTDOOR" find the number which is the same as the score at the top. If your score is not shown, draw a line *between* the scores above and below your own. Use the numbers under M if you are a boy and the numbers under F if you are a girl. Draw a line through this number from one side to the other of the entire column under OUTDOOR. Do the same thing for the scores at the top of each of the other columns. If a score is larger than any number in the column, draw a line across the top of the column; if it is smaller, draw a line across the bottom.

3. With your pencil blacken the entire space between the lines you have drawn and the bottom of the chart. The result is your profile for the *Kuder Preference Record—Vocational*.

   An interpretation of the scores will be found on page 35.

   This page is to be kept by your counselor.

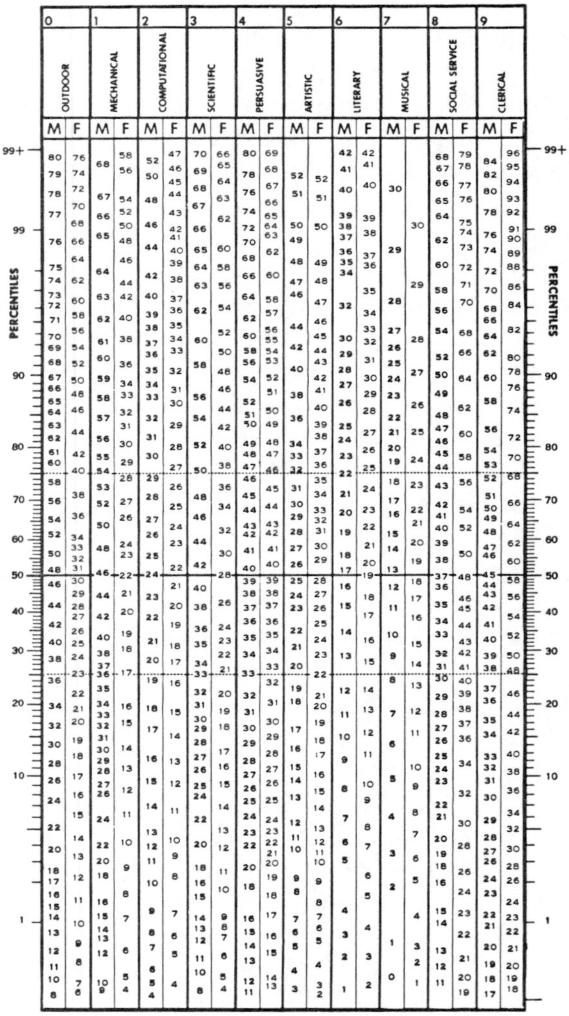

7-298 – FORM 21

SRA   Science Research Associates, Inc.
259 East Erie Street, Chicago, Illinois 60611

A Subsidiary of IBM

keys have been developed with criterion validities of as high as .53 (Knauft, 1949). Expressing Strong's findings in another way, Knauft suggests that a person with an "A" rating in an occupation has about 3.6 chances to 1 of entering that occupation, while those with "C" ratings have about 5 chances to 1 of not entering the occupation. Thus, while the criterion validity coefficients are not as high as we would like, it is obvious that the SVIB provides a valuable supplement when prediction of job satisfaction and turnover is important.

Kuder Preference Record

If one studies the historical development of interest inventories, it becomes apparent that the early work had a highly practical orientation. It approached the problem from a strictly empirical view, that is, the validation procedure focused on criterion validation. However, criterion validity has some shortcomings. One such shortcoming is that any change in population can result in a change in the validity coefficient. For example, if, in the original validation group, males and females were equally represented, a marked change in these proportions could affect the criterion validity. Also, since there are many possible criteria, establishing many coefficients can be a vexing problem. As an example, Strong was faced with developing a scoring key for many different occupations. However, if one takes the position that interest traits can be identified, inferences about vocational choice can be made from the pattern of responses. A test that reflects this approach is the Kuder Preference Record–Vocational. There are other Kuder scales (Personal and Occupational), but the Kuder-Vocational has been most effective, and is most widely used.

The Kuder-Vocational has been used in high school and college counseling programs. It was designed for use with junior high through college-age students, in contrast to the SVIB, which is for age 17 years and older. The Kuder was developed to provide relatively independent interest categories from which inferences could be made about vocational choices. The following ten vocational interest categories were specified: Outdoor, Mechanical, Computational, Scientific, Persuasive, Artistic, Literary, Musical, Social Service, and Clerical, as shown in Figure 10.2. Each of the ten scores has a description and suggested vocational areas. For example, a high score on the Outdoor scale means the individual prefers work that keeps him outside a great deal of the time, usually working with animals and growing things. Suggested occupations are forest ranger, naturalist, and farmer. Suggested occupations for individuals scoring high on the Mechanical scale are automobile repairman, watchmaker, drill press operator, and engineer. This particular form can be used for both males and females, as indicated.

In plotting a profile for an individual, the scores on the ten scales are recorded in the space at the top of the profile chart. Depending on the sex of the individual, the scores are plotted in either the M or F columns. A line is drawn through the score on a given scale, and the entire space between this line and the bottom of the chart is darkened. This results in ten "bars" of varying height. The relative heights indicate the areas of greater and lesser interest, the higher bars indicating greater interest. The percentiles indicated on the sides of the profile are norms based on over 3,000 individuals for each normative group. The two dotted lines at the 25th and 75th percentiles were selected to indicate a middle grouping of 50 percent of the normative group. Scores falling between these two lines are arbitrarily designated as "average" level of interest.

In order to attain the relative independence of the ten Kuder scales, and to minimize faking, a forced-choice format was used. All the items in the Kuder-Vocational reflect an activity, and the subject responding to each item is confronted with an activity triad. In responding to the triad, he is forced to select the activity in the triad he *likes most,* and another that he *likes least.* Each triad reflects three different categories from the ten interest category scales. For example, one of the 168 activity triads is:

> Sell artist's supplies
> Grow seeds for florists
> Raise white mice for scientists

Since the S is forced to respond to each triad, each person makes the same number of selections and rejections, thereby systematically inflating or deflating various interest categories. This type of forced-choice format results in what has been called an *ipsative* score, as opposed to a *normative* score. That is, the pattern of interests is based on the individual himself, rather than on some normative group.

Consider a different interpretation of ipsative scoring. Suppose we wish to assess preferences for three interest categories, Artistic, Outdoor, and Scientific. When a S responds to this activity triad, a preference for "sell artist's supplies," and a dislike for "raise white mice for scientists," adds to the Artistic score. By successively presenting three interest categories with three different types of activities, a high Artistic score, a moderate Outdoor score, and a low Scientific score should result for an artistically inclined individual.

Ipsative scores have several interesting characteristics. Conceptually, ipsatizing has the effect of deviating the subtests from the *person's* (not subtest's) mean. Thus, the mean across all categories is the same for all individuals tested. The forced-choice format exerts some control over faking, minimizes between-person variation, and maximizes within-person variation. The minimization of between-person differences results in the suppressing of correlations among subtests. While this suppressing of subtest correlations facilitates individual profile analysis, the biasing effect brings into question other statistical computations based on the scores. In summary, ipsatization has the following four effects:

1. A slight control is exerted over faking.
2. Interest preferences are accentuated for ease of interpretation.
3. The interest profile is distorted in favor of one (or perhaps two) interests.
4. Minimization of person-to-person differences results in a downward biasing of correlation coefficients, so further statistical computations based on the scores reflect the biasing.

> **The Kuder-Vocational test contains ten relatively independent categories from which inferences to vocational choices are made. A forced-choice format is used, resulting in an ipsative score.**

The work on the Kuder-Vocational has generated the development of several forms, and a more recent interest inventory, the Kuder Occupational Interest Survey (OIS). The Kuder-Vocational forms were designed to meet varying needs and varying age groups. For example, Form C, which was published in 1948, contained Outdoor and Verification Scales, the need for these scales being recognized by the users of Form B.[1] It is not the purpose of this text to review numerous interest inventories or their forms. However, for comparison purposes, it is appropriate to consider the Kuder-OIS briefly.

The Kuder-OIS provides scores for 50 specific occupations. That is, instead of containing the more general scales of the Kuder-Vocational, such as Outdoor and Mechanical, the Kuder-OIS contains scales for specific occupations, such as Accountant and Nurse. Form DD (Kuder, 1966) is designed for use with college students. There are 100 items, each item consists of three activities. The respondent is asked to indicate his most-liked and least-liked activities. Thus, the item and test format is the same as that for the Kuder-Vocational. The keys for scoring the occupational scales were developed by comparing responses of individuals in general. Form DD also contains a Verification Scale. Occupational scales exist for both men and women. In addition to scores on the occupational scales, men receive a set of scores on College Major Scales. The latter are designed to assist in making decisions about potential fields of concentration. Women may also receive scores in occupational scales generally associated with men, and also under the College Major Scales. In that case, the occupation or major is one in which men predominate, but in which there are increasing opportunities for women.

---

[1]For a more detailed discussion of the development of various forms, see Kuder, 1964, pp. 11–14.

Comparison of the SVIB with the Kuder-Vocational and Kuder-OIS

These major interest inventories have some differences. Most importantly, the Kuder-Vocational has scores for interest traits, while the SVIB has scores for an occupation. The Kuder-Vocational is trait-oriented, while SVIB is criterion-oriented. With the Kuder-Vocational test, we can describe the person relative to scientific, artistic, or other constructs. We get a clearer picture of the individual relative to the constructs that underlie his interests. However, there are advantages to the criterion validation of the SVIB. Its relationship to a real-life occupational choice is more direct and explicit. Specific occupational choices can be considered and keyed to obtain a specific score. Second, the scoring scheme is different. The Kuder-Vocational has items arranged in forced-choice triads that yield ipsative scores, while the SVIB provides normative scores—scores to be compared with those of some external group to determine a person's interests in that group. Finally, the Kuder-Vocational is a self-scored instrument, while the SVIB is generally machine-scored commercially.

What are the advantages and disadvantages of the above differences? Clearly, a score based on the trait approach of the Kuder-Vocational allows for a more rational interpretation. The potential of a trait theory to describe a person in terms of scientific or artistic traits is logically defensible and compelling. However, the greater empirical success of the SVIB, and the lack of a highly effective theory of interests offsets the advantage of the Kuder-Vocational. Next, the forced-choice, ipsative format of the Kuder-Vocational was incorporated to minimize unreliability due to such factors as faking and acquiescence. However, the characteristics associated with ipsative scoring may or may not offset the slight advantage gained by the procedure. Finally, the self-scoring format of the Kuder-Vocational is highly innovative, much simpler, and more convenient than the complex scoring of the SVIB. Thus, these differences favor the more easily scored Kuder-Vocational with its compelling trait origins. The SVIB, on the other hand, has proven criterion validity and, unfortunately, a more complicated scoring scheme.

The SVIB and the Kuder interest inventories have been subjected to intensive investigation and research. Studies examining the correlations between scores on similarly named scales from different inventories have generally produced low to modest correlations at best. Zytowski (1968) studied such correlations between scales of the SVIB and the Kuder-OIS, and found a median correlation coefficient of .25. Certainly, one interpretation of this result is that predictions of a similarly named scale from one inventory to another would be poor; however, it does not necessarily indicate a lack of validity to an external criterion. Zytowski concludes that his findings do not suggest that any of the scales are invalid for the purposes for which they were designed.

Kuder (1969) provides an excellent explanation of why correlations between scores on similarly named scales from different inventories tend to be modest. There are, of course, the differences in rationale and scoring methods between the SVIB and the Kuder-OIS, and these would make low correlations very likely. Also, as Kuder points out, the SVIB scores are essentially difference scores, differentiating an occupational group from a general reference group. This has the effect of partialing out or removing the substantial core of interests that people have in common. The Kuder-OIS scores, on the other hand, are not difference scores. Therefore, in comparison, if the SVIB score contains a single factor, that of the occupation under study, the corresponding score on the Kuder-OIS contains two factors, that of the occupation and that of interests of people in general. With this difference in underlying structure of the scores, high correlations between the scores would not be expected.

Which, then, is the better interest inventory? Clearly, at this stage in the development of interest inventories, there is no simple or all-inclusive answer to the question. The use to be made of the test results certainly has a bearing on what inventory to use. Uses and interpretations are generally discussed in detail in the manual accompanying the test. Interest inventories exist for different age groups, and, in many cases, the specific forms vary with the age group. There is no "best" interest inventory, except as defined by the conditions of the specific situation. Therefore, the selection of an interest inventory must be a function of the situation and the preference of the user.

Stability of Interests

Any long-range use of interest inventories depends on the stability of the interests over time. Considerable research has been done in this area. Interests of elementary-school-age children tend to be unstable, and the usefulness of interest inventories with this group is questionable. Interests become increasingly stable with high-school-age students, and those of college-age persons are relatively stable.

Campbell (1969, p. 21) summarized studies dealing with the stability of the SVIB over time. Scores on the Occupational scales were studied using a test-retest situation. Correlations between scores obtained 30 days apart were slightly over .90, and dropped to about .75 over 20 years for adults. Scores for men first tested at age 16 correlated .55 with retest scores secured when the men were over 35 years of age. Over the four-year college span, correlations usually are in the .60's. It is clear that the older the individual is at the time of initial testing, the more stable the interests will tend to be. Also, the shorter the retest interval, the more the stability of interests. Of these two factors, the age at initial testing is the more important. When using the SVIB with persons under 21 years of age, the possibility of interest change and corresponding instability of scores exists and must be considered.

Another indication of stability, in addition to high test-retest correlations, would be the similarity of interest profiles. Strong (1955), in his retest study 18 years after college, found the similarity between profiles to be such that approximately 50 percent of the persons would receive the same occupational suggestions. In a study of the stability of interests within occupations, Campbell (1966) arrived at the following conclusions:

> ... there is considerable stability across time within occupations on interest measures, much more than one might expect intuitively. Further, these studies collectively imply that individuals in the 1930 culture were similar in their interest patterns to those in the 1964 culture, and that the mechanisms of occupational choice—whatever they may be—are fairly constant over long time periods. Somehow men with banking interest gravitated into the banking business 30 years ago, and men with those same interest patterns are found in the same jobs today [p. 1018].

A study (Herzberg & Bouton, 1954) of the stability of the Kuder-Vocational with 17- to 21-year-olds indicated correlations ranging from .50 to .84 for the various scales. Studies (Rosenberg, 1953) involving stability of various age groups vary somewhat in results; however, there is evidence that scores possess at least some degree of stability. In any event, the Kuder-Vocational indicates some stable differences in interest patterns for different occupations.

The stability of interest patterns relative to age is certainly not unexpected. With the beginning of high school, the student becomes exposed to adult occupations and pursuits more directly. There is increased focus on specific activities, courses, and the like. The student, at least to some extent, has the opportunity to pursue the activities he most enjoys, thus, not only specializing, but cultivating and deepening his interests. Certainly new interests may develop as the individual ages, but generally they are offshoots of, or at least related to, already existing interests.

Domain of Interests

Having considered interest measurement, let us return to interests in the cognitive-noncognitive domains. Recall that interests are motivational variables—a valence toward an activity. But, can the activity categories be simplified? What are the primary interest traits?

Before approaching interest traits or activity categories, we must recognize that trait identification is a function of people and tests. Different kinds of people manifest different interest traits, and different tests also measure different interest traits. Nevertheless, across investigations (using different samples and inventories), we should be able to identify some of the more important interest traits or categories.

Thurstone (1931) undertook the first multiple factor approach to interest trait identification. He identified four such dimensions: (1) interest in science, (2) interest in language, (3) interest in people, and (4) interest in business. Similarly, Ferguson, Humphreys, and Strong (1941) compared the SVIB and the Study of Values (Allport & Vernon, 1931), and identified five interest categories. Four of their five traits correspond roughly to Thurstone's findings. Other research has also provided some confirmation of the four Thurstone categories.

Pondering the question of interest traits, we see that we can define at least four motivational traits. From our knowledge of the primary cognitive abilities, we can combine abilities with interests to predict performance in some activity. Combining Vernon's description of the four most important human abilities (verbal, number, reasoning, and spatial) with Thurstone's interest categories, we obtain sixteen interest-ability combinations. We can view this as a 4 by 4 matrix with human abilities on one dimension and interest categories on the other. By attending to both interest and ability strengths and weaknesses, more effective counseling, for example, should be forthcoming.

The practical problem of obtaining this ability-interest matrix is facilitated by the use of tests, such as CTMM, which provide these ability scores. No widely accepted interest inventory, however, provides scores on the four interest traits. The work of Ferguson, Humphreys, and Strong (1941) provides a basis for obtaining these scores from the SVIB and Study of Values. Table 10.2 summarizes that work, and provides some information about the basic interest categories.

Another clue about the domain of interests can be found embedded in the rotation problem in factor analysis. Vernon (1949) also investigated the domain of interests, but he focused on maintaining the general factor (instead of rotating it out, as in the Thurstone tradition). He identified a general factor that he labeled *gregariousness*. Thus, Thurstone's findings can be defined as gregariousness associated with situations involving science, language, people, and business.

> Applying factor analysis to the measurement of interests seems to reveal a general factor labeled *gregariousness*. By rotation, this factor can be broken down into four categories, which reflect the extent of gregariousness related to each category.

Personality Assessment

The history of psychology is, in large part, a history of the study of personality and personality disorders. This history reflects an early attempt to generate theories of personality based on minimal data and crude measurements. Recently, there have been attempts to combine theory and data in an attempt to produce both more refined measures and theories.

223

Table 10.2 **Interest and Occupational Classification According to High and Low Scores on SVIB and Study of Values**

Interest	Occupation or Vocational Orientation	
	High Scores	Low Scores
People	Teacher YMCA Secretary CPA Office Worker	Physician
Business	Political	Economic
Language	Lawyer Physician Esthetic Theoretic	Office Worker Economic
Science	Chemist Physician Theoretic Teacher	Life Insurance Salesman Political Lawyer

Adapted from Ferguson, Humphreys, & Strong, 1941, pp. 200–201.

Early studies of personality attempted to categorize people into types. A type, according to Eysenck (1953a, p. 13), is a group of correlated traits, while a trait is a function of correlated behaviors. Thus, a delinquent or psychopath can be thought of as a type resulting from a pattern of behavior traits. Figure 10.3 is a representation of Eysenck's theory of the organization of personality. His hierarchy ranges from the specific response level to the type level. The specific response level is succeeded by the habitual response level, which, in turn, determines various traits. The individual's traits then determine the type.

The term *personality* has varied meanings among educators and psychologists. In the broadest sense, we might consider it as the sum total of an individual's cognitive and noncognitive characteristics. In a more restricted sense, we can refer to personality as the manner in which the individual behaves. In this sense, Guilford (1959a, p. 407) suggests that ability variables refer to how *well* an individual will perform; interests are motivational and reflect *what* a person will do; personality variables will reflect the *manner* in which a person does something. In this book, personality will be used generally in the restricted sense of the manner in which an individual does something.

Early attempts to study personality were quite consistent in subjectively identifying a component of personality, something akin to what we presently call extroversion-introversion. Kretschmer (1948), for example, observed that individuals could be ordered on a continuum from those who were extremely withdrawn (schizophrenics) to those who manifested extremely cyclical manic-depressive behaviors (cyclothymics). He also suggested that these characteristics existed in less extreme forms among normal individuals, for which he suggested the designations schizothymes and cyclothymes.

A second component of personality was identified that can be referred to as anxiety or emotionality. While these early efforts lacked a great deal of methodological sophistication, Hall and Lindsey (1970, pp. 380–416) partially confirmed and clarified earlier work. Thus, students beginning the study of personality assessment should expect to find subtests of extroversion-introversion and emotionality in existing tests.

The most straightforward approach to assessment of personality would be by directly observing an individual's behavior in real-life situations. Another approach would be to describe hypothetical situations for which an individual reports a typical response. This indirect approach to personality assessment is

Figure 10.3   Diagrammatic Representation of Hierarchical Organization of Personality

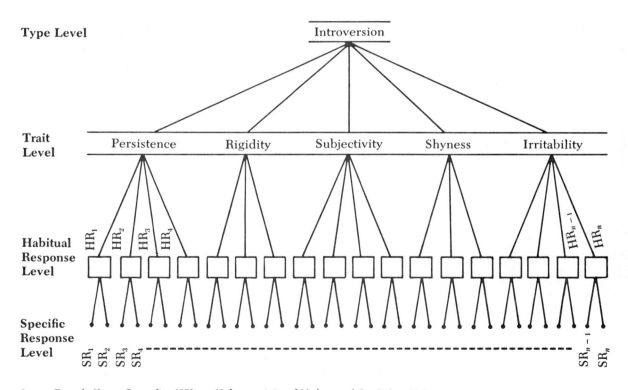

Source: Eysenck, *Human Personality*, 1953a, p. 13, by permission of Methuen and Co., Ltd., publishers.

the more common of the two. Note also that in both direct and indirect personality assessment, we are interested in assessing the typical behavior of that individual. That is, we are not trying to induce him to do his best, or to strive for a maximum performance, as with the testing of cognitive abilities.

In our discussion of interest inventories, emphasis was placed on validation procedures. That is, if validity is concerned with what a test is supposed to measure, the method of measurement must be related to that purpose. In the following discussion, we shall again consider two inventories, the Minnesota Multiphasic Personality Inventory (MMPI), which was developed using criterion validation methods, and the Sixteen Personality Factor Test (16PF), which was developed using trait or construct validation procedures.

Minnesota Multiphasic Personality Inventory: Criterion Validity

The MMPI is a paper-and-pencil inventory in which the individual is asked to respond to statements or items. It was developed for the specific purpose of distinguishing individuals considered normal from those suspected of demonstrating some degree of psychopathology. The inventory was developed by S. R. Hathaway, a clinical psychiatrist, and J. C. McKinley, a neuropsychiatrist, at the University of Minnesota.

The MMPI was designed to provide information on multiple phases of personality. Individuals are required to respond *True, False,* or *Cannot Say* to 550 items that represent ten clinical scales (including social introversion as a clinical scale) and four validity scales. Table 10.3 summarizes both the clinical and validity scales and presents interpretations of the scales.

The subtest scores are transformed to *T*-scores and plotted on a profile sheet to yield a pattern described as reflecting the multiple-phases of personality. Figure 10.4 presents sample inventory profiles. The profiles are interpreted in the usual sense in which the pattern of a given line represents the defined group.

> **The MMPI was designed to differentiate normal individuals from those possessing some degree of psychopathology. The inventory contains ten clinical scales and four validity scales.**

To develop the criterion validity of the MMPI scales, responses of over 800 hospitalized people classified into psychiatric criterion groups were compared with over 700 visitors to the hospital. These visitors were considered as the "normal" group. However, to avoid the limitation of a hospitalized versus nonhospitalized dichotomy, a hospitalized-normal versus hospitalized-psychiatric dichotomy was also studied. An item that discriminated (correlated) hospitalized

Table 10.3 The Validity and Clinical Scales of the MMPI

Scale	Interpretation
Validity Scales: Question (?)	A high score indicates evasiveness.
Lie (L)	Persons trying to present themselves in a favorable light (e.g., good, wholesome, honest) obtain high L scale elevations.
Faking (F)	High scores suggest carelessness, confusion, or "fake bad."
Correction (K)	An elevation on the K scale suggests a defensive test-taking attitude. Exceedingly low scores may indicate a lack of ability to deny symptomatology.
Clinical Scales: Hypochondriasis (Hs)	High scorers have been described as cynical, defeatist, and crabbed.
Depression (D)	High scorers usually are shy, despondent, and distressed.
Hysteria (Hy)	High scorers tend to complain of multiple symptoms.
Psychopathic Deviate (Pd)	Adjectives used to describe some high scorers are adventurous, courageous, and generous.
Masculinity-Femininity (Mf)	Among males, high scorers have been described as aesthetic and sensitive. High-scoring women have been described as rebellious, unrealistic, and indecisive.
Paranoia (Pa)	High scorers on this scale were characterized as shrewd, guarded, and worrisome.
Psychasthenia (Pt)	Fearful, rigid, anxious, and worrisome are some of the adjectives used to describe high Pt scorers.
Schizophrenia (Sc)	Adjectives such as withdrawn and unusual describe high Sc scorers.
Hypomania (Ma)	High scorers are called sociable, energetic, and impulsive.
Social Introversion (Si)	High scorers: modest, shy, and self-effacing. Low scorers: sociable, colorful, and ambitious.

Adapted from Kleinmuntz, 1967, p. 220.

Figure 10.4 Examples of Profiles of the MMPI

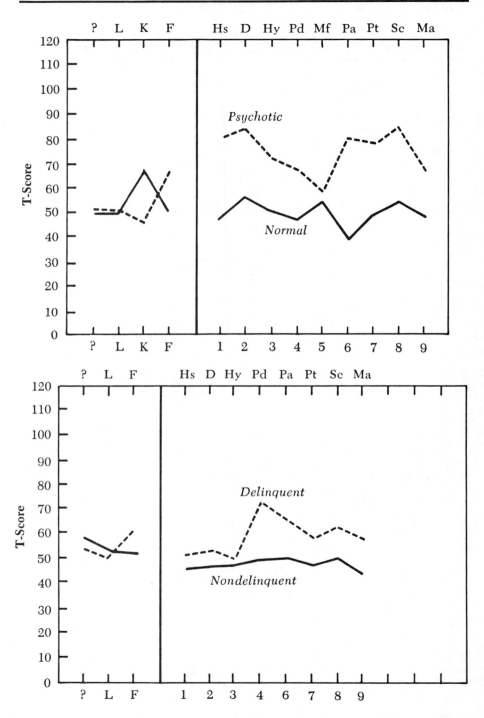

Sources: (top profiles) Weider, *Contributions Toward Medical Psychology*, V. 2, pp. 554, 563, copyright © 1953, The Ronald Press Co., New York; (bottom profiles) Hathaway & Monachesi, 1953, p. 32.

patients from nonhospitalized people was then checked for discrimination of hospitalized-normal from hospitalized-psychiatric individuals. These items were then included in the scale of the criterion group they discriminated. The non-hospitalized-normal group was supplemented with college students and WPA workers. Although the MMPI was originally developed for use with hospitalized psychiatric patients, it is used presently as a screening device for persons with personality problems. Also, the MMPI has been widely used as a research tool in a variety of situations.

With widespread use, some questions have been raised about the scoring of the MMPI. In developing the inventory, items were placed in the scoring key of a particular group on an empirical basis. The group, initially the hospitalized group, responded differently than the normal group. Items that discriminated a criterion group from a normal group were included in a scale of the group they discriminated. Because some items discriminated multiple groups, they are found in more than one scale. The overall effect of this procedure was the development of scales with undesirably high intercorrelations. Also, since homogeneity of items was not a primary goal of the MMPI development, all of the subtests do not measure internally consistent traits. A study of MMPI items shows that response patterns for some items reflect quite obvious clinical symptoms, although this is not true of all items. Responses to other items appear to have nothing to do with a particular psychiatric pattern. These are labeled *subtle items*. The obvious and the subtle items are not only different in nature, but are statistically uncorrelated. Knowledgeable groups, such as college students, can often recognize the more normally acceptable responses to the obvious items, and variations tend to arise from the subtle items. Thus, the scores may represent quite different personality manifestations than those of the hospitalized-psychiatric patients on which the scoring keys were originally established.

The development and publication of the MMPI was widely accepted in clinical circles The wide use of the test soon resulted in the recognition of various profiles of case studies. Also, many additional scales were constructed. The result was the *MMPI Atlas* (Hathaway & Meehl, 1951), which consisted of a wide variety of MMPI profiles and personality descriptions. Several such codebooks, which reviewed and summarized the various profiles, were quickly published to assist in MMPI interpretation. Summarizing the voluminous research and literature on the MMPI, clinician and psychometrician alike must acknowledge its contribution to the emerging field of personality measurement—both in theory and practice.

Sixteen Personality Factor Test: Construct Validity

While the MMPI was specifically designed to differentiate psychiatric criterion groups from a normal population, the Sixteen Personality Factor Test (16PF) was designed to assess the personality traits of normal subjects. It is a factor analytically developed personality inventory. In this way, it contrasts with the MMPI, which was primarily concerned with criterion validity. Utilizing factor analysis, Cattell (1957) has educed 16 dimensions of personality. Four composite "second-order" scores, from a combination of the 16 factors, were also obtained by using second-order factoring, that is, factoring of the subtests. The second-order scores are more general, and there is some loss of information in using them, compared with the initial factors. Nevertheless, the second-order scores do provide a convenient, capsule description of personality. The primary factors and the second-order 16PF composites are identified descriptively and discussed more fully later.

The 16PF was designed for use with young adults (from age 16 or 17 years) to late maturity. Parallel younger-age versions of the test can be used for personality assessment down through adolescence to age 6 or 7 years (the HSPQ, CPQ, and ESPQ tests). The 16PF is virtually self-administering, and can be used with groups and individuals. It is applicable to a wide range of educational levels, and is available in some 15 languages. Forms A and B of the 16PF, containing 187 items, are longer and more reliable, but reasonable reliability can also be obtained in the shorter Forms C and D, consisting of 105 items. Forms A and B assume a high school reading level, while Forms C and D are suitable for substantially lower reading levels. A "Low Literate" Form E is available for experimental use with culturally disadvantaged and intellectually limited subjects.

Whether longer or shorter forms of the 16PF are used, all forms measure 16 dimensions of personality. Each dimension is identified as a factor, and represented as a subtest score. The factors and the personality description associated with high and low scores are shown in Table 10.4.

The subtests are scaled using a sten transformation, and the resulting scores are plotted on a profile form, which provides an individual's profile on the 16 dimensions. Reliabilities of the subtests, as with most multifactor inventories, tend to be lower than desirable. As would be expected for personality tests, test-retest (stability) coefficients are lower than equivalence coefficients. Split-half reliabilities (Cattell & Eber, 1962, p. 6) for each of the 16 primary factor subtests range from .71 to .93, with an average around .84.

Using the principle that a test validity can be as high as the square root of the reliability, Cattell and Eber (1962, p. 8) also report the validity coefficients of the subtests as the square root of the internal consistency reliability estimates. These validity coefficients average about .91.

Second-order factors can also be obtained by combining the groups of subjects. The four principal, second-order factors are:

Anxiety: The score shows the level of anxiety in the commonly accepted sense, which may be either manifested for normal situational reasons or may be neurotic in origin, correlated with psychiatric evaluations of anxiety level.

Table 10.4 Personality Description of the High and Low Scorers on the 16PF Factors

Factor	A person with a low score on the factor is described as:	A person with a high score is described as:
A	RESERVED, detached, critical, cool	OUTGOING, warmhearted, easy-going, participating
B	LESS INTELLIGENT, concrete-thinking	MORE INTELLIGENT, abstract-thinking, bright
C	AFFECTED BY FEELINGS, emotionally less stable, easily upset	EMOTIONALLY STABLE, faces reality, calm
E	HUMBLE, mild, obedient, conforming	ASSERTIVE, independent, aggressive, stubborn
F	SOBER, prudent, serious, taciturn	HAPPY-GO-LUCKY, heedless, gay, enthusiastic
G	EXPEDIENT, a law to himself, by-passes obligations	CONSCIENTIOUS, preserving, staid, rule-bound
H	SHY, restrained, diffident, timid	VENTURESOME, socially bold, uninhibited, spontaneous
I	TOUGH-MINDED, self-reliant, realistic, no nonsense	TENDER-MINDED, dependent, overprotected, sensitive
L	TRUSTING, adaptable, free of jealousy, easy to get on with	SUSPICIOUS, self-opinionated, hard to fool
M	PRACTICAL, careful, conventional, regulated by external realities, proper	IMAGINATIVE, wrapped up in inner urgencies, careless of practical matters, bohemian
N	FORTHRIGHT, natural, artless, sentimental	SHREWD, calculating, worldly, penetrating
O	PLACID, self-assured, confident, serene	APPREHENSIVE, worrying, depressive, troubled
Q₁	CONSERVATIVE, respecting established ideas, tolerant of traditional difficulties	EXPERIMENTING, critical, liberal, analytical, free-thinking
Q₂	GROUP-DEPENDENT, a "joiner" and good follower	SELF-SUFFICIENT, prefers own decisions, resourceful
Q₃	CASUAL, careless of protocol, untidy, follows own urges	CONTROLLED, socially precise, self-disciplined, compulsive
Q₄	RELAXED, tranquil, torpid, unfrustrated	TENSE, driven, overwrought, fretful

These descriptions are found in *About the 16PF,* published by the Institute for Personality and Ability Testing, Champaign, Ill., a four-page, uncopyrighted brochure.

Extroversion vs. *Introversion:* A high score indicates a socially outgoing, uninhibited person, good at making contacts, while the low score reveals an introvert, both shy and self-sufficient.

Tough Poise vs. *Responsive Emotionality:* High "tough poise" scores mark an enterprising, decisive, imperturbable personality. The low scores point to a person more deeply emotionally sensitive, guided by emotions, and liable to more frustrations and depression.

Independence vs. *Dependence:* High scores signify an aggressive, independent, self-directing person; low scores, a group-dependent, agreeable, passive personality.

For example, scores for factors A, E, F, H, and Q_2 are weighted to obtain the second-order, extroversion-introversion factor, which is found in most personality inventories. In addition to these second-order factors, a masculinity-femininity factor can also be obtained. Second-order factors like those described have been identified in other inventories. While the combining of subtests results in a loss of some information, combining correlated subtests does result in increased reliability, and more generalized behavior descriptions.

The scoring of the 16PF is straightforward, requiring only two keys and the sten transformation. Faking and acquiescence are partially controlled by a few strategically located "buffer" items, and by utilizing items in which the socially desirable response is not obvious. Additionally, a Motivational Distortion (Md) scale is included, which can be used to identify extreme attempts at falsifying the responses. Norms for the 16PF are available with the test and are regularly updated and constantly expanded. A total of approximately 7,000 representative cases have been tested in developing the various norms. Separate norms exist for distinct groups, such as college students. Norms depend on the sex of the subjects and the form of the test being used.

What are the major uses of the 16PF in light of the interpretation of the scores? The test battery is useful because it samples the total personality. That is, it provides an index of intelligence as well as measures of extroversion-introversion and emotionality. The point is made that the 16PF provides information about both personality variables and about general ability, although it might be argued that general ability is somehow subsumed as part of personality. While the information provided by the test can be extremely valuable, more distinct information about verbal, numerical, and fluid abilities is desirable, and even necessary, in many situations.

The 16PF has found considerable use in vocational guidance and industrial selection. There are optimum job profiles available to assist the psychologist or guidance counselor. The 16PF profile has been developed for over 50 vocations, such as ministers, airline pilots, nurses, firemen—many quite diverse occupations. Research with the 16PF has established weights for predicting criteria, such as school achievement and leadership.

Clinical use of the 16PF is also quite extensive for initial screening and diagnosis of various disorders. Profiles exist for clinical criterion groups, such as alcoholics, psychotics, psychopaths, sociopaths, and many others. All in all, profiles are available for over 80 clinical criterion and occupational groups. These profiles are based on approximately 10,000 subjects.

Undoubtedly, the wide use of the 16PF is due primarily to two reasons. First, it provides comprehensive coverage of personality at various ages and with different educational levels. Second, research has related it clearly to fundamental personality structures. The 16PF is designed to measure the total personality and can be used with normal and abnormal subjects. Thus, its use in prediction has wide application for various settings: scholastic, vocational, and clinical. This eliminates the use of numerous separate tests, one for each specific prediction interest. However, this generality may sacrifice the precision obtainable by more specifically oriented tests. Continued research is, and undoubtedly will be, ongoing for some time on the interpretation and uses of the 16PF.

Summary

This chapter discussed the measurement of both interests and personality, and centered on the use of self-report inventories. The inventories are paper-and-pencil tests through which the individual describes himself. Personality traits can also be measured through the use of projective techniques. In contrast to self-report inventories, projective techniques require the individual to interpret objects or things other than himself (such as to respond to a picture or an ink blot, for example). Underlying the use of projective techniques is the assumption that an individual's responses are influenced by his needs, desires, motives, concerns, etc. Of course, particular response patterns require interpretation. The methodology of using projective techniques, such as direct interviewing of subjects suspected of having personality disorders, requires considerable training and experience. These techniques find their major use in clinical situations on an individual, rather than a group, basis. They are or should be used by trained clinicians.

We have already alluded to several problems associated with the measurement of interests and personality. Certainly, the problems of faking and acquiescence have been recognized. Faking may be controlled by the use of more subtle items.

Self-report inventories are susceptible to semantic problems, which can appear in two ways. The items may be ambiguous and open to interpretation by the individuals taking the inventory. Items including phrases such as "Do you usually participate in ... ?" or "Do you assume leadership in ... ?" involve interpretation by the individual. What does *usually* mean? What does it mean to *participate in*, or *assume leadership*? Not only can different subjects come up with different interpretations, but a single subject may change his interpretation between testings. This latter situation is evidenced by sizable percentages of different responses to the same items on two or more testing occasions.

A second way in which semantic difficulties appear is in communicating results among users. There may be confusion and ambiguity when naming and describing factors, for example. Generally, the meanings of interest and personality factors tend to be less clear than meanings of factors associated with human abilities. The lack of precision among terms associated with interests and personality requires careful attention to how a term is defined by a specific user, and how a term is used in a given situation.

The scores on self-report inventories may be affected by situational factors. An individual may give somewhat different responses when applying for a job than when performing on the job later. Varied instructions may result in different responses from the same individual.

While the present status of personality and interest measurement is not completely developed, a knowledge of basic dimensions is important to the practitioner. Certainly, knowing the interest categories: people, business, science, and language, and the personality dimensions: extroversion-introversion and anxiety, will facilitate learning about basic inventories. While it can be argued that these lists are incomplete, these dimensions appear to be the more basic ones.

In this chapter, we have used the terms *trait, dimension,* and *factor* interchangeably. Is a factor a trait? We have consistently taken the position that "intervening states" are inferences from behavior or categories of behavior. If a trait is an inference from behavior used to predict another criterion behavior, the concept of trait is highly useful. Also, it matters little, except for the sake of clarity, if we refer to it as a dimension, factor, construct, attribute, or trait. All are inferences from behavior that assist in predicting (and, in some sense, explaining) human behavior. Our use of the term implies a higher order habit, learning set, or predisposition to respond—nothing more, nothing less.

As one studies factors, traits, or what have you, it is immediately apparent that since behavior categories can be reduced, inferences from these categories result in more and more inferences or traits with less and less generality. This is an unresolvable problem. What is a primary trait? What is a second-order factor? The answers to these questions are framed in the data from which these inferences originated. If any answer exists at all, it must come from looking across studies to determine which traits continue to be identified. We have attempted to focus on those traits, cognitive and noncognitive, that are quite widely accepted.

How important are traits? It is obvious from our discussion that we think the concept of traits in the prediction of behavior has merit. Trait approaches to predicting behavior account for a maximum of about 50 percent of the variation in many criterion performances. Also, it can be inferred that situational variables and trait interactions are at least as important as traits themselves. Although too much emphasis could be put on a trait approach, the fact remains that in many situations, trait tests and trait theories can be widely used to advantage.

This chapter has introduced the student to the measurement of interests and personality through paper-and-pencil self-inventories that can be administered to a group or an individual. The interpretations of personality and interest measures are quite complex. Entire books are devoted to this topic, or to special facets of this topic. Noncognitive measurement is still in its infancy or, at best, its adolescence. This does not mean that measurement procedures are unsophisticated or simple. It means that a great deal of research and development is still required in this complex and difficult area of measurement.

Selected Readings

Allport, G. W. Traits revisited. *American Psychologist,* 1966, 21, 1–10.

Cattell, R. *The scientific analysis of personality.* Baltimore: Penguin Books, 1965.

Cattell, R., Eber, H., & Tatsuoka, M. *Handbook for the 16PF.* Champaign, Ill.: Institute for Personality and Ability Testing, 1970.

Dahlstrom, W., & Welsh, G. *An MMPI handbook: A guide to use in clinical practice and research.* Minneapolis: University of Minnesota Press, 1960.

Eysenck, H. *The structure of human personality.* New York: Wiley, 1953.

Hall, C., & Lindsey, G. *Theories of personality.* (2nd ed.) New York: Wiley, 1957, pp. 380–416.

Individual Review Questions

1. Prospective teachers are administered the Minnesota Teacher Attitude Inventory. Scores on this inventory are considered *cognitive/noncognitive* measures.

2. One individual, responding to an interest inventory, gives what he perceives as only socially acceptable responses regardless of how he feels. This inaccuracy in responding is called _____.

3. When responding to a personality inventory, an individual has a response set of agreeing with any issue on which he is undecided. This tendency in responding is an example of _____.

4. One problem in personality assessment is that specific methods of measurement cannot be separated from the traits being measured. The traits and methods used in assessing them are thus _____.

5. A personality inventory is constructed so the items are highly homogeneous. The validation procedure emphasized is that of *construct/criterion* validation.

6. In comparing cognitive and noncognitive measures, *cognitive/noncognitive* measures presently tend to possess the higher reliability.

ANSWERS
1. noncognitive
2. faking
3. acquiescence
4. confounded
5. construct
6. cognitive

235

7. A research psychologist puts greatest emphasis on clarifying and defining the personality traits being considered. The major concern here is with *construct/content/criterion* validity.

8. When testing an individual in an academic achievement area, she is generally instructed to strive for *maximum/typical* performance. However, if the same individual is administered a personality inventory, the results are assumed to reflect *maximum/typical* performance.

9. In measurement of a given personality trait, high *internal consistency/stability* reliability is desirable. However, depending on the situation, we may or may not want high *internal consistency/stability* reliability.

10. Strong's development of the Strong Vocational Interest Blank (SVIB) was based on *empirical/theoretical* procedures.

11. The SVIB was developed using *construct/criterion* validation procedures.

12. When using criterion validation procedures to develop an interest inventory for psychologists, the items to which the psychologists' responses are *different from/similar to* the responses of people in general would be of special interest.

13. While attempting to determine whether or not an item distinguishes between individuals in an occupation and those not in the occupation, the correlation between the responses to the item and the dichotomy of "occupation, not occupation" is the _____ of the item.

14. An individual receives a score of 50 on the Architect scale of the SVIB. This puts the individual at the _____ of the _____ group of architects.

15. Interest inventories developed using *construct/criterion* validation procedures are especially susceptible to changes in validity if there is a change in the population from the original norm group.

16. The Kuder Preference Record–Vocational was developed using *construct/criterion* validation procedures.

17. The Kuder-Vocational provides *general/occupational* interest categories.

18. The *Outdoor/Forest Ranger* scale is found on the Kuder-Vocational.

19. A score derived for an individual by a forced-choice technique, where the pattern of interests is based on the individual himself, is a(n) *ipsative/normative* score.

20. The forced-choice format tends to *decrease/increase* likelihood of faking.

21. The ten interest categories of the Kuder-Vocational tend to be relatively *dependent/independent.*

22. If we were concerned with the traits that describe an individual's interests, we would prefer the score on the *Kuder-Vocational/SVIB*.

23. The SVIB provides *ipsative/normative* scores, while the Kuder-Vocational provides *ipsative/normative* scores.

24. The *Kuder-Vocational/SVIB* has the more complex scoring procedures.

25. Through childhood into young adulthood, interests become *decreasingly/increasingly* stable with age.

26. In Thurstone's initial approach to identifying interest constructs, he identified _____ traits.

27. Vernon focused on a general factor in the factor analysis of interest scores. This general factor was labeled _____.

28. Considering Eysenck's concept of personality types and traits, a type consists of a group of correlated _____, and a trait is a function of correlated _____.

29. Early studies of personality were quite consistent in identifying a component that has become known as _____ _____.

30. The MMPI was developed using *construct/criterion* validation procedures, and the 16PF was developed using *construct/criterion* validation methods.

31. The MMPI was designed to secure information on *a dual phase/multiple phases/ a single phase* of personality.

32. The MMPI contains ten clinical scales and four _____ scales.

33. The determination of item discrimination in the MMPI was based on an *a priori/ empirical* approach.

34. When items of a personality inventory are found in two or more scales, the scales tend to have relatively *high/low* intercorrelations.

35. The 16PF was originally designed to assess the personality traits of *hospitalized/ morally delinquent/normal* individuals.

36. The 16PF was designed for use with *adolescents/small children/young adults*.

37. The subtest scores of the 16PF are scaled using a _____ transformation.

38. The 16PF, as the name implies, identifies 16 primary factors of personality. However, _____ second-order, or more general, factors are also identified and represented by scores.

ANSWERS

22. Kuder-Vocational
23. normative; ipsative
24. SVIB
25. increasingly
26. four
27. gregariousness
28. traits; behaviors
29. extroversion-introversion
30. criterion; construct
31. multiple phases
32. validity
33. empirical
34. high
35. normal
36. young adults
37. sten
38. four

Study Exercises

1. Distinguish between cognitive and noncognitive abilities.
2. Distinguish between personality and interest traits.
3. Some subtest intercorrelations, as presented in the *California Test of Personality Manual* (1953, p. 6), are listed. What evidence can you find to support the personality traits postulated by Cattell?

	1A	1B	1C	1D	1E	1F	2A	2B	2C	2D	2E	2F
1. Personal Adjustment												
A. Self-reliance	.33	.21	.32	.52	.43	.07	.39	.21	.18	.23	.17	
B. Sense of Personal Worth		.28	.63	.46	.29	.20	.47	.33	.31	.36	.26	
C. Sense of Personal Freedom			.40	.32	.21	.06	.22	.22	.46	.19	.21	
D. Feeling of Belonging				.51	.35	.13	.48	.32	.47	.37	.33	
E. Withdrawing Tendencies					.47	.15	.45	.46	.35	.39	.24	
F. Nervous Symptoms						.02	.25	.27	.32	.28	.19	
2. Social Adjustment												
A. Social Standards							.24	.34	.13	.19	.20	
B. Social Skills								.25	.21	.30	.32	
C. Anti-social Tendencies									.40	.40	.22	
D. Family Relations										.34	.28	
E. School Relations											.37	
F. Community Relations												

4. Distinguish between ipsative and normative scoring.
5. Consider the following factor matrix (from Thurstone, 1931, p. 201):

		I	II	III	IV
Advertising	1	−.48	.66	−.21	.22
Art	2	.45	.70	−.18	−.31
CPA	3	−.04	.32	.00	.56
Chemistry	4	.98	−.21	−.15	.06
Engineering	5	.84	−.36	−.22	.16
Law	6	−.23	.77	−.12	.44
Ministry	7	.09	.51	.62	−.30
Psychology	8	.77	.47	−.04	−.28
Teaching	9	.36	.15	.68	−.22
Life Insurance	10	−.82	−.02	.27	.45
Architecture	11	.83	.26	.16	.05
YMCA Secretary	12	−.23	.00	.90	−.37
Farming	13	.71	−.54	.01	.18
Purchasing Agent	14	−.05	−.79	.01	.44
Journalism	15	−.15	.84	−.28	.25
Personnel	16	−.30	−.26	.66	−.19
Real Estate	17	−.76	−.07	−.06	.58
Medicine	18	.71	.33	−.26	−.09

a. Identify Thurstone's factors for Business, Language, People, and Science.
b. Discuss the loadings of the following professions: Advertising, Chemistry, Psychology, Ministry, and Medicine.
c. Which two professions most clearly identify each factor?

6. Distinguish between the criterion and homogeneous keying of the SVIB and the Kuder-Vocational.
7. Discuss the logic of reporting a validity coefficient as the square root of the reliability (as done with the 16PF).
8. Consider the relatively low criterion validity coefficients of the SVIB. What evidence is there to suggest that while the coefficients are low, they still provide valuable information?

11   Test Construction

Thus far in this text, the emphasis has been on types and characteristics of psychological measures or tests. We have considered the measurement of specific human characteristics, and the reliability, validity, and norms associated with that measurement. Little attention has been given specifically to how a test is constructed. This chapter will present the general principles of test construction. Although we often associate test construction with some type of educational activity, such as preparing an achievement test in a specific academic area, the principles discussed in this chapter have wider application to a variety of forms of psychological measurement. These principles also may apply to some measures of personality and attitudes, as well as ability measures.

The principles and procedures discussed in this chapter apply to psychological measures that are based on the *linear model*. This model simply requires that test scores are obtained by summing scores with either equal or differential weighting over the items. That is, the test score is based on a linear combination of the responses to individual items. Nunnally (1970, p. 196) estimated that 95 percent of all psychological measures are based on the linear model.

One other general assumption has been made: the construction of any test reflects some purpose and some set of objectives. It is not our intent to argue the merits of particular purposes or statements of objectives. The assumption is that any test construction situation requires a purpose for constructing the test, and has objectives associated with its construction.

One final point. The discussion that follows may suggest that achievement-type items are under consideration. While this is so, the principles are general enough to cover most ability, personality, and other types of tests. Thus, while achievement tests are used to illustrate the test construction principles, the principles are general enough for wider application to many other types of tests.

Construction of Test Items

Suppose we have an adequate set of objectives, and, to some extent, have identified the outcomes, learning or otherwise, related to these objectives. For example, the objectives might reflect a unit of instruction in an academic area, or some other type of experience, designed to affect a subject's attitude. How do we construct good test items to measure any change? No single list of procedures will insure good items, but there are suggestions that should result in the production of better items, if they are followed.

First, the item should reflect the objective to be measured. The subject should know what type of performance is required of her. Confusing and ambiguous, as well as unnecessary, terminology should be avoided in the item. The item should not require performance for which the subject does not have the prerequisite skills. For example, in an achievement test, we should not require the subject to apply a set of principles if she has not been trained in the prerequisite skills, knowledge, or comprehension of these principles. Other necessary technical prerequisites may also be lacking; for instance, the subject cannot read or understand the item because the reading level is not suitable. She may know the content the item covers, but cannot respond correctly because she cannot understand the item. Assuming that we are not testing reading, the item has failed to do its job in this case.

> **Test items should reflect the objectives of a unit of instruction. Students should know the objectives, and what to expect on the test. Clarity of terminology is a necessary requirement for good item construction, and the subject should possess the necessary prerequisites for the performance required by the item.**

Items are often classified according to form. A commonly used classification scheme is the dichotomy *objective* and *essay* items. Objective items require a short response, but their objectivity lies in "the extent to which equally competent scorers get the same result." Multiple-choice items are objective items. The multiple-choice name is derived from the multiple options from which the examinee selects a response. There must be at least two alternatives predetermined by the test constructor, including one correct or best response.

Essay items require a much longer response, giving the examinee more latitude in content and form. Essay items are generally free-response items, in which the examinee supplies the response rather than simply identifying it among the alternatives. Scoring essay items usually involves some type of subjective judgment on the part of the scorer.

Some short-response items, such as filling in a blank, are considered both free-response and objective items. It is likely that equally competent scorers will get consistent results with short-answer, definite correct-response items.

The scoring of the response to an essay item should be made as objective as possible for between-scorer consistency. The fact that we classify items as objective or essay in this chapter does not imply that essay items are lacking in objectivity.

Constructing Forced-Choice Items

Forced-choice items include such forms as multiple-choice and true-false. They are items for which the examinee is not permitted to construct his own response. The multiple-choice form is flexible, and is widely used. The lead-in to a multiple-choice item is called the *stem*, and the set of alternatives is the *response*. Multiple-choice items, contrary to popular opinion, can be used effectively for higher-level thought processes than simple recall or knowledge-level responses. Multiple-choice items can be used to test objectives in application, analysis, and synthesis. It may be more difficult to construct items for the higher levels, but this should not dissuade the constructor from using multiple-choice items for testing objectives on these levels.

The wording of an item should be such that all of the content is used to determine the response. A strong association between a word or phrase in the stem and a word or phrase in the responses may result in only part of the content being used. Hawkes, Lindquist, and Mann (1936) illustrated this difficulty with the following example:

> *Original form:* The leader in the making of the compromise tariff of 1833 was (1) Clay, (2) Webster, (3) Jackson, (4) Taylor, (5) Harrison.
> *Rewritten form:* The leader in the tariff revision of 1833 was (1) Clay, (2) Webster, (3) Jackson, (4) Taylor, (5) Harrison [p. 77].

In the original form many students responded correctly because of the strong association between *compromise* and *Clay*. This was evident when less than half the students responded correctly as soon as the item appeared in the rewritten form. Matched test items are very susceptible to this difficulty—a single word provides the entire cue, and the rest of the phrase is essentially unused.

It is best to avoid textbook terminology and stereotyped situations in wording the item. For example, if the correct response to a definition item is the exact definition given in the text, the item requires little more than simple recall. It is better to construct an item that requires the examinee to apply a principle in a new situation, or to identify a definition in a novel form. Construct the item so that selecting the correct response requires an understanding of the principle or term.

The contrast between the stereotyped, factual approach and the novel, interpretive approach is provided by the following two items:

1. Unified control over supply or demand which will permit the regulation of price is known as:
   (a) the law of supply and demand.
   (b) a monopoly.
   (c) specialization.
   (d) an unfavorable balance of trade.
2. Which of the following men may be said to have a monopoly?
   (a) Mr. A., who owns all the tin mines in the world.
   (b) Mr. B., who makes a business of buying and selling stock on the New York Stock Exchange.
   (c) Mr. C., who sells only one article, shoes, in his store.
   (d) Mr. D., who owns the largest gold mine in the world [University Evaluation and Examination Service, 1948, p. 3].

Clearly the first item contains in its stem the textbook definition of monopoly. If the examinee has memorized the definition, he can quickly recognize familiar words. In the second item, the examinee must understand the term *monopoly* to arrive at the correct response. The alternatives are novel and plausible, and the test constructor can put in any desired degree of discrimination between the alternatives.

> **In constructing multiple-choice items, design the alternatives so the examinee must demonstrate an understanding or application of the principle, rather than simply recalling a textbook definition or some key terms used in stating the principle.**

The incorrect responses, or distractors, in an item should not be so unreasonable that the correct response can be recognized by elimination of the incorrect ones; it is possible to use a best answer. More than one, or all of the responses, could be at least partially correct, but one is definitely the best response. This approach requires a greater depth of understanding and closer discrimination than the completely correct or incorrect alternatives. The examinee may eliminate incorrect responses due to subtle weaknesses within them. In this case, such elimination is not undesirable, especially if the objective of the item was to recognize such subtle weaknesses. In any event, incorrect responses should not be eliminated for superficial reasons, such as inconsistent grammar between the stem and an incorrect response.

When one presents items containing definitions, it is better to put the definition in the response than in the stem. This way the examinee must select the definition rather than simply select the term. An even better approach is to have the examinee interpret the meaning of the term. For example, consider a definition of *patent*. To put the definition in the response, we could phrase the stem as, "What is a patent?" This would be followed by several alternatives, one of which is correct or best. For an interpretive approach, the item might be:

> Which of the following practices tends *most* to defeat the purpose for which patents are given?
> (a) forming corporations to make use of patents.
> (b) purchasing patents in order to keep them from being used.
> (c) preventing patents from being renewed more than once.
> (d) requiring all patents to be obtained at a central office in Washington, D.C. [University Evaluation and Examination Service, 1948, p. 4].

In order to correctly respond to this item, the examinee must know what a patent is and understand its purpose. Note the use of the word *most* in the stem. Moreover, note that none of the responses contains direct clues to the meaning of *patent*.

The stem of a multiple-choice item should contain the central content of the item, and any qualifications to the content. Item stems should stand alone and not receive part of their content from other items. All alternatives in the response should be grammatically consistent with the stem. Alternatives should be homogeneous in both grammar and structural form. Confusion can arise with negatively stated stems, and these should be avoided. Brevity of items also tends to enhance communication and lessen confusion.

The homogeneity of the alternative responses relative to grammar and form is very important. The responses should also be homogeneous in linguistic difficulty and technical level. Avoid terms that are clearly too technical for the context, because the responses in which they appear might be eliminated superficially. Terms not yet introduced in prior instruction should be avoided, since students may eliminate directly any responses with clearly unfamiliar terms. If responses vary greatly in length, some may be immediately recognized as being inconsistent with the context.

> **Homogeneous alternative responses for multiple-choice items must be considered in item construction. Responses should be homogeneous in form, length, grammar, technical level, and linguistic difficulty.**

The content of the item, not the form, should determine the response for the student. Telltale words or phrases can provide unwanted clues. Words like *sometimes, absolutely,* and *never* should be avoided, if possible. They are especially likely to appear in true-false items. Very specific and emphatic terms tend to go with items that contain false statements; weaker terms tend to be included in true statements.

In the construction of true-false items, many of the suggestions for multiple-choice items also apply. The statements in the item should be unambiguous. It is best to avoid exact textbook terminology. Keep statements brief, and limit each to a single concept; do not run together statements that are partially true and partially false. Consider, for example, the statement that "mercury and sodium chloride are metals." The student may know the content, but may be uncertain of the desired response. If the statement is partially true, should he respond "True"? Trick statements may elicit an incorrect response due to a superficial technicality rather than a lack of knowledge; they should be avoided.

When using forced-choice test items, all the information in the item and its response is provided by the examiner. The examinee is required to use the information and make his choices. The matter of how the examinee uses the information is controlled, to some extent, by the test constructor when constructing the items. Poorly constructed items may provide undesirable clues or information that permit the examinee to respond in ways not intended. Confusing items may handicap the examinee by not adequately providing all the information needed. It is essential that items be carefully constructed so the content of the items can be used in the manner desired; that is, so the items can meet the purpose for which the test was developed.

Constructing Short, Free-Response Items

Short, free-response items generally require answering a question with a short response, possibly one phrase or one sentence; or by providing a missing word or phrase in an otherwise complete statement, known as a completion item. The usual clarity in presenting the statement applies. Indefinite statements should be avoided; for example, "World War II took place in _____." The student is hard pressed to respond. Does the item call for a period of time? Or location? An improved phrasing would be, "The European hostilities of World War II took place during the period _____." In addition, statements should not become cumbersome, confusing, or mutilated in order to place the blanks.

Constructing Other Short-Response Items

Other types of short-response items that find occasional use in test construction are *matching items* and *ordering items*. Matching items typically consist of two columns of short statements in which single statements from each column are to be paired. Ordering items may require arranging several events in chrono-logical order.

Matching items must be so presented that the student understands the criterion for the matching. Unwarranted clues should be avoided, and the item content (the statements) should be homogeneous. We might, for example, have a listing of battles in one column and the dates for the battles in another. But we would not include battles and countries in one column, and dates and statesmen in the other. Usually the statements in a column are systematically arranged, as in alphabetical order. The number of matching items should be considered; usually there are not more than 10 to 15 statements per column. An excessive number tends to waste time, and decreases homogeneity of the statements. In items that involve ordering statements, homogeneity of content is again important. Lack of homogeneity tends to provide extraneous clues. Columns in a matching exercise should be clearly labeled.

Use of Essay Items

Essay items, or examinations consisting exclusively of essay items, are used for classroom testing. The items per se may not be difficult to construct. Usually they are designed to elicit a relatively long response, possibly one or more para-graphs. The actual item may be quite short and straightforward. Usually such items are included to test levels of knowledge, such as analysis, application, or synthesis. If an essay item requires only recall, generally it can be replaced by a series of short-answer items. Why do we continue using essay items? There is strong opinion that certain purposes can be met only through the use of essay items, such as demonstrating analysis. Actually, there is very little research evidence regarding the effectiveness of and necessity for using essay items.

Few test constructors will use essay items for simple recall; yet, unless they are carefully constructed to elicit higher-level outcomes, essay items may reduce to being only factual-knowledge items. Phrasing the directions to the student in an essay item must be done so the form or level of response expected is very specific. For example, the student must be told to list, compare, describe, or whatever. This initial direction is very important. It implies that information exists, independent of the student's knowledge, and that the information is to be used in a given way. For example, it is a mistake to phrase an item: "Write what you know about the war between the Jews and Arabs during 1967." The item is far too broad, and has no focus. Also, it does not specifically call for any learning outcomes, except possibly factual recall. Even more disastrous, the response cannot be scored or graded. No matter what the student writes, his response must be correct. Even if the student responds, "I know nothing about this war," it is a correct response, since he is doing as directed in the item. Correspondingly, beginning an item "What do you think..." is a similar mistake in item construction.

Generally, in constructing essay items, it is better to use more items focused on a specific point and requiring shorter responses, than to have a few, very broad items. More items and shorter responses tend to give the student more direction, and tend to restrict the responses to those intended. We may also identify and partition the specific content to which we want the student to respond. For example, we may construct an item:

> Contrast the circumstances of the 1967 war between Israel and the Arab nations with respect to:
> (a) military resources on both sides.
> (b) internal support within the nations.
> (c) the role of the United States and Russia.

This item informs the student what activity is expected of him, and directs his attention to the points desired. Without such additional direction, the student may, or may not, select the points desired by the examiner.

> **In constructing essay items, define the specific activity desired, and give the student all necessary directions. More items with shorter anticipated responses will tend to meet these criteria.**

The biggest difficulty with essay items comes in their scoring and grading. Most essay items involve an element, usually substantial, of subjective evaluation on the part of the scorer. There may be problems of both objectivity and consistency in scoring—not only between scorers, but also for the same scorer at different times. It is imperative that a list of criteria, as objective as possible, be developed prior to the scoring, and that scorers adhere closely to the criteria. More explicit items with shorter anticipated responses tend to minimize subjectivity, and make the scoring more objective.

Scoring difficulties make for low reliability of subjective tests. A multiple-choice or short-response test can be scored more reliably than an essay test. Also, given the broader sampling of content in the short-response test, it tends to be more valid than the essay test. Of course, the decision to use a short-response or essay-type test should be a function of the material to be covered and the outcomes to be tested. There are some topics that logically require essay tests, while short-response items are more appropriate for other topics. All things being equal, however, multiple-choice items can be scored more easily, can cover a broader range of content, and can be designed to sample a higher level of content than most other types of tests.

Whether short-response or essay items are being constructed, the test constructor should formulate the items carefully and avoid "throwing the items together." Items should be clear, concise, and long enough to convey the meaning intended. Long items with several parts should have the parts clearly distinguished to avoid confusion. Unless it is a purpose of the test, the student's performance should not be determined by his ability to unravel the technical aspects of responding to an item. Complicated items may be difficult, not because of the content, but because of complexity of form or terminology. Items should be carefully checked to avoid this situation.

When one constructs items for an anticipated test, it is well to organize and outline the content to be covered by the test. Objectives should indicate the examinee performance expected. Each item should be carefully prepared and reworked if necessary. It is advantageous to have a pool of items from which to make final selections for the test.

Putting the Test. Together

Assuming the test constructor has a pool of adequately written items, there are straightforward procedures for assembling a test to make it more convenient for all concerned. The items should be presented so they are easy to understand and simple to respond to. With true-false items, we can indicate by parentheses or a line where the student is to respond, usually with either T or F. The responses can be put in a column either to the right or left of the items. For completion items, the spaces for responding can be placed in a column to the right of the items. If more than one space is required for an item, the spaces can be coded by number, for example:

Scores in the standard unit normal distribution have a mean of ___(1)___ and a standard deviation of ___(2)___.

(1) _____
(2) _____

Note that spaces or blanks for responding are all of equal size so the subject does not infer the length of the correct response from the size of the blank.

The items should use the simplest and most straightforward form for recording the response. We have already mentioned the T or F for true-false items. Completion items require filling in the appropriate blank. Multiple-choice items can have a column for responding, as with true-false items. The student then puts the number or letter corresponding to his selection in the space for the item answer.

With relatively long tests consisting entirely of multiple-choice items, a separate answer sheet may be used on which the student darkens a square corresponding to his answer for each item. Test publishers commonly use such answer sheets so they can be machine-scored. In these cases, the student must be able to make the connection between the items on the test copy and the answer sheet. This may be somewhat complicated for younger children, say 6- and 7-year-old youngsters. If this happens, separate answer sheets should not be used. Even with older children, technical difficulties can arise. For example, an item on the test may be skipped because of difficulty, but the corresponding response space is not skipped on the answer sheet. When this occurs, all the following responses will not correspond with their test items. Whenever separate answer sheets are employed, their use should be carefully explained to the students, and possible technical pitfalls should be mentioned.

Usually, all items of a specific type are placed together in the test. Such placement facilitates the scoring and the review of the test. More important, it enables the student to develop a set for the particular form, rather than fluctuating back and forth between different types placed in a random or haphazard arrangement. Placing similar items together requires less attention to the techniques of responding, and allows greater concentration on the content of the items. Certainly, we can include more than one type of item in a test; doing so provides some variety for the student and also gives the test constructor more latitude than if he were limited to a single type of item.

After the test is put together, it must be administered, taken, and scored. All of these operations can result in various types of error. Error contributes to decreased reliability and increased standard error of measurement. It follows, then, that these factors should be controlled to the greatest extent possible.

Minimizing Error Variance

To minimize test administration errors, the test should be accompanied by clear and concise directions. To avoid omissions in the instructions, it is better to have the instructions written even if they will be presented orally. The examinee should know what to do if he encounters certain situations. For example, if he does not know an answer, should he guess or omit the item? The examinee should have ample time (unless it is a timed or speeded test), and should not have his anxiety level raised more than is normally caused by a testing situation.

Doppelt (1954) discussed guessing as a source of error variation. With achievement tests, we may use a correction-for-chance (chance guessing) formula rather than counting correct responses only. This formula corrects for omission rather than for guessing, as such. It is commonly used, and applies to items with two or more options:

$$\text{Score} = R - \frac{W}{O - 1}, \tag{11.1}$$

where:

$\quad$ Score $=$ corrected score
$\qquad R =$ number of correct responses
$\qquad W =$ number of incorrect responses
$\qquad O =$ number of options in each item.

Applying this formula for our four-option items, we would have: Score $= R - W/3$. Note that with formula 11.1, items that are omitted do not count as incorrect responses.

What is the effect of guessing on the individual's score and the overall test results? Obviously, there will be more correct responses than if guessing had not occurred. We also know that there is considerable variation in the tendency to guess from one individual to another. We can attempt to control this variation by giving very explicit directions that the examinee is to respond to every item; that is, to guess if the correct response is not known.

The question still remains whether formula 11.1 should be used. Since the formula corrects for omissions, if few items are omitted, applying the formula will have little effect on the ranking of scores. If there is marked difference in the number of items omitted by students, the correction resulting from use of the formula will affect the scores and their relative positions.

Under any conditions, formula 11.1 is an approximate adjustment, because the formula is based on two assumptions, which, for all practical purposes, are rarely, if ever, completely met. These assumptions are: (1) the student either knows the right answer or guesses, but does not respond on the basis of misinformation, and (2) all alternate responses are equally attractive to a student who does not know the correct response. We know that many students have partial information, and can eliminate one or more incorrect responses. Also, test constructors often structure items so misinformation leads to an incorrect response rather than a guess.

There can be "psychological" reasons for applying the formula. Obviously, if the student has been told that his score will be corrected, it should be corrected. Guessing is more of a problem when items have fewer alternatives, such as two, rather than more alternatives, such as five answers, for multiple-choice items. If there are fewer alternatives on the test items, without the correction, the poorer students may be misled by the uncorrected score; that is, the uncorrected score may seem to represent considerably more knowledge than they actually possess. Therefore, with two or three alternatives per item, the correction is recommended even if there are few omissions. Speeded tests present more of a problem for guessing than do power tests. General consensus is that for tests consisting of items with more alternatives and adequate time, there is little gained by applying the correction; simply indicating the score in terms of the number correct is quite satisfactory.

The scoring of a test also introduces opportunity for error. Any scoring procedure should be kept as simple as possible. With short-answer, objective exams, the scoring can usually be done very efficiently. Weighting items is usually an unnecessary procedure. Guilford (1954), summarizing empirical results of differential weighting, concluded:

Differential weighting of items is therefore most effective in short tests and pays little dividends when there are more than 10 to 20 items. . . . In a long test it matters little what set of weights is used, provided they are of appropriate algebraic sign. Thus, weights of 1 for all items in long tests of ability are quite appropriate [p. 447].

The scoring of essay questions tends to be less objective than that of short-answer items. Nevertheless, the scorer should develop a list of points or criteria to be used in scoring. Prior to scoring any tests, the scorer should know what constitutes a correct response, and any rules for scoring should be defined. If scoring rules do not remain consistent throughout the scoring, the individual's score may become more a function of the paper's position in the pile than of actual performance.

Item Analysis

We have considered different types of items and how they may be organized into a test. Until items are administered to a group of subjects and scored, there is no empirical information about the adequacy of individual items or the test. Certainly, in the case of an achievement test, content validity is of major importance, and is established primarily on a logical, rather than an empirical, basis. Nevertheless, item analysis can provide important information for test construction.

When an item analysis is undertaken, two indices or item characteristics are generally obtained: the item discrimination index, and the item difficulty index. The item discrimination index is a measure of how well performance on an item correlates with some internal or external criterion scores. Usually an external criterion is not available, and an internal criterion is used. This internal criterion can be the total test score, or preferably, the subtest score in which the item is included, assuming the test is divided into two or more subtests. In this case, the item discrimination index tells us the degree to which an item correlates with other items (the similarity of items). The item difficulty index tells us if an item is too difficult or too easy. Information provided by the difficulty index is applicable where maximum dispersion is required; for example, with norm-referenced, ability, and achievement tests. However, in some situations, the difficulty index may not apply. Both of these indices will be discussed further when we consider norm- and criterion-referenced testing.

To initiate an item analysis, it is desirable to have an item pool at least double the final test length. To lessen the possibility of chance fluctuation in the item analysis, Nunnally (1970, p. 201) suggested that the items be administered to at least 300 subjects, and that there be at least five times as many subjects as items. A single instructor is usually not about to initiate such an extensive analysis. Nevertheless, if item analysis information is desired, the instructor should be aware of possible limitations in the stability of the statistics generated.

Appropriate use of item analysis information may not be easy. Inappropriate use is not uncommon, and interpretation of item analysis results requires great care.

The Item Discrimination Index: Internal Criterion

One important characteristic of the item discrimination index is the extent to which it differentiates between the high and low performers on the test. An index with this discrimination can be obtained by correlating the performance on the item with the total test or subtest score. Thus, one type of item discrimination index consists of a correlation coefficient. Assuming that an item can be scored right or wrong, and that the total test or subtest score assumes at least interval scale measurement, we have the conditions for applying the point-biserial correlation coefficient. The point-biserial correlation coefficient is the product-moment correlation when one variable is dichotomous, and the other variable is continuous and measured on at least an interval scale.

There are several computational formulas for figuring the point-biserial correlation coefficient. Our preference is:

$$r_{pbi} = \frac{\overline{X}_p - \overline{X}}{S} \sqrt{p/q},\tag{11.2}$$

where:

$\overline{X}_p$ = the mean of the scores on the continuous variable (total test) of the individuals passing the item

$\overline{X}$ = the mean of all scores on the continuous variable

S = the standard deviation of all scores on the continuous variable

p = the proportion of individuals responding correctly to the item

$q = 1 - p.$

In computing item discrimination indices, we generate the item–total test or item-subtest correlation coefficients—the point-biserial r's. These coefficients are then studied for magnitude. Items with high point-biserial r's are usually retained, and those with low or negative r's rejected. An item with a high coefficient is retained because the high coefficient indicates similarity (over the group of examinees) between performance on the item and performance on the total test or subtest. Recall from Chapter 5 that such similarity contributes to reliability.

> **High item-test correlations contribute to test reliability. Retaining items with high coefficients and rejecting items with low or negative coefficients generally increase the reliability estimates of the test.**

If an item has a near zero or negative correlation with the total test score, we generally discard it. Such low correlations tend to decrease test reliability. However, before routinely discarding items with low point-biserial r's, study them carefully first to discover if they are unique in measuring content to be represented in the test. If so, additional items of similar content should be added to the test.

> Routinely discarding items that have low item–total test correlations can result in a test with higher reliability, but lower criterion or content validity.

An important principle in measurement suggests that the more similar the set of items, the *higher* the reliability. Paradoxically, there are situations in which *lower* correlations are required to maximize certain types of validity. If a test is to measure a number of concepts, all item–total test correlations might not be high. Certainly, this will be true if only two or three items are used to measure one of the concepts embedded in the test items. Since validity is of paramount importance in all test construction, adding or deleting items must be done with discretion. High and low point-biserial r's are technical information that must be cautiously used when constructing a test.

> Higher criterion and content validity may be achieved when item–total test score correlations are relatively lower. High item-test correlations, while contributing to reliability, do not necessarily provide evidence of high test validity.

This poses an obvious dilemma for the test constructor. One solution is to group similar items (those sampling similar concepts) into subtests. Then, item-subtest correlations, rather than item–total test correlations, are computed to provide evidence of reliability and validity. High correlation coefficients will confirm that the subtest items being sampled are reliable and, by the nature of the subtest construction, likely valid. By using item-subtest correlations, both clusters of reliable items and sampling of various concepts are obtained.

> When item-subtest correlations are used to construct tests, high correlations provide evidence of high reliability. To the degree that each subtest samples a relevant concept, the high correlations can also contribute to evidence of test validity.

The Item Discrimination Index: External Criterion

Item discrimination indices are correlations between items and some external or internal criterion. Using an internal criterion, say test score, results in an index that assists in the maximization of reliability—but not necessarily criterion validity. Sometimes it is possible to obtain scores on some external criterion, and the item-criterion correlations also provide item discrimination indices. If this external criterion is also the criterion the test is being validated against, these item discrimination indices can be used to select items to maximize the criterion validity of the test.

For example, suppose we wish to design a test to predict masculinity-femininity. We could correlate items with the male-female dichotomy, hoping to obtain items to which males respond "yes" (or "no") and females respond "no" (or "yes"). Items with high discrimination indices (which have a high correlation with this external criterion) can be used to create a test with high criterion validity. In situations where purpose requires high criterion validity, the external criterion can be used for an analysis of test items. However, in situations where purpose requires content or construct validation, an internal criterion is often used. Thus, the selection of an external or internal criterion must be a function of the purpose for which the test has been designed.

> **When the purpose for constructing the test dictates criterion validation, items can be validated against the external criterion that the test is designed to predict.**

What constitutes a minimum correlation coefficient for retaining an item? There is no single answer to this question, but some guidelines have been suggested. If a test constructor requires a minimum number of items for the final version of the test, and there is no opportunity to develop additional items, about the only course of action is to select the required number of items from those with the highest point-biserial r's. Suppose we have a subtest consisting of 100 multiple-choice items that is part of a large achievement test. We would expect the correlations to range from zero to about .40, with correlations above .20 considered adequate. If the number of items required meets this criterion, an adequate pool of items exists. If not, the test constructor has little option but to develop a larger item pool, and reapply the item analysis.

In Chapter 5, the importance of difficulty level and item homogeneity was discussed in the framework of reliability theory. Moderate difficulty level and high item intercorrelations resulted in maximum internal consistency reliability. Depending on test validation procedures, high item intercorrelations may or may not result in better test validity. Nevertheless, it is important that we be able to specify information about the difficulty level and the discrimination characteristics of an item.

The Item Difficulty Index

First, unless criterion referencing is being used, very hard items or very easy items generally contribute little to a test. In Chapter 5, the variance of an item was the proportion passing the item, multiplied by the proportion failing the item: $S_i^2 = p_i q_i$. If an item is of moderate difficulty so that p_i is approximately equal to q_i (both around .5), maximum dispersion is produced. (The range for moderate difficulty is generally considered to be .3 to .7.) Conversely, if the item is very difficult or very easy, little dispersion is produced. Since most traditional concepts of reliability and validity are dispersion-based, moderate difficulty items are generally desirable.

Suppose an ability test or a standardized achievement test is being developed. In order to assess *differences* in human performances, dispersion is crucial. In such a case, items of moderate difficulty level are sought, because they maximize differences between individuals.

On the other hand, suppose an instructor had committed himself and his students to a program of mastering all concepts or content in a subject. If, in fact, all concepts were mastered, an item analysis would indicate that most items, if not all, were too easy. In this case, items of moderate difficulty would not be desirable, and discrimination would be of little value.

> **Items of moderate difficulty level should be used in situations where dispersion is required. However, this rule is not appropriate for mastery learning, where dispersion is minimized.**

Computational Procedures for Item Analysis

The item discrimination index is a correlation coefficient, and the magnitude of this coefficient indicates how well an item discriminates between the high and low performers by some standard. There are other computational approaches to obtaining measures of item discrimination and item difficulty. Using an internal criterion, a computational approach for obtaining such indices has been suggested by Kelley (1939) and by Cureton (1957). The computation involves the difference between correct and incorrect responses of the upper 27 percent and the lower 27 percent of the individuals taking the test. The performances of the middle 46 percent of the examinees do not enter into the analysis. This measure is called the index of discrimination. If we compare an upper and a lower group, we know the item will discriminate more accurately than if we simply compared the upper one-half or 50 percent with the lower one-half. Why do we include 27 percent in each group, instead of, say, 10 percent or 30 percent?

Let us assume that there is a positive correlation between performance on the item and performance on the test. This means that a greater proportion of high-scoring students will have responded correctly to the item than did low-scoring students. However, the item more accurately discriminates between individuals who score on opposite sides of the mean, and whose scores lie farther from the mean, than it does for individuals who score close to the mean. Let p_u be the proportion of students in the upper (high test scores) group passing the item, and let p_l represent the corresponding proportion of the lower group. The difference between p_u and p_l will be greater if we use only extreme scores. However, the difference, $p_u - p_l$, has a standard deviation or standard error.[1] As the difference $(p_u - p_l)$ increases, the standard error of the difference increases. We want a large difference for discrimination, but a small standard error for precision. The combination of the magnitude of the standard error and the magnitude of the difference maximizes the discrimination of the item when 27 percent of the scores is included in each of the extreme groups.

The item analysis procedure is relatively straightforward and can be done easily by individual instructors. The computational procedure for the item analysis is:

1. Arrange the answer sheets in order from low to high test score. Determine 27 percent of the total number of papers; let k represent this number. (We cannot include part of a paper; therefore, k may be approximately 27 percent, but k must be an integer.) Identify the two subgroups of test papers: the k with the higher scores, and the k with lower scores.

2. For each item, count the number of correct and incorrect responses to the item given by members of the higher group. Do the same for the lower group, keeping the counts for the groups separate. Repeat this procedure for each item in the test, and record the counts opposite their respective responses. (The recording can be done on a test copy.)

3. Add the correct responses to each item for both the upper and lower groups. Divide this sum by the maximum possible correct responses, that is, $2k$. Express this quotient as a percentage. This percentage is the *index of item difficulty.*

4. Subtract the lower group's correct responses to each item from those of the upper group. Divide this difference by the maximum possible difference, namely, k. This quotient, a decimal fraction, is the *index of discrimination.*

The item analysis procedure provides us with the index of item difficulty and the index of discrimination for each item. The index of item difficulty is based on the responses of both upper and lower groups combined. If very few individuals responded correctly, the item would be difficult; conversely, if most individuals

---

[1] The statistic $p_u - p_l$ has a theoretical distribution of possible values if we select repeated random samples and compute it. The standard deviation of such a distribution is called the *standard error of the difference.*

responded correctly, the item would be easy. The item analysis provides the ratio of the total number of correct responses to the item to the maximum number of possible correct responses. This ratio is expressed as a quotient, and is multiplied by 100 to obtain a percentage. Its maximum value is 100 percent, indicating that all students in both groups responded correctly. The higher the numerical value of the index, the easier the item. In essence, this index is an inverse measure, in that the increasing value of the index indicates decreasing difficulty.

> **The index of item difficulty is expressed as a percentage derived from the ratio of the total number of correct responses in both upper and lower groups to the maximum possible number of correct responses for the two groups.**

The index of discrimination, as the name suggests, indicates how well the item discriminates between subjects in the upper and lower groups. (This index is commonly designated by D.) As Step 4 shows, we compute the difference[2] $(p_u - p_l)$. If all subjects in the upper group responded correctly, and all those in the lower group incorrectly, $p_u - p_l$ would equal 1.00, which is the maximum possible value of the index.

> **The index of discrimination of an item is expressed as a decimal fraction derived from the quotient of the difference between the number of correct responses in the upper and lower groups (upper minus lower) divided by the maximum possible difference, k, for the two groups.**

If the number of correct responses is the same for both groups, the item has an index of discrimination of 0.00; that is, the item does not discriminate. Negative discrimination can also occur if more correct responses are found in the lower group than in the upper group.

These two indices are not completely independent of each other. Items that are too difficult or too easy cannot possibly be good discriminators, because it is impossible to secure a large difference in number of correct responses between the upper and lower groups. Test reliability is generally enhanced by high discrimination indices, because they reflect high item similarity.

The item analysis just discussed uses an internal criterion, namely, the total test score or subtest scores, for determining the upper and lower groups. Thus, the whole process actually hinges on the assumption that the entire test or sub-

---

[2]Let C_u and C_l be the numbers of correct responses in the upper and lower groups, respectively. Step 4 indicates that we divide $C_u - C_l$ by k; or $(C_u - C_l)/k$. But $(C_u - C_l)/k = C_u/k - C_l/k$, which, by definition, is $p_u - p_l$.

test is good. When we select highly discriminating items using these internal criteria, we obtain a test whose items are valid measures of what the entire test or subtest measures. Therefore, in this way, the item analysis is a procedure of item validation. It does not follow directly that the test as a whole has improved in validity. However, since selecting highly discriminating items tends to increase reliability—a necessary condition for validity—selecting these items will probably, but not necessarily, increase validity as well.

Item analysis procedures are based on empirical results. If a test is used only once, item analysis provides information in retrospect. In this sense, it is not extremely useful except in judging past adequacy of the test. However, if tests or items are reused, or if there is opportunity for trying out a test, the information from the item analysis should be useful in making adjustments or improving the test. Then, decisions on the retention and revision of specific items can be made. Items with negative or zero discrimination should be discarded. It is unlikely that only a given number of the items with the highest discrimination will be retained. Some easy and some difficult items are commonly included for reasons mentioned earlier. Ebel (1956) suggests that classroom test items should have indices of discrimination of .30 or more. Moreover, the final test as a whole should still reflect the content and learning objectives that underlie the test.

Test items can be critiqued by knowledgeable people, if such people are available. If a test has been given, it may be possible to have those who have taken it critique the test. Such a critique often reveals poorly constructed items—those that are ambiguous, irrelevant, or difficult to understand. Often, unsuitable items can be reworded or restructured to make them usable. If not, they should be discarded.

Speeded Tests

Our discussion of test construction thus far has dealt with *power* tests. A power test is one where even given additional time, the examinees would improve their scores little, if any. A *speed* test, on the other hand, puts restrictive time limits on the examinees. The items of a speed test usually have difficulty levels around .95; that is, they are very easy. The variance in the scores on a speed test is obtained from the time limit, not the difficulty levels of the items. A typing test is a good example of a speeded test.

With a power test, we can base an estimate of reliability on an internal consistency measure, such as the Kuder-Richardson formula 20 (formula 5.9). The theory of reliability relates directly to the intercorrelations of the items. In a speed test, the examinee is limited in the number of items that can be attempted. Therefore, the magnitude and pattern of item intercorrelations become a function of the positioning of the items in the test, and the time limits. If items are positioned either early in the test, or near the end of the test, they will have difficulty levels close to 100 and 0 percent, respectively. They would tend to have very low inter-correlations, and low correlations with the total score. Items positioned near the middle of the test would tend to have high intercorrelations, and high correlations with total score. Therefore, constructing speeded tests must involve principles different from those for developing power tests.

Whether constructing power or speeded tests, an item pool is a requirement. In contrast to power tests, the reliability of speeded tests is not as directly related to the number of items, but more to the time limits. A shorter test may be more reliable, if it provides the most reliable distribution of scores. Therefore, the size of the item pool is an intuitive estimate to a large degree.

Measures of internal consistency are inappropriate as indicators of reliability for speeded tests. A measure of reliability is obtained by the correlation between alternate forms. (Also, odd-even split-half forms may be used.) Reliability of speeded tests depends on the time limits that produce the most reliable score distributions. Rather than computing various reliability coefficients using alternate forms of various sizes to find the most desirable, another procedure can be used. For speed tests, the reliabilities based on different time limits are closely related to the variances of the distributions of scores produced by the time limits. The larger the variances, the higher will be the test reliability. Hence, the time limit that results in the largest variance should be selected.

> **When a test is given under speeded conditions, reliability estimates are generally spuriously high. The parallel forms reliability estimate is most appropriate for speeded tests.**

Criterion-Referenced Versus Norm-Referenced Testing

For some years now, instructional specialists have distinguished between norm-referenced and criterion-referenced testing. The distinction between these two types of testing (Popham & Husek, 1971) is concerned with how an individual's test performance is evaluated. Performance on a norm-referenced test is evaluated by focusing on an individual's performance relative to the performance of those in a norm group. In contrast, a criterion-referenced test focuses on an individual's performance relative to some criterion standard. A criterion standard, for example, might be to get 80 percent of the items on a test correct. Criterion-referenced testing is a logical development of the movement to measure behavioral objectives. Once behavioral objectives have been specified, testing determines whether mastery has been attained, and testing is criterion-referenced.

The distinction between criterion-referenced and norm-referenced testing has brought some traditional principles of test construction into question. Indeed, *some* specialists have suggested that traditional test theory is inadequate for criterion-referenced measurement. We doubt that this is so; however, the two referencing approaches do require a clear understanding of the relative appropriateness of various measurement concepts. That is, it is apparent that some classical concepts developed for norm-referencing are quite inappropriate for criterion-referencing. Also, because there has been a preoccupation with norm-referencing in the past, criterion-referencing needs some further clarification.

Characteristics of Norm-Referenced Measurement

Traditionally, psychological measurements have been evaluated using the norm-referenced model, that is, an individual's score is evaluated relative to other people in the norm group. Because dispersion is essential to norm-referencing, variance becomes an extremely important concept. Indeed, many conceptions of reliability and validity are based on the concept of variance.

> **Norm-referenced testing occurs when an individual's test performance is evaluated by comparing it with other individuals in some normative reference group.**

As an example of norm-referencing, if the purpose of testing is to screen candidates for their numerical ability, individual performance is measured relative to the performance of others in that group. To evaluate the performance of an individual relative to others in the group, variance is required. How does the individual's score compare with others in the normative distribution? In order to position the score, we must know something about distribution variance. Furthermore, most classical conceptions of norms, reliability, and validity are variance-based. Norm-referencing requires variance, and in most cases, maximization of this variance is desirable.

Consider another variance-based example of how norm-referencing might be used. Suppose assessment of the numerical ability of a group of individuals is desired. First, numerical ability is a construct embedded in the reliable variation of the group; that is, numerical ability is a construct derived from variance-based correlational procedures. Dispersion is essential for the initial identification of a construct such as numerical ability. Furthermore, once a test of numerical ability has been constructed, norms and reliability considerations also require dispersion. Thus, the identification and assessment of human abilities presently require norm-referenced evaluation procedures.

Given that norm-referencing requires dispersion, the item analysis procedures discussed earlier in this chapter were generally developed to maximize test variance. Indeed, the difficulty level and discrimination indices were devised to maximize item variance and similarity, respectively. When used properly, item analysis procedures result in increased reliability and validity due to increased dispersion.

Just as with validity, purpose plays a major role in determining whether norm- or criterion-referenced measurement is the appropriate procedure. Obviously, the question arises, Are there situations for which maximum variance is not desired? Or, correspondingly, it would be interesting to know if there are situations in which the purpose requires minimum or zero variance. Such a situation arises when mastery learning is a goal, and in this situation criterion-referencing is appropriate. Thus, norm- and criterion-referencing can be considered on a purpose continuum, where the extremes are maximum and zero variance.

> **Norm-referencing and criterion-referencing can be viewed as the extremes of a purpose continuum on which maximum variance and zero variance, respectively, are desired.**

Characteristics of Criterion-Referenced Measurement

Criterion-referenced evaluation generally is used when mastery learning is a goal of instruction, and the measurement procedure is devised to assess whether mastery of objectives was obtained. One of the anticipated, if not actual, outcomes of the use of criterion-referenced measures is that the items tend to have high p-values; that is, a high proportion of individuals tend to pass each item. The result is a skewed distribution with near zero variance. As the variance approaches zero, any correlational concepts associated with the test also tend toward zero. Under the condition of complete mastery, variance and correlation-based measurement concepts become zero or indeterminate, respectively.

Consider some examples of what might happen to specific measurement concepts under conditions of mastery learning. In theory, since everyone is expected (sooner or later) to pass a criterion-referenced item, the variance of the test and items would approach zero as the p-values of each increase. As a consequence, the discrimination index would be indeterminate.

Furthermore, criterion-referenced tests tend to have low reliability. To understand the effect of criterion-referencing on reliability, recall our discussion of range of talent. Test theory suggests that reliability is the proportion of systematic variation in a test. When teaching is for mastery, the systematic variance of a test is minimized. If the theoretical item p-values are all 1, systematic or reliable variance is 0, and the variance of a test will be due to error. Indeed, in this case, an appropriate error index is the standard error of measurement. Thus, for criterion-referenced measurement, classical reliability is logically (according to test theory principles) an inappropriate statistic.

The standard error of measurement is a logically appropriate index for use with criterion-referenced measurement. However, since standard error of measurement is computed from $S_x \sqrt{1 - r_{xx'}}$ (formula 4.10), with $r_{xx'}$ at zero, the standard error of measurement is as large as the standard deviation of the test. Thus, under the condition of complete mastery, any obtained test variance is theoretically error variance. That is, according to test theory, under complete mastery, any obtained variance in a test is error variance. In that case the standard deviation of a test is the standard error of measurement.

What is the effect of criterion-referencing on the standard error of measurement with empirical data? In practice criterion-referencing often results in a highly skewed distribution of scores; that is, most individuals obtain mastery, but some do not. To compute the standard error of measurement, we can use procedures outlined by Lord (1959) and Swineford (1959). Lord indicated that when KR-20 was inserted into the standard error of measurement formula for items of moderate difficulty, the error of measurement approaches $3/7 \sqrt{n}$ (where n is the number of items). Swineford's theoretical paper supports Lord's work, and gives the standard error of measurement as:

$$S_e = \sqrt{pq(1 - \bar{r}_{ij})} \sqrt{n}. \tag{11.3}$$

Since $\bar{r}_{ij}$ will be essentially zero under mastery, the error of measurement for criterion-referenced measurement will reduce to:

$$S_e = \sqrt{pq} \sqrt{n}. \tag{11.4}$$

If mastery is obtained, the standard error of measurement should be 0. However, if items have an average difficulty of .8 or .9, the standard error of measurement will be about $.4 \sqrt{n}$, or $.3 \sqrt{n}$, respectively. The point to be made is that the classical conception of reliability is logically inappropriate in criterion-referencing. However, a more appropriate measure of error is the standard error of measurement approximated by formula 11.4.

Other writers have proposed various approaches to the reliability dilemma for criterion-referenced tests. Shavelson, Block, and Ravitch (1972) suggest that traditional reliability procedures be applied to the individual subscales of a test, each subscale representing a unidimensional trait or skill continuum. Of course, subscale reliability will be less than total score reliability. However, for each subscale, a classification scheme for the examinees can be developed. For example, anyone scoring less than one standard error of measurement below the criterion score would be classified as nonmastery, and a retraining program would be prescribed. Of course, anyone reaching criterion would be classified as mastery. Individuals performing between mastery and nonmastery could receive additional parallel items until their appropriate classification is determined. Dividing the test into subtests and following this procedure avoids the problem of examinees passing the total test, but not reaching criterion on some of the skills or knowledge represented by individual subtests. Two subjects could obtain identical total scores, but represent markedly different mastery (or nonmastery) levels. Then, too, the instructor can use the subscale information for diagnostic purposes, if necessary.

What of the validity of criterion-referenced tests? We discussed the concepts of content, criterion, and construct validity previously. A criterion-referenced test is generally geared toward instructional or behavioral objectives. Thus, we find that the test validation must be based on content validity, that is, the test must stand alone as a measure of the objectives.

One of the principles of test theory is that a reliability coefficient places an upper boundary on the *validity coefficient* of a test. That is, a test must be reliable to have criterion (and, perhaps, construct) validity. However, we have seen that classical reliability is inappropriate for criterion-referencing. So, also, is the notion of criterion validity. Rather, a criterion-referenced test must be valid by the nature of its content; it must have content validity that does not require dispersion.

In summary, the distinction between criterion-referenced and norm-referenced testing raises some interesting questions. Dispersion-based measurement concepts are simply not appropriate for criterion-referenced measures. However, content validity can be built into a criterion-referenced test, and the standard error of measurement is an appropriate index of error. The development of procedures for analyzing criterion-referenced tests is in its infancy, and new ideas and procedures are certain to be developed. As each is reported, it must stand the test of professional scrutiny, and not all will survive. An understanding of traditional test theory principles will clarify much of the thinking about the problem, and will provide the foundation for further work.

Summary

In this chapter, we have discussed the major principles of test construction, and the procedures that can be used to analyze test results. The construction of test items largely follows a logical procedure, avoiding various pitfalls that might decrease item effectiveness.

Item analysis procedures were discussed, including the determination of difficulty level and the index of discrimination for the item. The correlation between performance on an item and the total or subtest score was seen as a useful measure of the adequacy of the item. Minor points, such as the weighting of items, were considered, and special characteristics of speeded tests were identified.

Finally, criterion-referenced and norm-referenced testing were contrasted, and traditional test theory and procedures, as they apply to criterion-referenced testing, were discussed.

Suggested Readings

Downie, N. M. *Fundamentals of measurement.* (2nd ed.) New York: Oxford University Press, 1967, Chapters 6–11.

Ebel, R. Criterion-referenced measurements: Limitations. *School Review,* 1971, 79, 282–288.

Ebel, R. *Measuring educational achievement.* Englewood Cliffs: Prentice-Hall, 1965, Chapters 1–2.

Gronlund, N. E. *Measurement and evaluation in teaching.* (2nd ed.) New York: Macmillan, 1971, pp. 3–56.

Livingston, S. Criterion-referenced applications of classical test theory. *Journal of Educational Measurement,* 1972, 1, 13–26.

Nunnally, J. C. *Introduction to psychological measurement.* New York: McGraw-Hill, 1970, Chapter 8.

Popham, W. J. (Ed.) *Criterion-referenced measurement.* Englewood Cliffs: Educational Technology Publications, 1971.

Shavelson, R., Block, J., & Ravitch, M. Criterion-referenced testing: Comments on reliability. *Journal of Educational Measurement,* 1972, 9, 133–137.

Individual Review Questions

1. When test scores are obtained by summing scores over items in some manner, we are using a _____ model for measurement.

2. An item in a physics test, requiring the student to diagram a circuit, is missed by 90 percent of the class because the terminology is unfamiliar. What is the error in this item?

3. When we compute an item discrimination index against an internal criterion, we _____ performance on an item with total test performance.

4. Generally, in test construction, if we increase the similarity of the items, we tend to *decrease/increase* the test reliability.

5. High item–total test score correlation coefficients *do/do not* necessarily increase criterion validity.

6. In order to attain maximum internal consistency reliability, the test items should be of *high/low/moderate* difficulty level.

7. Items of *high/low/moderate* difficulty level tend to maximize the dispersion of the test scores.

8. An instructor sets complete student mastery of the test items as a goal. This goal is attained and the instructor (mistakenly) computes difficulty indices for the items. The difficulty indices would be _____ percent.

ANSWERS
1. linear
2. Prerequisite skills are unwarrantedly assumed.
3. correlate
4. increase
5. do not
6. moderate
7. moderate
8. 100

9. Items near the beginning of a speeded test would tend to have item difficulty levels near *0/50/100* percent.

10. Instruction in a chemistry course has emphasized the application of atomic theory. A subsequent test includes only knowledge-level items dealing with atomic theory. The test is lacking or low in _____ validity.

11. An item for which the student does not have the option of constructing his own response is a _____ _____ item.

12. The objectivity of a test item *does/does not* lie in the length of response required to answer the item correctly.

13. Which is the better item, and for what reason?
    (a) The science of providing information for decision-making is:
        (1) measurement.
        (2) evaluation.
        (3) data-processing.
        (4) testing.
    or
    (b) Evaluation, by definition, is:
        (1) the end of project data collection.
        (2) the science of providing information for decision-making.
        (3) the comparison of performance of experimental program students with that of regular program students.
        (4) the construction of criteria for behavioral objectives.

14. If a true or false response is required, what is wrong with the following item: "Reliability and validity are defined as consistency of measurement"?

15. What is the weakness of the following completion item: "United States' business during the 1930s was _____"?

16. If possible, the arrangement of items in a test should be in order of *decreasing/ increasing* difficulty.

17. One possible difficulty with essay items is lack of consistency between scorers. Lack of such consistency means that the item lacks _____.

18. A test for which the time limit is not a factor influencing the student's performance is a _____ test.

19. An item to which one-half of the Ss taking the test respond correctly is said to have _____ _____ difficulty.

20. The distribution of scores on a test is markedly skewed toward the low end of the scale of measurement. This indicates that the test is too *difficult/easy* for the examinees.

ANSWERS
9. 100
10. content
11. forced-choice
12. does not
13. (b), since the definition is in the response
14. The item is partially true and partially false.
15. The stem is an indefinite statement.
16. increasing
17. objectivity
18. power
19. 50 percent
20. easy

21. A test that is too difficult does not discriminate the *less/more* able students, and one that is too easy does not discriminate the *less/more* able students.

22. The overall effect of guessing on an individual's test score is to *lower/raise* the score.

23. As the number of alternatives per item increases, the correction for guessing tends to have a *greater/lesser* effect on the test scores.

24. An increase of item intercorrelations tends to *decrease/increase* the reliability of the test.

25. A percentage derived from the quotient of the sum of correct responses of both the upper and lower 27 percent of scores divided by the maximum possible correct responses of both the upper and lower 27 percent is called the index of item _____.

26. In an item analysis of a test, there are 50 scores in each of the upper and lower 27 percent groups. Eight individuals in the lower group and 40 in the upper group responded correctly to Item 18. The index of item difficulty for Item 18 is_____.

27. The index of discrimination is expressed as a *percentage/quotient*.

28. On a given item to which 100 students have responded, 25 of the upper group and 11 of the lower group responded correctly. The index of discrimination for the item is _____.

29. The index of item difficulty for the item discussed in the immediately preceding question is _____.

30. The index of item difficulty increases in value as *fewer/greater* numbers of students respond correctly to the item.

31. The maximum value for the index of item difficulty is 100 percent, indicating a very *difficult/easy* item.

32. The maximum value of the index of discrimination is _____. This maximum value is obtained only under the condition that all of the *lower/upper* group respond incorrectly, and all of the *lower/upper* group, correctly.

33. If there are more correct responses to an item in the lower than upper group, the item is a _____ discriminator.

34. The inclusion of highly discriminating items in a test tends to *decrease/increase* the reliability of the test.

35. If performance is evaluated by comparing the test scores of an individual to scores of other individuals in the group, the test is *criterion-/norm-* referenced.

ANSWERS

21. less; more
22. raise
23. lesser
24. increase
25. difficulty
26. 48%
27. quotient
28. .52
29. 67%
30. greater
31. easy
32. 1.00; lower; upper
33. negative
34. increase
35. norm-

36. The equivalence reliability estimate of a criterion-referenced test should approach *0.0/.5/1.0* because, due to mastery, the systematic variation tends to be eliminated.

37. The most appropriate index of reliability for criterion-referenced measurement is the *standard error of measurement/KR-20/KR-21*.

38. A classroom teacher requires 90 percent mastery of the objectives for a unit. Testing to determine whether this level of performance is attained would be *criterion-/norm-* referenced testing.

39. A student asks a counselor to secure information about his own cognitive abilities. The counselor administers the Differential Aptitude Test. This is an example of *criterion-/norm-* referenced testing.

40. As a test development technique, item analysis is more appropriate for *criterion-/ norm-* referenced testing than for *criterion-/norm-* referenced testing.

41. A criterion-referenced test is generally validated through *construct/content/ criterion* validation procedures.

42. When we evaluate an individual's score with reference to its position in the distribution of scores of some defined group, we are using *criterion-/norm-* referenced measurement.

43. Variance or dispersion is essential in determining characteristics of *criterion-/ norm-* referenced tests.

44. When considering concepts of reliability and item analysis in norm-referenced measurement, we generally desire to *maximize/minimize* variance.

45. Criterion-referenced measures tend to have *high/low* p-values as individuals approach mastery.

46. If we correlated the scores on a criterion-referenced test on which almost all examinees had attained mastery with the scores on another performance test with large variance, the correlation coefficient would tend to be close to *0/.5/1.00*.

Study Exercises

1. A student takes a test with 75 multiple-choice items, each of which contains five options. He has 41 correct responses, has 24 incorrect responses, and omitted the remaining items. What would his score be after correcting for chance or omissions? Identify the two assumptions under which the formula for correction applies. (These two assumptions are rarely met in practice.)

2. A test is administered to 159 students. An item analysis is conducted, and the number of correct responses to an item is determined for the 27 percent high scorers and 27 percent low scorers. On a given item, 38 of the high scorers and 6 low scorers

ANSWERS
36. 0.0
37. standard error of measurement
38. criterion-
39. norm-
40. norm-; criterion-
41. content
42. norm-
43. norm-
44. maximize
45. high
46. 0

1. 35
2. index of item difficulty, 51%; index of discrimination, .74

responded correctly. (No one omitted the item.) Compute the index of item difficulty and the index of discrimination for this item.

3. Identify the inadequacy or poor construction in each of the following items:

   a. An elephant is a _____.

   b. The United States exploded the first atomic bomb in _____.

   c. Correlating performance on a test with subsequent performance on a job, in order to determine the predictive value of a test, would be a procedure for dealing with:

      (1) construct validity.

      (2) predictive validity.

      (3) reliability.

      (4) behavioral objectives.

   d. The freezing point of water is about 32° F.

4. An instructor gives a 10-item test to 30 students. The 27 percent high and 27 percent low scorers had the following numbers of correct responses on the items. Compute the indices of item difficulty and item discrimination for the items, and decide which individual items should be retained for future tests.

	Number correct responses	
Item	High group	Low group
1	6	2
2	5	5
3	8	0
4	3	7
5	7	1
6	6	3
7	6	4
8	5	6
9	1	0
10	4	2

5. Consider the following test score data for a given item:

Total Score	Incorrect	Correct
20	/	///
19	//	////
18	//	/////
17	///	////
16	///	/////
15	/////	///
14	////	///
13	/////	//
12	///	//
11	///	//

a. How many individuals took the test?

b. How many people will be in the upper 27 percent group?

c. Using the upper and lower 27 percent method, compute the item discrimination index.

d. Using the upper and lower 27 percent method, compute the index of item difficulty.

ANSWERS

4.	Difficulty	Discrimination
1	50%	.50
2	62.5%	.00
3	50%	1.00
4	62.5%	−.50
5	50%	.75
6	56.3%	.38
7	62.5%	.25
8	68.8%	−.13
9	6.3%	.13
10	37.5%	.25

On the basis of statistical data only, retain items 1, 3, 5, and 6.

5. (a) 64; (b) 17; (c) .35; (d) 53%

6. Compute the item-test correlation from the data in problem 5.
7. Fifty subjects take an exam; 30 score correctly on Item A, and 20 do not. The means of total test scores for those scoring correctly and incorrectly on Item A were 80.7 and 72.3, respectively. The standard deviation of the total test scores was 11.2. Compute the point-biserial r between performance on Item A and the total test scores. What conclusions can be made about the discrimination value of Item A?
8. The following information is secured from a 10-item test administered to 20 individuals. The standard deviation of the distribution of test scores was 3.25. Determine the point-biserial r between item performance and test performance for the following items.

   Item A. Fifteen individuals responded correctly, and their test score mean was 6.0. The 5 responding incorrectly had a test score mean of 5.6.

   Item B. Only 1 individual responded correctly and his test score mean was 9.0. The remaining 19 individuals had a test score mean of 5.73.

   Item C. Ten individuals responded correctly and their test score mean was 7.0. The test score mean of those responding incorrectly was 4.8.

   Item D. Eight individuals responded correctly with a test score mean of 6.5. Those responding incorrectly had a test score mean of 5.5.

   Compare the items on their discrimination values.
9. Two hundred subjects take an exam. In an item analysis, the responses of the upper and lower 27 percent groups are considered. On Item J, 15 subjects in the lower group and 40 subjects in the upper group responded correctly. Compute the index of item difficulty for Item J.
10. Compute the index of discrimination for Item J in the preceding question.

ANSWERS
6. .26
7. .37
8. (a) .05; (b) .22; (c) .34; (d) .15
9. 50.9%
10. .46

Glossary

Ability: (*See* Construct)

Ability test: A test designed for the specific purpose of assessing present psychological abilities or traits. For example, many tests of general mental ability (such as SCAT or CTMM) are designed to yield information about specific primary mental abilities.

Achievement test: A test designed for the specific purpose of assessing prior learning. Generally, achievement tests are given to assess the effect of curricular treatments.

Aptitude: (*See* Construct)

Aptitude test: A test designed for the specific purpose of predicting some criterion performance. Examples are the Differential Aptitude Test, used for counseling college-bound students, and the General Aptitude Test Battery, used for counseling primarily vocation-bound individuals.

Area transformation: A conversion of raw scores to a new set of scores that indicates a given area in the distribution (usually the area below the point). In the conversion, the equality of the difference between scores and the shape of the distribution is usually not retained. After this transformation, arithmetic operations should not be applied to the transformed scores.

Attribute: (*See* Construct)

Basal age: On the Stanford-Binet test, the highest mental age level at and below which the subject passes all of the items.

Behavioral objectives: Objectives so stated that the outcome is described in terms of the learner's desired behavior.

Bipolar factor: A factor on which some tests in the factor matrix have high positive loadings and some tests have high negative loadings.

Ceiling: The upper limit of an ability that can be assessed by a test. With the Stanford-Binet test, it is the first MA level in which all items were missed.

Centroid method: A mathematical procedure used for extracting factors from test data.

Coefficient of equivalence: The correlation coefficient between the performance of a given group on two parallel forms of a test administered simultaneously, or approximately so—parallel forms reliability.

Coefficient of stability: The correlation coefficient between the performance of a given group on a single test administered on two different occasions—test-retest reliability.

Communality: For a specified variable in a factor matrix, communality is the sum of the squared loadings across the given factors; the proportion of the variance due to the factors for a given test.

Constant: A characteristic that has the same value or is the same for all individuals under consideration.

Construct: A characteristic inferred from behavior, and attributed to an individual. In this sense, an ability, trait, attribute, or aptitude all reflect an intervening state inferred from various behavior categories.

Construct validity: The method of validation that establishes the degree to which a particular test measures specified psychological constructs. For example, a test of intelligence might reflect the constructs suggested by a specific theory of intelligence. The Raven's Matrices test has construct validity because it reflects the Spearman-Burt-Vernon theory of intelligence.

Content validity: The method of validation that, through a logical analysis of the test content, establishes whether the test measures those principles it is supposed to measure. For example, an achievement test must reflect the content or principles embedded in that achievement domain.

Correction for attenuation: A correction for test unreliability applied when computing a validity coefficient. The correction provides an estimate of validity if one or both measures (test and criterion) are perfectly reliable.

Criterion keying: A test construction orientation in which item validity is directed toward the correlation of each item to some external criterion (*see* Discrimination index, and Item analysis). In this way, the criterion validity of the total test becomes paramount and a function of the item validities.

Criterion-referenced measurement: A test construction orientation in which items reflecting specific objectives are written with learner mastery as a goal. Thus, performance is not relative to some other score (as with norm-referencing), but is referenced to some criterion. The validity of a test must be embedded in its content, and psychometric concepts based on systematic dispersion are inappropriate.

Criterion validity: The method of validation that, through correlation, predicts the degree to which a particular test will predict some specified criterion performance. For example, an academic aptitude test might correlate .55 with college grade point average, and this test would have criterion validity, because it is empirically related to the criterion performance.

Covariance: The average product of the deviation scores for two variables.

Difficulty index: The proportion (percentage) of individuals passing a given test item; the larger the index, the easier the item.

Discrimination index: A quotient or decimal fraction that indicates how well an item discriminated between the low and high scorers on some criterion. The quotient can be determined by dividing the observed difference in correct responses of the groups by the maximum possible difference. The criterion can be internal (as the total test score), or external (as teacher ratings).

Error score: The part of an obtained test score that is due to nonsystematic sources. Nonsystematic sources include scoring errors, rating errors, recording errors, etc.

Error variance: The average of the squared deviations of a set of error scores from their mean; the unreliable variance of a test.

Evaluation: The provision of information through formal means, using criteria, measurement, and statistics, to serve as a rational basis for making judgments in decision-making situations.

Factor: A hypothetical trait, ability, or construct inferred from test data. In most situations, matrices of intercorrelations of test data are analyzed to determine the factors accounting for the intercorrelations among the variables.

Factor matrix: A matrix with as many rows as variables under study, and as many columns as factors. The numbers in the matrix are the loadings or correlations between the variables and the factors. The numbers are also the coordinates of the tests in an orthogonal reference system.

"g" factor: A general factor identified in hierarchical factor theory as the ability to educe relationships.

General factor: A factor on which all tests in the factor matrix have modest to high loadings. Since all tests correlate with the factor, the inference is made that some hypothetical general ability is related to all of the test variables.

Group factor: A factor on which some group of tests in the factor matrix has modest to high loadings, and at least one test has a zero or low loading.

Histogram: A graphical representation of the scores in a distribution with frequency of occurrence plotted for each score in the form of a rectangle; the areas of the rectangles are proportional to the frequencies of the scores.

Homogeneous keying: A test construction orientation in which item validity is directed toward the correlation of each item to the total test score (*see* Discrimination index, and Item analysis). In this way, high item-test correlations result in homogeneous sets of items grouped into subtests that reflect traits or constructs.

Intelligence quotient: The ratio of mental age to chronological age, times 100; more recently, *deviation IQ* has been defined as an individual's score relative to the mean of a representative group of people of similar chronological age.

Interests: An attitude or valence toward an activity.

Internal consistency reliability: The index that is the average of all possible split-half reliability estimates. This index reflects the degree to which a group of items are measuring the same thing. Internal consistency can be computed from the KR-20 formula.

Interval scale: A measurement scale that, in addition to ordering scores, also establishes equal units on the scale so distances between any two scores are of a known magnitude; also called equal-unit scale.

Ipsative score: The scoring scheme in which subtest performance is contrasted with the individual's average subtest performance rather than with the average of a reference group, as in normative scoring.

Item analysis: The procedure for evaluating items for a norm-referenced test. The procedure usually results in determining the difficulty and discrimination indices for each item. Mostly, the purpose of the procedure is to identify items that do not contribute to the dispersion necessary for reliable norm-referenced tests.

Kuder-Richardson formula 20 (KR-20): A formula for estimating the internal consistency reliability of a test that provides the average reliability estimate for all possible split-half reliability estimates of the test (formula 5.9).

Linear relationship: A relationship between two variables that can be described adequately by a linear pattern of points in a scattergram.

Linear transformation: A conversion of scores that preserves the equality of the differences and the shape of the distribution that can change the mean, variance, and standard deviation of the scores.

Loading: The product-moment correlation between a test and a hypothetical, idealized (perfectly reliable) measure of a theoretical factor.

Mean: The sum of the scores in a distribution divided by the number of scores in the distribution.

Measurement: The assignment of numerals to objects or events according to rules.

Measures of central tendency: Points in a distribution that indicate where the distribution tends to center on the score scale.

Measures of dispersion: Indices that indicate the amount of spread or variability in the distribution.

Median: The point or score in a distribution below which 50 percent of the scores are located.

Mode: The score in a distribution that has the greatest frequency of occurrence.

Nominal scale: A measurement scale that classifies its elements into two or more categories to indicate that the elements are different, but does not classify them according to order or magnitude.

Normal distribution: A family of bell-shaped, symmetrical distributions, generally expressed as a curve.

Normative score: The scoring scheme in which the individual's performance is contrasted with the average of a reference group called the normative group.

Norm-referenced measurement: A test construction orientation in which the items are written to maximize dispersion of examinee scores. The concepts of reliability and validity are embedded in the variance of the test. Thus, maximum reliability and validity are attained by maximizing test variation, and measurements are generally interpreted by their relative position in some normative group.

Norms: Descriptive statistics that summarize the test performance of a reference group of individuals. Norms have various forms, such as percentiles, grade norms, and age norms.

Objective test: A test in which all scorers get the same results when scoring the test performance.

Obtained score: The raw score that consists of both a nonerror and an error component.

Obtained variance: The average of the squared deviations of a set of raw (obtained) scores about their mean. Obtained variance results from both systematic and nonsystematic sources.

Omnibus test: A test in which items reflecting many mental abilities are presented in a single composite test, rather than being systematically grouped into subtests. As an example, an omnibus mental ability test will contain many important abilities. This type of test yields a single score, and can have quite generalizable criterion validity, because the items can correlate with many criterion performances. An omnibus test can be contrasted with one that is internally consistent.

Ordinal scale: A measurement scale that classifies and ranks elements or scores in some order.

Percentile: A raw score point. The 84th percentile is the raw score value that has 84 percent of the scores in the distribution below that raw score point. Since a percentile is a raw score point, percentiles are distributed the same as the raw scores.

Percentile rank: The percentage of cases below a given score point or percentile. A percentile is a raw score, while percentile rank is the percentage of cases below that score point. Percentile ranks undergo a nonlinear transformation; that is, the relative distances between the raw scores and between the percentile ranks are not necessarily the same. Regardless of the shape of the distribution of the raw scores, the shape of the distribution of the percentile ranks is rectangular.

Personality: The noncognitive aspect of behavior associated with the manner in which a person does something. For example, is the person withdrawn, compulsive, etc.? A broader definition might include the sum total of one's cognitive and noncognitive characteristics.

Power test: A test for which performance would increase little, if any, if additional time were provided for responding to the test items.

Product-moment correlation coefficient: An index of the relationship between two variables (formula 2.6).

Profile: A graphic representation of two or more scores for an individual (or single group of individuals, such as a class; or two or more groups on a single measure) presented so the relative positions of the scores can be readily identified. Scores presented in a profile are converted to a common scale, such as grade equivalents, T-scores, stens, etc.

Range: One plus the difference between the two extreme scores of a distribution.

Ratio scale: A measurement scale that contains equal units, and also establishes an absolute zero for the scale.

Reliability: The degree to which a test is consistent in its measurements. Consistency is usually defined as being: over time (stability reliability), over items (equivalence reliability), or internally consistent (internal consistency reliability).

Reliability coefficient: The coefficient of correlation between parallel forms of the same test (equivalence reliability coefficient), between the same test on different occasions (stability reliability coefficient), or the average correlation coefficient from all possible split-halves corrected for length (internal consistency coefficient). All are correctly referred to as reliability coefficients, but each measures a different aspect of test consistency.

Spearman-Brown Prophecy Formula: A formula used for specifying the relationship between reliability and test length (formula 5.1). Given the reliability of a test of a specified length, the reliability of a longer (or shorter) test can be estimated, providing the items to be added (or subtracted) are representative of the original test.

Specific variance: Reliably measured variance that does not correlate with the criterion, or that is not due to any common factors.

Speeded test: A test for which performance is dependent on the number of items completed within a specified time limit. Items on a speeded test have a difficulty index approaching 1.0.

Split-half reliability coefficient: A coefficient for estimating the reliability of a test by splitting it into comparable halves, correlating the scores from the halves, and adjusting for length using the Spearman-Brown formula.

Standard deviation: A one-dimensional measure of dispersion; the square root of the average squared deviations of a set of scores from their mean.

Standard error of estimate: The standard deviation of the distribution of error scores associated with prediction, an error score being the difference between an observed and a predicted score.

Standard error of measurement: A standard deviation; the estimate of the magnitude of the error in a test score; the square root of the error variance of a test.

Standard scores: Scores transformed to have a given mean and standard deviation. Commonly used standard scores are z-scores, T-scores, sten scores, and stanine scores.

Stanine score: A linearly transformed standard score yielding nine single-digit scores with a mean of 5 and a standard deviation of 2.

Sten score: A linearly transformed standard score yielding ten single-digit scores with a mean of 5.5 and a standard deviation of 2.

T-score: A linearly transformed standard score having a mean of 50 and a standard deviation of 10.

Test: A device for the quantitative assessment of educational and psychological attributes of an individual. Operationally, a test generally secures a sample of human behavior.

True score: The difference between an obtained and an error score; the hypothetical mean score that would be obtained from repeating measurements on the same test for the same individual.

True variance: The average of the squared deviations of a set of true (perfectly reliable) scores from their mean.

Unit normal curve: The normal curve (distribution) with a mean of 0, a standard deviation of 1, and an area of 1.

Validity: The degree to which a test measures what it is supposed to measure. Three commonly cited aspects of the validation procedure are content, construct, and criterion validity. Since different purposes require the measurement of different constructs, various methods of validating a test might assume more importance initially. That is, while an intelligence test might require a focus on certain human abilities initially; later, both the content and criterion aspects of validation also become important.

Variable: A characteristic that takes on different values for the individual under consideration.

Variance: A two-dimensional measure of dispersion; the average of the squared deviations of a set of scores from their mean.

z-score: A score giving the number of standard deviations above or below the mean. The z-score is a linearly transformed standard score having a mean of 0 and a standard deviation of 1.

Bibliography

Allport, G. W., & Vernon, P. E. *A study of values.* Boston: Houghton Mifflin, 1931.

American Psychological Association. Technical recommendations for psychological tests and diagnostic techniques. *Psychological Bulletin Supplement,* 1954, 51, Part 2, 1–38.

American Psychological Association. *Standards for educational and psychological tests and manuals.* Washington, D.C.: American Psychological Assn., 1966.

American Psychological Association. Psychological assessment and public policy. *American Psychologist,* 1970, 25, 264–266.

American Psychological Association, Ad Hoc Committee on Ethical Standards in Psychological Research. *Ethical principles in the conduct of research with human participants.* Washington, D.C.: American Psychological Assn., 1973.

Anastasi, A. Psychology, psychologists, and psychological testing. *American Psychologist,* 1967, 22, 297–306.

Bayley, N. Consistency and variability in the growth of intelligence from birth to eighteen. *Journal of Genetic Psychology,* 1949, 75, 165–196.

Bennett, J., Seashore, H., & Wesman, A. *Differential aptitude tests, third edition manual.* New York: Psychological Corporation, 1959.

Binet, A., & Simon, T. *The development of intelligence in children.* Translated by E. S. Kite. Department of Research No. 11. Vineland, N.J.: Training School, 1916.

Blommers, P., & Lindquist, E. F. *Elementary statistical methods.* Boston: Houghton Mifflin, 1960.

Bolles, R. *Theory of motivation.* New York: Harper & Row, 1967.

Buros, O. (Ed.) *The sixth mental measurements yearbook.* Highland Park, N.J.: Gryphon Press, 1965.

Burt, C. The structure of the mind: A review of the results of factor analysis. *British Journal of Educational Psychology,* 1949, 19, 110–111, 176–199.

California Test of Mental Maturity Manual. Los Angeles: California Test Bureau, 1957.

California Test of Personality Manual. All levels forms AA and BB. (1953 rev.) Monterey: California Test Bureau, 1953.

Campbell, D. The stability of vocational interests within occupations over long time spans. *Personnel and Guidance Journal,* 1966, 44, 1012–1019.

Campbell, D. *Strong vocational interest blanks, 1969 manual supplement.* Stanford: Stanford University Press, 1969.

Campbell, D., & Fiske, D. Convergent and discriminant validation by the multitrait-multimethod matrix. *Psychological Bulletin,* 1959, 56, 81–105.

Cattell, R. *Personality and motivation structure and measurement.* Yonkers: World Book, 1957.

Cattell, R. Validity and reliability: A proposed more basic set of concepts. *Journal of Educational Psychology,* 1964, 55, 1–22.

Cattell, R. Are IQ tests intelligent? *Psychology Today,* 1968, March, 56–62.

Cattell, R., & Eber, H. *Manual for forms A and B—sixteen personality factor questionnaire.* Champaign, Ill.: Institute for Personality and Ability Testing, 1962.

Cronbach, L. Coefficient alpha and the internal structure of tests. *Psychometrika,* 1951, 16, 297–334.

Cronbach, L. *Essentials of psychological testing.* (2nd ed.) New York: Harper & Row, 1960.

Cronbach, L., & Meehl, P. Construct validity in psychological tests. *Psychological Bulletin,* 1955, 52, 281–302.

Cureton, E. The upper and lower twenty-seven percent rule. *Psychometrika,* 1957, 22, 293–296.

Davis, P. C. A factor analysis of the Wechsler-Bellevue scale. *Educational and Psychological Measurement,* 1956, 16, 127–146.

Doppelt, J. *Expectancy tables—a way of interpreting test validity.* Test Service Bulletin No. 38. New York: Psychological Corporation, 1949.

Doppelt, J. *Better than chance.* Test Service Bulletin No. 45. New York: Psychological Corporation, 1953.

Doppelt, J. *The correction for guessing.* Test Service Bulletin No. 46. New York: Psychological Corporation, 1954.

Doppelt, J. *How accurate is a test score.* Test Service Bulletin No. 50. New York: Psychological Corporation, 1956.

Ebel, R. *Measuring educational achievement.* Englewood Cliffs: Prentice-Hall, 1956.

Eysenck, H. *The structure of human personality.* London: Methuen, 1953. (a)

Eysenck, H. *Uses and abuses of psychology.* Baltimore: Penguin Books, 1953. (b)

Ferguson, G. Learning and human ability: A theoretical approach. In P. DuBois, & G. Mayo (Eds.), *Research strategies for evaluating training.* AERA Monograph Series in Curriculum Evaluation. Chicago: Rand McNally, 1970.

Ferguson, L., Humphreys, L., & Strong, E. A factorial analysis of interests and values. *Journal of Educational Psychology,* 1941, 32, 197–204.

Flavell, J. H. *The developmental psychology of Jean Piaget.* Princeton: Van Nostrand, 1963.

French, J. W., Ekstrom, R. B., & Price, L. A. *Manual for kit of reference tests for cognitive factors.* Princeton: Educational Testing Service, 1963.

Glass, G., & Stanley, J. *Statistical methods in education and psychology.* Englewood Cliffs: Prentice-Hall, 1970.

Guilford, J. *Psychometric methods.* (2nd ed.) New York: McGraw-Hill, 1954.

Guilford, J. *Personality.* New York: McGraw-Hill, 1959. (a)

Guilford, J. Three faces of intellect. *American Psychologist,* 1959, 14, 469–479. (b)

Gulliksen, H. *Theory of mental tests.* New York: Wiley, 1950.

Hall, C., & Lindsey, G. *Theories of personality.* (2nd ed.) New York: Wiley, 1970.

Hathaway, S., & Meehl, P. *An atlas for the clinical use of the MMPI.* Minneapolis: University of Minnesota Press, 1951.

Hathaway, S., & Monachesi, E. *Analyzing and predicting juvenile delinquency with the MMPI.* Minneapolis: University of Minnesota Press, 1953.

Hawkes, H., Lindquist, E., & Mann, C. *The construction and use of achievement examinations.* Boston: Houghton Mifflin, 1936.

Herzberg, F., & Bouton, A. A further study of the stability of the Kuder-preference record. *Educational and Psychological Measurement,* 1954, 14, 326–331.

Hofstaetter, P. The changing composition of intelligence: A study in T-technique. *Journal of Genetic Psychology,* 1954, 85, 159–164.

Holtzman, W. Recurring dilemmas in personality assessment. *Journal of Projective Techniques,* 1964, 28, 144–150.

Hoyt, C. Test reliability estimated by analysis of variance. *Psychometrika,* 1941, 6, 153–160.

Kaiser, H. Review of Virginia L. Senders, *Measurement and statistics. Psychometrika,* 1960, 25, 411–413.

Kelley, T. The selection of upper and lower groups for the validation of test items. *Journal of Educational Psychology,* 1939, 30, 17–24.

Kleinmuntz, B. *Personality measurement: An introduction.* Homewood, Ill.: Dorsey Press, 1967.

Knauft, E. A selection battery for bake-shop managers. *Journal of Applied Psychology,* 1949, 33, 304–315.

Kretschmer, E. *Korperbau and Charakter.* Berlin: Springer, 1948. (*Physique and character.* 2nd ed. New York: Humanities Press, 1951.)

Kuder, G. F. *Administrators manual, Kuder preference record-vocational.* Chicago: Science Research Associates, 1960.

Kuder, G. F. *Kuder-E, general interest survey manual.* Chicago: Science Research Associates, 1964.

Kuder, G. F. *Kuder-DD occupational interest survey.* Chicago: Science Research Associates, 1966.

Kuder, G. F. A note on the comparability of occupational scores from different interest inventories. *Measurement and Evaluation in Guidance,* 1969, 2, 94–100.

Kuder, G. F., & Richardson, M. The theory of the estimation of test reliability. *Psychometrika,* 1937, 2, 151–160.

Lawley, D., & Maxwell, A. *Factor analysis as a statistical method.* London: Butterworth, 1963.

Lindquist, E., & Hieronymous, A. *Iowa tests of basic skills: Manual for administrators, supervisors, and counselors.* Boston: Houghton Mifflin, 1964.

Loevinger, J. The attenuation paradox in test theory. *Psychological Bulletin,* 1954, 51, 493–504.

Loevinger, J. Objective tests as instruments of psychological theory. *Psychological Reports*, 1957, 3, 635–694.

Lord, F. Tests of the same length do have the same standard error of measurement. *Educational and Psychological Measurement*, 1959, 19, 233–239.

McCorquodale, K., & Meehl, P. On a distinction between hypothetical constructs and intervening variables. *Psychological Review*, 1948, 55, 95–101.

McNemar, Q. Lost: Our intelligence? Why? *American Psychologist*, 1964, 9, 857–860.

Magnusson, D. *Test theory.* Translated by Hunter Mabon. Reading, Mass.: Addison-Wesley, 1966.

Mehrens, W., & Lehmann, I. *Standardized tests in education.* New York: Holt, Rinehart & Winston, 1969.

Nunnally, J. *Psychometric theory.* New York: McGraw-Hill, 1967.

Nunnally, J. *Introduction to psychological measurement.* New York: McGraw-Hill, 1970.

Popham, W., & Husek, T. Implications of criterion-referenced measurement. In W. Popham (Ed.), *Criterion-referenced measurement.* Englewood Cliffs: Educational Technology Publications, 1971.

Ritter, R. Effective counseling for engineering freshmen. *Journal of Engineering Education*, 1954, June, 636–641.

Rosenberg, N. Stability and maturation of Kuder interest patterns during high school. *Educational and Psychological Measurement*, 1953, 13, 449–458.

Royer, L. The great response-style myth. *Psychological Bulletin*, 1965, 63, 129–156.

Rozeboom, W. *Foundations of the theory of prediction.* Homewood, Ill.: Dorsey Press, 1966.

SCAT Series II, Cooperative School and College Ability Tests, Handbook. Princeton: Educational Testing Service, 1967.

SCAT-Technical Report. Princeton: Educational Testing Service, 1957.

Shavelson, R., Block, J., & Ravitch, M. Criterion-referenced testing: Comments on reliability. *Journal of Educational Measurement*, 1972, 5, 133–137.

Spearman, C. General intelligence: Objectively determined and measured. *American Journal of Psychology*, 1904, 115, 201–292.

Stevens, S. S. Mathematics, measurement, and psychophysics. In S. S. Stevens (Ed.), *Handbook of experimental psychology.* New York: Wiley, 1951.

Strong, E. K., Jr. *Vocational interests of men and women.* Stanford: Stanford University Press, 1943.

Strong, E. K., Jr. *Vocational interests eighteen years after college.* Minneapolis: University of Minnesota Press, 1955.

Strong, E. K., Jr. *Manual for vocational interest blank for men.* Stanford: Stanford University Press, 1966.

Swineford, F. Note on "Tests of the same length do have the same error of measurement"! *Educational and Psychological Measurement*, 1959, 19, 241–242.

Terman, L., & Merrill, M. *Measuring intelligence.* Boston: Houghton Mifflin, 1960.

Thorndike, R. *The concepts of over and underachievement.* New York: Teachers College Bureau, 1963.

Thurstone, L. L. A multiple factor study of vocational interests. *Personnel Journal,* 1931, 10, 198–205.

Thurstone, L. L. The factorial isolation of primary abilities. *Psychometrika,* 1936, 1(3), 175–182.

Thurstone, L. L. *Multiple factor analysis.* Chicago: University of Chicago Press, 1947.

Thurstone, L. L. *The differential growth of mental abilities.* No. 14. Chapel Hill: University of North Carolina Psychometric Laboratory, 1955.

University Evaluation and Examination Service. *Suggestions for test construction.* Technical Bulletin No. 1. Iowa City: University of Iowa Press, 1948.

Vernon, P. E. Classifying high-grade occupational interests. *Journal of Abnormal and Social Psychology,* 1949, 44, 85–96.

Vernon, P. E. *The structure of human abilities.* London: Methuen, 1950.

Wechsler, D. *Manual for the Wechsler adult intelligence scale.* New York: Psychological Corporation, 1955.

Weider, A. (Ed.) *Contributions toward medical psychology.* Vol. 2. New York: Ronald Press, 1953.

Wert, J. E. *Educational statistics.* New York: McGraw-Hill, 1938.

Wesman, A. Intelligent testing. *American Psychologist,* 1968, 12, 267–274.

Zytowski, D. Relationship of equivalent scales of three interest inventories. *Personnel and Guidance Journal,* 1968, 44, 44–49.

Appendix A

TABLE OF THE NORMAL CURVE

$\frac{x}{\sigma}$	Area	Ordinate	$\frac{x}{\sigma}$	Area	Ordinate	$\frac{x}{\sigma}$	Area	Ordinate	$\frac{x}{\sigma}$	Area	Ordinate
.00	.0000	.3989	.35	.1368	.3752	.70	.2580	.3123	1.05	.3531	.2299
.01	.0040	.3989	.36	.1406	.3739	.71	.2611	.3101	1.06	.3554	.2275
.02	.0080	.3989	.37	.1443	.3725	.72	.2642	.3079	1.07	.3577	.2251
.03	.0120	.3988	.38	.1480	.3712	.73	.2673	.3056	1.08	.3599	.2227
.04	.0160	.3986	.39	.1517	.3697	.74	.2703	.3034	1.09	.3621	.2203
.05	.0199	.3984	.40	.1554	.3683	.75	.2734	.3011	1.10	.3643	.2179
.06	.0239	.3982	.41	.1591	.3668	.76	.2764	.2989	1.11	.3665	.2155
.07	.0279	.3980	.42	.1628	.3653	.77	.2794	.2966	1.12	.3686	.2131
.08	.0319	.3977	.43	.1664	.3637	.78	.2823	.2943	1.13	.3708	.2107
.09	.0359	.3973	.44	.1700	.3621	.79	.2852	.2920	1.14	.3729	.2083
.10	.0398	.3970	.45	.1736	.3605	.80	.2881	.2897	1.15	.3749	.2059
.11	.0438	.3965	.46	.1772	.3589	.81	.2910	.2874	1.16	.3770	.2036
.12	.0478	.3961	.47	.1808	.3572	.82	.2939	.2850	1.17	.3790	.2012
.13	.0517	.3956	.48	.1844	.3555	.83	.2967	.2827	1.18	.3810	.1989
.14	.0557	.3951	.49	.1879	.3538	.84	.2995	.2803	1.19	.3830	.1965
.15	.0596	.3945	.50	.1915	.3521	.85	.3023	.2780	1.20	.3849	.1942
.16	.0636	.3939	.51	.1950	.3503	.86	.3051	.2756	1.21	.3869	.1919
.17	.0675	.3932	.52	.1985	.3485	.87	.3078	.2732	1.22	.3888	.1895
.18	.0714	.3925	.53	.2019	.3467	.88	.3106	.2709	1.23	.3907	.1872
.19	.0753	.3918	.54	.2054	.3448	.89	.3133	.2685	1.24	.3925	.1849
.20	.0793	.3910	.55	.2088	.3429	.90	.3159	.2661	1.25	.3944	.1826
.21	.0832	.3902	.56	.2123	.3410	.91	.3186	.2637	1.26	.3962	.1804
.22	.0871	.3894	.57	.2157	.3391	.92	.3212	.2613	1.27	.3980	.1781
.23	.0910	.3885	.58	.2190	.3372	.93	.3238	.2589	1.28	.3997	.1758
.24	.0948	.3876	.59	.2224	.3352	.94	.3264	.2565	1.29	.4015	.1736
.25	.0987	.3867	.60	.2257	.3332	.95	.3289	.2541	1.30	.4032	.1714
.26	.1026	.3857	.61	.2291	.3312	.96	.3315	.2516	1.31	.4049	.1691
.27	.1064	.3847	.62	.2324	.3292	.97	.3340	.2492	1.32	.4066	.1669
.28	.1103	.3836	.63	.2357	.3271	.98	.3365	.2468	1.33	.4082	.1647
.29	.1141	.3825	.64	.2389	.3251	.99	.3389	.2444	1.34	.4099	.1626
.30	.1179	.3814	.65	.2422	.3230	1.00	.3413	.2420	1.35	.4115	.1604
.31	.1217	.3802	.66	.2454	.3209	1.01	.3438	.2396	1.36	.4131	.1582
.32	.1255	.3790	.67	.2486	.3187	1.02	.3461	.2371	1.37	.4147	.1561
.33	.1293	.3778	.68	.2517	.3166	1.03	.3485	.2347	1.38	.4162	.1539
.34	.1331	.3765	.69	.2549	.3144	1.04	.3508	.2323	1.39	.4177	.1518

$\dfrac{x}{\sigma}$	Area	Ordinate	$\dfrac{x}{\sigma}$	Area	Ordinate	$\dfrac{x}{\sigma}$	Area	Ordinate	$\dfrac{x}{\sigma}$	Area	Ordinate
1.40	.4192	.1497	1.80	.4641	.0790	2.20	.4861	.0355	2.60	.4953	.0136
1.41	.4207	.1476	1.81	.4649	.0775	2.21	.4864	.0347	2.61	.4955	.0132
1.42	.4222	.1456	1.82	.4656	.0761	2.22	.4868	.0339	2.62	.4956	.0129
1.43	.4236	.1435	1.83	.4664	.0748	2.23	.4871	.0332	2.63	.4957	.0126
1.44	.4251	.1415	1.84	.4671	.0734	2.24	.4875	.0325	2.64	.4959	.0122
1.45	.4265	.1394	1.85	.4678	.0721	2.25	.4878	.0317	2.65	.4960	.0119
1.46	.4279	.1374	1.86	.4686	.0707	2.26	.4881	.0310	2.66	.4961	.0116
1.47	.4292	.1354	1.87	.4693	.0694	2.27	.4884	.0303	2.67	.4962	.0113
1.48	.4306	.1334	1.88	.4699	.0681	2.28	.4887	.0297	2.68	.4963	.0110
1.49	.4319	.1315	1.89	.4706	.0669	2.29	.4890	.0290	2.69	.4964	.0107
1.50	.4332	.1295	1.90	.4713	.0656	2.30	.4893	.0283	2.70	.4965	.0104
1.51	.4345	.1276	1.91	.4719	.0644	2.31	.4896	.0277	2.71	.4966	.0101
1.52	.4357	.1257	1.92	.4726	.0632	2.32	.4898	.0270	2.72	.4967	.0099
1.53	.4370	.1238	1.93	.4732	.0620	2.33	.4901	.0264	2.73	.4968	.0096
1.54	.4382	.1219	1.94	.4738	.0608	2.34	.4904	.0258	2.74	.4969	.0093
1.55	.4394	.1200	1.95	.4744	.0596	2.35	.4906	.0252	2.75	.4970	.0091
1.56	.4406	.1182	1.96	.4750	.0584	2.36	.4909	.0246	2.76	.4971	.0088
1.57	.4418	.1163	1.97	.4756	.0573	2.37	.4911	.0241	2.77	.4972	.0086
1.58	.4429	.1145	1.98	.4761	.0562	2.38	.4913	.0235	2.78	.4973	.0084
1.59	.4441	.1127	1.99	.4767	.0551	2.39	.4916	.0229	2.79	.4974	.0081
1.60	.4452	.1109	2.00	.4772	.0540	2.40	.4918	.0224	2.80	.4974	.0079
1.61	.4463	.1092	2.01	.4778	.0529	2.41	.4920	.0219	2.81	.4975	.0077
1.62	.4474	.1074	2.02	.4783	.0519	2.42	.4922	.0213	2.82	.4976	.0075
1.63	.4484	.1057	2.03	.4788	.0508	2.43	.4925	.0208	2.83	.4977	.0073
1.64	.4495	.1040	2.04	.4793	.0498	2.44	.4927	.0203	2.84	.4977	.0071
1.65	.4505	.1023	2.05	.4798	.0488	2.45	.4929	.0198	2.85	.4978	.0069
1.66	.4515	.1006	2.06	.4803	.0478	2.46	.4931	.0194	2.86	.4979	.0067
1.67	.4525	.0989	2.07	.4808	.0468	2.47	.4932	.0189	2.87	.4979	.0065
1.68	.4535	.0973	2.08	.4812	.0459	2.48	.4934	.0184	2.88	.4980	.0063
1.69	.4545	.0957	2.09	.4817	.0449	2.49	.4936	.0180	2.89	.4981	.0061
1.70	.4554	.0940	2.10	.4821	.0440	2.50	.4938	.0175	2.90	.4981	.0060
1.71	.4564	.0925	2.11	.4826	.0431	2.51	.4940	.0171	2.91	.4982	.0058
1.72	.4573	.0909	2.12	.4830	.0422	2.52	.4941	.0167	2.92	.4982	.0056
1.73	.4582	.0893	2.13	.4834	.0413	2.53	.4943	.0163	2.93	.4983	.0055
1.74	.4591	.0878	2.14	.4838	.0404	2.54	.4945	.0158	2.94	.4984	.0053
1.75	.4599	.0863	2.15	.4842	.0395	2.55	.4946	.0154	2.95	.4984	.0051
1.76	.4608	.0848	2.16	.4846	.0387	2.56	.4948	.0151	2.96	.4985	.0050
1.77	.4616	.0833	2.17	.4850	.0379	2.57	.4949	.0147	2.97	.4985	.0048
1.78	.4625	.0818	2.18	.4854	.0371	2.58	.4951	.0143	2.98	.4986	.0047
1.79	.4633	.0804	2.19	.4857	.0363	2.59	.4952	.0139	2.99	.4986	.0046
									3.00	.4987	.0044

Appendix B
SUMMATION: NOTATION AND OPERATIONS

This appendix illustrates notation and the operations associated with summation to avoid marked digression from the major content of the text. The operations are simply identified and illustrated; mathematical proofs are not provided. Students possessing a background in elementary statistics undoubtedly are familiar with the operations, but may want to review them if they have been neglected through disuse.

The symbol Σ is sometimes called the *summation operator;* it means *to sum over whatever follows immediately in the expression.* For example, suppose we have five numbers designated by X's: $X_1 = 3$, $X_2 = 7$, $X_3 = 4$, $X_4 = 2$, $X_5 = 8$. If we want to sum the X's, we designate this by:

$$\sum_{i=1}^{5} X_i,$$

in which X_i is the general symbol for the number; the notation under the Σ indicates to begin summing with number X_1; and the 5 above the Σ indicates to continue through number X_5. Thus, for this example:

$$\sum_{i=1}^{5} X_i = X_1 + X_2 + X_3 + X_4 + X_5 = 3 + 7 + 4 + 2 + 8 = 24.$$

In general, the notation

$$\sum_{i=1}^{N} X_i$$

means to begin summing with the first number and conclude with the Nth. Often the notations above and below the Σ are omitted; when they are, Σ means to sum from the first through the Nth number. Although seldom used in a measurement context, we could sum part of the scores, and so indicate in the Σ notation. For example, in the above five numbers, if the sum of only the second and third numbers were desired, it could be designated by:

$$\sum_{i=2}^{3} X_i = 7 + 4 = 11.$$

This is the general summation operation. Let us consider some operations associated with summation of scores.

Operation 1. Applying the summation operator, Σ, to the products resulting from multiplying a set of numbers by a constant is equal to the constant multiplied by the sum of the numbers.

Let 2 be the constant, and the numbers be: $X_1 = 1$, $X_2 = 3$, $X_3 = 4$, and $X_4 = 7$. To apply this operation, these numbers could be written: 2(1), 2(3), 2(4), and 2(7). To find the sum of the numbers, we have:

$$\sum_{i=1}^{4} (2)X_i = 2(1) + 2(3) + 2(4) + 2(7) = 2\sum_{i=1}^{4} X_i = 2(1 + 3 + 4 + 7) = 30.$$

In general notation, this operation is symbolized by:

$$\sum_{i=1}^{N} CX_i = C\sum_{i=1}^{N} X_i.$$

Operation 2. Applying the summation operator, Σ, to a series of constant scores is equal to the product of N times the constant score.

Suppose $X_1 = 4$, $X_2 = 4$, and $X_3 = 4$, that is, all three scores are equal to the constant 4. Then,

$$\sum_{i=1}^{3} X_i = 4 + 4 + 4 = \sum_{i=1}^{3} C = 4(3) = 12;$$

and in general notation,

$$\sum_{i=1}^{N} C = NC.$$

Operation 3. Applying the summation operator, Σ, to the algebraic sum of two (or more) scores of a single individual, and then summing these sums over the N individuals is the same as summing each of the two (or more) scores separately over the N individuals, and then summing the sums.

Suppose we have four individuals, each with an X and Y score:

Individual	1	2	3	4
X	2	5	3	1
Y	7	9	6	5

$$\sum_{i=1}^{4}(X_i + Y_i) = [(X_1 + Y_1) + (X_2 + Y_2) + (X_3 + Y_3) + (X_4 + Y_4)]$$
$$= 9 + 14 + 9 + 6 = 38;$$

and

$$\sum_{i=1}^{4} X_i + \sum_{i=1}^{4} Y_i = X_1 + X_2 + X_3 + X_4 + Y_1 + Y_2 + Y_3 + Y_4$$
$$= 2 + 5 + 3 + 1 + 7 + 9 + 6 + 5 = 38.$$

In general notation:

$$\sum_{i=1}^{N}(X_i + Y_i) = \sum_{i=1}^{N} X_i + \sum_{i=1}^{N} Y_i.$$

As an illustration of applying the Σ operator, suppose we consider $\Sigma_{i=1}^{N}$ $(X_i - \overline{X})$. By applying operation 3,

$$\sum_{i=1}^{N}(X_i - \overline{X}) = \sum_{i=1}^{N} X_i - \sum_{i=1}^{N} \overline{X},$$

but for any given set of scores, $\overline{X}$ is a constant. Therefore, applying operation 2:

$$\sum_{i=1}^{N}(X_i - \overline{X}) = \sum_{i=1}^{N} X_i - N\overline{X}.$$

Given the numbers: 3, 4, 5, 5, 6, 7, we note that the mean of this set is 5. Substituting numbers into the example:

$$\sum_{i=1}^{6}(X_i - \overline{X}) = -2 + (-1) + 0 + 0 + 1 + 2 = 0.$$

$$\sum_{i=1}^{6} X_i - N\overline{X} = (3 + 4 + 5 + 5 + 6 + 7) - 6(5) = 0$$

This also illustrates that the algebraic sum of the deviations around the mean is zero.

The summation operator also applies to expressions raised to powers, such as squares, cubes, etc. Consider

$$\sum_{i=1}^{N} (X_i - \overline{X})^2.$$

The term $(X_i - \overline{X})$ can be squared to give $X_i^2 - 2\overline{X} X_i - \overline{X}^2$. Therefore,

$$\sum_{i=1}^{N} (X_i - \overline{X})^2 = \sum_{i=1}^{N} (X_i^2 - 2\overline{X} X_i + \overline{X}^2)$$

$$= \sum_{i=1}^{N} X_i^2 - \sum 2\overline{X} X_i + \sum \overline{X}^2,$$

by operation 3. But 2, $\overline{X}$, and $\overline{X}^2$ are constants for any given set of numbers. Therefore,

$$\sum_{i=1}^{N} (X_i - \overline{X})^2 = \sum_{i=1}^{N} X_i^2 - 2\overline{X} \left(\sum_{i=1}^{N} X_i \right) + \sum_{i=1}^{N} \overline{X}^2,$$

by operation 1, and

$$\sum_{i=1}^{N} (X_i - \overline{X})^2 = \sum_{i=1}^{N} X_i^2 - 2\overline{X} \left(\sum_{i=1}^{N} X_i \right) + N\overline{X}^2,$$

by operation 2. We know from the relationship between the sum and the mean that

$$\sum_{i=1}^{N} X_i = N\overline{X}.$$

Therefore, substituting into the middle term of the right side of the equation:

$$\sum_{i=1}^{N} (X_i - \overline{X})^2 = \sum_{i=1}^{N} X_i^2 - 2\overline{X}(N\overline{X}) + N\overline{X}^2$$

$$= \sum_{i=1}^{N} X_i^2 - 2N\overline{X}^2 + N\overline{X}^2,$$

and by collecting terms:

$$\sum_{i=1}^{N} X_i{}^2 - 2N\overline{X}{}^2 + N\overline{X}{}^2 = \sum_{i=1}^{N} X_i{}^2 - N\overline{X}{}^2.$$

Substitution for a quantity or factor represented by a Σ is also illustrated in this example.

Using the set of six numbers above, we can illustrate:

$$\sum_{i=1}^{6} (X_i - \overline{X})^2 = (-2)^2 + (-1)^2 + (0)^2 + (0)^2 + (1)^2 + (2)^2 = 10.$$

$$\sum_{i=1}^{6} X_i{}^2 - N\overline{X}{}^2 = (9 + 16 + 25 + 25 + 36 + 49) - 6(25)$$
$$= 160 - 150 = 10,$$

called *the sum of squares* for X.

Thus far we have considered the use of a single operator with a single subscript on whatever is being summed. Similarly, we can use double summation operations with symbols having two subscripts.

Suppose we have three distinct groups of subjects, with five subjects in each group, and a score on some variable, X, for each subject. We can represent the 15 scores in a two-dimensional data array in which the three rows represent the three groups, and five columns represent the first, second, ..., to the fifth scores in each group. We let the first subscript on any X indicate the group (row), and the second subscript indicate the score (column).

Scores on X

Group 1	$X_{11}, X_{12}, X_{13}, X_{14}, X_{15}$
Group 2	$X_{21}, X_{22}, X_{23}, X_{24}, X_{25}$
Group 3	$X_{31}, X_{32}, X_{33}, X_{34}, X_{35}$

We have a double subscript on any given score, the first subscript indicating the group in which the score occurs, and the second indicating the score in the group. We can let j symbolize the number of the score in the group, and i the number of the group. With this X_{ij} notation, j can take on values from 1 through 5, and i values from 1 through 3. There are, of course, 15 ij combinations for subscripts. If we wanted to sum all 15 scores, we could first sum the five scores in each group, then sum the sums of the three groups, giving what we will call a *grand sum*, that is:

the sum of group 1 is $\quad\displaystyle\sum_{j=1}^{5} X_{1j},$

and that of group 2 is $\quad\displaystyle\sum_{j=1}^{5} X_{2j},$

and that of group 3 is $\quad\displaystyle\sum_{j=1}^{5} X_{3j}.$

Then, the sum of the three groups is given by the grand sum:

$$\sum_{j=1}^{5} X_{1j} + \sum_{j=1}^{5} X_{2j} + \sum_{j=1}^{5} X_{3j}.$$

Since we are summing, we can designate this grand sum by:

$$\text{Grand Sum} = \sum_{i=1}^{3}\left(\sum_{j=1}^{5} X_{ij}\right) = \sum_{i=1}^{3}\sum_{j=1}^{5} X_{ij}.$$

This final notation tells us to:

1. sum the five X scores in each group, represented by the subscript j, and
2. sum these sums for the three groups, represented by the subscript i.

In applying the notation $\sum_{i=1}^{3}\sum_{j=1}^{5} X_{ij}$, it should be noted that the first Σ goes with the first subscript, in this case i, and the second Σ goes with the second subscript, in this case j. However, in doing the operations, we actually work from "the inside out," so to speak, since we apply the $\sum_{j=1}^{5}$ first, and then the $\sum_{i=1}^{3}$. That is, we sum within the groups before we can sum over the groups.

Suppose we move to a general notation, and let n be the total number of groups, each group containing J observations or scores. The grand sum would then be given by:

$$\text{Grand Sum} = \sum_{i=1}^{n}\sum_{j=1}^{J} X_{ij}.$$

Note that it is not necessary for all groups to have the same number of scores. If the groups have different numbers of scores, we symbolize this by putting a J_i above the Σ operator instead of J. The J_i simply indicates the number of scores in the ith group, i being a general symbol indicating the group. In a computational exercise, we would insert the appropriate number for the groups 1 through n.

Let us consider again the sum of squares for X:

$$\sum_{i=1}^{n} \sum_{j=1}^{J} (X_{ij} - \overline{X}_i)^2.$$

This expression with the double summation operator directs us to perform the following operations:

1. Subtract from each score in a given group the mean of that group $(\overline{X}_i)$.
2. Square these deviations, one for each score in the group, and sum the squared deviations for the given group.
3. Repeat operations 1 and 2 for all the groups, 1 through n, arriving at n sums.
4. Sum the n sums, as indicated by the operator $\Sigma_{i=1}^{n}$.

We can also rewrite the expression:

$$\sum_{i=1}^{n} \sum_{j=1}^{J} (X_{ij} - \overline{X}_i)^2 = \sum_{i=1}^{n} \sum_{j=1}^{J} (X_{ij}^2 - 2\overline{X}_i X_{ij} + \overline{X}_i^2),$$

by simply squaring the terms. Now, moving the Σ operator closer to the parentheses across the terms in the parentheses, we get:

$$\sum_{i=1}^{n} \left(\sum_{j=1}^{J} X_{ij}^2 - 2\overline{X}_i \sum_{j=1}^{J} X_{ij} + J\overline{X}_i^2 \right).$$

Note, for the middle term, we can move $\overline{X}_i$ in front of the operator, because for any given group, $\overline{X}_i$ is a constant, and the Σ operator we moved across the parentheses sums only on j; for the final term, $\overline{X}_i^2$ is a constant for any given group, so instead of summing it, we can simply multiply by J, the number of scores in the group. Clearing away the parentheses and moving the second Σ operator into each term, we get:

$$\sum_{i=1}^{n} \sum_{j=1}^{J} X_{ij}^2 - 2 \sum_{i=1}^{n} \overline{X}_i \sum_{j=1}^{J} X_{ij} + J \sum_{i=1}^{n} \overline{X}_i^2.$$

Consider the middle term: we know that the sum of the scores in any one group equals J times the mean of that group. That is

$$\sum_{j=1}^{J} X_{ij} = J\overline{X}_i$$

for the ith group. Therefore, substituting this into the above expression, we get

$$\sum_{i=1}^{n}\sum_{j=1}^{J} X_{ij}^2 - 2\sum_{i=1}^{n}\overline{X}_i(J\overline{X}_i) + J\sum_{i=1}^{n}\overline{X}_i^2 = \sum_{i=1}^{n}\sum_{j=1}^{J} X_{ij}^2 - 2J\sum_{i=1}^{n}\overline{X}_i^2 + J\sum_{i=1}^{n}\overline{X}_i^2.$$

We see that the second and third terms are alike now, and can be combined to equal

$$-J\sum_{i=1}^{n}\overline{X}_i^2.$$

Therefore:

$$\sum_{i=1}^{n}\sum_{j=1}^{J}(X_{ij} - \overline{X}_i)^2 = \sum_{i=1}^{n}\sum_{j=1}^{J} X_{ij}^2 - J\sum_{i=1}^{n}\overline{X}_i^2.$$

The right side of this equation is a more convenient computational form, and gives the same result in any application. It directs us to perform the following operations:

1. Square each score in a given group, and sum the scores for that group.
2. Do operation 1 for the n groups, obtaining n sums.
3. Sum the n sums obtained in operation 2. (The $\sum_{i=1}^{n}$ directs us to do this.)
4. Square the n group means, and sum these squared means.
5. Multiply the sum of operation 4 by J.
6. Subtract the result of operation 5 from the sum of operation 3.

In order to illustrate the above calculation of the sum of squares using a double summation, let us assume:

Scores

Group 1   5, 7, 9, 11, 13
Group 2   21, 22, 23, 24, 25

In this illustration, $n = 2$, $J = 5$, $\overline{X}_1 = 9$, $\overline{X}_2 = 23$.

Using the deviation form:

$$\sum_{j=1}^{J}(X_{1j} - \overline{X}_1)^2 = \sum_{j=1}^{5}(X_{1j} - \overline{X}_1)^2$$

$$= (-4)^2 + (-2)^2 + (0)^2 + (2)^2 + (4)^2 = 40,$$

which is the sum of the squares of the scores for group 1.

$$\sum_{j=1}^{5} (X_{2j} - \overline{X}_2)^2 = (-2)^2 + (-1)^2 + (0)^2 + (1)^2 + (2)^2 = 10,$$

which is the sum of the squares of the scores for group 2. Summing these two sums, we get

$$\sum_{i=1}^{2} \sum_{j=1}^{5} (X_{ij} - \overline{X}_i)^2 = 40 + 10 = 50.$$

Applying the computational form, we get

$$\sum_{i=1}^{2} \sum_{j=1}^{5} X_{ij}^2 - 5 \sum_{i=1}^{2} \overline{X}_i^2.$$

Square the scores in group 1 and sum them: $25 + 49 + 81 + 121 + 169 = 445$; and do the same for the scores in group 2: $441 + 484 + 529 + 576 + 625 = 2{,}655$. Summing these two sums, we get 3,100. This completes the determination of

$$\sum_{i=1}^{2} \sum_{j=1}^{5} X_{ij}^2.$$

The next step is to square the two group means ($\overline{X}_i$'s), giving 81 and 529; add these two squares, giving 610; and multiply this sum by 5, giving 3,050. This completes the determination of

$$5 \sum_{i=1}^{2} \overline{X}_i^2.$$

Therefore:

$$\sum_{i=1}^{2} \sum_{j=1}^{5} X_{ij}^2 - 5 \sum_{i=1}^{2} \overline{X}_i^2 = 3{,}100 - 3{,}050 = 50,$$

the result consistent with our earlier result applying the deviation form for calculation of the sum of squares for X.

These operations and illustrations, applied in various appropriate combinations, should adequately cover the summation notation discussed in the text.

Name Index

Adcock, C., 167
Allport, G., 223, 235, 277
Anastasi, A., 6, 128, 277

Bayley, N., 74, 201, 277
Bennett, J., 188, 277
Binet, A., 188, 277
Block, J., 262, 264, 280
Blommers, P., 277
Bolles, R., 138, 145, 277
Bouton, A., 222, 279
Bradley, J., 34
Brown, F., 80, 103, 128
Buros, O., 201, 277
Burt, C., 161, 277

Campbell, D., 142, 143, 209, 214, 221, 222, 277
Cattell, R., 128, 133, 176, 192, 193, 201, 203, 205, 206, 230, 235, 238, 277, 278
Coombs, C., 8
Cronbach, L., 98, 128, 140, 141, 145, 176, 278
Cureton, E., 225, 255, 278

Dahlstrom, W., 235
Davis, P., 198, 278
Doppelt, J., 77, 112, 117, 118, 249, 278
Downie, N., 264
DuBois, P., 278

Ebel, R., 80, 103, 128, 258, 264, 278
Eber, H., 230, 235, 278
Ekstrom, R., 160, 278
Eysenck, H., 7, 224, 225, 235, 237, 278

Ferguson, G., 34, 175, 278
Ferguson, L., 223, 224, 278
Festinger, L., 145
Fiske, D., 142, 143, 209, 277
Flavell, J., 173, 278
French, J., 160, 278

Glass, G., 13, 23, 278
Gronlund, N., 264
Guilford, J., 80, 103, 153, 165, 167, 174, 224, 250, 278
Gulliksen, H., 80, 110, 278

Hall, C., 225, 235, 279
Harris, C. W., 80, 128, 201
Hathaway, S., 226, 228, 229, 279
Hawkes, H., 242, 279
Helmstadter, G., 59, 80, 103
Herzberg, F., 222, 279
Hieronymous, A., 136, 279
Hofstaetter, P., 190, 279
Holtzman, W., 209, 279
Hoyt, C., 80, 98, 279
Humphreys, L., 223, 224, 278
Hunt, J. McV., 201
Husek, T., 259, 280

Kaiser, H., 7, 279
Katz, D., 145
Kaufman, A., 128
Kelley, T., 225, 255, 279
Kerlinger, F., 167
Kite, E., 277
Kleinmuntz, B., 227, 279
Knauft, E., 217, 279
Kretschmer, E., 224, 279
Kuder, G., 98, 100, 211, 212, 216, 219, 221, 279

Lawley, D., 170, 279
Lehmann, I., 176, 201, 280
Lindquist, E., 136, 242, 277, 279
Lindsey, G., 225, 235, 279
Livingston, S., 264
Loevinger, J., 7, 124, 125, 145, 279, 280
Lord, F., 262, 280

McClelland, J., 34
McCorquodale, K., 145, 172, 280

McKinley, J. C., 226
McNemar, Q., 178, 201, 280
Magnusson, D., 101, 103, 280
Mann, C., 242, 279
Maxwell, A., 170, 279
Mayo, G., 278
Meehl, P., 140, 141, 145, 172, 229, 278, 279, 280
Mehrens, W., 176, 201, 280
Merrill, M., 195, 280
Monachesi, E., 228, 279

Nunnally, J., 13, 31, 80, 111, 209, 240, 251, 264, 280

Peak, H., 145
Piaget, J., 173, 192, 201, 202, 278
Popham, W. J., 34, 259, 264, 280
Price, L., 160, 278

Ravitch, M., 262, 264, 280
Richardson, M., 98, 100, 279
Ricks, J. H., Jr., 59
Ritter, R., 115, 280
Rosenberg, N., 222, 280
Royer, L., 209, 280
Rozeboom, W., 109, 280

Seashore, H., 59, 188, 277
Senders, V., 279
Shavelson, R., 262, 264, 280
Simon, T., 188, 277
Spearman, C., 161, 280
Spence, J., 34, 59
Stanley, J., 13, 23, 278
Stevens, S., 2, 3, 8, 145, 280
Strong, E. K., Jr., 211, 213, 214, 215, 217, 222, 223, 224, 236, 278, 280
Swineford, F., 262, 280

Tatsuoka, M., 235
Terman, L., 195, 280
Thomson, G., 167
Thorndike, R., 128, 177, 281
Thurstone, L., 164, 174, 178, 187, 223, 237, 238, 281

Vernon, P. E., 161, 162, 163, 165, 173, 176, 178, 201, 223, 237, 277, 281

Wechsler, D., 192, 196, 198, 199, 281
Weider, A., 228, 281
Welsh, G., 235
Wert, J., 281, 283
Wesman, A., 7, 103, 188, 201, 277, 281

Zytowski, D., 220, 281

Subject Index

Ability:
  cognitive, 7, 173–175
  definition of, 271
  measurement of, 172–184
  noncognitive, 7, 208
Ability profile, 181, 275
Ability test, 7, 175, 271
  ability continuum, 175, 176, 192
  aptitude-achievement distinction,
    184–186
  group tests of general mental
    ability, 176–184
  individual tests of general mental
    ability, 188–201
Achievement test, 7, 184–186, 271
Acquiescence, 209
Aptitude test, 7, 184–188, 271
Area transformations, 50–52, 271
Attribute, 7, 271

Basal age, 189, 271
Bipolar factor, 156, 271

California Test of Mental Maturity
    (CTMM), 181–184, 204, 223
  manual, 182
  short-form test (57-S Form), 183
  subtests, 182–184
*California Test of Personality
    Manual*, 238
Ceiling, 189, 271
Centroid factoring method,
    152–154, 271
Coefficient of equivalence, 72–75, 271
Coefficient of stability, 72–75, 271
Communality, 158, 271
Composite variance, 92–93
Constant, 11, 271
  effect of adding to scores, 23, 24
  effect of multiplying on scores, 23, 24
Construct, 7, 172, 272

Construct validity, 133, 134,
    137–145, 272
  logic of, 138–142
  method for establishing, 142–144
  as related to purpose, 133, 134,
    137, 138
Content validity, 133–137, 272
  as related to purpose, 135
  steps for developing, 136, 137
Correction for attenuation, 122, 272
Correction for guessing, 249–251
Correlation:
  biserial, 252
  as covariance, 26–28
  product-moment, 28–34
Covariance, 26–28, 272
Criterion, definition of, 110, 112
Criterion-keying, 211, 272
Criterion-referenced measurement,
    4, 259–263, 272
Criterion validity, 109–128, 272
  as determined by an expectancy
    table, 117–118
  factors influencing, 118–128
  as predictable variance, 113–117
  as related to purpose, 110, 111, 137
  as related to reliability, 119–127

Differential Aptitude Test (DAT),
    186–188, 205, 207
  subtests, 186–188

Essay test items, definition
    of, 241–242
Expectancy tables, 117, 118

Factor analysis, 150–167, 273
  centroid factoring, 152–154, 271
  communality, 158
  computation of factors, 150–154
  factor matrix, 154, 273

Factor analysis (*continued*)
    naming of factors, 159–161
    reading a factor matrix, 155–161
    related to theories of human
        abilities, 161–167
    rotational transformation, 154–155
    types of factors, 156
    variance due to factors, 157
Faking, 209

General Aptitude Test Battery (GATB),
    186–188, 205, 207
General factor, 156, 273
Gregariousness, as a general interest
        factor, 223
Group factor, 156, 273

Hierarchical factor theory, 161–164
Histogram, 14, 273
Homogeneous keying, 211, 273

Intelligence:
    crystallized, 192, 193
    fluid, 192, 193
Intelligence quotient:
    deviation IQ, 192–194, 273
    ratio IQ, 191, 273
Interest inventories, 211–223
    domain of interests, 222–223
    measurement of interests, 211–221
    stability of interests, 221–222
Interests, 208, 273
Internal consistency reliability,
    98–100, 273
Ipsative scoring, 218, 273
Item:
    analysis, 251–258, 273
    construction, 241–248
    difficulty, 93–96, 251, 255–258, 272
    discrimination, 251, 252–258, 261,
        263, 272
    effect of item similarity on
        reliability, 92–96
    effect of item similarity on
        validity, 124–127

Kuder Occupational Interest
        Survey, 219–220
    comparison with SVIB, 220–221

Kuder Preference Record-Vocational,
    211, 212, 216, 217–219, 222, 236,
    237, 239
    comparison with SVIB, 220–221
Kuder-Richardson reliability estimate,
    98–100, 273

Linear model, 240
Linear transformations, 42–50, 274
Loading, 152, 274

Matching test items, definition
    of, 245–246
Mean, 14, 15, 274
Measurement, 1–8
    definition of, 2, 11, 274
Measurement scales, 12–14
    interval scale, 13, 273
    levels of, 12
    nominal scale, 12, 274
    ordinal scale, 12, 13, 274
    ratio scale, 13, 275
Measures of central tendency,
    14–17, 274
Measures of dispersion, 17–23, 274
Median, 14–16, 274
Minnesota Multiphasic Personality
        Inventory (MMPI), 226–230, 237
    Atlas, 229
    clinical scales, 226, 227
    validity scales, 226, 227
Minnesota Teacher Attitude
        Inventory, 235
Mode, 14, 15, 274
Multiple-choice test items, definition
    of, 241
Multitrait-multimethod
        matrix, 142–144

Normal curve, 25, 26, 43–50, 274
Normative group, 196
Normative score, 218, 220, 274
Norm-referenced measurement, 4,
    259–261, 274
Norms, 53–59
    age norms, 56, 57
    definition of, 53, 274
    development of, 57–59
    grade norms, 56, 57

percentile norms, 53
standard score norms, 54

Objective, behavioral, 259
Objective test items, definition of, 241

Percentile ranks:
  computation of, 51
  definition of, 50, 275
  transformation of, 52
Percentiles, 50–52, 275
Personality assessment:
  definition of, 8, 224
  traits measured in, 224–226
Point-biserial correlation coefficient, 252, 253, 269
Power test, 258, 259, 275
Primary mental abilities
    theory, 164–167
  stability of primary abilities, 173
Privacy, invasion of, 6
Projective techniques, definition of, 233

Range, 17, 275
Range of talent:
  effect on reliability, 89–92
  effect on standard error of
    measurement, 89–92
  effect on validity, 127–128
Raven's Progressive Matrices, 172, 176–178, 181, 202–204, 206
Regression effect, 196
Reliability:
  definition of, 275
  empirical estimation of, 96–100
  equivalence reliability, 72–75
  factors influencing, 84–96
  internal consistency, 98–100
  relationship to validity, 119–127
  stability reliability, 72–75
  theory of, 64–71
Response, in a multiple-choice
    item, 242
Response set, definition of, 209

School and College Ability Test
    (SCAT), 176–181, 202–204, 206
  Series II Handbook, 179, 180

Selection ratio, 118
Sixteen Personality Factor Test (16PF),
    226, 229–233, 237, 239
  description of factors, 230–232
  forms, 230
  Motivational Distortion scale, 232
Spearman-Brown prophecy formula,
    85–89, 275
Speed test, 258–259, 265, 275
Standard deviation, 17, 20–23, 276
Standard error of difference, 100–102,
    200, 256
Standard error of measurement, 75–79
  definition of, 77, 276
  factors influencing, 84–96
  illustration of, 194–196,
    249, 261–263
  logic of, 77–79
  relationship to reliability, 75–77
Stanford-Binet test (S-B), 188–192,
    194–196, 201, 205–206
  Form L, 195
  Form M, 195
Stanine scores, 48–50, 276
Stem, in a multiple-choice item, 242
Sten scores, 47–48, 276
Strong-Campbell Interest Inventory
    (SCII), 214, 215
  Basic Interest Scales, 215
  Occupational Scales, 215
Strong Vocational Interest Blank
    (SVIB), 211–215, 217, 220–224,
    236–237, 239
  Engineer Scale, 213, 215
  occupational scales, 212–215, 221
Study of values, 223, 224
Summation notation, 15, 16, 284–293

T-score, 46, 47, 276
Taylor Manifest Anxiety Scale
    (TMAS), 172
Test construction, 240–269
Trait, 7

Validity:
  construct validity, 133, 134, 137–145
  content validity, 133–137
  criterion validity, 109–128

Validity (*continued*)
  definition of, 109, 110, 276
  factors influencing, 118–128
  of noncognitive measures, 210
  as related to purpose, 5
  relationship to reliability, 119–127
Variable, 11, 276
  continuous, 14
  dependent, 12
  discrete, 14

  independent, 12
  organismic, 12
Variance, 17–20
  computation of, 19, 20
  definition of, 19, 276

Wechsler Adult Intelligence Scale
  (WAIS), 192, 196–201, 206

z-scores, 24, 25, 42–46, 276

Printed in U.S.A.

BCDEFGHIJ-D-898765 4321